Paris 1900

OKLAHOMA CITY MUSEUM OF ART

Notes:

Oklahoma City Museum of Art
Chairman: Virginia Meade Fox
President and Chief Executive: Carolyn Hill
Chief Curator: Hardy S. George

Publication:
Editor and Curator: Hardy S. George
Co-curator: Gabriel P. Weisberg
Assistant to the Curator: Lauren C. Lucht
Copyeditor: Jeffery J. Pavelka
Designer: Eric H. Anderson
Registration: Matthew C. Leininger

Published by the Oklahoma City Museum of Art
Donald W. Reynolds Visual Arts Center
415 Couch Drive, Oklahoma City, Oklahoma 73102
Telephone: 405-236-3100
www.okcmoa.com

Distributed by the University of Washington Press,
P.O. Box 50096, Seattle, Washington 98145-5096
www.washington.edu/uwpress

Library of Congress Control Number: 2007939736
ISBN: 0911919082

Cover image:
CAT. 22; p. 93
Jules Chéret (French, 1836-1932)
Jardin de Paris, ca. 1895
Lent by The Minneapolis Institute of Arts,
Gift of Bruce B. Dayton, P.85.4

The publishers have endeavored to credit all known
persons holding copyright or reproduction rights for
illustrations in this book.

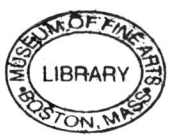

Paris 1900

OKLAHOMA CITY MUSEUM OF ART

CONTENTS

Introduction and Acknowledgments

Carolyn Hill

Paris in 1900 was a snapshot of international rivalry. Envious of such successes as the World's Columbian Exposition, Chicago 1893, and concerned that its reputation as *the* international art capital was declining, Paris mounted a fierce initiative, the Exposition Universelle (1900). In a mammoth effort that encompassed history and future equally, 210 pavilions occupying about a fourth of Paris set out to celebrate the nineteenth-century values of imperialism and eclecticism while staking claim in leadership toward the future and modernism. Although the aims of the event were to showcase the city's supremacy in education and instruction, fine and decorative arts, technology, labor, State welfare, and hygiene, the emphasis on the 1889 Exposition, which centered on machinery, had shifted, giving far more attention to the arts. Art nouveau, at its height at the time, was a significant movement.

Paris 1900 explores important aspects of the fin-de-siècle period including the socio-economic and technological activities that caused Paris to emerge as the center for artistic creativity in all of Europe, and how innovations in all of the arts produced a culturally rich period at the turn of the century. The exhibition is organized in six sections: works associated with the Exposition Universelle; decorative objects representing French art pottery; paintings and prints influenced by Japanese art; works expressing dreams and dreamlike states; works representing the revival of aristocratic taste associated with eighteenth-century French art; and posters and magazine covers, commercial lithographs which drew attention to everything from theatre, circus, and cabaret to advertisements for cigarettes and perfume. In a climate of tensions borne of opposites, the fin-de-siècle epoch was synonymous with powerfully new political movements defined by the rejection of an old, oppressive and fatigued imperial order. At the same time, an optimism for a new order would aspire to sever the distinction of high and low art, combine beauty and utility, introduce art into the lives of the fast developing middle class, and turn to nature as the model for design. This way of approaching modern society and new production methods swept over all of the arts, where design was once a separate art form,

DETAIL: Georges de Feure (French, 1868-1943) (see cat. 32; p. 85)
Paris Almanach, 1894
Lithograph
Dr. Gabriel and Yvonne Weisberg Collection

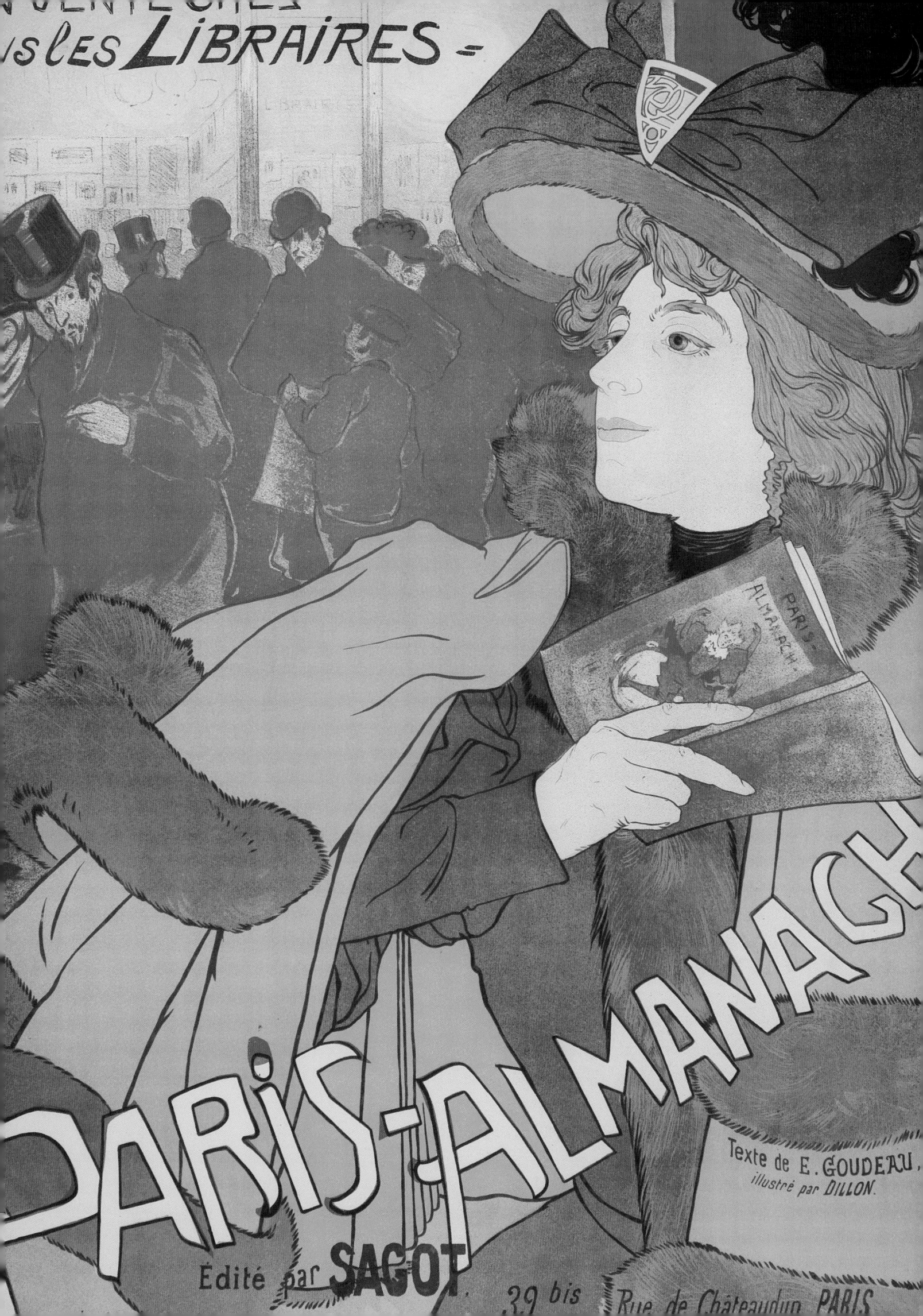

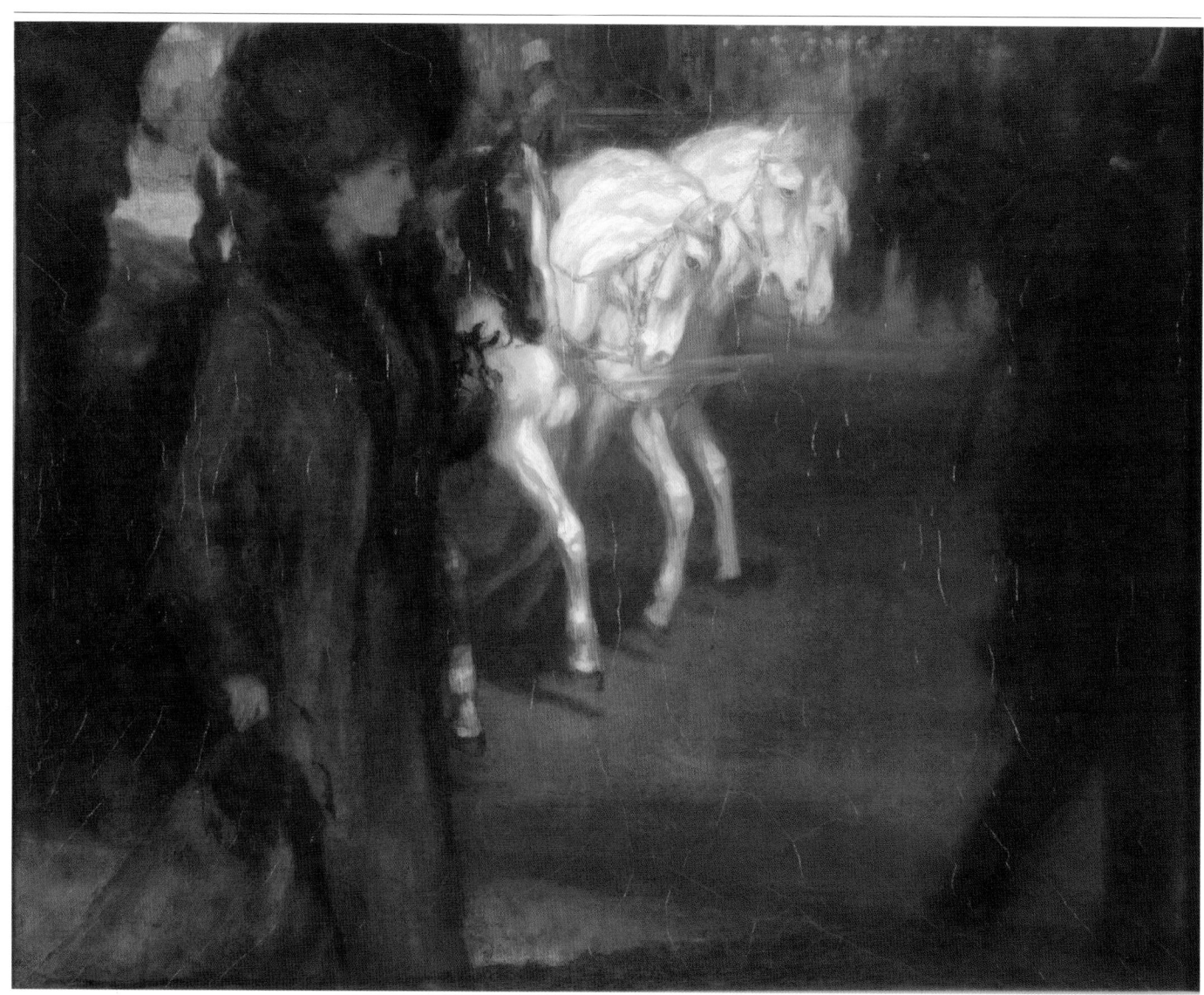

CAT. I   Louis Anquetin (French, 1861–1932)

City Scene, ca. 1905

Oil on canvas, 25¼ x 32 in. (64.13 x 81.28 cm)

Jane Voorhees Zimmerli Art Museum; Rutgers, The State University of

New Jersey; Purchased in Memory of Andrew Korzun, 1981

Photograph by Jack Abraham; 84.099.001

co-mingling with architecture, interior decoration, and craftsmanship separated from mechanical production. And, Paris was determined to demonstrate its superiority in the arts and industry.

Siegfried Bing's influential L'Art Nouveau pavilion, a building at the Exposition designed by André Arfvidson, included rooms designed by artists Edward Colonna, Georges de Feure, and Eugène Gaillard. Supporting the idea that art nouveau was French and had its roots in rococo art and architecture of the Ancien Régime, particularly the period of Louis XV, the graceful organic design of art nouveau revealed its eighteenth-century origins. One of the most prolific designers of this period, Georges de Feure's versatility as an artist and designer caught the attention of Bing, who discovered his work in the Paris salons. Whether art glass, silverware, jewelry, porcelain and pottery, fine furniture, paintings, or many known graphic arts and posters, de Feure's designs were noted for the suggestion of an elegant sensuality, as seen in his lithograph *Paris Almanach*, (cat. 32; p. 85). Specializing in images of seductive femmes fatales dressed in modish gowns and trailing garments that sometimes recalled the kimono clad women in Japanese prints, de Feure captured the essence of the feminine spirit, and showed a fascination with the decorative elements and exoticism found in Japanese art.

The influence of Japanese art on French ceramists involved not only such aesthetic themes as flowers, serpents, and women, but also the revival of superb craftsmanship associated with forms and glazes. Viewed as equals to other art forms, period ceramics, designed as independent works of art, helped further the international renaissance in the applied arts. Eduard Stellmacher's *Amphora Eastern Dragon Vase* (cat. 109; p. 144) is a ready reference to the serpentine twisting movements of the whiplash curve, a stylistic motif inspired by Japanese designs. Large pottery companies, including the Sèvres National Manufactory, employed many talented French master potters. Ernest Chaplet was one of the most inventive, having begun working as an apprentice porcelain painter at Sèvres at the age of thirteen. Amidst thriving business, bold technical and artistic innovations, and their creative relationships with one another, a number of brilliant master potters produced some of the best ceramics in Western history.

After Japan's two hundred years of isolation, its art slowly began to circulate throughout Europe, the result of a 1854 trade treaty between the United States and Japan. Western artists, fascinated by Japanese use of nature as a primary source, flat perspectives, and woodblock coloring, embraced this new and unusual art, and began to absorb it, integrating it into their own creations. Swift to capitalize on an obvious entrepreneurial opportunity, Siegfried Bing had bought art from Japan for many years selling it in his Paris shops. Not surprisingly, Georges de Feure, Louis Legrand, and others who exhibited their work in Bing's Salon de l'Art Nouveau starting in 1895, absorbed the Japanese aesthetic, and incorporated it in their own creations. Such works were shown in his extensive pavilion at the Exposition Universelle in Paris. The Japanese woodblocks by Andō Hiroshige (cat. 49; p. 38) included in this exhibition as reference, are excellent examples of nature as motif, and meticulously rendered block colors on flat surfaces. Similarities may be found in Henri Rivière's *L'Isle des cygnes* (cats. 91, 92; p. 108) or paintings by Charles Guilloux. Their flattened perspectives and fluid line may be associated with Japanese color woodblock prints of the early nineteenth century. It appears certain Japanese prints had a significant and influential impact on turn-of-the-century art.

Closely aligned, the symbolist and "Les Nabis" artists were represented in Bing's pavilion as well. In a nod to the early beginnings of psychiatry and hypnosis, the themes of dreams and dreamlike states were explored. French painter and writer Maurice Denis, a member of the symbolist movement and Les Nabis group, published an article in support of his group titled *Definition of Neo-Traditionalism,* which contained some of the principles of modern art. Denis's *Avril* drawing (cat. 27; p. 32), a subject of reverie and fantasy, no doubt was inspired by new forms of Christian mysticism and the new scientific interest in psychiatry and the investigation of dreams as a means of connecting with the unconscious.

In his well-known proposal for the definition of paint-ing, Denis said: "Remember that a picture, before being a battle horse, a nude, an anecdote or whatnot, is essential-ly a flat surface covered with colors assembled in a certain order." Influenced by Gauguin, who employed symbols with psychological subtlety that sets him apart from many other symbolists, Denis took Gauguin's use of flat color, and sometimes incorporated decorative abstraction, more so than his teacher. Artists associated with Denis and Les Nabis, and others whose works found their way into the *peinture du l'âme* ("painters of the soul") exhibitions, and Joséphin Péladan's Salon de la Rose + Croix, produced paintings that worked well with the modern and historical-ly eclectic interiors of the 1890s. This idea was paramount in fin-de-siècle designs that stressed harmony between ar-chitecture, interior decor, finishings, and objets d'art.

Jules Chéret, who was influenced by rococo art, championed the idea of the color lithograph poster as an advertising medium and as a work of art. In addition to an apprenticeship in lithography and an art course at the École Nationale de Dessin, Chéret studied the techniques of various artists, past and present, by frequenting Paris museums. Influenced by scenes of frivolity depicted in the works of such rococo artists as Jean-Honoré Fragonard (1702-1806) and Jean-Antoine Watteau (1684-1721), Chéret created advertising posters, initially just to earn a living as he pursued painting, but eventually as his sole artistic effort. Responding to demand, he expanded his business from highly successful posters for cabarets, music halls, and theatres such as Les Folies-Bergère and the Moulin Rouge, to products of any kind, becom-ing a major advertising voice for such clients as railroad companies and many manufacturing businesses. As his work gained popularity and his designs of free-spirited females found larger audiences, many assigned him the role of "father of the women's liberation." Interestingly, Gustave Charpentier, French composer best known for his opera *Louise*, inspired by texts by Charles Baude-laire and Voltaire, composed *Louise* in Paris where it was accepted for production by the Opéra-Comique. A realistic portrait of Parisian working-class life, *Louise* is

associated with the theme of women's liberation, as well. Charpentier and his colleague Camille Saint-Saëns were very much a part of the collective sentiment for reviving classical ideals and the aristocratic taste associated with rococo art. Saint-Saëns rejected ideas associated with not only the impressionist painters, but also the impression-ist composer Claude Debussy. His well-known *Piano Concerto No. 5*, which ranks with Charpentier's *Louise*, and the poster designs by Chéret (cat. 22; p. 93) as well as a watercolor by Adolphe Willette of a *Girl on a Swing* (cat. 123), which might have been inspired by Jean-Hon-oré Fragonard's *The Swing* (1766, Wallace Collection, London), are excellent examples of the rococo revival. Colored lithograph posters were starting to receive rec-ognition as works of art. The 1890s is associated with the flowering of the poster as illustrated advertisement. The highly skilled artists working in this genre are Chéret, Théophile-Alexandre Steinlen, Alphonse Mucha, Willette, and Henri de Toulouse-Lautrec.

Steinlen, who was part of the Montmartre art scene, had worked earlier as a fabric designer in the industrial city of Mulhouse. Although he was influenced by Émile Zola's caustic realism, his art cannot be easily classi-fied. He portrayed the cabaret dancer Loïe Fuller for the cover of *Gil Blas Illustré*, street entertainers, as well as the social unrest and misery associated with the poorer parts of Montmartre, and he has been seen as something of a chronicler, and social satirist. At times, like Zola, he mocked the manners and values of the Paris working class, and at times exhibited a great deal of sympathy for the downtrodden. He made lithograph posters for caba-rets, and others to advertise commercial products.

Mucha began as a choir boy and amateur musician in his birthplace of Moravia in the modern Czech Republic. It was the art he could admire in the local churches that inspired his determination to become a painter. Arriving in Paris, in 1887, he began his career on a meager and unpredictable income as an artist drawing illustrations for popular magazines (cat. 67), and balancing successes and failures while sharing a studio with Gauguin. He enjoyed a circle of artists, musicians, and theatrical personalities,

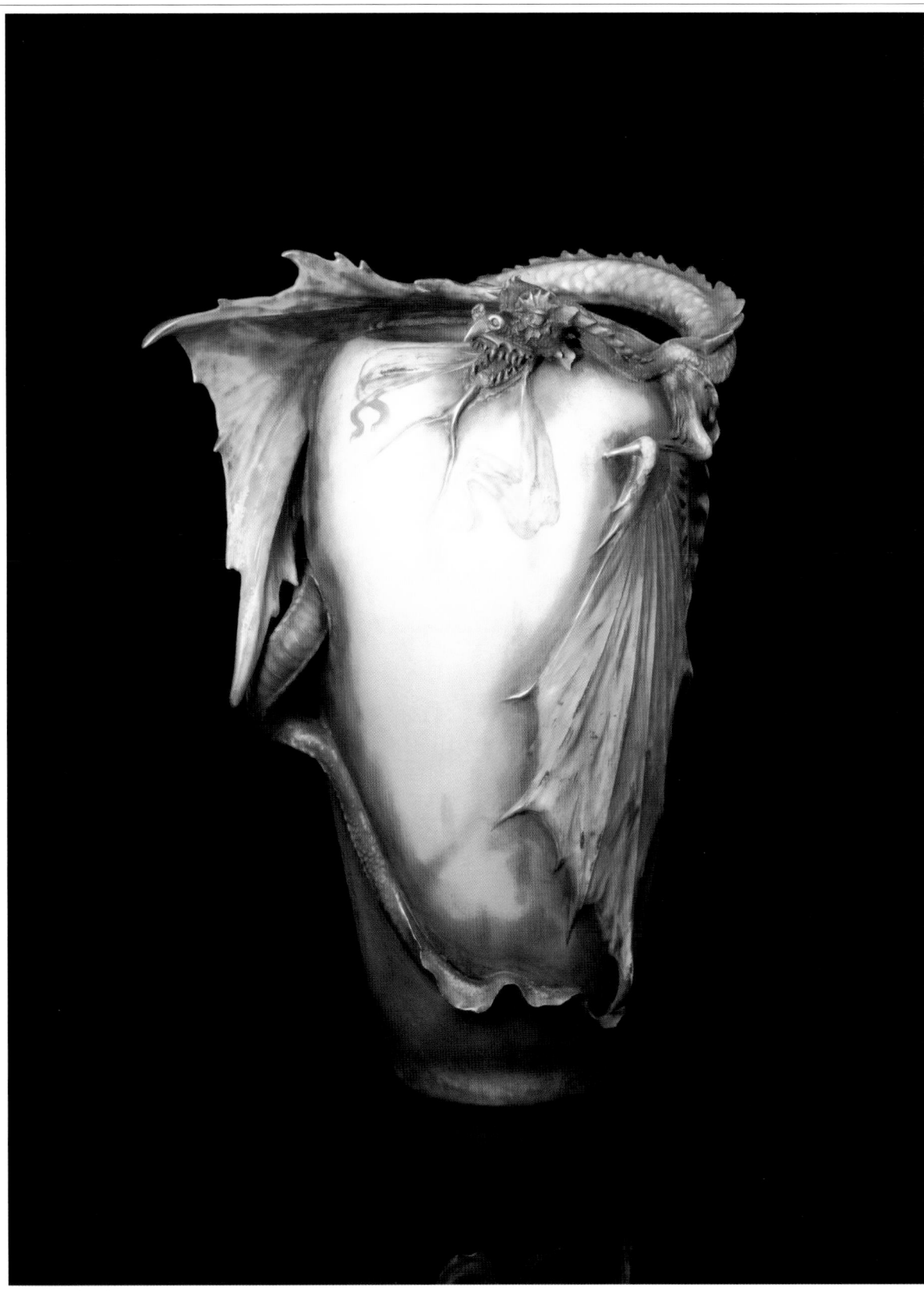

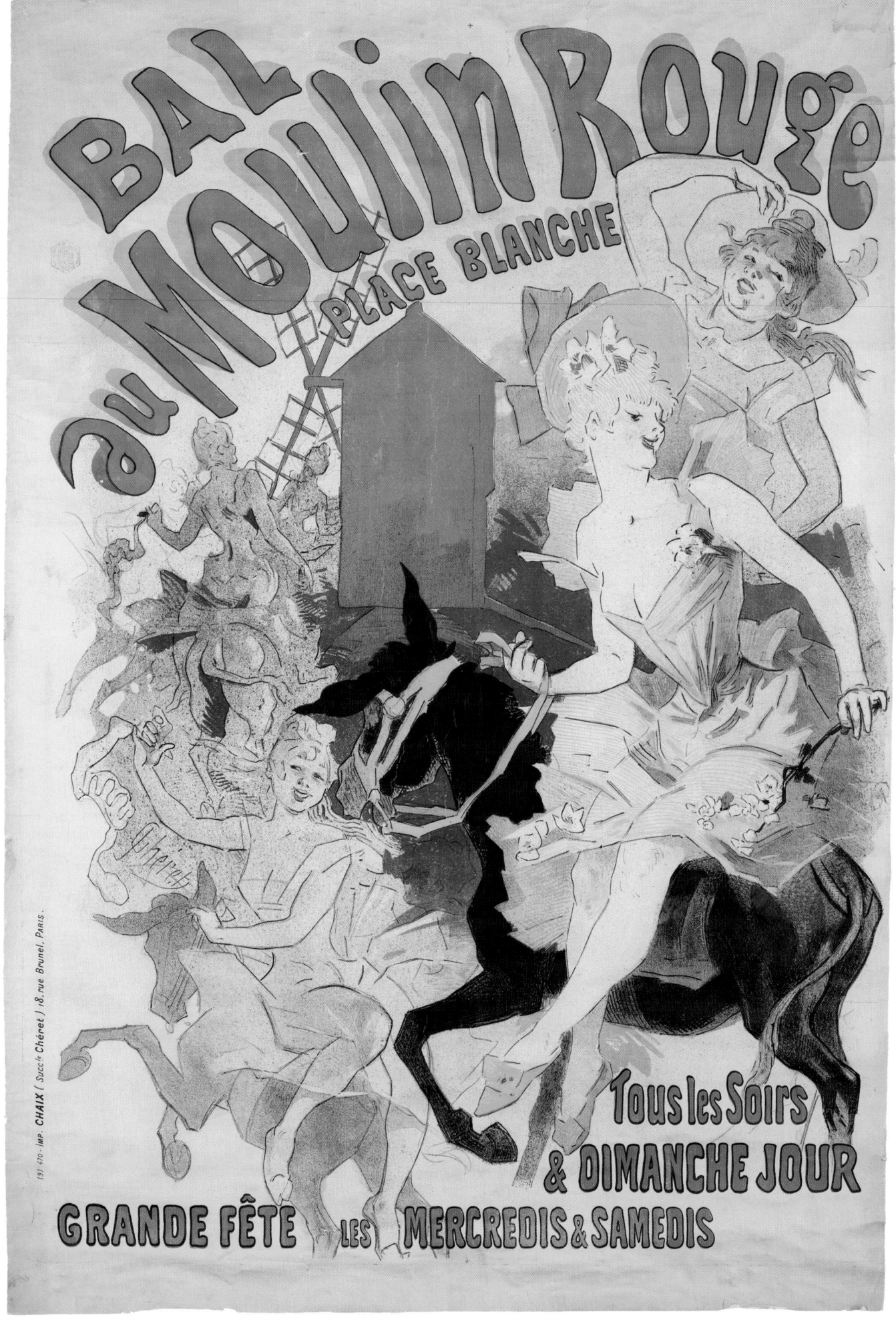

CAT. 20   Jules Chéret (French, 1836-1932)
Bal au Moulin Rouge, 1892
Color lithograph, 50¼ x 35¼ in. (127.6 x 89.5 cm)
Lent by The Minneapolis Institute of Arts,
The Modernism Collection, gift of Norwest Bank Minnesota, P.98.33.1

while formulating his ideas of what his art would become. Called on to create a poster for a Sarah Bernhardt play, he rejected the commercial style of other popular poster artists in favor of his own unique design. The almost life-size image was a sensation that made his name a household word.

Appropriately, the exhibition concludes with a section given over to posters and magazine covers, a fitting conclusion acknowledging the immense role of art books, magazine publications, and printmaking in disseminating art to a swiftly growing middle class. Perhaps no artist is more closely associated with the poster, and the influence of Japanese woodblock prints, as well as the nightlife of Montmarte's cabarets, dance halls, restaurants, and brothels: Toulouse-Lautrec. His *Moulin Rouge, La Goulue* (cat. 110; p. 89) is an iconic image for the Parisian cabaret, the persona of Paris and its many manifestations, and for the ascent of the merger of commerce and art in the poster revolution.

> He did not overturn reality to discover truth, where there was nothing. He contented himself with looking. He did not see, as many do, what we seem to be, but what we are. Then, with a sureness of hand and a boldness at once sensitive and firm, he revealed us to ourselves....fixed forever by the artist's pitiless pencil. (Obituary in the *Journal de Paris*)

The idea of the exhibition grew out of a conversation with Hardy S. George, Ph.D., Museum Chief Curator; Gabriel P. Weisberg, Ph.D.; and myself. *Paris 1900* is the result of the museum's interest in organizing an exhibition of European objects. Discussions between Dr. George, and colleague Dr. Weisberg, centered on the unique artistic milieu that was Paris at the turn of the century, and led to the idea of the two art historians co-curating the exhibition. As the organizing co-curator and catalogue editor, Dr. George extends his deepest appreciation to Dr. Weisberg for his expertise and continuing interest in the museum's exhibitions program. Many have contributed to its success, principally Dr. Weisberg,

Dr. George, and his invaluable curatorial assistant Lauren Lucht. Both extend special thanks to Matthew C. Leininger, Jim Meeks, Ernesto Sánchez Villarreal, Christina Hicks, Chandra Boyd, Amy Young, Nicole Emmons, and John Calabrisi for their roles in presenting the exhibition. For their work in funding and marketing the exhibition and catalogue, we extend our gratitude to Kenneth Lindquist, Jim Eastep, Leslie Spears, Whitney Cross, and Christen Conger. To all others at the Oklahoma City Museum of Art who helped in the organization of the project, our thanks. The enthusiastic support of the Exhibitions Committee, Frank Hill, Chair, and the Board of Trustees is especially appreciated. Special thanks also to Elizabeth J. Fowler, Ph.D., Assistant Professor of Art and Design History, Syracuse University; Sarah Sik, Ph.D. student in Art History, University of Minnesota; and Dr. Weisberg for their essays which have contributed significantly to the catalogue. Catalogue copyeditor Jeffery J. Pavelka and Eric Anderson, catalogue designer and helpful colleague, deserve special thanks for their very able assistance.

Finally, we gratefully acknowledge the Kirkpatrick Foundation for its leadership role as the Presenting Exhibition Sponsor, and the Inasmuch Foundation for its unfailing support as the Presenting Season Sponsor. For the invaluable partnership of leading season sponsors, we offer profound thanks to Chesapeake Energy Corporation, Devon Energy Corporation, and the Oklahoma Arts Council. For important season sponsorships of American Fidelity Foundation, GlobalHealth, MidFirst Bank, OGE Energy Corporation, and SandRidge Energy, Inc., we offer our deepest appreciation. For generous assistance in marketing the exhibition, we thank Cox Communications and *The Oklahoman*. We acknowledge, as well, Sarkeys Foundation and Sonic, America's Drive-In, for their generous support given through arts education endowments.

The Sacred and Profane: An Exploration of Interiors in Fin-de-Siècle Art

Hardy S. George

In Paris during the last decade of the nineteenth century, domestic interiors were given a great deal of attention by architects, designers, and artists. On one level this represents an admiration for the luxury and elegance of the intimate decor associated with the reign of Louis XV. This is combined with an interest in unifying design, ceramics, furniture, and painting to create a total sense of harmony and intimacy no longer available in the fast moving and disjointed rhythms of the over-populated city in an age of enormous change brought about by the noisy clatter of new technology. Perhaps the search for a fulfilling overall unity in new art [art nouveau] cannot only be attributed to Charles-Pierre Baudelaire's synthetism and Richard Wagner's ideas about an all-embracing work of art [*Gesamtkunstwerk*]. This was propelled by the same optimism and utopian thinking associated with the social reformers and theoretical anarchists of the second half of the century: Pierre Joseph Proudhon (1809-1865), Émile Zola (1840-1902), and Peter Kropotkin (1842-1921). Along with domestic and public interiors decorated with murals by such artists as Maurice Denis, Alphonse Osbert, and Jules Chéret, there are public interiors of cabarets, music halls, and theatres portrayed by Henri de Toulouse-Lautrec and Théophile-Alexandre Steinlen.

The Exposition Universelle et Internationale (1900), celebrating the opening of a new century, is also associated with the maturation of the complex and sensual beauty of art nouveau's convoluted style of architecture and interior decoration. While the Paris Exposition Universelle of 1889 gave emphasis to machinery as well as industrial iron and glass construction marking technological advances of the time, the Paris 1900 exhibition gave more attention to the arts; graphic works, paintings, and sculpture, as well as glass, ceramics, and jewelry, reflecting the verve and dynamism of the fin de siècle. In the 1900 exhibition, Siegfried Bing (1838-1905) reintroduced in his "L'Art Nouveau pavilion" a more graceful and organic form of interior design. With the increasing growth of French nationalism in the 1890s, Bing clearly placed the emphasis on associating art nouveau's stylistic roots with rococo art, architecture, and decoration of the closing years of the Ancien Régime and the reign of Louis XV.

DETAIL Alphonse Mucha (Czech, 1860-1939) (see cat. 73; p. 52)
Job, 1898
Color lithograph on paper mounted on linen
Courtesy J. Raj K. Dhawan

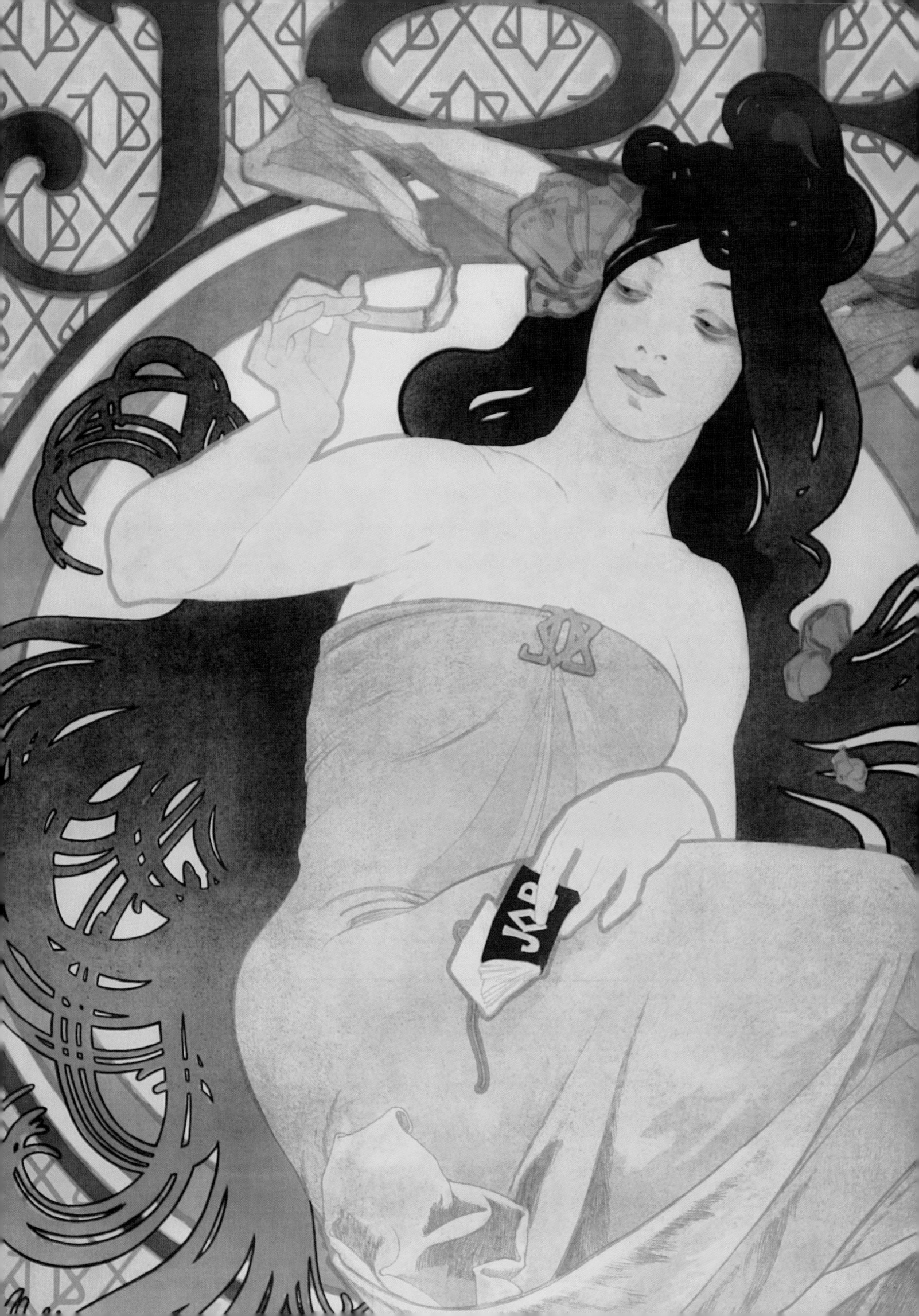

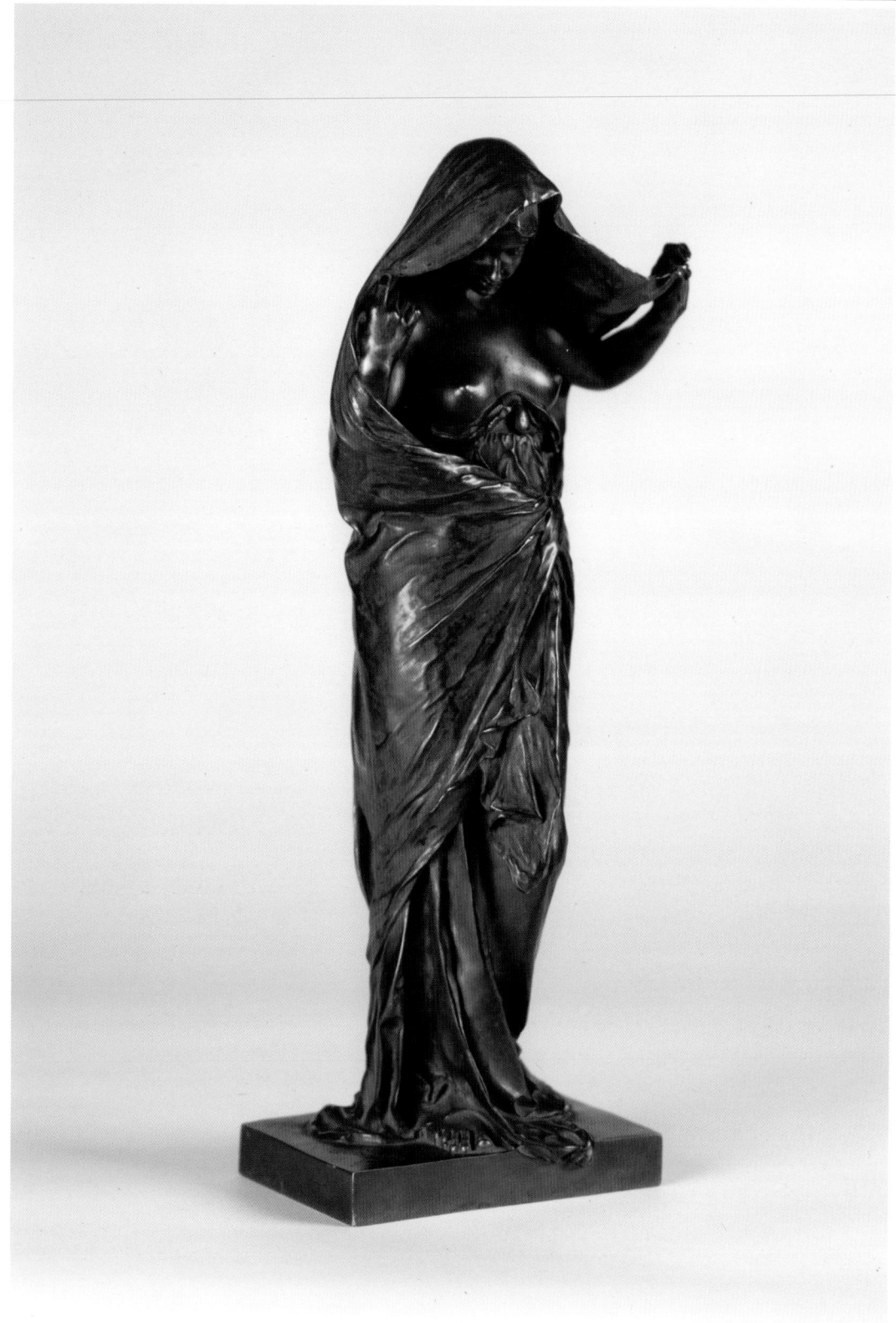

CAT. 3   Ernest Barrias (French, 1841-1905)
La Nature se dévoilant devant la Science [Nature Unveiling
Herself Before Science], ca. 1899
17 x 8 x 4 in. (43.2 x 20.3 x 10.2 cm)
Private Collection

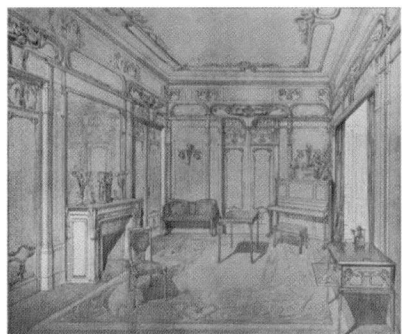

Bing chose artists and designers whose work would clearly evoke the spirit of French eighteenth-century art. His L'Art Nouveau pavilion featured interiors by the furniture maker and jewelry designer Edward Colonna, a sitting room in gold and blue with rococo inspired décor (fig. 1), and a *petit salon de dame* with gilded screens and hung with silk tapestries by the painter and printmaker Georges de Feure. A bedroom was designed by Eugène Gaillard. There were also paintings and decorative works that were chosen by Bing as a suitable addition to the overall harmony of the various rooms. He urged artists to work together in creating unified and organic interiors. What were the further developments, if any, of this idea of a harmonious interior with arts and crafts playing equally important roles in the overall design? How did this idea evolve, and what were its origins? In this development did painting continue to play its traditional and dominant role or did it become more a part of the decor? The Oklahoma City Museum of Art's exhibition includes a number of artists whose work can be associated with the various styles and the inventiveness that made the 1900 Paris Exposition Universelle the high point in the development of fin-de-siècle art, and how innovations in all of the arts produced a particularly rich moment in time. Who were the artists whose works were best suited to play a harmonious part in the total interior decor, as purportedly late eighteenth-century painting did, or was the idea of creating a total work of art, made up of furnishings, sculpture, architectural design, and painting, an ideal never fully realized? Did mystical and spiritual subject matter have a role to play in the quest for the total work of art?

Louis-Ernest Barrias worked on the sculptural decorations of the Paris Opera. At the 1872 Salon Barrias he exhibited a classical work in marble titled the *Oath of Spartacus*. People identified the work with the aftermath of the Franco-Prussian War (1870-1871). His *Defense of Paris in 1870* for the town of Courbevoie, Hauts-de-Seine, was exhibited in the Salon of 1881. A female figure in the work, representing the town, supports a wounded soldier. In 1893, Barrias did a bronze figure of the war hero *Anatole de la Forge* for the Père-Lachaise Cemetery. His *La Nature se dévoilant devant la Science* [Nature Unveiling Herself before Science] while personifying nature (life) and praising the progress of science, there is something funerary about her solemn pose (cat. 3).[1] This was first conceived for the Bordeaux Medical Faculty and was exhibited in the Salon of 1893. A number of versions seem to have been cast. One full-size version is in the Neurological Institute of the Royal Victoria Hospital in Montreal, another with a mixture of colored marbles and onyx (1899) now in the Musée d'Orsay in Paris. Like other large-scale bronzes made for public places, small ones, like the statuette in the exhibition, were caste for domestic interiors. *La Nature* would have added to the air of mystery in the art nouveau inner sanctum.

A mysterious environment, with provocative furnishings that included a selection of works of art appears to have been considered a kind of sanctuary offering refuge from the world. At the same time, the most careful visual arrangement or combination of art objects might emit energy vibrations that could well play havoc with the sensitive nerves of the collector and inhabitant. This idea of Dr. Jean-Martin Charcot's was endorsed in Edmond de Goncourt's *Maison d'un Artiste*. Artists and authors, associated with the reaction against realism and naturalism in the 1880s, such as Joris-Karl Huysmans and Maurice Denis, were motivated to portray, describe, condone, and create or help with the creation of such environments. In 1890, when the artist Charles Maurin traveled to the Château de Bouzols in the environs of Puy to paint the portraits of the count and countess of Brive, he wrote to his fellow artist Félix Vallotton: "I am in an ideal château for an Edgard Poë [sic], or a Huysmans, …"[2]

During roughly the same time span associated with the growth of art nouveau there was a parallel theoretical development concerned with the synthesis of all art forms, including music, poetry, and literature, which, through various combinations, could make up a total work of art. Richard Wagner, in writing about the

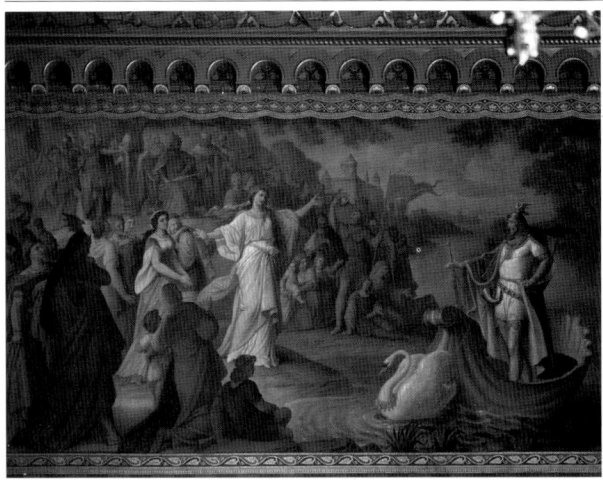

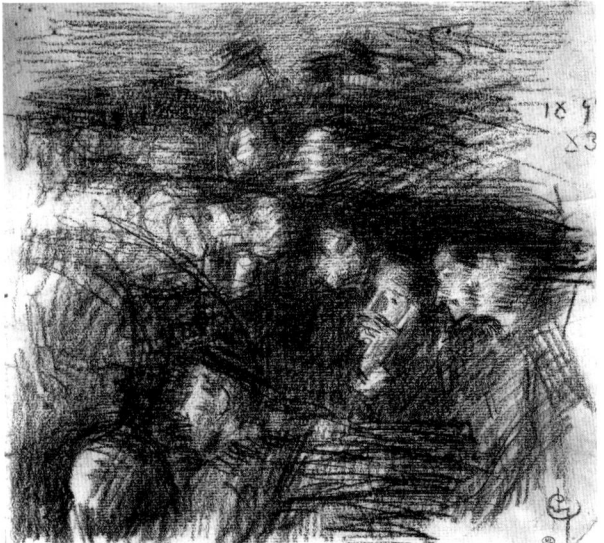

creation of a new type of musical drama as a unified work made up of visual, poetic, and literary or legendary components, first employed the term *Gesamtkunstwerk*. This term was used for an all-encompassing work in which drama, music, poetry, song, and paintings would be united into a new and complete art form. He expounded on this in his *Das Kunstwerk der Zukunft* [The Artwork of the Future], published in 1849. In his operas *Parsifal* (1877-1882) and *Lohengrin*, Wagner saw his principal characters as symbols rather than distinct individuals. *Parsifal* is a religious work celebrating the Eucharist. Lohengrin, as the son of Parsifal, is predestined to pursue the life of a knight of the Holy Grail. Ludwig II was the composer's most important admirer and benefactor. Wagner's operas were performed privately at the Bavarian king's nineteenth-century (1868-1886), fairy-tale castle of Neuschwanstein for his solitary pleasure. The Singer's Hall was decorated with frescoes depicting the life of Parsifal and in the salon scenes from the legend of Lohengrin were painted on coarse linen to create the appearance of tapestries. Ludwig II identified himself with Parsifal, the legendary Grail King. For the Salon, Ludwig commissioned Wilhelm Hauschid (1827-1887) to paint *The Miracle of the Grail* (1880-1881), and August von Heckel (1824-1883) to paint *Lohengrin's Arrival* in a boat drawn by a silver swan to defend Elsa, the King of Brabant's daughter, in a duel with the malevolent Count Telramund (fig. 2).

When achieved, if ever, this perfect synthesis of the arts would be greater and more meaningful than its individual parts. Wagner's idea that music of the future must be part of a synthesis of all the arts, and the implied possibility of achieving this in his operas had a far-reaching influence, as well as the intense and mysterious experience created by the "endless melody" and the unprecedented manner of combining music and drama. Because of France's humiliating defeat by the Germans in the Franco-Prussian War, there was great opposition to the presentation of Wagner's operas in Paris, in the last decades of the nineteenth century. Yet his "revelation of infinite splendour" in *Lohengrin* and other operas attracted

FIG. 2   August von Heckel (German, 1824-1883)
Lohengrin's Arrival, 1880-1881
Fresco , size not available, Neuschwanstein Castle (Fuessen),
Bavaria, Germany. Photograph: Alfredo Dagli Orti
Bildarchiv Preussischer Kulturbesitz/Art Resource,
New York

FIG. 3   Ernest Laurent (French, 1859-1929)
Etude pour Scène au bord du ruisseau, ou Le Concert Colonne
[Study for Scene at the Brook, or Concert Colonne], 1883
Black chalk on paper, $9\frac{7}{16}$ x $10\frac{5}{8}$ in. (24.02 x 27.04 cm)
Musée du Louvre, Cabinet des Dessins, Paris
Photograph in a Private Collection

the attention of a number of artist whose works were associated with the idealists and Salon de la Rose + Croix exhibitions held in the 1880s and 1890s. While the performances of Wagner's musical dramas were rare, Ernest Laurent was able to depict an enraptured audience listening to Beethoven's *Pastoral Symphony* at Concert Colonne (fig. 3) and Georges Seurat supposedly listening to the same music performed at that concert (fig. 4). Works such as these describe an interest in German Romantic music among artists seeking the experience of a meaningful synthesis in the arts.

Joséphin Péladan, the flamboyant founder of the Rosicrusian religious cult, employed the title "l'ordre de la Rose + Croix, du Temple et du Graal." Fantin Latour submitted a lithograph of the "Prelude to Lohengrin" (*Prélude de Lohengrin*) to the Salon of 1882 and a painting of this Wagnerian subject to the Salon of 1892. He also did several drawings and lithographs based on Wagner's *Parsifal*. Odilon Redon, made pastels, charcoal drawings, and lithographs of Wagnerian subjects (fig. 5). While music continued to be the dominant art form in Wagner's operas, his ideas concerning the future development of a *Gesamtkunstwerk* infiltrated the visual arts. In looking through photographs of art nouveau museum installations of interiors of the 1890s something always seems not quite right. The architecture does not always seem to do justice to the furniture, or visa versa. If there are paintings on the walls, many times they seem inappropriate. The ideal combination of setting, decoration, and music seems to only have been fully realized in theatre, opera, or literature. In spite of the imperfections of this utopian task, painters associated with Maurice Denis and "Les Nabis" as well as the idealists and other artists who exhibited with the Salon de la Rose + Croix and Le Barc de Boutteville played an important role in this synthesis of the arts. At the same time, it seems worthwhile to examine this sensitive issue of painting as decoration and the part it played in the total ensemble of the fin-de-siècle interior.

Joséphin Péladan's first Salon de la Rose + Croix was held in the Durand-Ruel gallery, which in the 1870s had promoted the work of the impressionists, but had

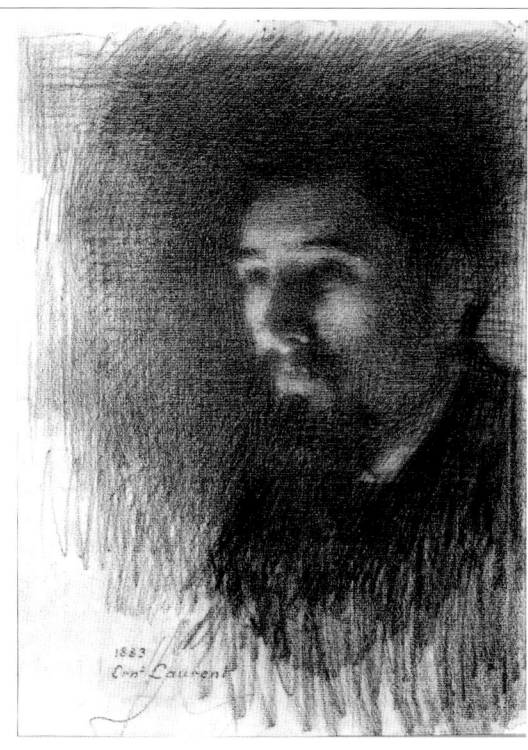

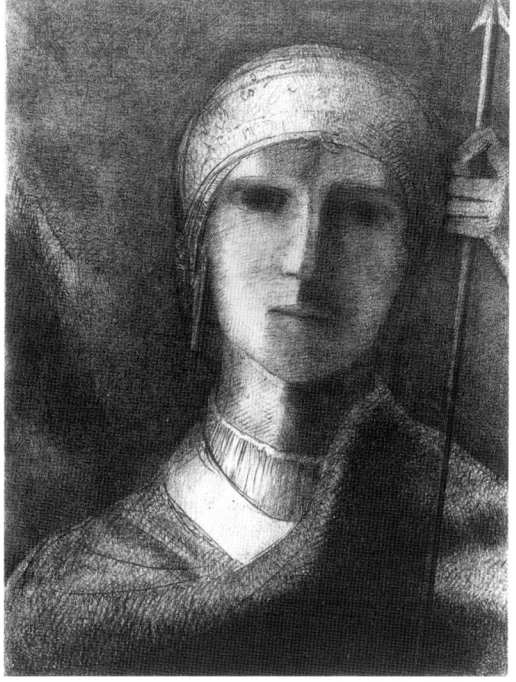

FIG. 4   Ernest Laurent (French, 1859-1929)
Portrait of Georges Seurat, 1883
Black chalk on paper, 15¾ x 12¹⁄₁₆ in. (40.09 x 31.02 cm)
Private Collection Musée du Louvre, Cabinet des Dessins, Paris
Photograph in a Private Collection

FIG. 5   Odilon Redon (French, 1840-1916)
Parsifal, 1892
Lithograph, 12⅝ x 9⁷⁄₁₆ in. (32 x 24 cm)
Private Collection

been "constantly on the verge of ruin"[3] in the mid-1880s, agreed to have this exhibition in their gallery. It took three days and nights to hang the show.[4] There was great enthusiasm for the exhibition, which was supposed to bring about the regeneration of art. An enormous crowd of over 22,600 visitors came, and 274 carriages were counted. It was necessary for the police to stop traffic in the area until late in the afternoon. The decoration of the interior was most important to Péladan. It was designed to convey the total meaning and spirit of the exhibition. The rooms of the gallery were filled with flowers. A brass ensemble played the prelude to *Parsifal*. The catalogue contained Péladan's reminder: "Artist, you are priest … Artist, you are king … Artist, you are magus. …"[5]

The essential aspects of *Gesamtkunstwerk* are found in ecclesiastical architecture of the Middle Ages. The Gothic church or cathedral, as a total work of art, made up of pictures, wall paintings, sculpture, stained glass, and at times music, could evoke a heavenly or otherworldly experience. Suger, Abbot of Saint-Denis (1081-1151), first an oblate at Saint-Denis Abbey near Paris, left behind a rare account (published in Paris, in 1867) of the construction activity and the value placed on embellishments of the abbey. It explains how the beauty of the sanctified interior space could offer shelter from worldly cares and stimulate the contemplation of spiritual realms:

> Thus, when – out of my delight in the beauty of the house of God – the loveliness of the many-colored gems has called me from external cares, and worthy meditation has induced me to reflect, transferring that which is material to that which is immaterial, on the diversity of the sacred virtues: then it seems to me that I see myself dwelling, as it were, in some strange region of the universe which neither exists entirely in the slime of the earth nor entirely in the purity of Heaven; and that, by the grace of God, I can be transported from this inferior to that higher world in an anagogical manner.[6]

In the 1890s, the aesthetic experience of the total makeup of the interior, and its inexplicable sense of mystery, was further encouraged by Wagner's ideas concerning opera as a complete theatrical, musical, visual, and spiritual experience. Early ideas concerning the domestic interior, and its aesthetic contents, as a total work of art can also be found in the ideas and writings of William Morris (1834-1896), the principal founder of the English Arts and Crafts movement, and in the writings and lectures of the French architect Eugène-Emmanuel Viollet-le-Duc (1814-1879), the chief restorer of French medieval monuments in France (for example, Notre-Dame de Paris, Vézelay, Saint-Denis and Château de Pierrefonds, see cat. 121). Morris established Morris-Marshall-Faulkner in 1861 to produce furniture, wallpaper, tile, stained glass, ceramics, and fabrics with common elements of decor and design. Viollet-le-Duc thought of the architect as a conductor directing and writing the score for an orchestral work involving the various skills of artists, sculptors, and craftsmen.

Viollet-le-Duc believed it was possible to work in the manner of the medieval master mason, in coordinating the efforts of artists, stone carvers, and craftsmen, giving the architectural project a sense of overall unity. He employed these ideas in carrying out the construction and decoration of his first major project, the restoration of Notre-Dame de Paris. Part of the restoration called for the replacement of the missing statues of saints and French kings which had been pulled down during the Revolution. The tracery of the rose windows required attention. Viollet-le-Duc felt that "nothing equals the richness of these transparent pictures," and that "in a restoration like that of Notre-Dame it is impossible not to try to harmonize all the accessory objects with the design of the edifice, above all when they are really important."[7] For this reason he wanted to "replace the convoluted grills and the bad taste of the galleries with grills more in sympathy with the architecture they accompany."[8] The murals for Notre-Dame are reproduced in chromolithography in Viollet-le-Duc's 1870 lavish color folio titled *Peintures Murales des Chapelles de Notre-Dame de Paris* (cat. 120). The mural paintings for this project as well as the ones for Château de Pierrefonds (cat. 121; p. 22), were supervised by Maurice Ouradou (1822-1884), who was married to Viollet-le-

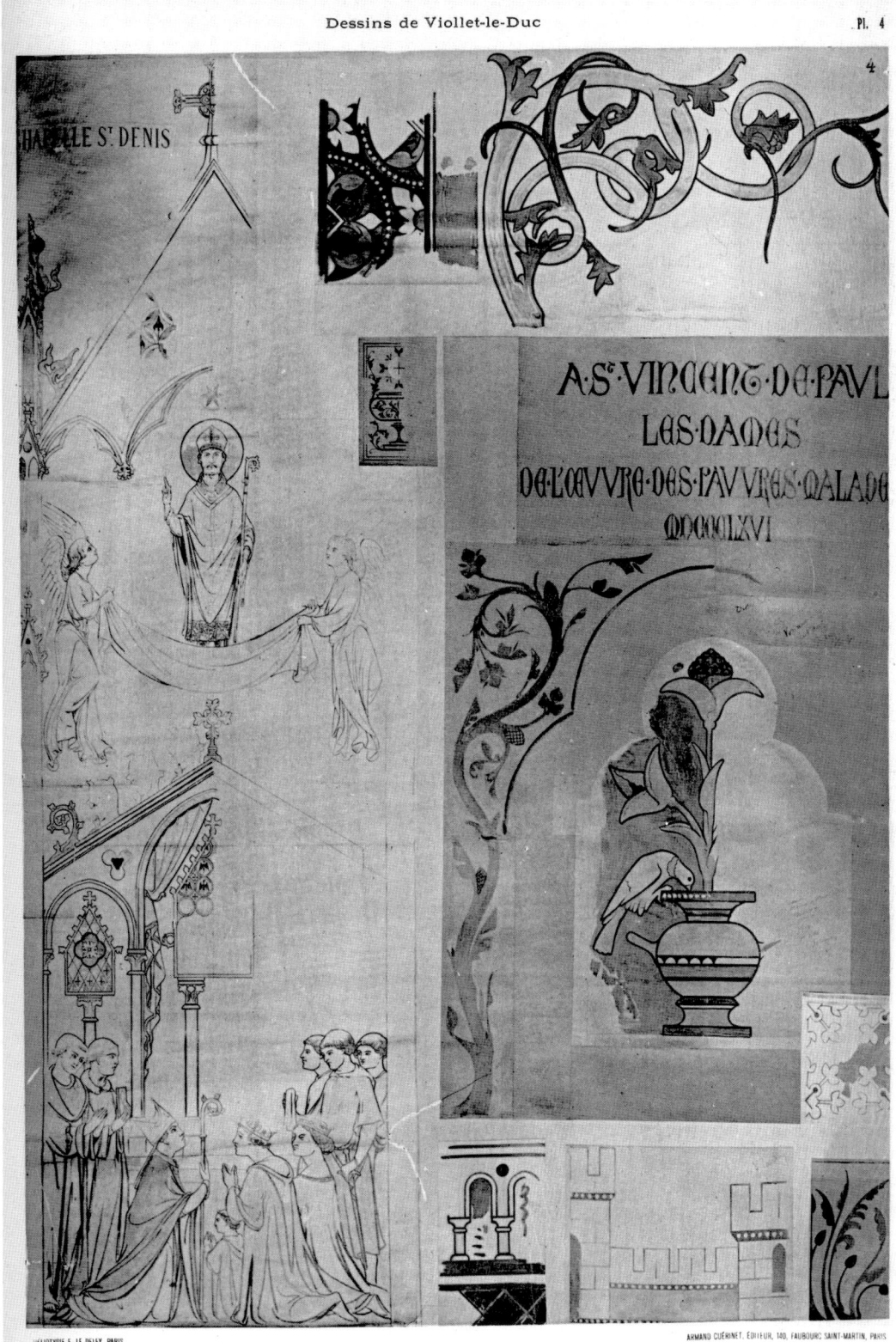

CAT. 120 Eugène-Emmanuel Viollet-le-Duc (French 1814-1879)
Designs for murals in the St. Denis Chapel of Notre-Dame, Paris.
Restoration work began 1845 and was completed 1864. *Dessins inédits de Viollet-le-Duc*, vol. I. Paris : A. Guérinet, [18—?-1902]
15½ x 11¾ in. (39.46 x 29.91 cm)
Architecture Collections, University of Oklahoma Libraries

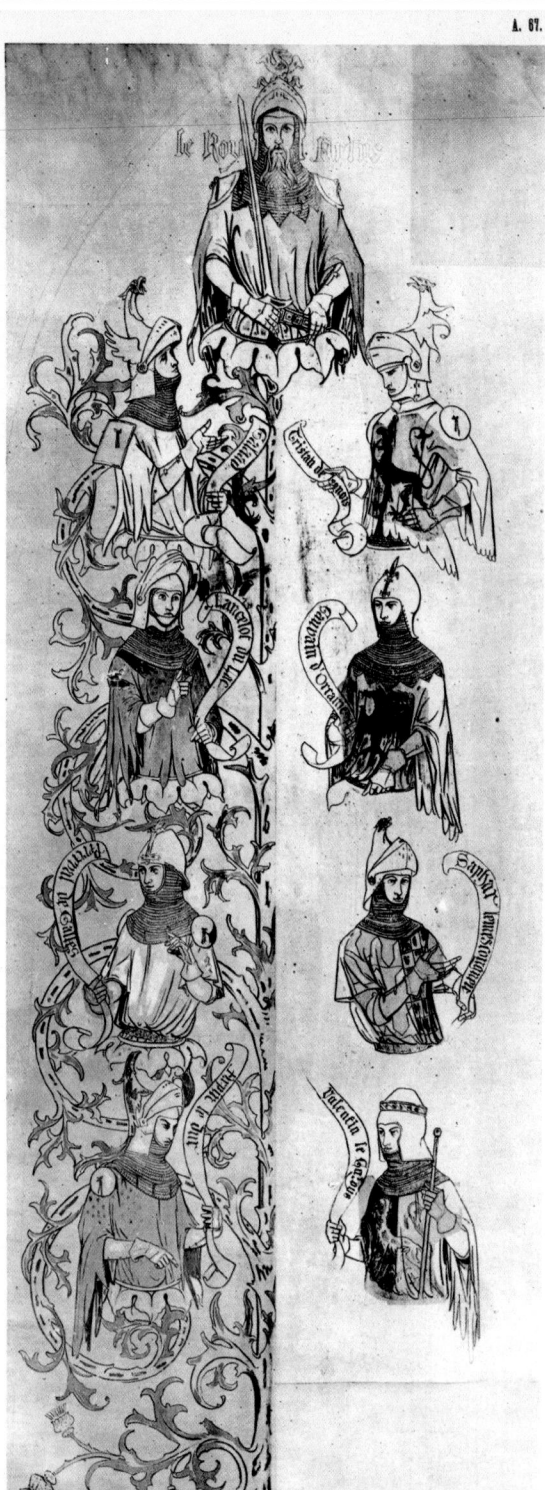

CAT. 121 Eugène-Emmanuel Viollet-le-Duc (French 1814-1879)

Designs for mural decorations in the Château de Pierrefonds. Restoration work began
1857 and continued until Viollet-le-Duc's death in 1879. *Dessins inédits de Viollet-le-Duc*,
vol. II. Paris : A. Guérinet, [18— ?-1902]; 15½ x 11¾ in. (39.46 x 29.91 cm)
Architecture Collections, University of Oklahoma Libraries

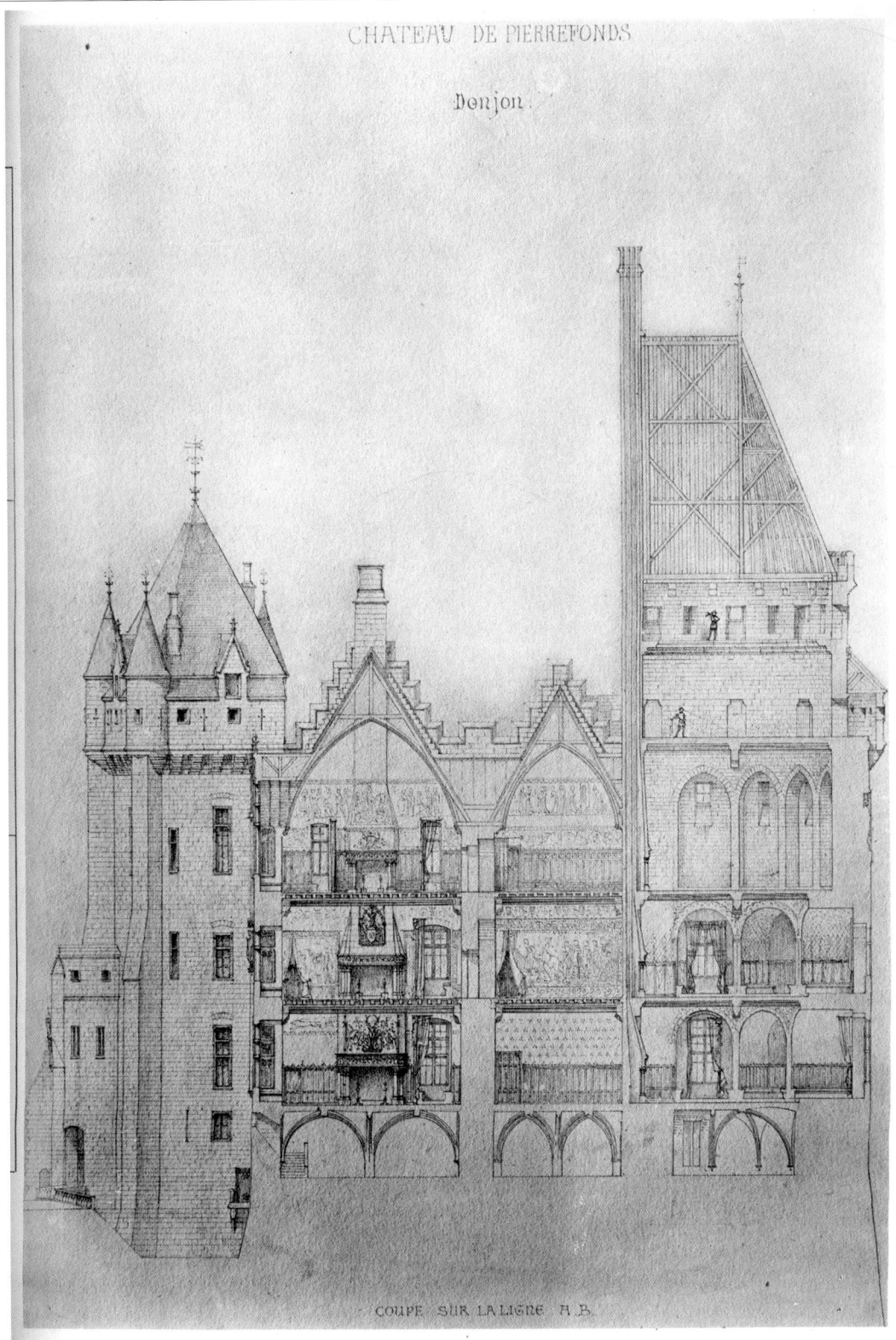

CHATEAU DE PIERREFONDS

Denjon.

COUPE SUR LA LIGNE A.B.

A. GUÉRINET, Editeur, 130, faubourg St-Martin, Paris.

Imp. phot. ARON, Paris.

CHATEAU DE PIERREFONDS

CAT. 121   Cover design showing placement Viollet-le-Duc's mural designs.
Dessins inédits de Viollet-le-Duc, vol. II. Paris : A. Guérinet,
[18— ?-1902]; 15½ x 11¾ in. (39.46 x 29.91 cm)
Architecture Collections, University of Oklahoma Libraries

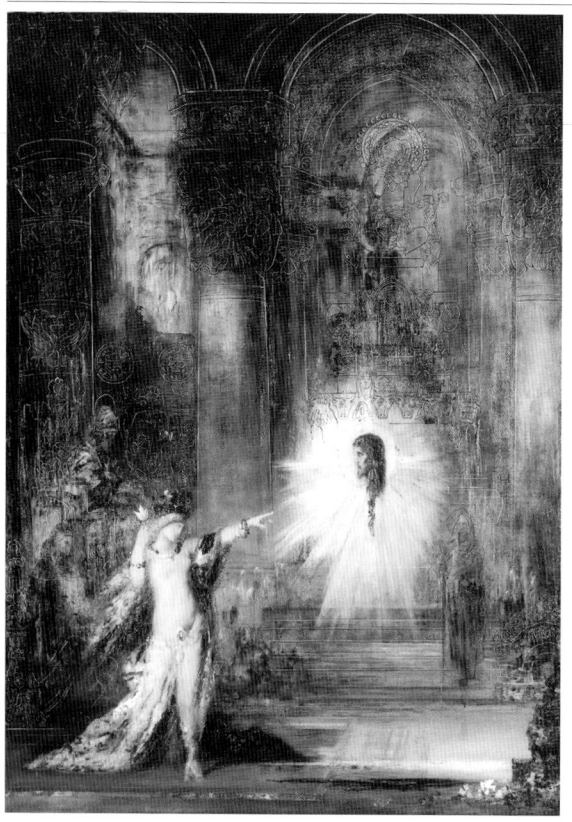

Duc's daughter Sophie. Although the murals have a cool precision and strident color associated with Viollet-le-Duc's confident and rational approach to the art of restoration, motifs like the vine patterns in the chapels, and the floral motifs in the empress's bedroom at Pierrefonds are associated with the first step toward art nouveau design.[9]

The concept of a complete rapport between the exterior-interior design of an architectural work, has spiritual, mystical, and psychological connotations. Also, the emphasis placed on the harmonious relationship of the interior and its decorous contents – furniture, art objects, sculpture, and painting – has been associated with a renewed interest in rococo art and architecture. There was an enhanced and cultivated appreciation of the total ensemble of art and design in eighteenth-century rococo interiors associated with the reign of Louis XV. Edmond and Jules de Goncourt's publications such as *Portraits intimes du XVIIIe siècle* (Paris, 1857) and especially Edmond's *Maison d'un Artiste* (2 vols. Paris, 1881), have been not only associated with the rococo revival, but most importantly, with the beginnings of a new aesthetic model, based on early nineteenth-century romantic concepts of individual creativity and genius, which put the humble eighteenth-century craftsmen, associated with the making of ceramics, woodwork, and furniture, on the same level as architects and painters.[10] The Goncourts' romantic appreciation of eighteenth-century art, expressed in their writings about aristocratic culture of the time of Louis XV, as well as Edmond's publication on their collection of eighteenth-century art, have been associated with the development of the art nouveau concept of "the interior as an organic ensemble."[11] Retreat from the world and hyperaesthetic sensitivity became the aristocratic affect of certain artists, authors, and collectors influenced by the writings and romantic stance of the Goncourts.

Joris-Karl Huysmans, author of the important 1884 symbolist novel *À rebours* [Against Nature or Against the Grain], was an admirer of the Goncourts and was inspired by Edmond's *Maison d'un Artiste*. Duc Floressas des Esseintes, the highly neurotic and extremely sensitive Baudelairien, who is the chief protagonist of the novel, seems to be a combination of Edmond Goncourt and the

FIG. 6   Gustave Moreau (French, 1826-1898)
L'apparition [The Apparition], ca. 1874-1876
Oil on canvas, 55⅞ x 40⁹⁄₁₆ in. (142 x 103 cm)
Musée Gustave Moreau, Paris
Photograph in a Private Collection

symbolist poet and aristocratic dandy Count Robert de
Montesquiou-Fezensac. In Huysmans' *À rebours*, des Esseintes buys an isolated villa on a hillside above the vil-
lage of Fontenay-aux-Roses in order to escape the vulgar
crowds, noise, and distractions of Paris. He decides to
"immerse himself in the peaceful silence of his house."[12]
He finds refuge from the turbulent life of the city and
makes inventive use of interior spaces constructed for
their psychological impact as a substitute for experiences
of the outside world. In renovating the villa, a room
was created "where mirror echoed mirror, and every
wall reflected an endless succession of pink boudoirs."[13]
Here, des Esseintes "enjoyed, in this voluptuous setting,
peculiar satisfactions – pleasures which were in a way
heightened and intensified by the recollection of past af-
flictions and bygone troubles."[14] His villa had a dining
room that resembled a ship's cabin with floorboards of
pitch pine and a small window opening that looked like a
porthole. This part of the special effects installation was
designed to create the artificial sensation of travel. For
des Esseintes, the actual experience of travel had become
a bothersome waste of time.

Robert, Compte de Montesquiou-Fezensac lived in
a house on rue Franklin with bizarre furnishings that
might have inspired des Esseintes's fictional house. The
symbolist poet Stéphane Mallarmé visited the home
of Robert de Montesquiou in 1883 and must have told
Huysmans what he had seen in "Ali-Baba's Cave ... The
sledge on a snow-white bearskin, the silk socks displayed
in a glass case, the church furniture and the gilded tor-
toise."[15] Robert de Montesquiou, known as "the bat,"
also appears as Baron de Charlus in Marcel Proust's *A la
recherche du temps perdu* [Remembrance of Things Past]
(1913-1927). Most important, however, is the influence of
the poetry of Baudelaire, especially his ideas concerning
synthesis and correspondences, or the interrelationship
of sense impressions. This is made evident in des Esseintes's "mouth-organ" made of an arrangement of li-
queur casks that could offer taste sensations equal to that
of colors mixed on a palette, and in creating moods and
sense experiences, sometimes associated with the past,
though the colors and materials of carefully selected fab-

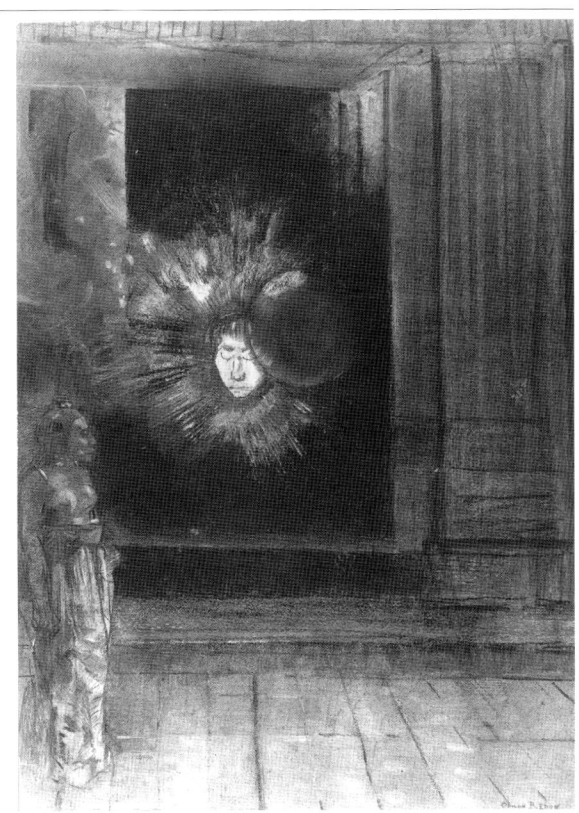

FIG. 7   Odilon Redon (French, 1840-1916)
L'apparition [The Apparition] , 1883
Charcoal heightened in white, 22¹³⁄₁₆ x 17⁵⁄₁₆ in. (58 x 44 cm)
Musée des Beaux-Arts, Bordeaux
Photograph in a Private Collection

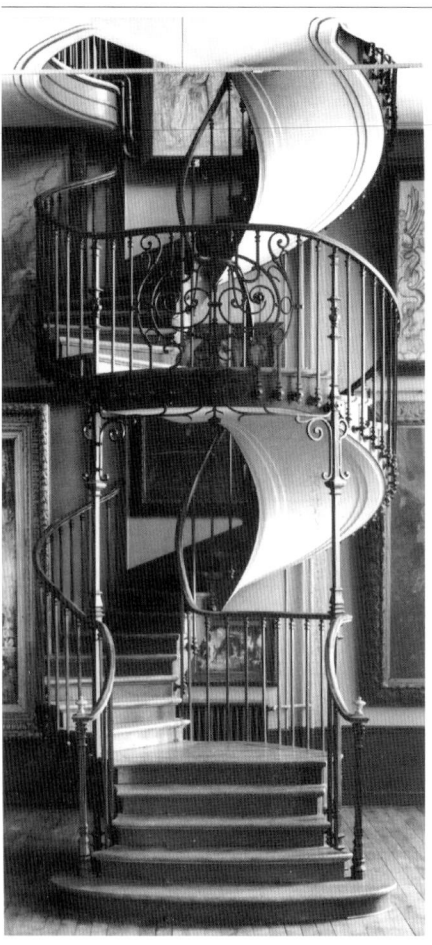

rics and furnishings. When the architect finished the renovation of the building at Fontenay, des Esseintes "gave long and careful consideration to the entire series of available colours. What he wanted was [sic] colours which would appear stronger and clearer in artificial light. He did not particularly care if they looked crude or insipid in daylight, for he lived most of his life at night, ..."[16] Special decor and paraphernalia were needed to evoke synthetic experiences associated with the senses (sight, taste, and smell). For the pink, mirrored boudoir he bought "delicate carved furniture in pale Japanese camphor-wood" and a "canopy of pink Indian satin" which would give soft warm tints to the flesh.[17] Des Esseintes hung the watercolor version of Gustave Moreau's *L'apparition* (fig. 6; p. 24) next to the painting of *Salomé dansant* [Salome Dancing] so that he could "try to puzzle out the antecedents of this great artist, this mystical pagan, this illuminee who could shut out the modern world so completely as to behold, in the heart of present-day Paris, the awful visions and magical apotheoses of the other ages."[18] He also selected Odilon Redon's *L'apparition* (fig. 7; p. 25), a variation on the subject of Salome's apparition of the head of St. John the Baptist by Moreau – there is a greater sense of the dreamlike mystery in this drawing – along with works by Jacques Callot and Rodolphe Bresdin. These were chosen for the *frisson*, created by their chilling and macabre subject matter, hardly a decorative part of the total ensemble.

The Paris studio and house of Gustave Moreau (fig. 8), also known as the "Wizard of St. Lazare," appears to have been a sanctuary for the artist. The studio, for many successful late nineteenth-century artists, became both a show place and a sanctuary. Fernand Khnopff (1858-1921), Alphonse Mucha, and Sarah Bernhardt had dwellings and studios with art objects, furnishings, and curiosities of all kinds. Khnopff's fin-de-siècle house and studio in Brussels (fig. 9), compared with Mucha's Paris studio (fig. 10), is relatively austere, yet it is a good example of the sanctuary-atelier of the 1890s, which included an altar dedicated to Hypnos (the son of Night

FIG. 8   Gustave Moreau (French, 1826-1898)
         View of the large studio on the 3rd floor with the spiral staircase built
         by Albert Lafon in 1895. Photograph by René-Gabriel Ojéda. Musée
         Gustave Moreau, Paris, France
         Réunion des Musées Nationaux/Art Resource, New York

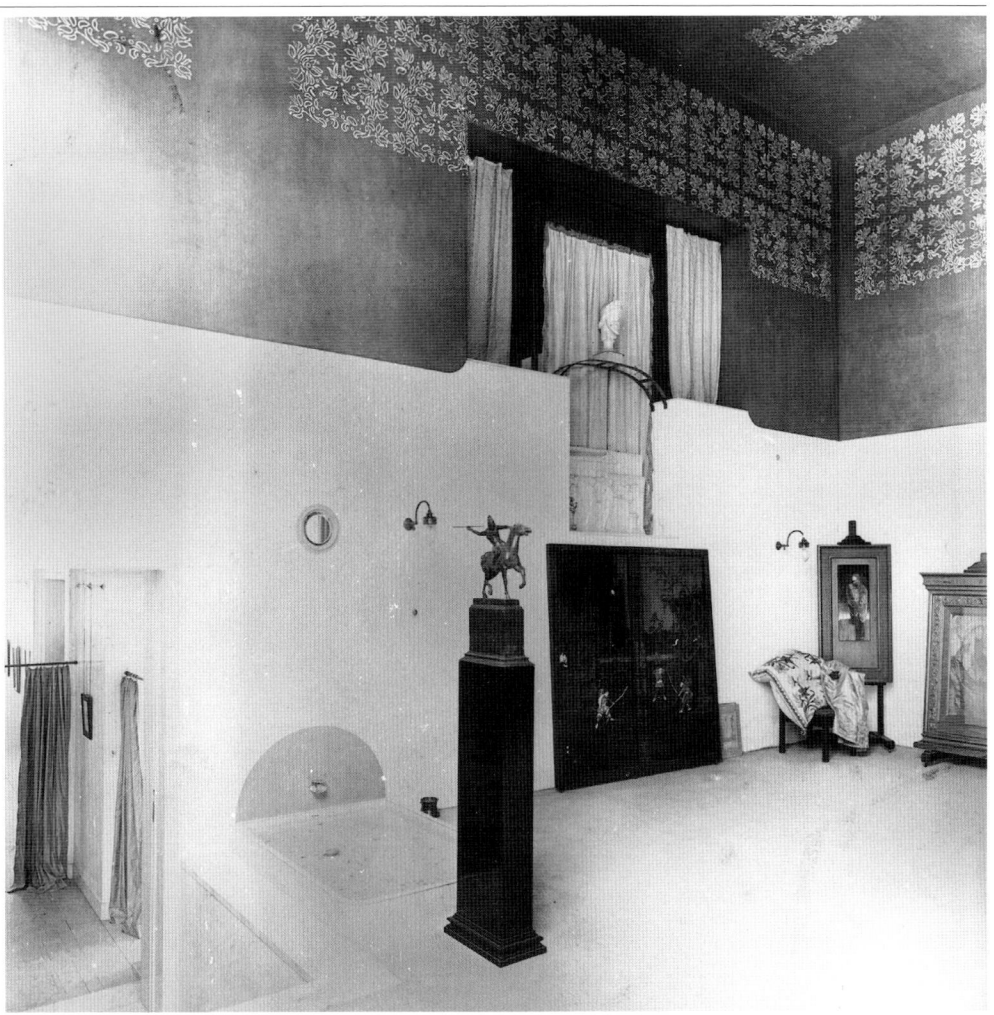

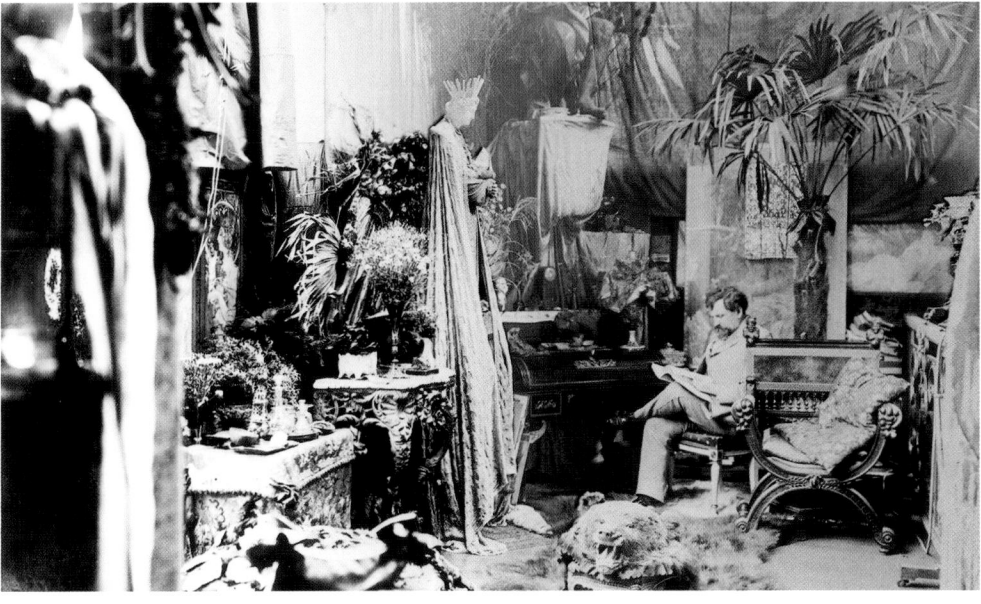

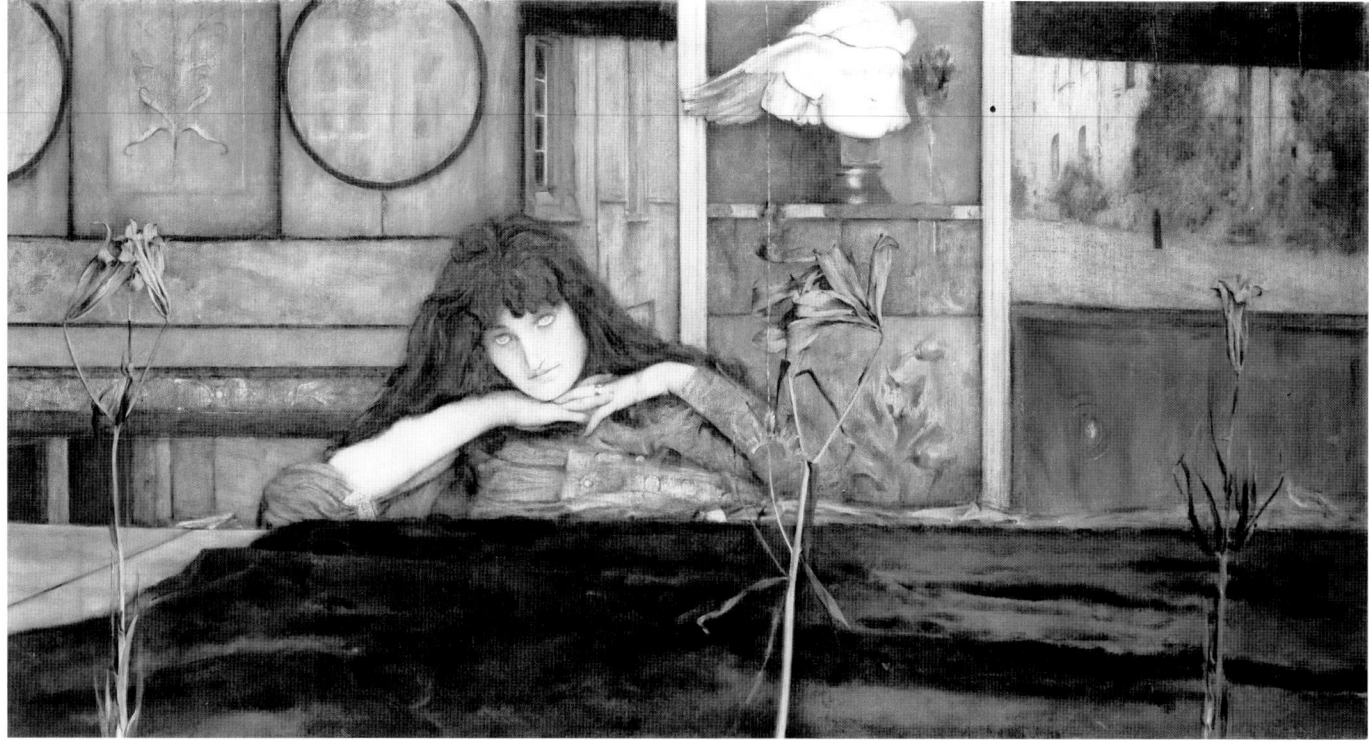

and twin brother of Death).[19] Nestor Eemans, Khnopff's biographer, described the appearance of the artist's studio where Khnopff sought solitude, and compared it with des Esseintes's rejection of society in Huysmans' *À rebours*. At the beginning of his career, Khnopff, like Denis, Bonnard, and Vuillard, displayed a preference for intimate scenes of domestic life. In 1892, he completed a painting titled *I Lock My Door Upon Myself*, or *A Recluse* the second title given to the picture (fig. 11). It was inspired by the poetry of Christina Rossetti. A complete edition of her poems appeared a year before Khnopff carried out the painting. Certain passages of Rossetti's poem "Memory" evoke imagery and ideas which might be associated with the painting. The opening passage of the second part of this poem seems the most relevant:

> I have a room where into no one enters
> Save I myself alone:
> There sits a blessed memory on a throne,
> There my life centres.

In Khnopff's painting a woman is shown seated behind a table in a state of ennui or quietly enduring her melancholia. On the wall there is a painting of a deserted street in which stands a solitary figure. The head of Hypnos with its tinted blue wing is on a shelf next to the painting. This head is also found in other works, as well as in a photograph of the artist, where it appears as a kind of household god or votive motif surmounting his occult altar (fig. 12).[20] On the base of Hypnos, continuing below at the back of the altar, an inscription reads *On n'a que soi* [One knows only oneself]. On the ceiling in mosaic is Khnopff's astrological sign, Libra. This idea of the studio as an alchemist's laboratory, or secret shrine, where the

FIG. 11   Fernand Khnopff (Belgian, 1858-1921)
I Lock the Door Upon Myself, 1891
Oil on canvas, 28¾ x 54¼ in. (50 x 150 cm)
Neue Pinakothek, Munich
Photograph in a private collection

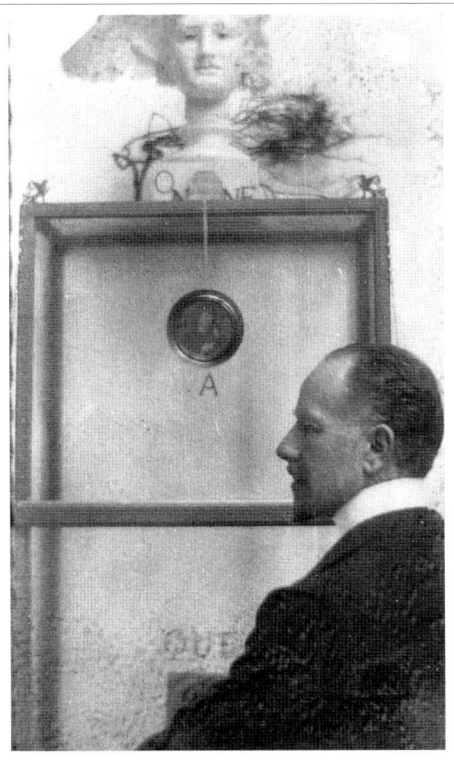

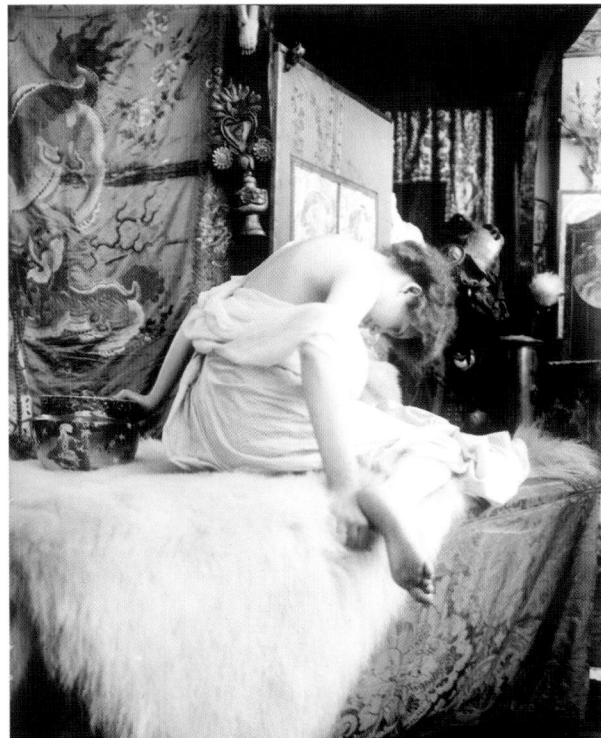

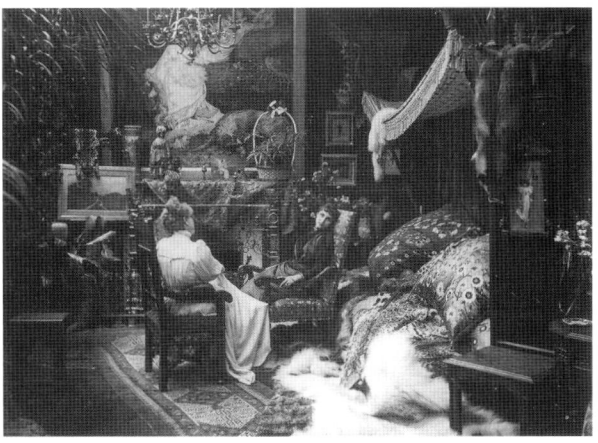

magical process of creation takes place, developed during the Romantic period. For example, there were contemporary accounts of J.M.W. Turner's London studio as being the dusty refuge of a secretive genius. The late nineteenth-century studios with their bizarre decor seem to give definition to the romantic conception of the artist as one who is capable of withdrawing from the material demands of life and like an alchemist reveals things which cannot be seen by those who are caught up in the practical tasks of the workaday world.

Mucha's studio on rue du Val-de-Grâce (fig. 10), like the apartment of his patroness Sarah Bernhardt (fig. 14), was something of a mish-mash of Asian, Turkish textiles and vases, Persian carpets, as well as bear-skins and stuffed birds along with "Renaissance, baroque, and Empire" furniture.[21] Unfortunately, this type of setting hardly exhibited the elevated harmony of sculpture, painting, and furnishings that represented Bing's ideal art nouveau interior, which Mucha would at times simulate with his dressed-up model and studio props (fig. 13).

FIG. 13   Model in Mucha's studio rue de Val-de-Grâce
Photograph, ca. 1900
©Mucha Trust 2007

FIG. 12   Fernand Khnopff (Belgian, 1858-1921)
Photograph of Khnopff in front of shrine
Private Collection

FIG. 14   Paul Nadar
Studio of Sarah Bernhardt on the Boulevard Péreire, n.d.
Gelatin silver print, 8¼ x 10⅝ in. (21 x 27 cm)
Centre des Monuments Nationaux

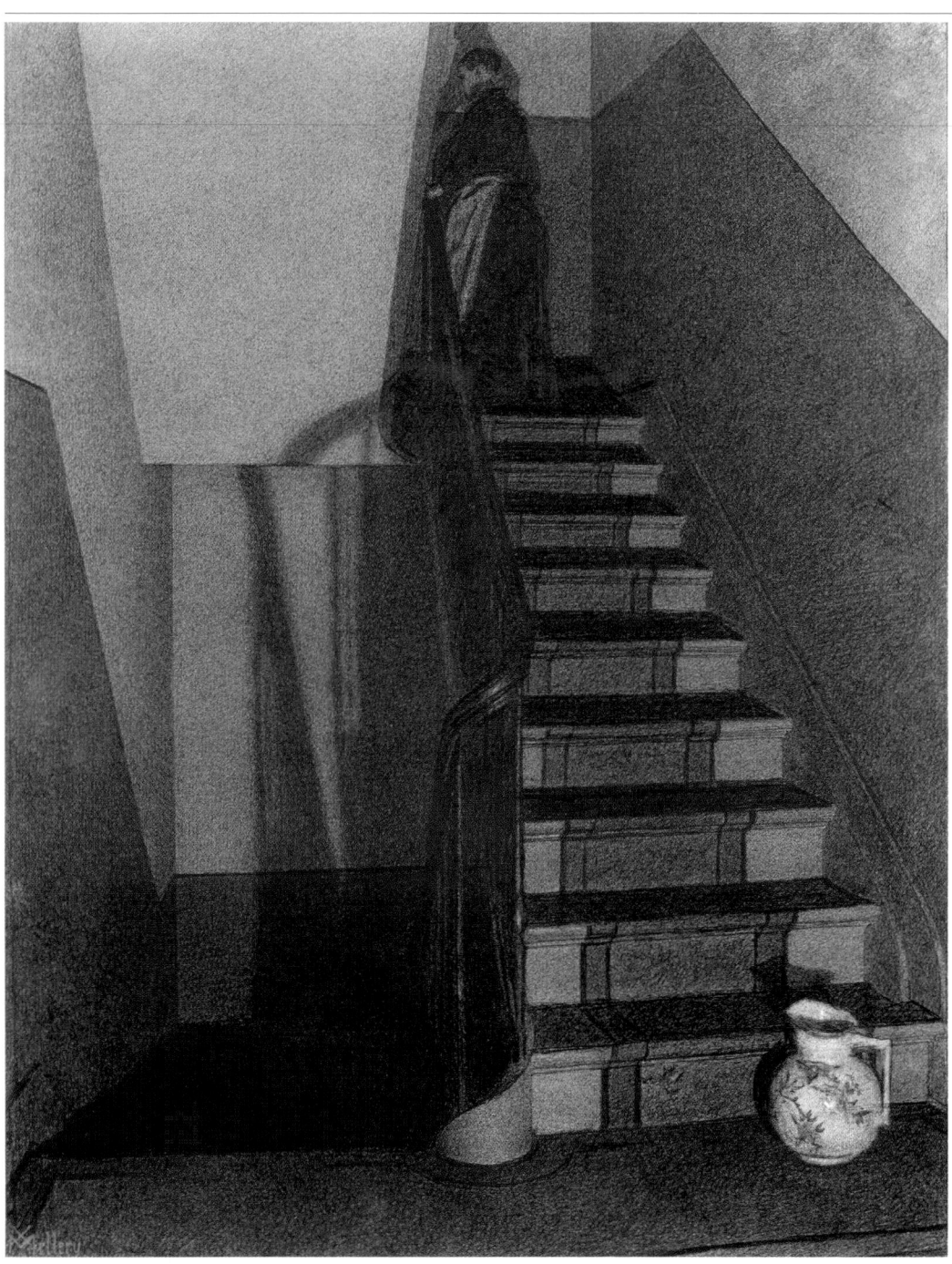

FIG. 15   Xavier Mellery (Belgian, 1845-1921)

L'escalier au pot blanc [Staircase with White Pitcher], ca. 1889

Chalk on paper, 22⅜ x 17¾ in. (57 x 45 cm)

Koninklijk Museum voor Schone Kunsten, Antwerp

KMSKA- Image Courtesy of Reproductiefonds-Lukas

Marcel Proust's psychological investigation of his memories and feelings surrounding an almost extinct fin-de-siècle culture in *A la recherche du temps perdu* [Remembrance of Things Past], includes an examination of the tastes of the period for eighteenth-century decor and Japanese art, as well as a satirization of less informed tastes and ideas concerning period furnishings. Unlike Edmond Goncourt or Joris-Karl Huysmans, in Proust's quest to capture and examine the indecipherable mystery of the human condition he was looking back on the habits and values of a society which he was very much a part of. In places the art and interior decor is used in portraying the elusive and complex persona of his chief protagonist, the aristocratic Swann, and the less complicated makeup of his wife Odette. In Proust's recollections of domestic scenes in the country house of his parents at Combray, and the Paris apartment of Swann and Odette, he describes the nuance of feeling and mood evoked by these mysterious interiors. Artists known for their paintings of interiors, who were also Proust's contemporaries, sought pictorial equivalence for these subjective feelings. Xavier Mellery (1843-1921) (fig. 15), Fernand Khnopff, Eugène Carrière (cat. 15; p. 34), Maurice Denis, and the *intimistes* Pierre Bonnard and Edouard Vuillard were known for their private and personal interiors of this kind. Their work was also associated with poetry which expressed the sentiments of the most secret realms of the soul. Interior decoration, decor, and collecting objects of art, however, did not escape Proust's satirical and caustic humor. Odette was beginning to see the importance of stylistic unity in interior furnishings and recognizing the prominent status of eighteenth-century decor. She claimed to be fond of "antiques," and:

> assumed a rapturous and knowing air when she confessed how she loved to spend the whole day "rummaging" in curio shops, hunting for "bric-à-brac" and "period" things. ... she spoke to Swann once about a friend to whose house she had been invited, and had found that everything in it was "of

the period." Swann could not get her to tell him what "period" it was. But after thinking the matter over she replied that it was "mediaeval"; by which she meant that the walls were paneled. Some time later she spoke to him again of her friend, and added, in the hesitant tone ... "Her dining room ... is ... eighteenth century!" ... She mentioned it again, a third time, when she showed Swann a card with the name and address of the man who had designed the dining-room, and whom she wanted to send for when she had enough money, to see whether he couldn't do one for her too; not one like that, of course, but ... with tall side-boards, Renaissance furniture and fireplaces like the chateau at Blois.[22]

Proust strikes a more serious note when he describes the placement and unifying content of M. De Guermantes's collection of paintings by a contemporary artist named Elstirs (identified as Whistler). While the fin-de-siècle interior with its sense of overall unity did not seem to interest Proust, here he appears intrigued by the homogeneity of his imagined creation of a perfectly unified collection of works probably based on his knowledge of Whistler's nocturne paintings:

> I had before me fragments of that world of new and strange colours which was no more than the projection of that great painter's peculiar vision, ... The parts of the walls that were covered by paintings of his [Elstirs], all homogeneous with one another, were like the luminous images of a magic lantern which in this instance was the brain of the artist, ...[23]

The late nineteenth-century followers of the mural painter Puvis de Chavanne, Maurice Denis (cat. 27; p. 32), and Alphonse Osbert (cat. 83; p. 33) shared with him in their decorative works his simplicity and sense of quietude and religious spirituality. Denis and Osbert painted murals for private homes, public buildings, and churches. The works of both artists have also been associated with

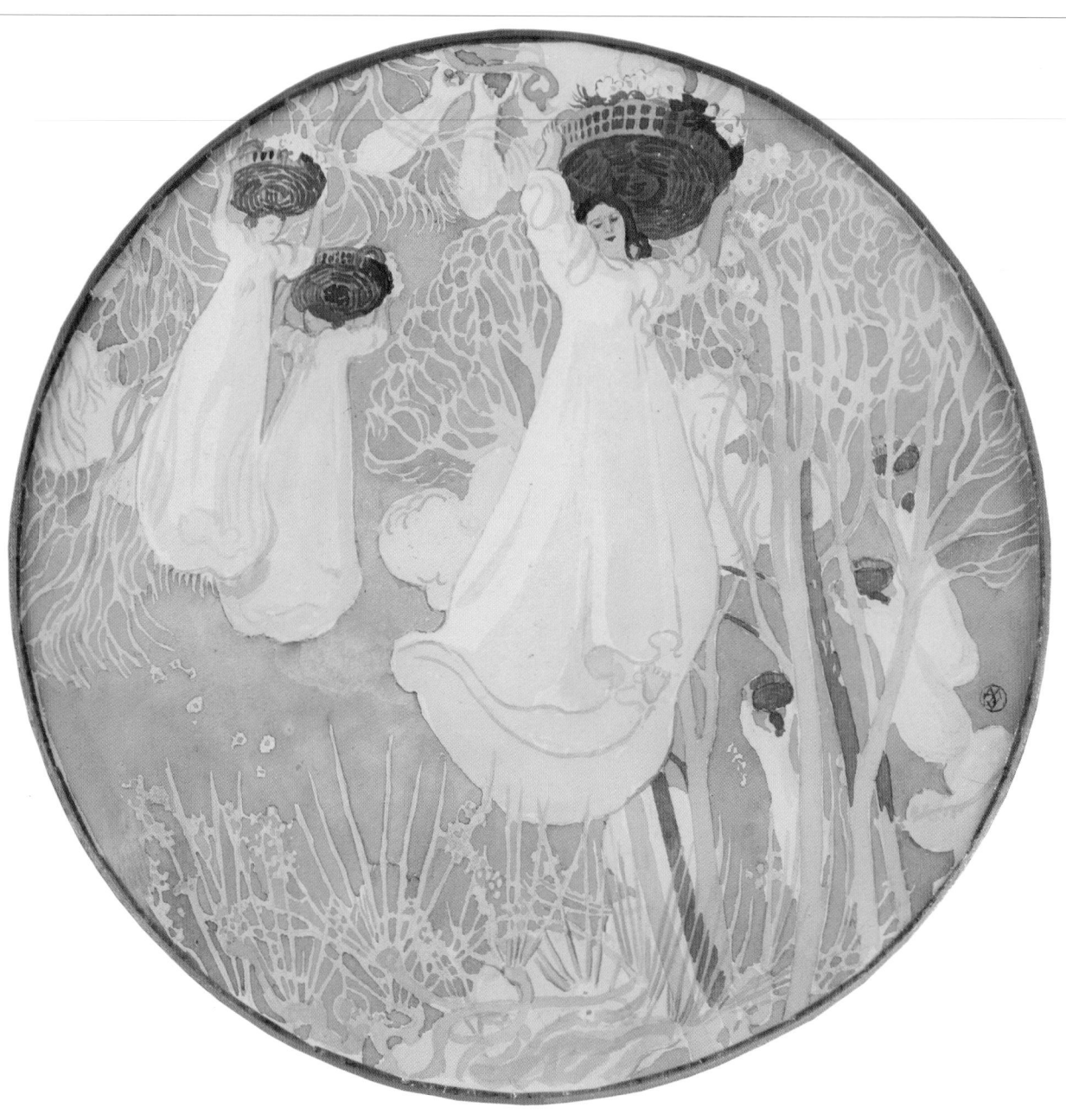

CAT. 27   Maurice Denis (French, 1870-1943)
Avril, after 1894 (1907?)
Drawing, ink wash heightened with white on paper,
diam. 7¼ in. (18.5 cm)
Russell Collection, Amsterdam

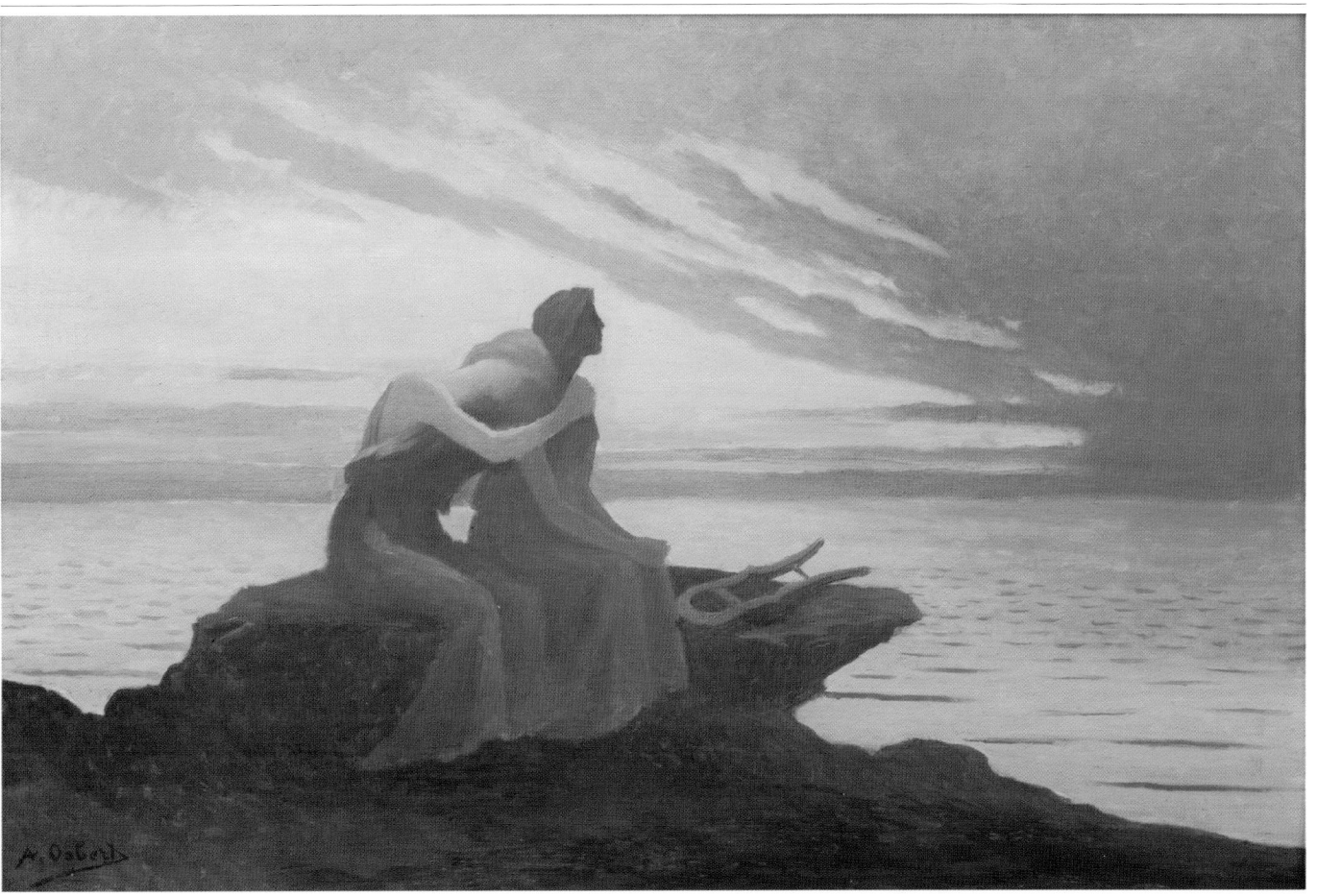

CAT. 83   Alphonse Osbert (French, 1857-1939)
Crepuscule du Soir, ca. 1900
Oil on panel, 14⅜ x 22¹⁄₁₆ in. (36.5 x 56 cm)
Russell Collection, Amsterdam

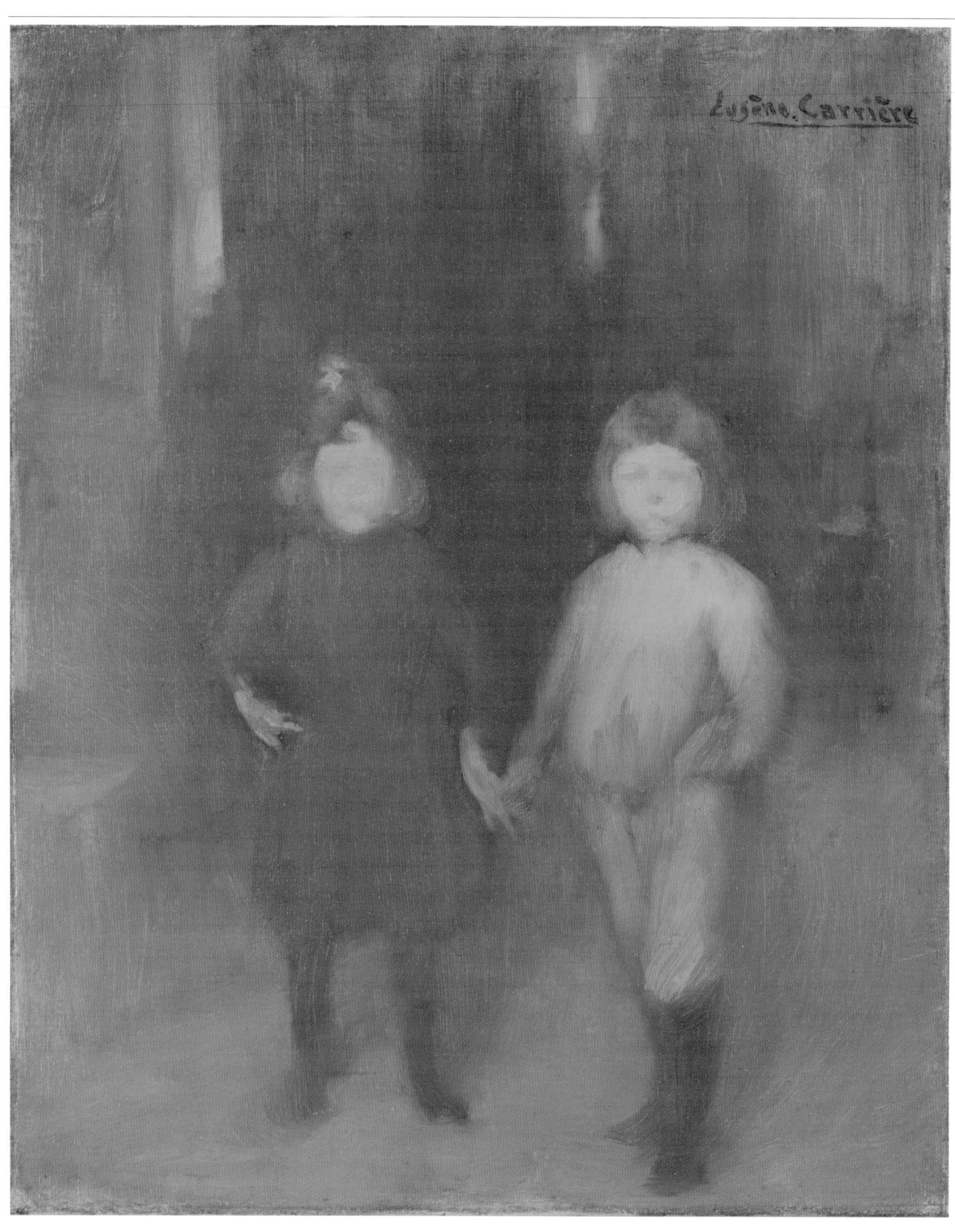

CAT. 15   Eugène Carrière (French, 1849-1906)
Jean-René and Lucie Carrière, ca. 1898-1900
Oil on canvas, 18¼ x 15¹⁄₁₆ in. (46.35 x 39.67 cm)
Wadsworth Atheneum Museum of Art, Hartford, Connecticut.
Gift of Ivan Loiseau

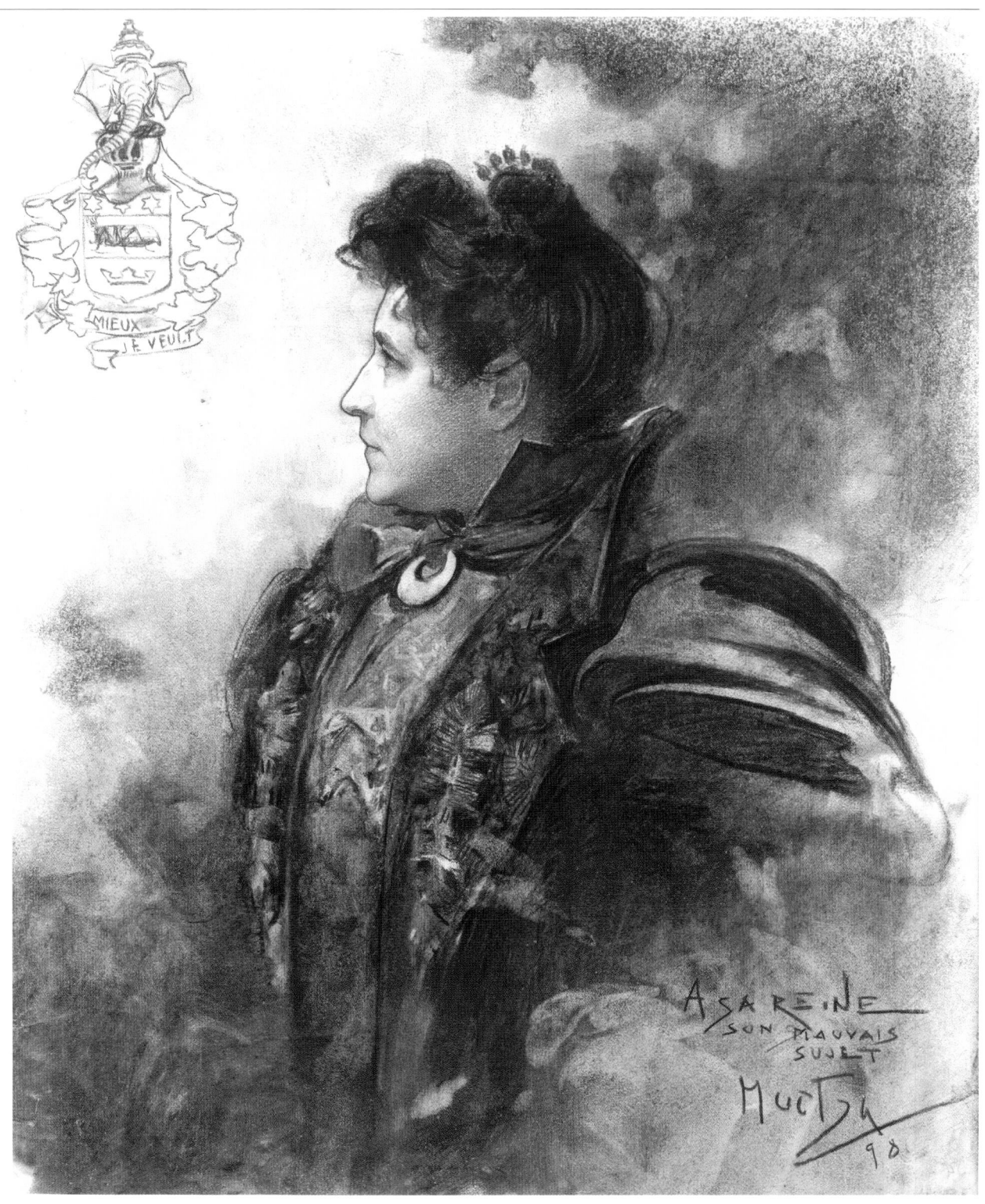

CAT. 74 Alphonse Mucha (Czech, 1860-1939)
Portrait of Sarah Bernhardt, 1898
Charcoal on paper, 18¹¹/₁₆ x 21⅝ in. (55 x 47.5 cm)
Russell Collection, Amsterdam

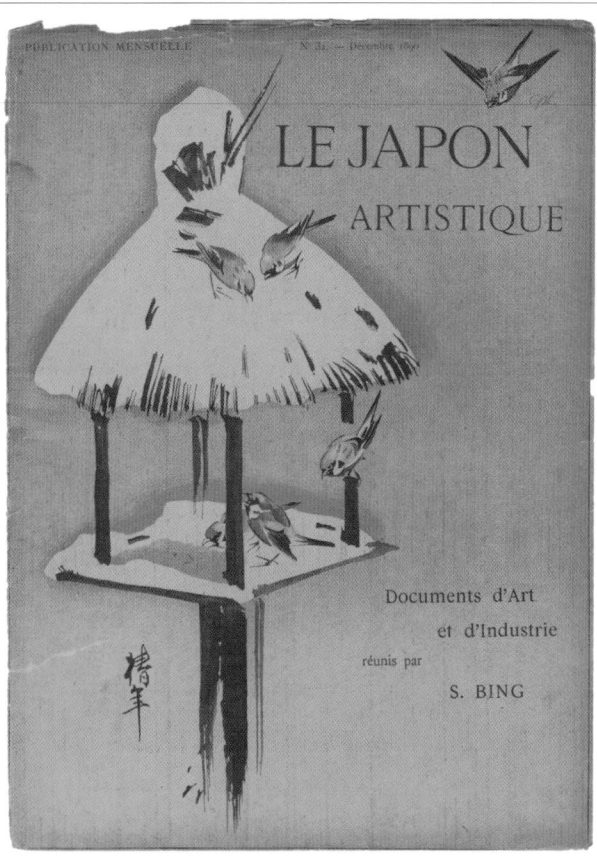

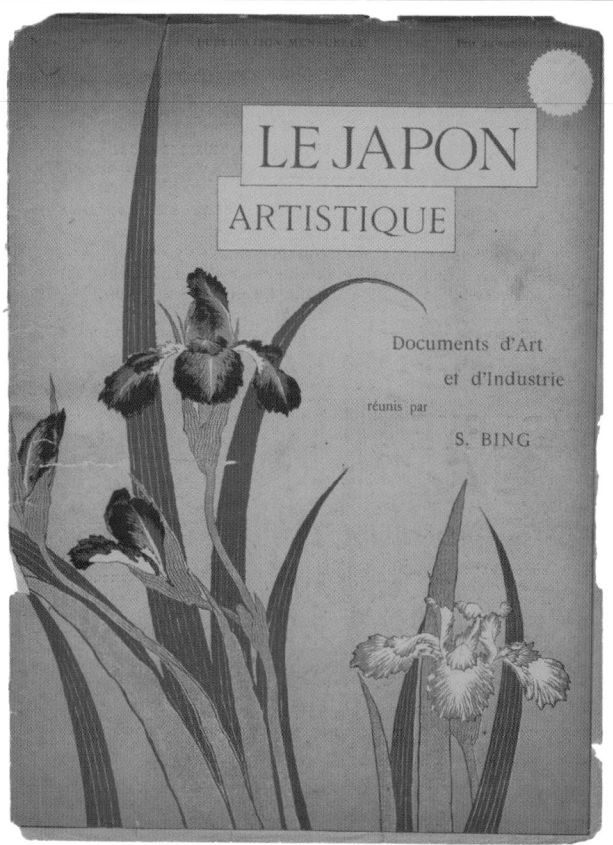

CAT. 50   *Le Japon Artistique* (cover), no. 32 (December 1890)
13 x 9⅝ in. (33 x 24.4 cm)
Dr. Gabriel and Yvonne Weisberg Collection

CAT. 51   *Le Japon Artistique* (cover), no. 24 (April 1890)
13 x 9⅝ in. (33 x 24.4 cm)
Dr. Gabriel and Yvonne Weisberg Collection

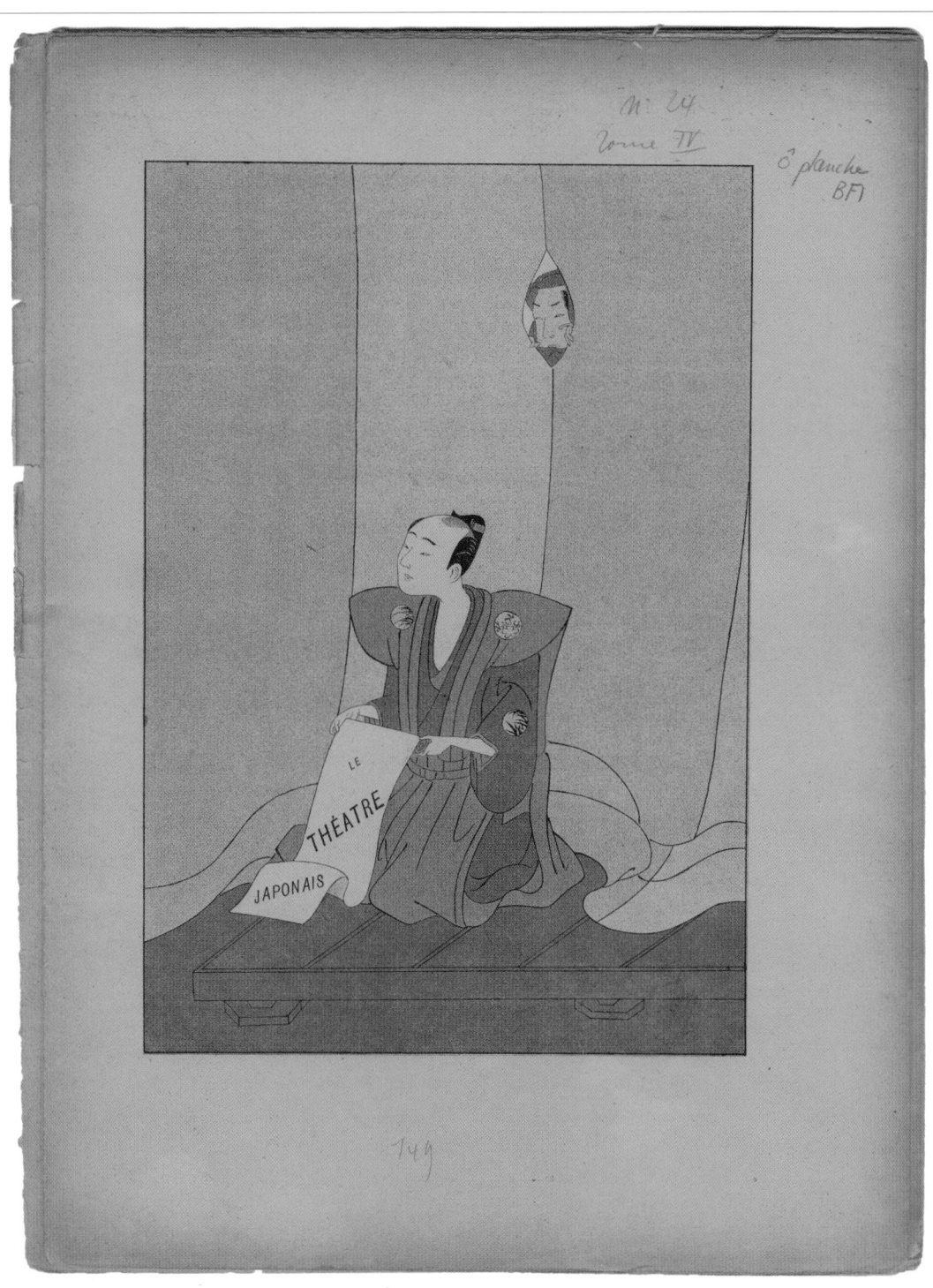

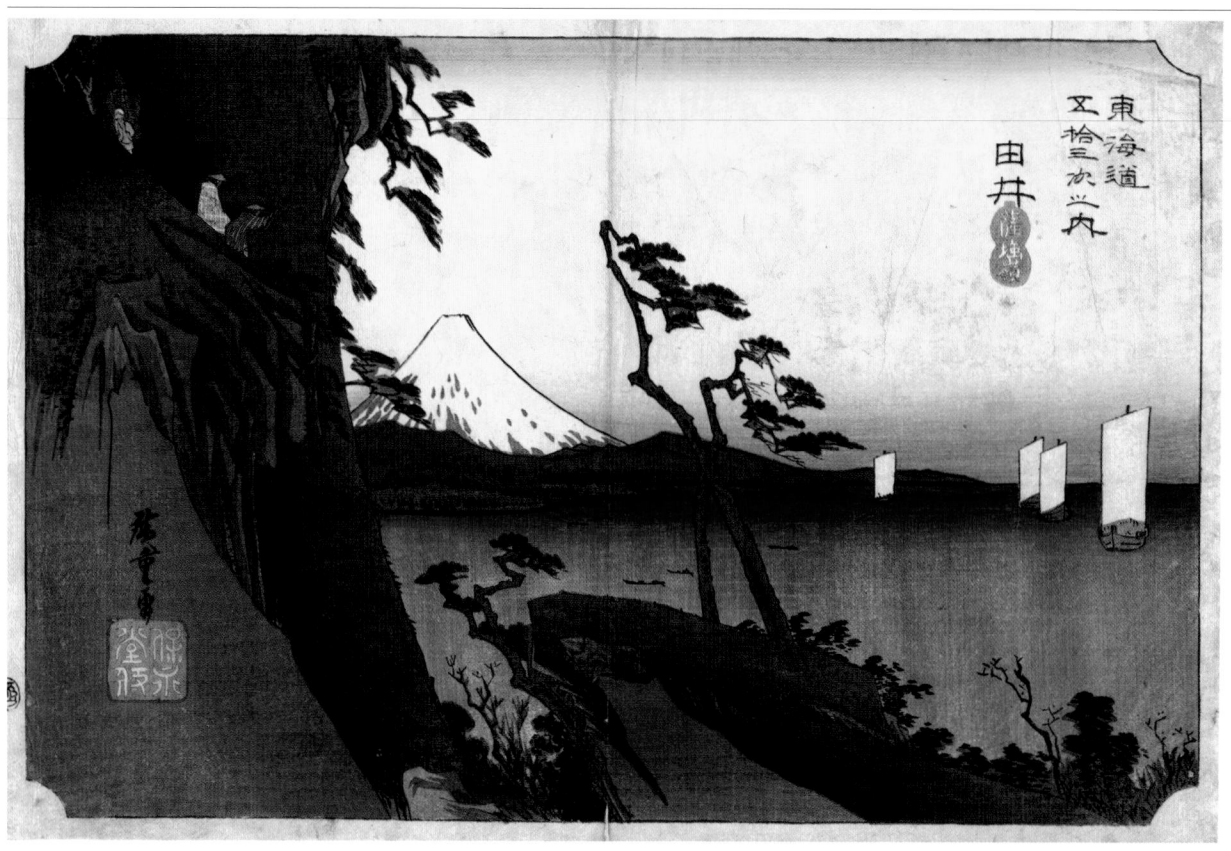

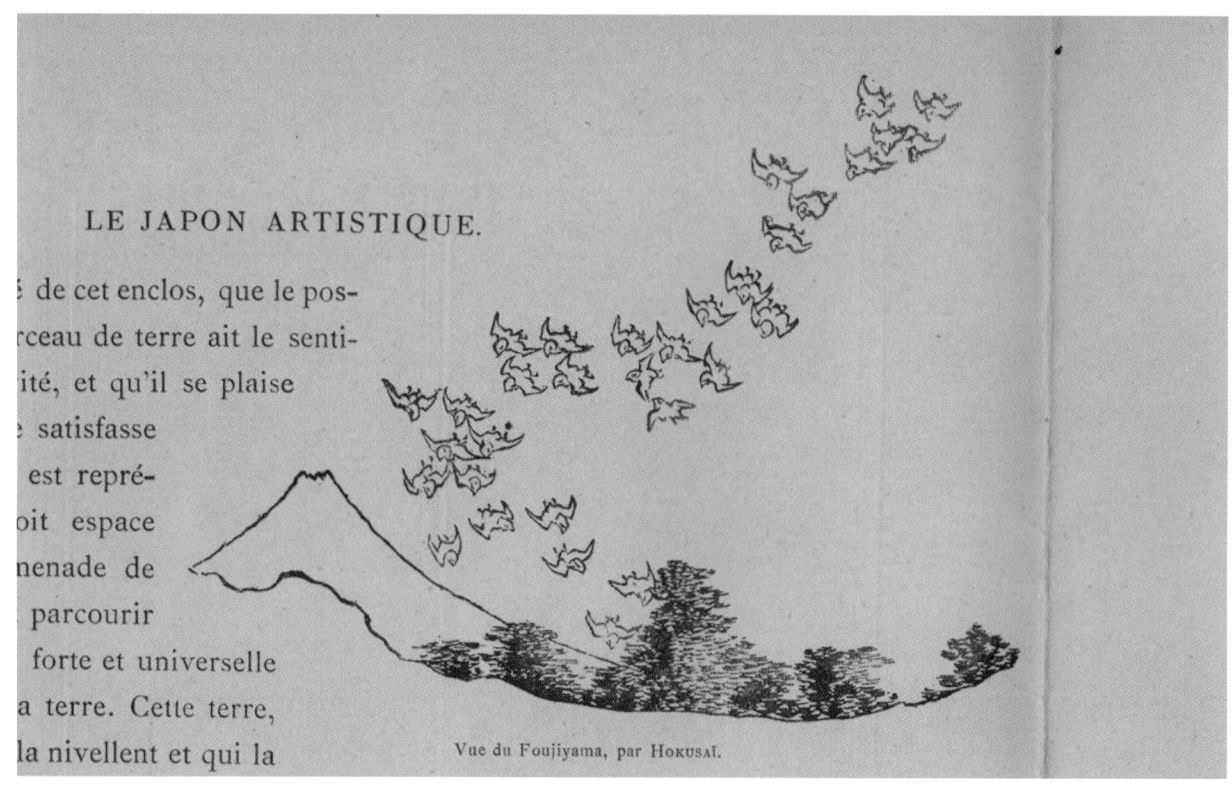

LE JAPON ARTISTIQUE.

e de cet enclos, que le pos-
rceau de terre ait le senti-
ité, et qu'il se plaise

e satisfasse

est repré-

oit espace

nenade de

parcourir

forte et universelle

a terre. Cette terre,

la nivellent et qui la

Vue du Foujiyama, par HOKUSAÏ.

CAT. 49   Andō Hiroshige (Japanese, 1797-1858)

The Pine Forest of Mio in Suruga Province:

"Thirty-six Views of Mount Fuji" series, 1858

Color woodblock print, 13⅜ x 8¾ in. (33.97 x 22.23 cm)

Private Collection

CAT. 50   *Le Japon Artistique*, no. 32 (December 1890)

"Vue du Foujiyama par Hokusai" in: "Les paysagistes Japonais"

article by Gustave Geffroy.

13 x 9⅝ in. (33 x 24.4 cm)

Dr. Gabriel and Yvonne Weisberg Collection

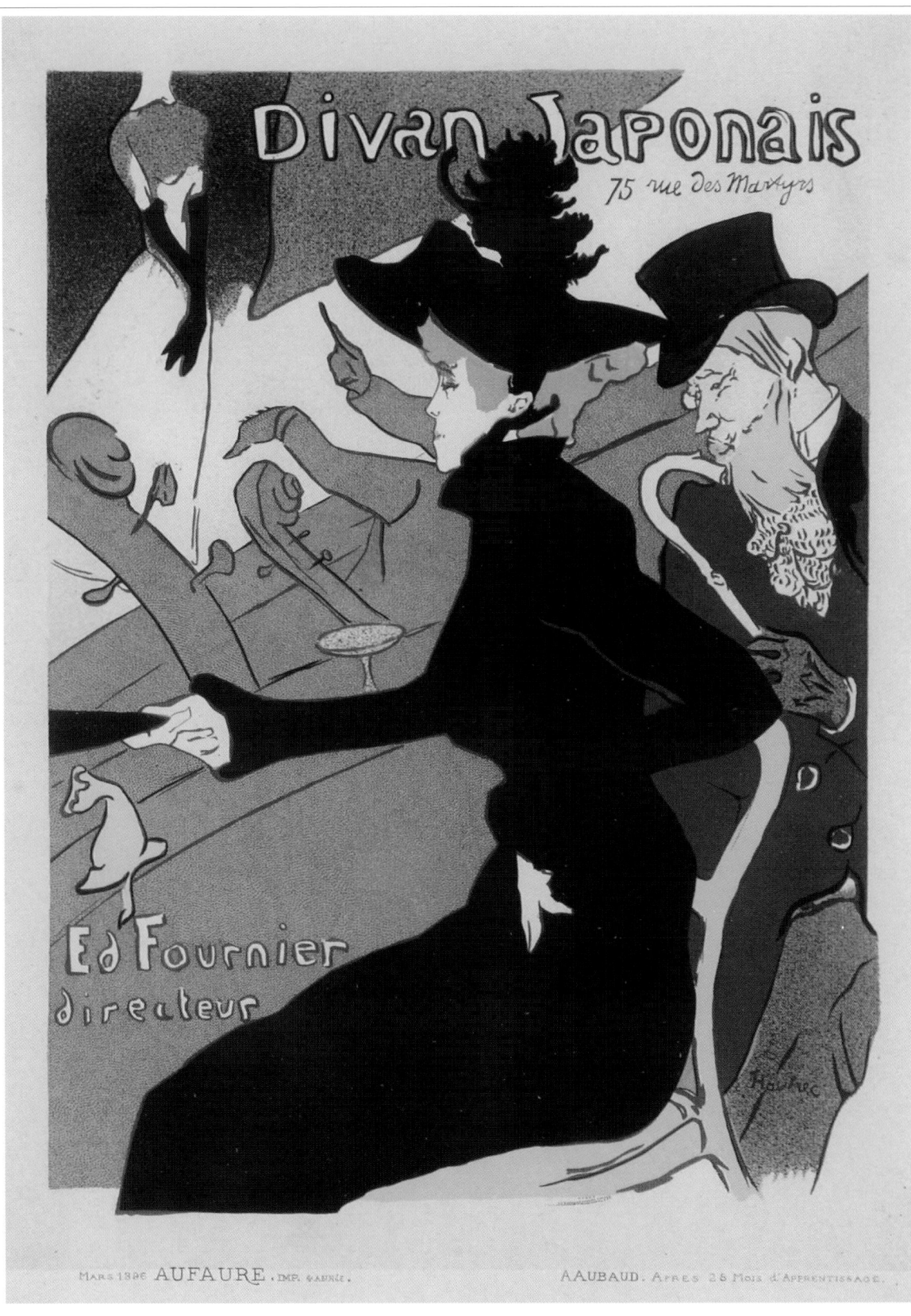

CAT. 118 Henri de Toulouse-Lautrec (French, 1964-1901)
Divan Japonais, 1896
Color lithograph, 11 x 8 in. (28 x 20.36 cm)
Courtesy J. Raj K. Dhawan

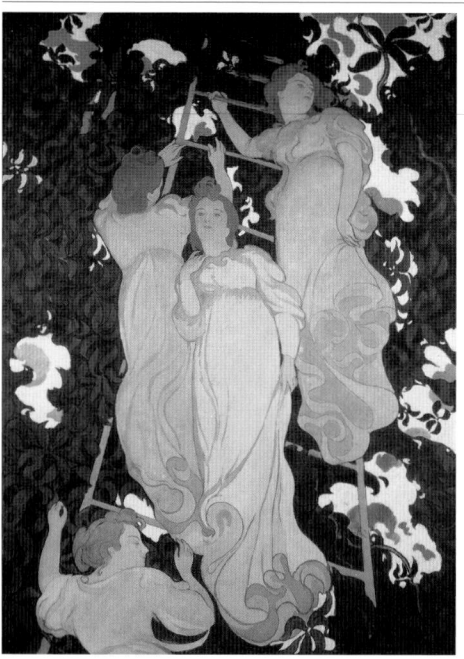

the sense of overall unity and decorative qualities making up the essential ingredients of synthetism and cloisonnism in the 1880s and 1890s. Denis, along with his teacher at the Académie Julien, Paul Serussier, and his fellow students who established the brotherhood known as Les Nabis (from the Hebrew word for "prophets") were spiritual followers of the Pre-Raphaelites. The principal influence, however, came from Japanese art and the related flatness and expressive color.

In Siegfried Bing's first issue of his journal *Le Japon Artistique* (1888), he emphasized the importance of Japanese art (cat. 49; p. 38) as a new force which would greatly influence developments in Europe. In 1890, he had an extensive *ukiyo-e* print exhibition that included the Japanese landscapists Hiroshige, Hokusai, Kiyonaga, Toyonobu, Harunobu, Shunsho, Sharaku, and Utamaro. The show was accompanied by an issue of *Le Japon Artistique* with illustrations of woodblock prints and an article by Gustave Geffroy on *Les Paysagistes Japonais* [the Japanese Landscapists] with references to work of Hokusai (cat. 50; p. 38) and Hiroshige.

Gauguin's flat contrasting fields of color and his use of decorative line owe a great deal to Japanese color prints. The structured and enclosed forms of his cloisonnism, introduced in the religious Brittany paintings of 1888, had a considerable effect on Les Nabis. Also, Georges Seurat had reestablished the importance of line and form in his influential works of the late 1880s in which contour, as well as decorative and expressive line and color, were emphasized. These works reveal the influence of the decorative flatness of Japanese woodblock prints, which is combined with expressive color, linear curves, and arabesques evoking emotions of gaiety, sadness, or calm.

The decorative and arabesque line plays an important part in Maurice Denis's music-related prints and paintings of the early 1890s showing women in long flowing gowns recalling the work of the English Pre-Raphaelites. Long gowns and the serpentine line appear in Denis's costume sketches for Maeterlinck's *Sept Princesses* (1891), the 1892 frontispiece for Debussy's

FIG. 16   Maurice Denis (French, 1870-1943)
L'échelle dans le feuillage [Ladder in the Foliage], 1892
Ceiling painting, Oil on canvas mounted on board
92½ x 67¾ in. (235 x 172 cm)
Musée départemental Maurice Denis "Le Prieuré"

La Damoiselle élue (based on "The Blessed Damozel" a poem by Dante Gabriel Rossetti). The floating figures in long gowns in the 1892 ceiling painting commissioned by Henry Lerolle of *L'échelle dans le feuillage* [Ladder in the Foliage] (fig. 16), have been compared with the angels in Jacob's dream (Gen., 28:12). Denis's related ceiling tondo, titled *Avril* (1894), was painted for the composer Ernest Chausson (fig. 17). Denis's highly finished drawing for, or after, the Chausson ceiling painting, is also titled *Avril* (cat. 27; p. 32). The drawing, like the painting, has been seen as "entirely Art Nouveau"[24] and makes use of baroque perspective to indicate the ascension of the gowned figures toward the heavens. In the lithograph, published in *L'Estampe originale*, two women, similarly attired, float through the air holding baskets on their heads. The theme of female figures in long gowns floating freely in the air occurs a number of times in his graphic work. He not only used the subject for the 1892 lithograph of *La Damoiselle élue*, but again in the same year, in a poster for *La Dépêche de Toulouse* (a Toulouse newspaper), and for a vignette on the list of his own works exhibited in 1893 at Le Barc de Boutteville gallery in Paris.

Alphonse Osbert had solid academic training, and for a while fell under the influence of seventeenth-century Spanish art (Velázquez and Ribera). Starting in 1881, he exhibited classical works at the Salon. His technique was transformed little by little with the influence of impressionism which caused him to use higher-keyed colors and to paint his landscapes directly before nature. After 1887, he fell under the influence of symbolist poetry and Puvis de Chavannes. He also had a friendly relationship with Seurat, Aman-Jean, and Séon. He soon gave up his impressionist naturalism for more imaginary subjects influenced by poetry and biblical stories like those of Puvis. He also shared Seurat's and Aman-Jean's interest in the disintegration of tone and the symbolic use of line, and employed the divisionist technique, and a range of hues – blue, violet, yellow, and green – associated with neo-impressionism and pointillism. In 1888, he filled his pictures with a spiritual light and employed a method of working

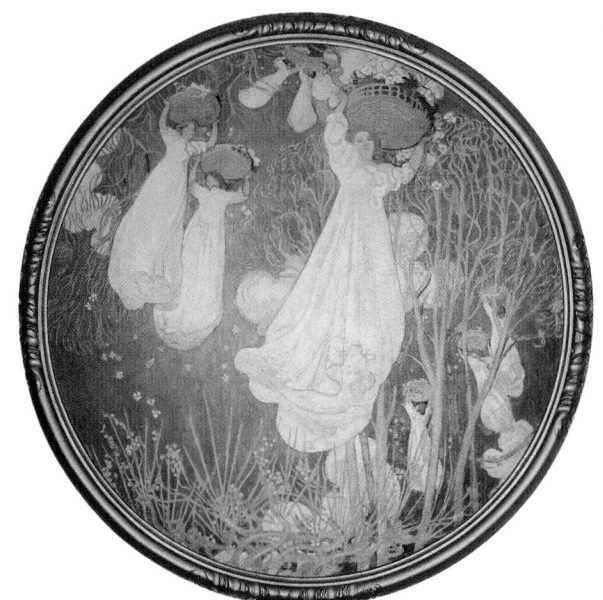

FIG. 17   Maurice Denis (French, 1870-1943)
Avril [April], 1894
Painting, 78¾ in. (200 cm)
Musée départemental Maurice Denis "Le Prieuré"

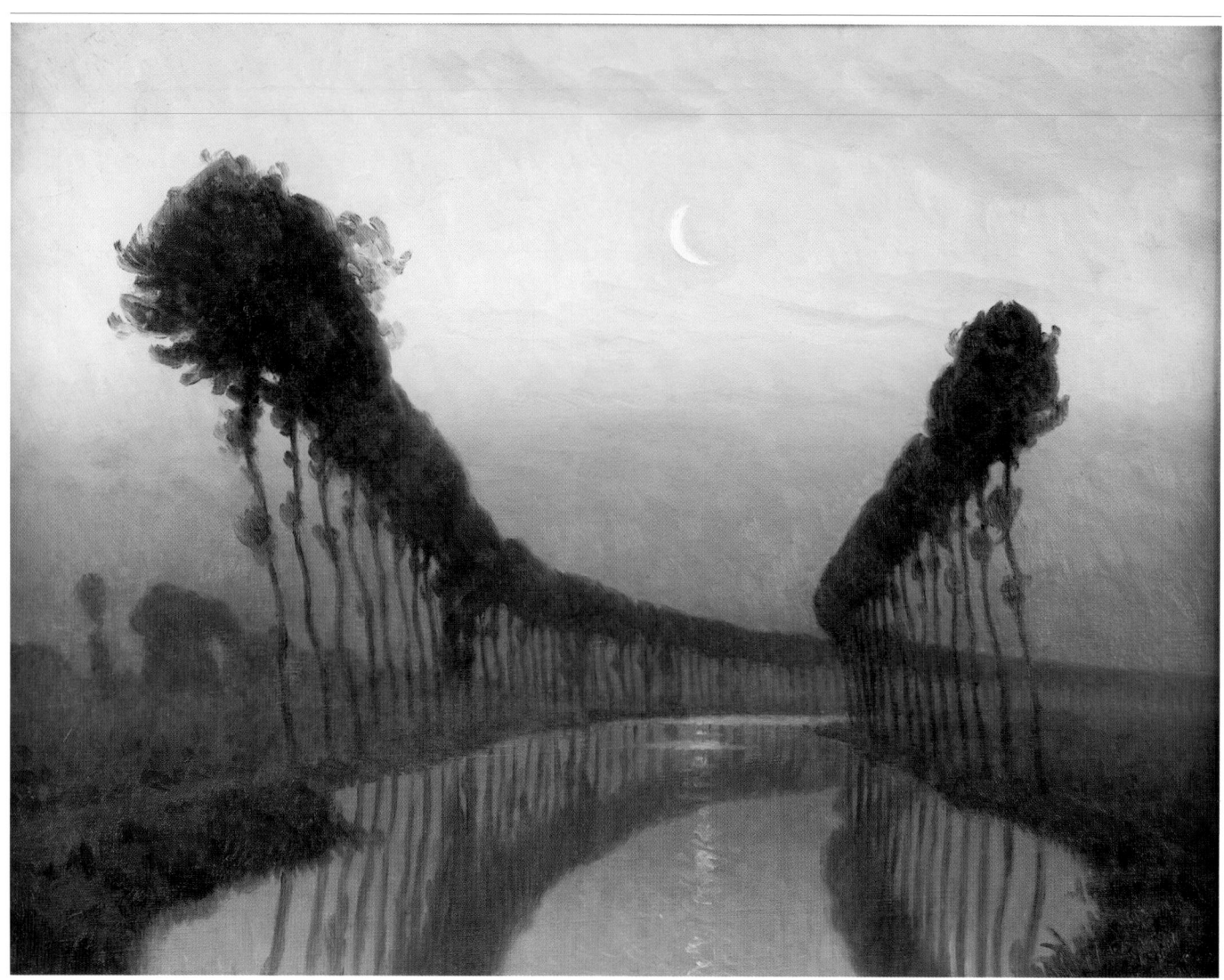

CAT. 42   Charles Guilloux (French, 1866-1946)
L'Allée d'eau [The Waterway], 1895
Oil on board, 17 $^{11}/_{16}$ x 23 $^{7}/_{16}$ in. (45 x 59.5 cm)
Russell Collection, Amsterdam

that was partly Nabi and partly neo-impressionist, and in his use of color and form, created a poetic iconography. His visionary landscapes included women often dressed in long white gowns carrying lyres, alone or in groups, immobile and silent (cat. 83; p. 33). Melancholy women and dream landscapes evoke under his brush human sentiments and the beauty of nature. His credo was: "Je veux arriver à la Simplicité même, au grand Silence." Osbert exhibited in the Salon de la Société nationale, founded by Puvis de Chavannes to replace the official Salon. In 1891, he was at Saint-Germain-en-Laye with Maurice Denis and Les Nabis, and in Paris he exhibited with this group several times at Le Barc de Boutteville. In 1890, he took part in the Comité des Artistes indépendants with Seurat, Luce, and Signac. He participated in all the exhibitions of the Salon de la Rose + Croix. Osbert was praised for the sweetness and serenity characterizing his twilight paintings [Soirs] staffed with "dreamy virgins." Many of his subjects of this kind were associated with Jeanne d'Arc or Sainte Geneviéve, the patron saint of Paris. His work also appeared among the paintings of les peintres de l'âme [the painters of the soul] in 1896, at the Salon des Cent, at Siegfried Bing's Salon de l'Art Nouveau and the Salon d'Art religieux organized in Brussels by the revue Durendal. Osbert was considered a decorator and painter of frescoes, and he was given several commissions for murals in public buildings in the city of Vichy and for the Conservatoire de Musique of Paris.

The relatively unknown and self-taught artist Charles Guilloux painted symbolist landscapes which relate stylistically to Osbert and particularly to Charles-Marie Dulac, Charles Lacoste, and other painters who painted decorative and imaginary and idealized landscapes.[25] These highly stylized symbolist works were particularly well suited for enhancing the total unity and sense of mystery associated with the fin-de-siècle domestic interior. In the 1890s, Guilloux exhibited his work with other artists associated with "the painters of the soul" in the Sociétaire des Independants and exhibitions at Le Barc de Boutteville.[26] In the early 1890s,

the uniqueness of Guilloux's decorative and stylized landscape painting was recognized immediately by Aubert Aurier, Gustave Geffroy, Roger-Marx, and others. His unique synthetism consists of rhythmic and expressive lines, the elimination of detail, and overall use of poetic color harmonies to convey lasting impressions of the artist's contemplative mental images of nature observed.

Guilloux's three river views with general titles, L'Allée d'eau [A Waterway] (cat. 42), L'Inondation (cat. 39; p. 44), and Paysage orageux [Stormy Landscape] (cat. 40; p. 45),[27] related to time of day and climate conditions. Cathérine Verleysen associates these landscapes with places Guilloux knew along the Seine, near the villages of Frette-sur-Seine and Herblay, where the artist lived with his family, near Bougival and Chatou. Interestingly, these are places, particularly Bougival and Chatou, which were frequented earlier by impressionists such as Renoir and Monet. The shoreline views could have been partially inspired by areas that he knew along the river Marne (Lagny, Mary, or Champigny), as well as Brittany (Saint-Michel-en-Grève, Tredez, Locquémeau).[28] Guilloux's Notre Dame vue des Quais (cat. 41; p. 46) may belong to the series of six paintings titled Le tournant de la Seine,[29] shown at Le Barc de Boutteville in 1893, and another group exhibited in the same gallery, in 1896, titled La Seine à Saint-Denis. The misty effects with soft reflections of light on the river bring to mind Whistler's nocturnes of the 1870s that originated from observations made on the Seine towards dusk and at night. This technique was based on Horace Lecoq de Boisbaudran's (1802-1897) unusual teaching method of visual memory training. Whistler's work was known in France, and he was one of the early devotees of Japanese art and decoration and part of the Mallarmé symbolist circle in the 1880s. Guilloux's gentle, limpid effects of evening light, with flat barges anchored offshore on the Thames combines the style of the early nineteenth-century print with the atmospheric effects of Whistler.[30] There was not only a need for artificial landscape subjects for turn-of-the-century interiors, but also portraits of illustrious individuals surrounded by all their worldly comforts.

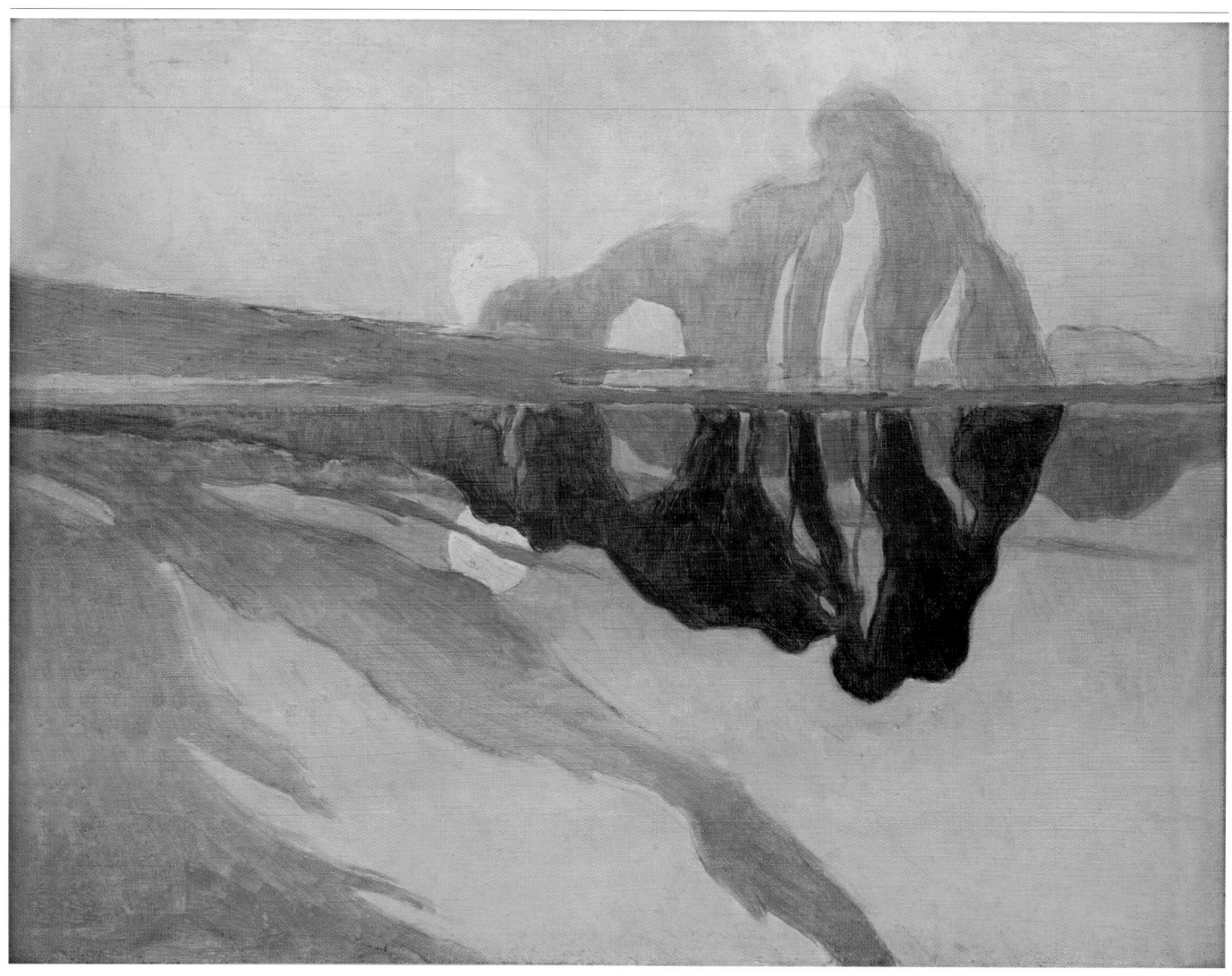

CAT. 39   Charles Guilloux (French, 1866-1946)
L'Inondation, ca.1892
Oil on paper laid down on board,
9⁷⁄₁₆ x 13 in. (24 x 33 cm)
Russell Collection, Amsterdam

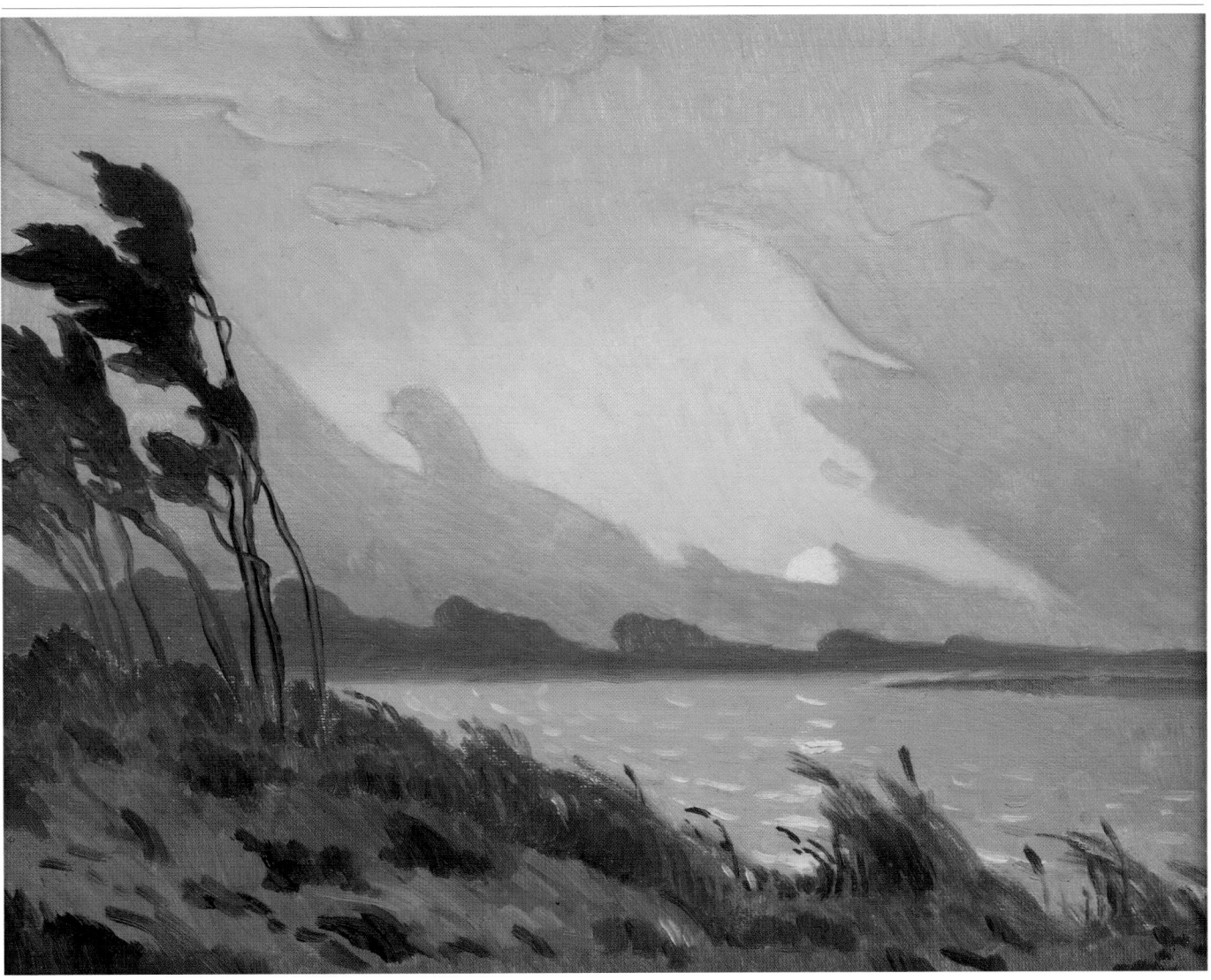

CAT. 40   Charles Guilloux (French, 1866-1946)
Paysage orageux [Stormy Landscape], ca.1892-1895
Oil on canvas, 10⅝ x 13¾ in. (27 x 35 cm)
Russell Collection, Amsterdam

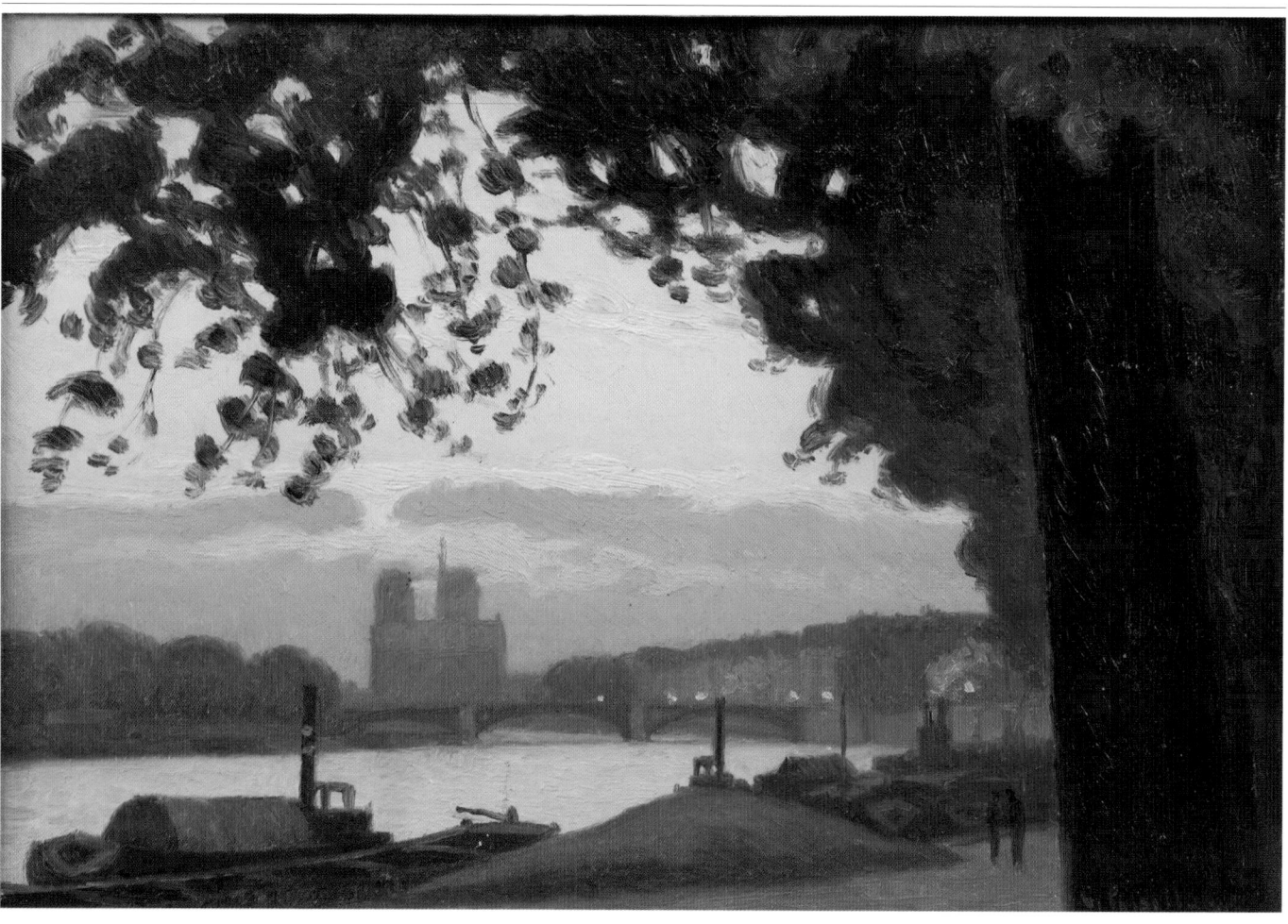

CAT. 41   Charles Guilloux (French, 1866-1946)
Notre Dame vue des Quais, 1894
Oil on board, 9$^{13}\!/_{16}$ x 13 in. (25 x 33 cm)
Russell Collection, Amsterdam

Sarah Bernhardt, a major talent in the French theatre of this period, as well as a sculptress of no mean
talent, was memorialized not only by Georges Clarin
(1843-1919) and Alphonse Mucha, but also by Jules
Chéret, Eugène Grasset, Leonetto Cappiello, Alfred
Stevens, Jean-León Gérôme, Edmond Lachenal, René
Lalique, the photographer Paul Nadar, and others. Sara
Bernhardt also made a *Self-portrait as Roland's Daughter*
in terra-cotta, and a *Self-portrait as a Sphinx* and had it
cast in bronze as part of a fantastic inkwell (fig. 18) which
became part of her interior decor. It was, however, Mucha, who was best known for his portraits of Bernhardt.
One of Mucha's "composed" photographs of a sump-
tuously attired model complemented by the decorous
furnishings of his Val-de-Grâce studio (fig. 19; p. 49)
appears related to photographs of Sarah Bernhardt in a
flowing dress that complements her luxurious Paris interior in much the same manner (fig. 20; p. 49).

In one of his earliest lithograph posters of 1894, he
portrayed her as *Gismonda* in Victorien Sardou's play by
the same name, and another of her for *La dame aux camé-
lias*, *Lorenzaccio*, *La Tosca*, *Médée*, and *Hamlet*. In these
posters Bernhardt is portrayed as a statuesque figure,
standing in a shallow arched niche with a surrounding
frame decorated with floral and whiplash ornaments,
characteristic of art nouveau decoration. The framing
architectural motif is reminiscent of the ones on or in
Renaissance and medieval churches containing statues of
saints and Old Testament prophets. In the early poster for
Gismonda her name appears on the arch of the niche and
the name of the theatre on the base. Mucha repeats this
composition for other theatre posters, and the ones an-
nouncing Sarah Bernhardt's visits to North America (cat.
65; p. 53). In the later ones the name of the theatre below
was replaced by "American Tour" with the names of the
agents underneath. Mucha's posters mark the zenith of
Bernhardt's acting career and her tours of North America
were part of her stellar climb to universal recognition.

Along with Mucha's niche motif used to frame the
figure of Bernhardt in costumes associated with her various roles, he employed another type of architectural form

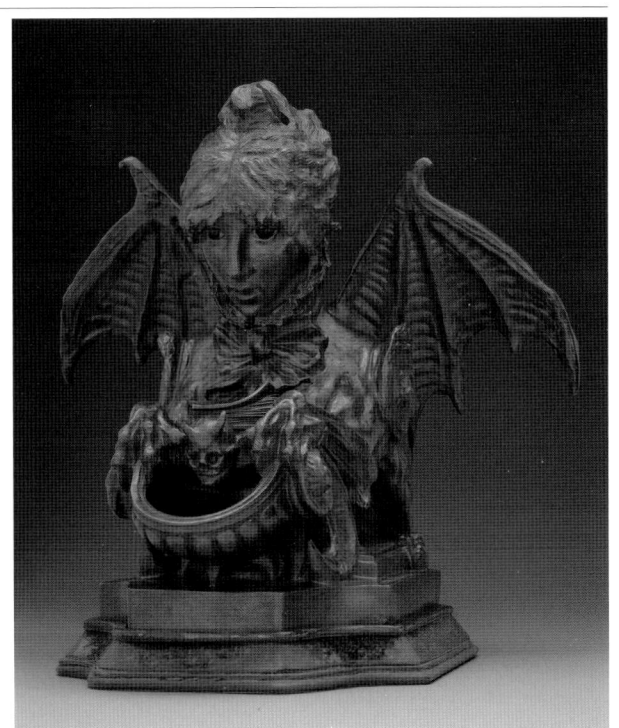

FIG. 18   Sarah Bernhardt (French, 1844-1923)
Fantastic Inkwell (Self-Portrait as a Sphinx), 1880
Metal, bronze, 12½ x 13¾ x 12½ in. (31.8 x 34.9 x 31.8 cm)
Museum of Fine Arts, Boston
Helen and Alice Colburn Fund, 1973.551

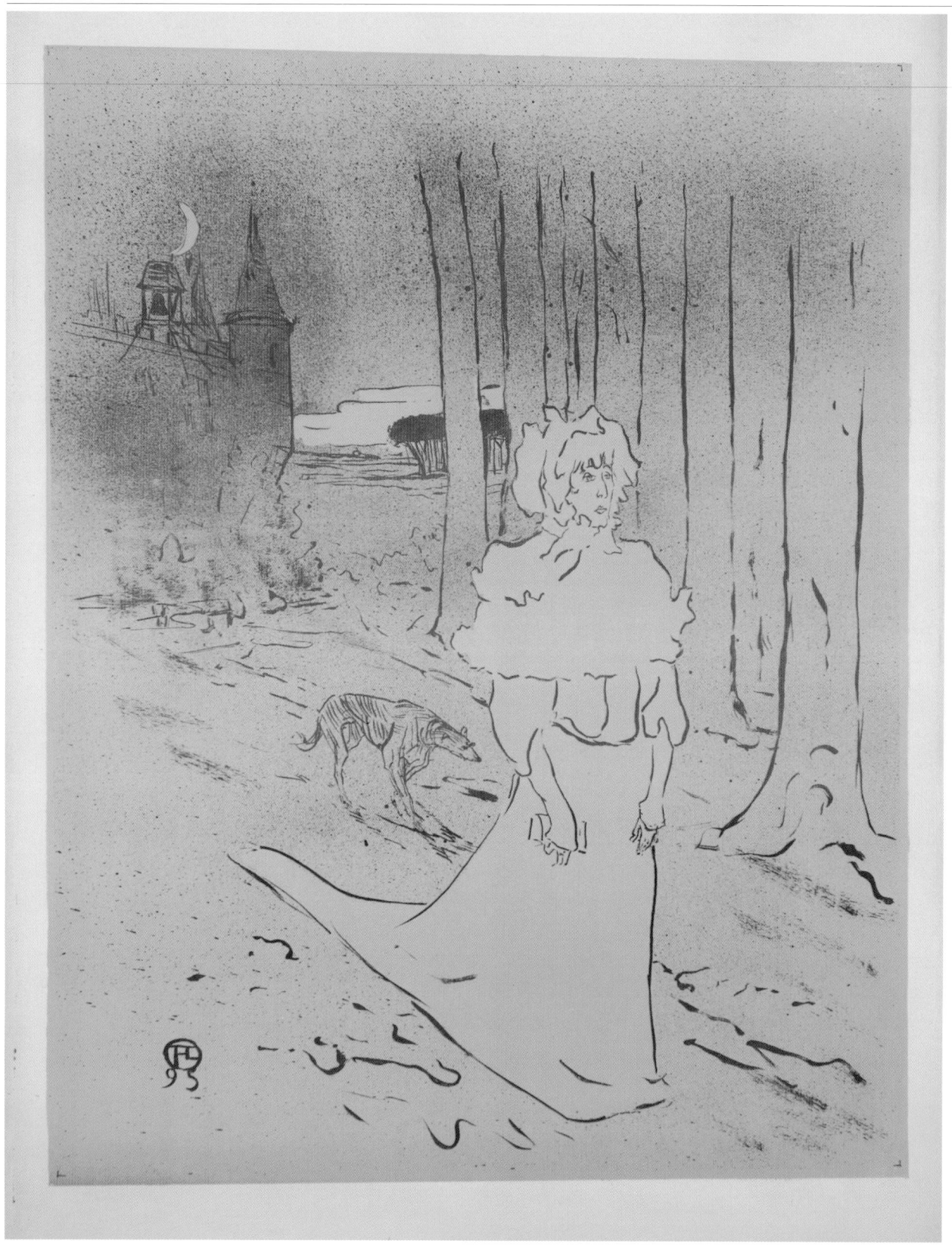

CAT. 116 Henri de Toulouse-Lautrec (French, 1864-1901)
La Chatelaine ou 'Le Tocsin', [The Chatelaine, or 'Le Tocsin'] 1895
Lithograph, 25⁹⁄₁₆ x 19¾ in. (65 x 50.1 cm)
Jane Voorhees Zimmerli Art Museum

as a setting for the diva holding Job cigarette papers (cat. 73) and demonstrating their even burn; one of his most famous commercial product posters. The product name Job also serves as a repetitive motif on the mosaic-like pattern surrounding the round opening. The circular motif has not only been taken to represent perfection, but also Mucha's "compulsive erotic symbolism."[31] These architectural motifs, with their shallow sense of space, framing his statuesque and monumental figures, hardly represent interior spaces.

The 1895-1900 period was Mucha's most productive. He continued to illustrate books and design wallpaper and decorative panels, but his posters remained of foremost importance. For the Exposition Universelle in 1900 he designed a jewelry shop for Georges Fouquet (1862-1957), a Houbignant perfumery, as well as a pavilion for Bosnia and Herzegovina,[32] and he designed Le Pavillon de l'Homme, in which he gave free reign to his imagination. This never-to-be-realized pavilion, futuristic in design, with sweeping lines and a large global dome representing the planet Earth appears to be based on Byzantine ecclesiastical architecture. In the working out of the sculptural and spatial plans for the proposed Le Pavillon de l'Homme, as well as the natural decor for his exposition stalls for the Parfumerie Houbigant and the jeweler George Fouquet, Mucha developed ideas that he used later in the design and construction of the Georges Fouquet jewelry boutique on rue Royale (1900-1901) across from Maxim's. Several photographs and drawings tell us about this richly conceived plan (figs. 22-24; pp. 55, 56, 57). The decoration of the walls and the ceiling, the mantelpiece, the wall-mounted display cases, the fountain that served as a base for the bronze female figure, the mirrors, the curtains, and the tapestries, were all conceived by Mucha. Behind the circular counter on the back wall, a circular motif was created by the large fanned tail of a peacock, bringing to mind the central motif of Whistler's Peacock Room design (fig. 21; p. 54) for Frederick R. Leyland's London home (1876-1877). The also charming female figure, inside the Fouquet boutique, to the right of the peacock, the hallmark of *Le Style*

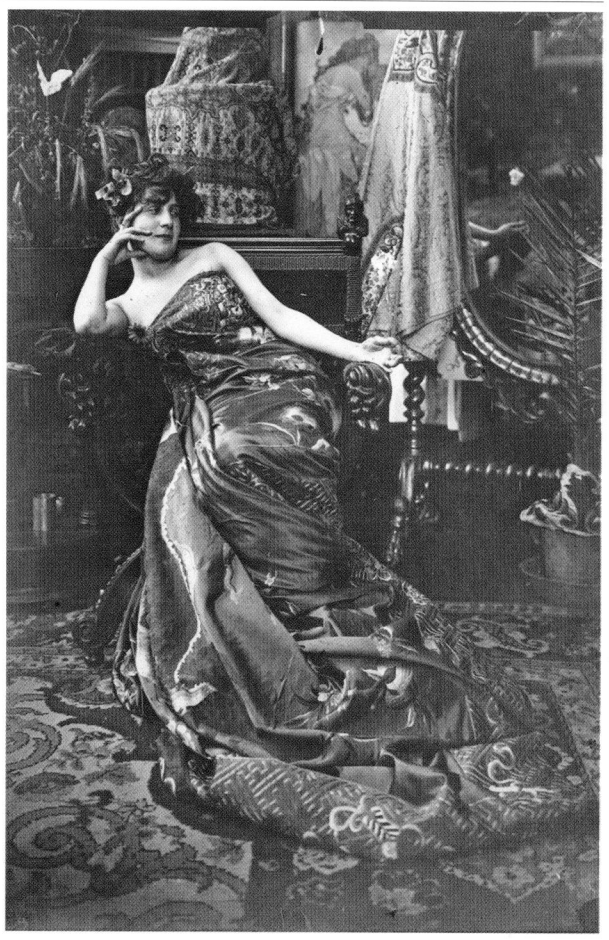

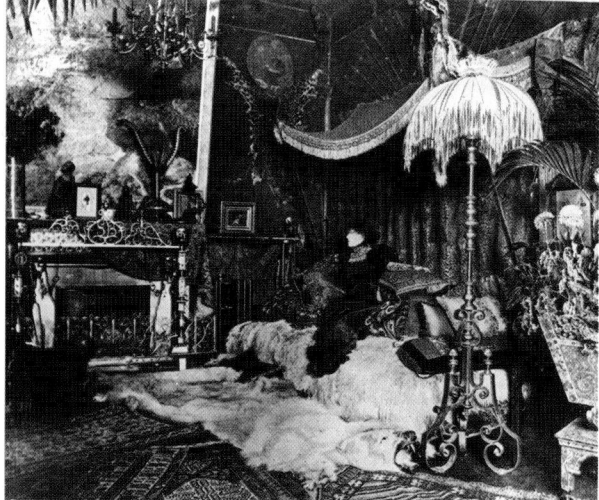

FIG. 19   Model in Mucha's studio rue de Val-de-Grâce
Photograph, ca. 1900
©Mucha Trust 2007

FIG. 20   Sarah Bernhardt at Home, n.d.
Photograph
From the Mander & Mitchenson Theatre Collection, London

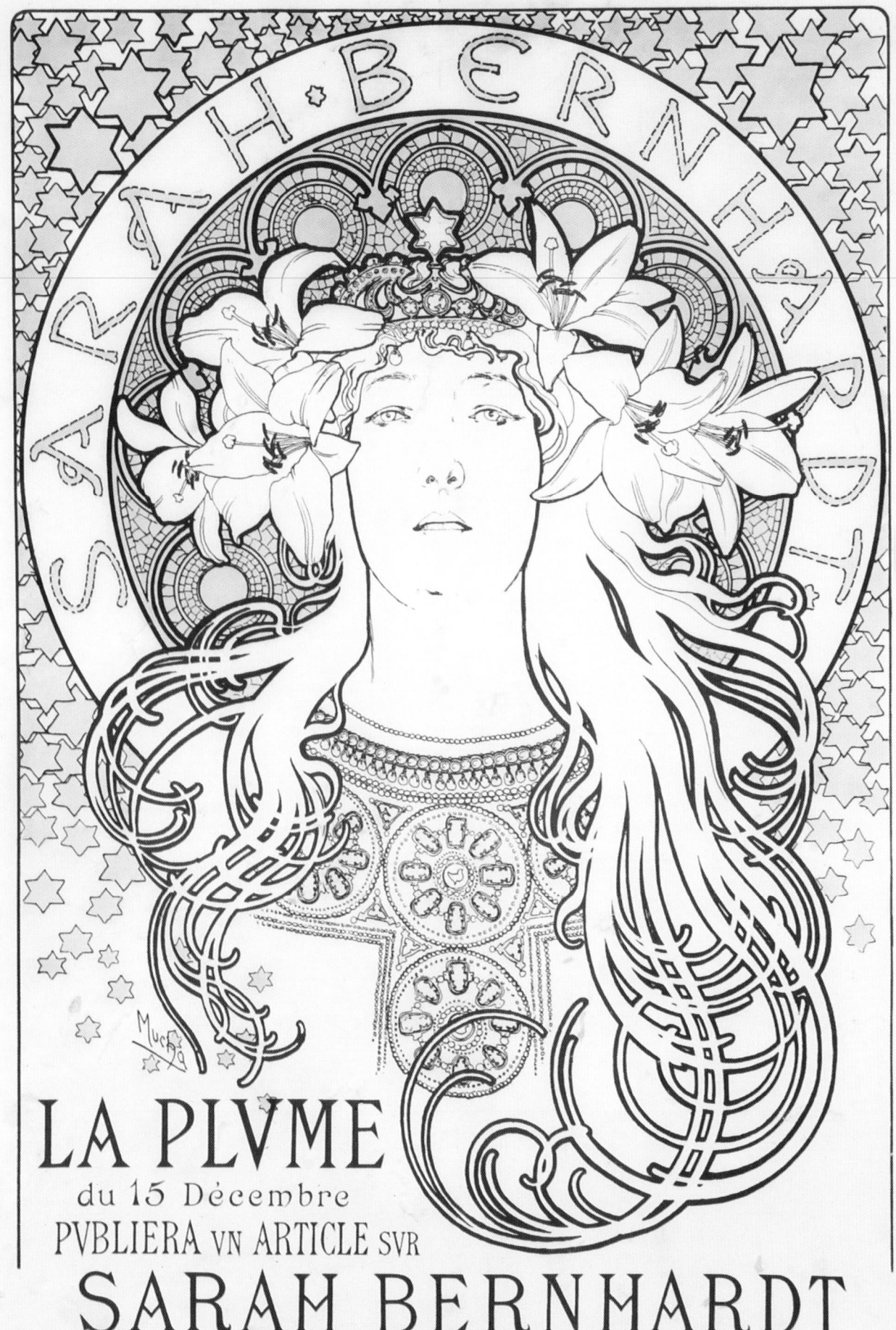

CAT. 70   Alphonse Mucha (Czech, 1860-1939)

Sarah Bernhardt, La Plume, 1897

Lithograph (proof), 25¾ x 18 in. (65.4 x 45.7 cm)

Courtesy J. Raj K. Dhawan through Galerie Michael,

Beverly Hills, California

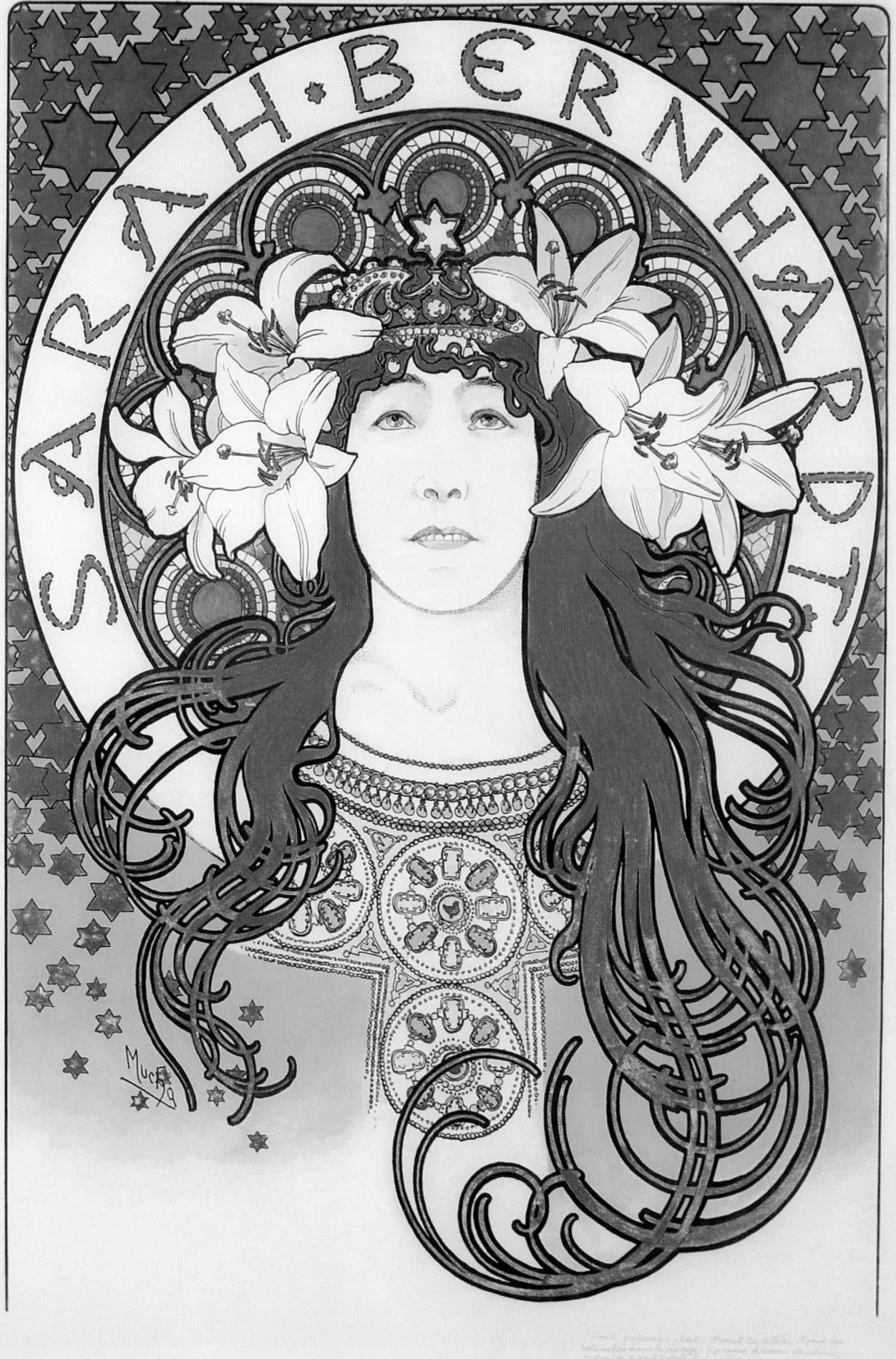

CAT. 69   Alphonse Mucha (Czech, 1860-1939)
Sarah Bernhardt, La Plume, 1897
Colored lithograph, 23 x 16 in. (58.42 x 40.64 cm)
Courtesy J. Raj K. Dhawan through Galerie Michael,
Beverly Hills, California

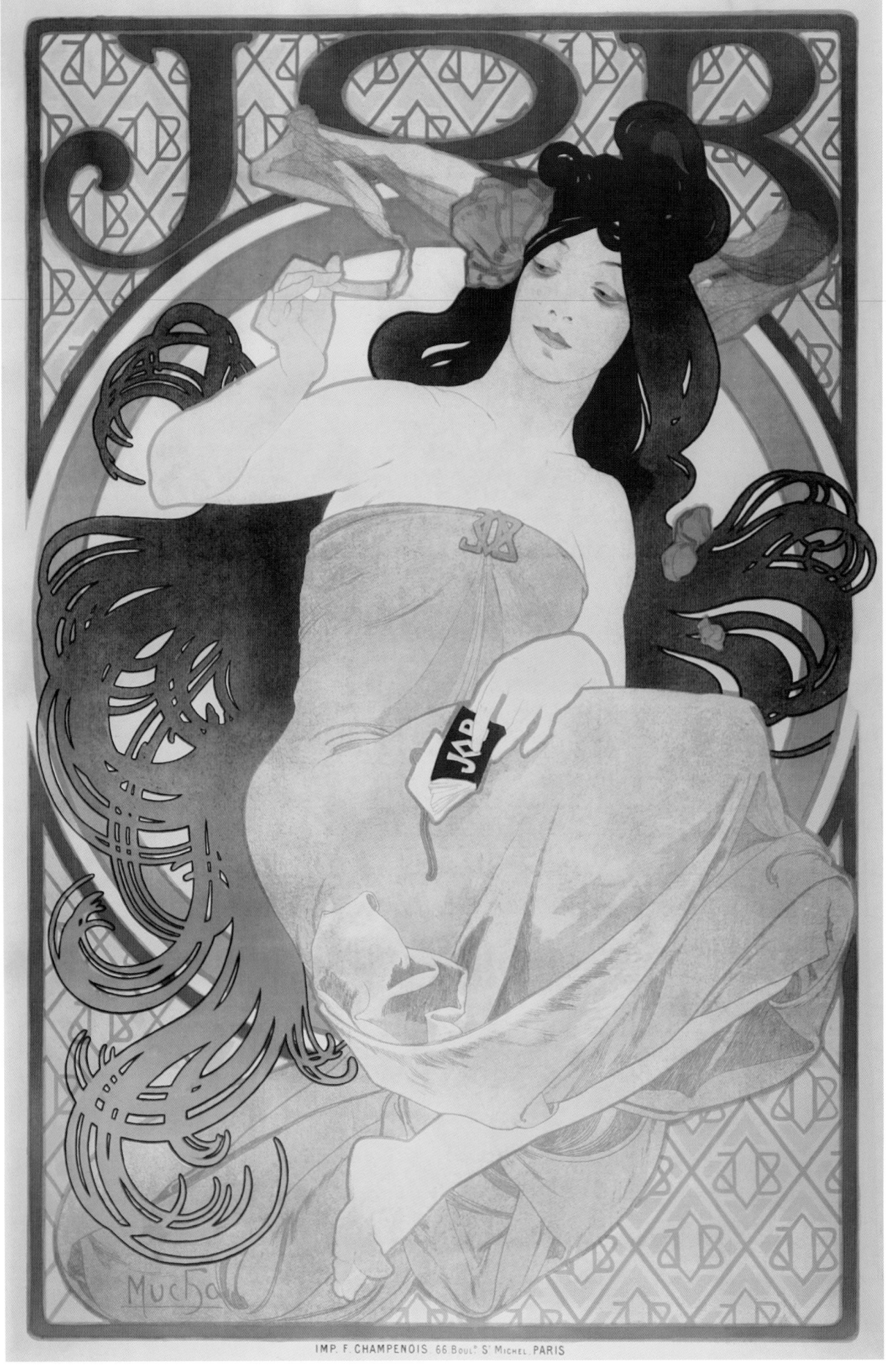

IMP. F. CHAMPENOIS. 66. Boul^d St Michel. PARIS

CAT. 73   Alphonse Mucha (Czech, 1860-1939)
Job, 1898
Color lithograph on paper mounted on linen
58¹³/₁₆ x 37¹¹/₁₆ in. (149.35 x 100.84 cm)
Courtesy J. Raj K. Dhawan

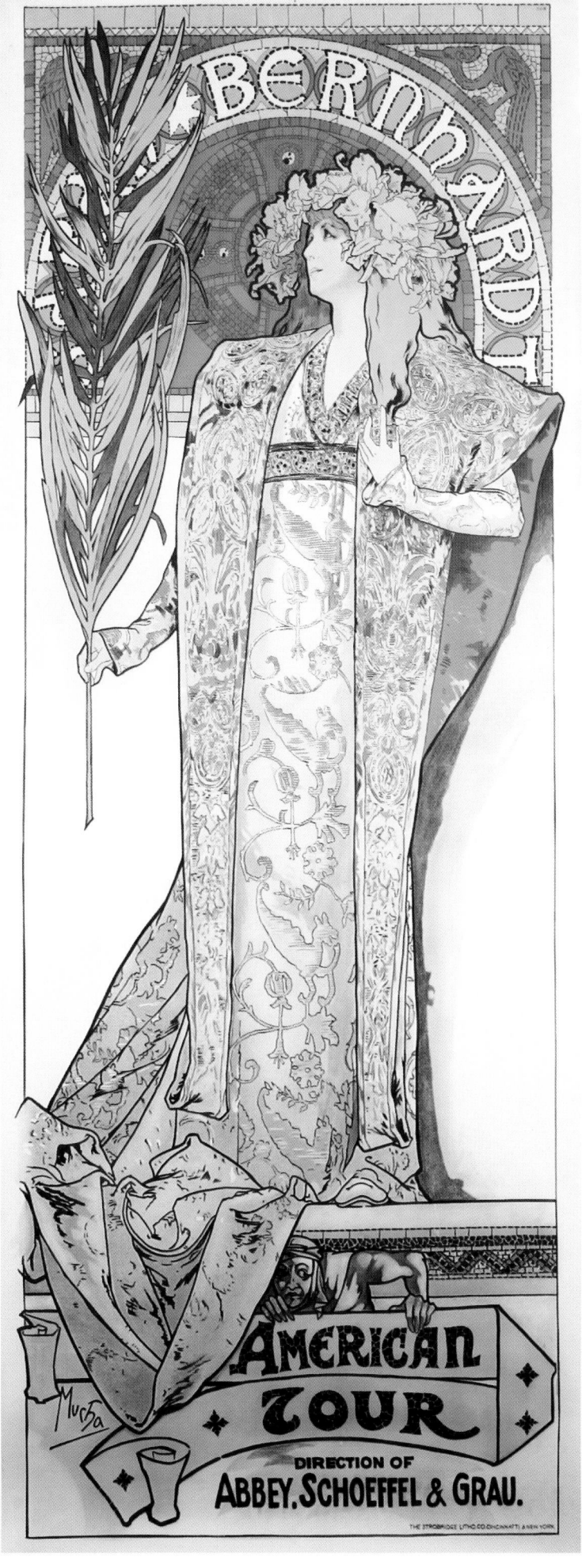

CAT. 65   Alphonse Mucha (Czech, 1860-1939)
Bernhardt American Tour, 1895
Color lithograph on linen,
78¼ x 29¼ in. (198.8 x 74.3 cm)
Courtesy J. Raj K. Dhawan through Galerie Michael,
Beverly Hills, California

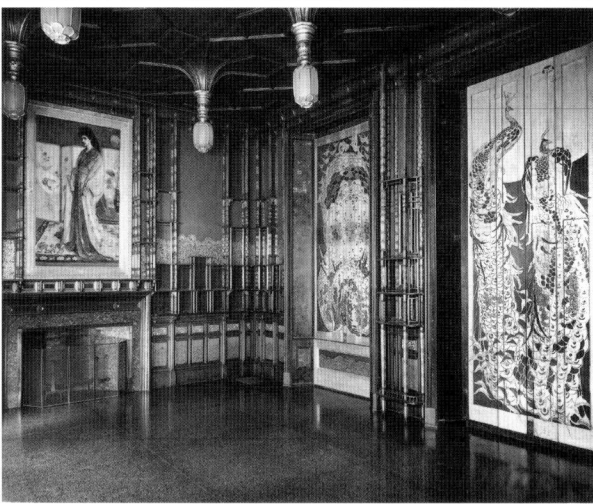

Mucha, also occupies a central place in the relief on the exterior of the building (fig. 22), but plays a less prominent role in the interior.

The first ideas for the interior design of Georges Fouquet jewelry boutique appear to have derived from Mucha's earlier designs for Parfumerie Houbigant. In a lost Houbigant drawing, known only by a photograph in the Jirí Mucha collection, a *femme-fleur* is seated on a throne against a huge circular peacock fan. To her left and right there are full-length female, poster-type figures in decorative niche-like frames. The shape of the large peacock fan is repeated lower down in radiant flowering stalks to the left and right of the central figure.[33] Here we have something of the exurberant sensualism of his poster art that is also found in his interior design for the Fouquet jewelry boutique (fig. 23; p. 56).

In the overall decor and design in the boutique there is a sense of perfect harmony, a place suited to the display of the jeweler's art. By the early 1920s, tastes had changed, and the modern style was no longer modern. Nevertheless, Fouquet understood the importance of Mucha's creation and when the decor was dismantled in 1923 he had it stored in a furniture warehouse for more than a decade. In 1936, the shop windows and other items were given to the Musée des Arts décoratifs, and in 1941, and again in 1949, Fouquet gave the principal parts of the design and Mucha's related drawings to the Musée Carnavalet, where the interior has been marvelously re-

installed so that visitors can actually walk through it.[34] In the 1901 Fouquet boutique, Mucha achieved the consummate synthesis of the art and decor, bringing together the sacred and profane, in his creation of an otherworldly commercial boutique. To initiate such a union can be an impossible task.

Decorative paintings, by Denis and Osbert, containing symbolic and allegorical subject matter, were commissioned by private patrons for domestic interiors. Interestingly enough some of these patrons were musicians and composers and some of the murals had themes related to music. Chéret, the poster artist, also painted murals for private homes, with subject matter related to the gaiety and eighteenth-century frivolity found in his Montmartre posters for cabarets, dance halls, and bars. Other poster artists, such as Toulouse-Lautrec, were content with the commercial possibilities offered by the color lithograph.

As with other artists in Montmartre his studio and living quarters were principally a place to work and sleep. The fraternity of artists and poets, described in Henri Murger's *Scènes de la vie de Bohème*, a highly successful novel published in 1848 about artistic life in the Latin Quarter, was brought up-to-date and made more appropriate to Montmartre in Puccini's opera *La Bohème* (staged in 1898). Lautrec's environment of choice could hardly be associated with the physical comforts, period furnishings, and objects of art which stimulated Proust's

FIG. 21   James Abbott McNeill Whistler (American, 1834-1903)
Harmony in Blue and Gold: The Peacock Room
Smithsonian Institution
Freer Gallery of Art, Washington, D.C.
Photograph in a Private Collection

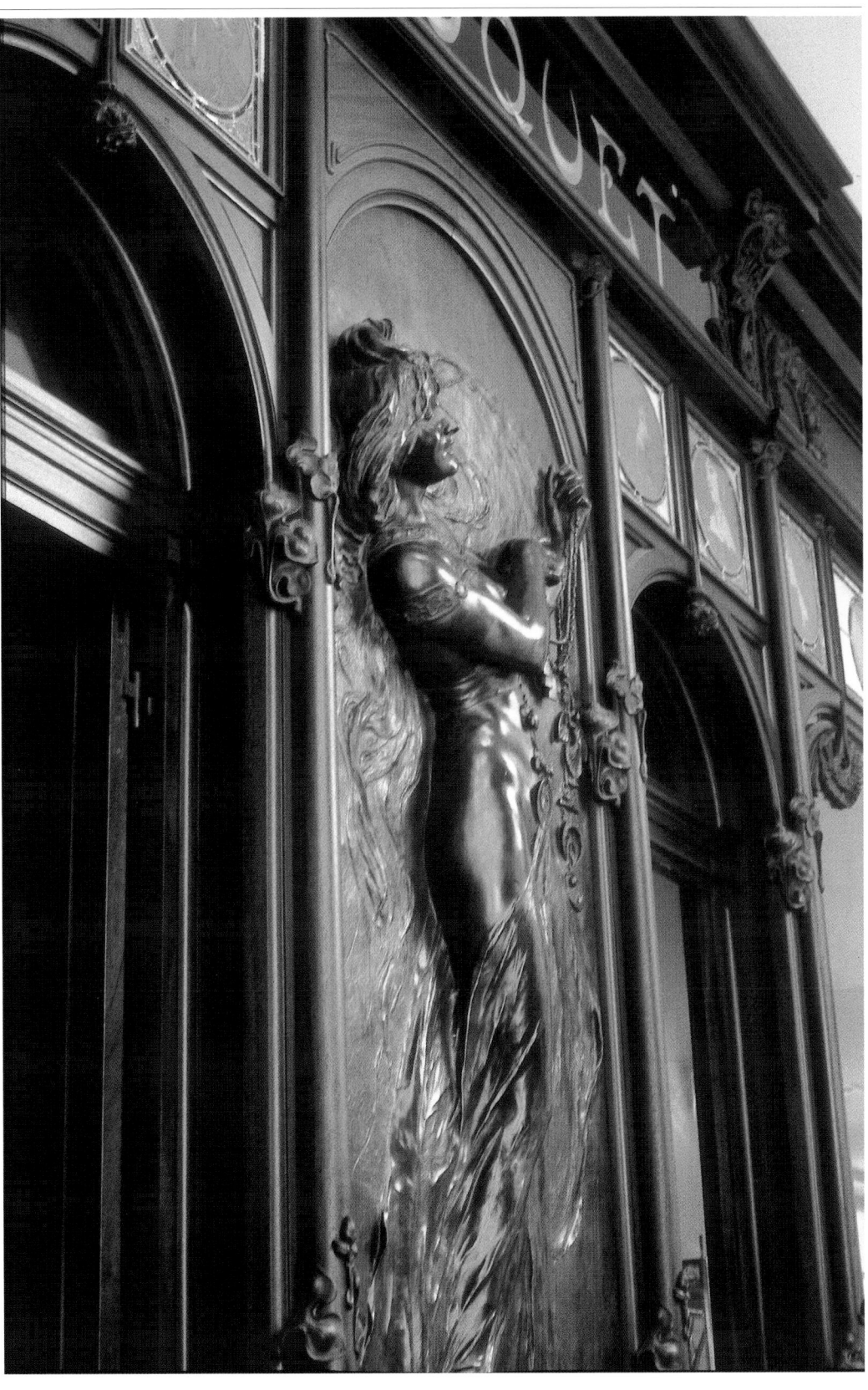

FIG. 22   Alphonse Mucha (Czech, 1860-1939)

Fouquet Boutique Exterior

Carnavalet Museum, Paris

Photograph courtesy of Yvonne Weisberg

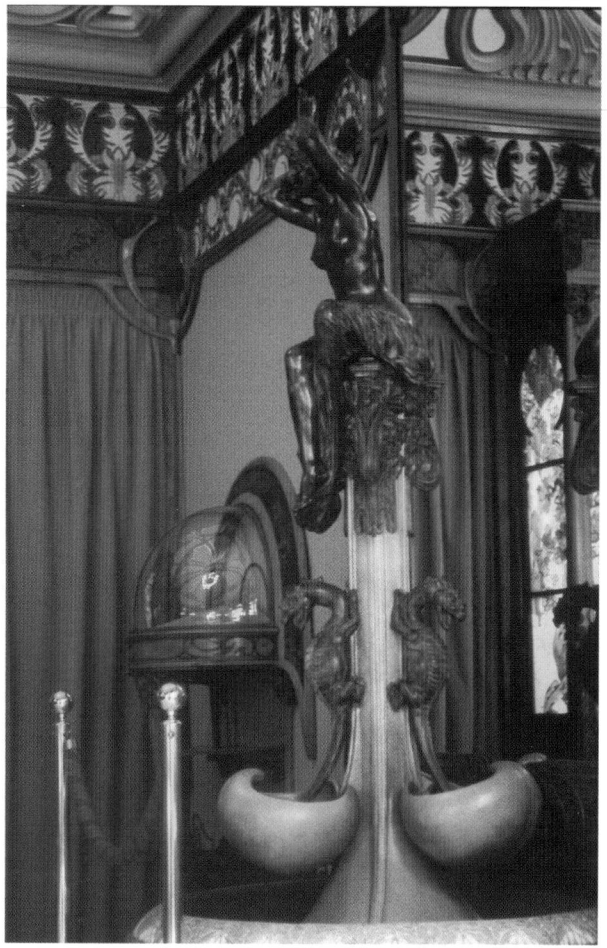

FIG. 23　Alphonse Mucha (Czech, 1860-1939)
Fouquet Boutique Interior
Carnavalet Museum, Paris
Photograph courtesy of Yvonne Weisberg

recollections and speculation concerning the life of the soul. Lautrec did not require the props and furnishings seen in the period photographs of Mucha's studio. For Lautrec, the bar and cabaret served as a living room, a *salon de conversation*, a congenial place to meet friends and to observe and make sketches of the entertainers and clients. This caused Mucha to later remark disapprovingly on Lautrec being too fond of night life. The Montmartre *lieu de rendez-vous* attracted artists and literati and people from all walks of life. In the café and bar it was possible to socialize, read, ignore all others in the privacy of one's own thoughts, or simply enjoy the passing scene. The cabaret could be a combination of a bar and vaudeville theatre which offered the entertainment of talented singers, comedians, and dancers. Many of the well-known entertainers, Aristide Bruant (cat. 111; p. 87), Yvette Guilbert, La Goulue (cat. 110; p. 89), Jane Avril (cat. 113; p. 88), Loïe Fuller, May Belford, and May Milton were portrayed in Lautrec's sketches, lithographs, and paintings. Each had their own individual style and personality, which Lautrec duly emphasized in his work.

The introduction of the *cabaret artistique* in the late 1870s provided popular entertainment on a level of professionalism previously unknown. La Grande Pinte was one of the first, established in 1878 by an art dealer named Laplace who knew a considerable number of artists in Montmartre and felt that the drab cafés in the Quarter were unworthy of their patronage. He thought it was disgraceful "that artists should be obliged to sit shut in between plain white walls, at ordinary marble tables similar to those at which bankers and grocers drink."[35] A number of new upscale *cabaret concerts* followed the establishment of La Grande Pinte; Le Chat Noir, Le Divan Japonais, and Le Mirliton. Lautrec set up a studio in Montmartre, at the age of twenty-one in 1885, and began to acquaint himself with the exhilaration offered by the cabarets, cafés, and bars in his *quartier*. La Grande Pinte, as a popular place where artists, poets, and writers could mix with wealthy and elegantly dressed Parisians, was in decline and had been replaced by Rodolphe Salis's Chat Noir, established in 1881. Lautrec, however, did not frequent the Chat Noir. He found the clients too pretentious and disliked the affected manners of Salis who addressed

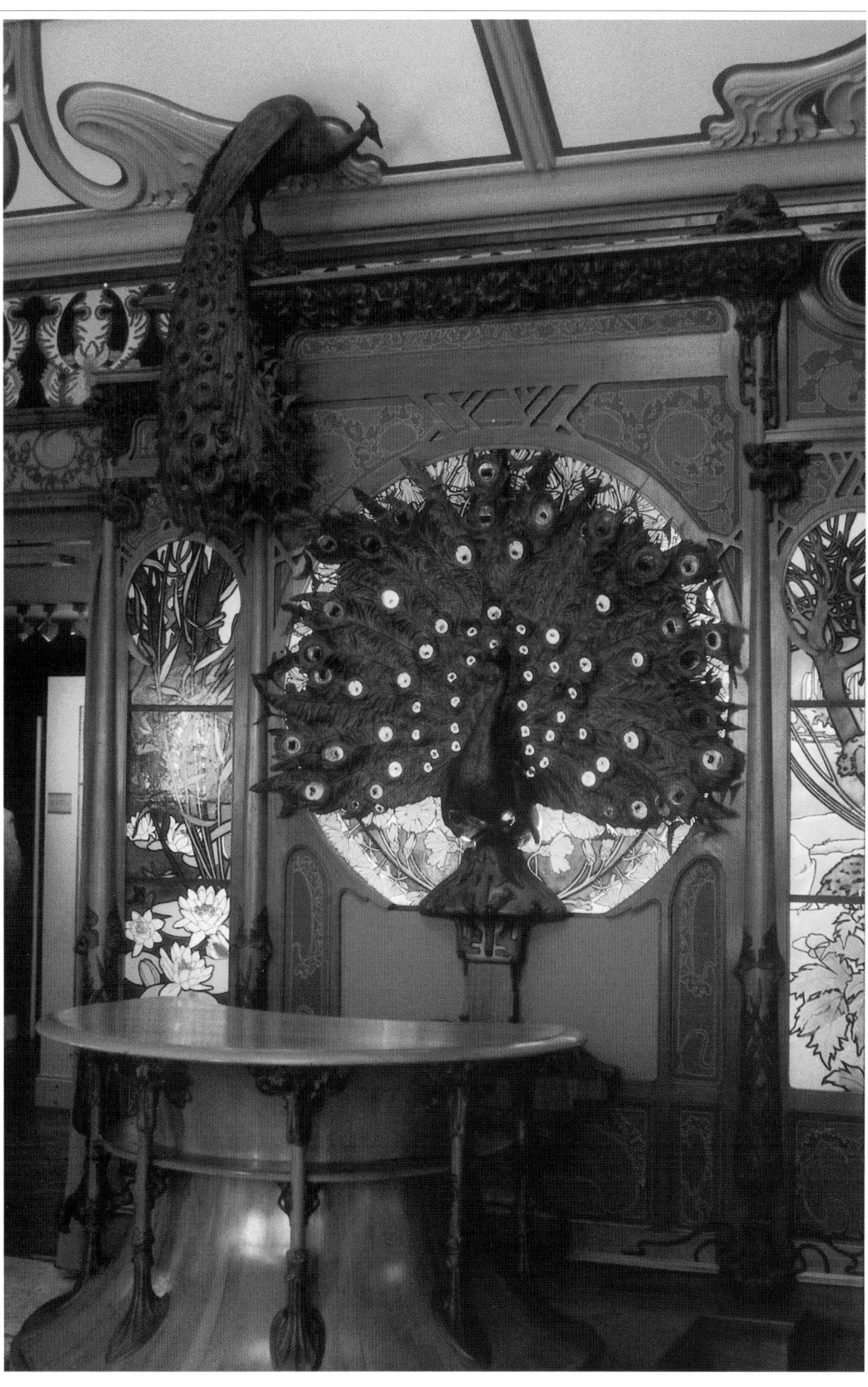

FIG. 24 Alphonse Mucha (Czech, 1860-1939)

Fouquet Boutique Interior

Carnavalet Museum, Paris

Photograph courtesy of Yvonne Weisberg

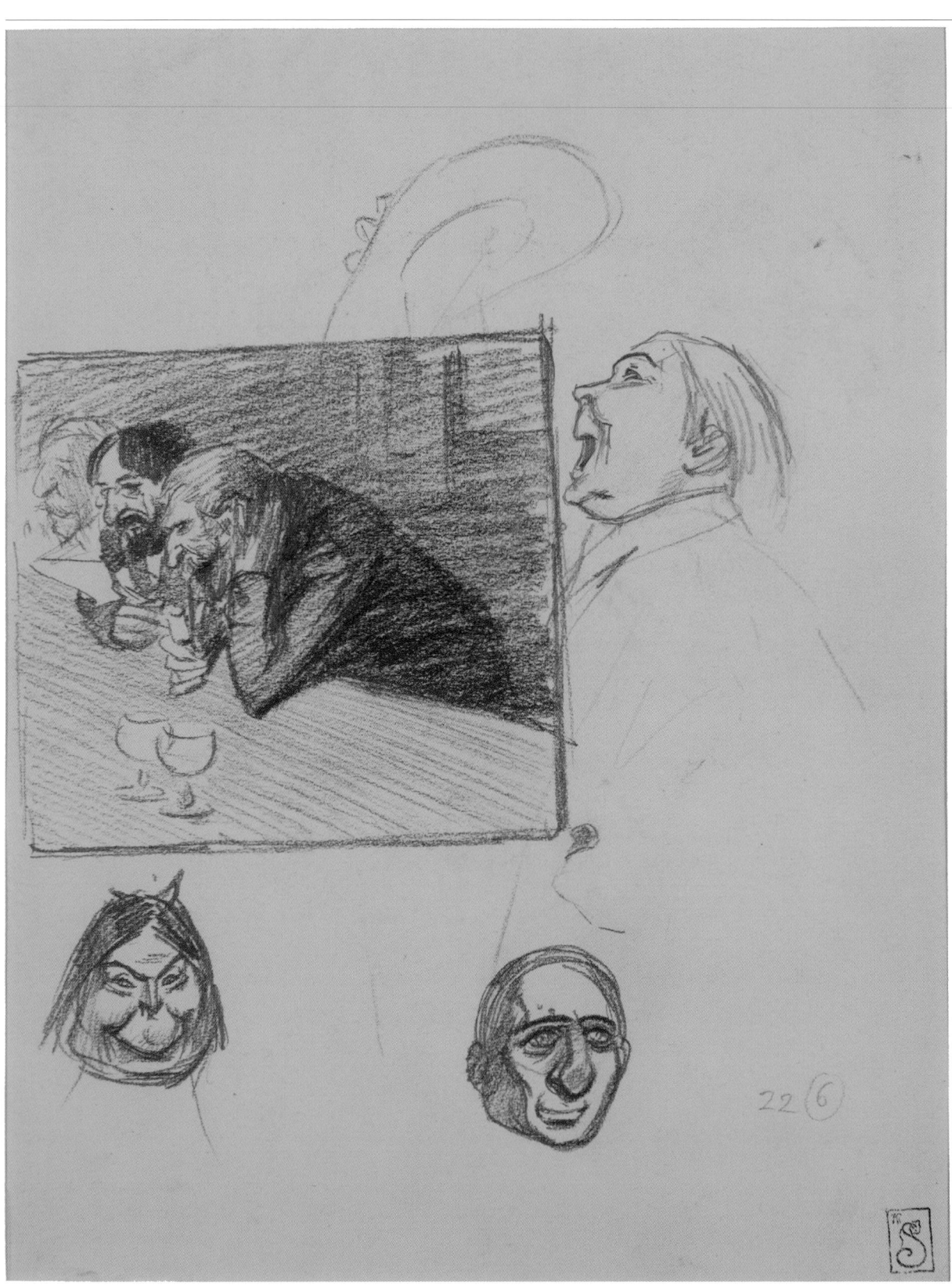

his customers as *messeigneurs* or *gentes dames*. Lautrec preferred the more down to earth atmosphere of Le Mirliton, a *cabaret artistique* owned by Aristide Bruant who was a singer and entertainer, and a composer of songs about the poor districts of the city.

A fascinating drawing by Théophile Steinlen shows Bruant singing (cat. 108), lifting his broad-brimmed, black-felt hat high above his head, and a small study on the same page of two men, leaning forward over the countertop of the bar, who seem to be conversing and look as if they have been drinking heavily. As the cabaret owner and entertainer Bruant always wore a black-velvet jacket and trousers, knee-length black leather boots, and a red scarf thrown over his shoulders. When on the street he wore a long black cape. This is how he is shown in Lautrec's lithograph posters advertising his cabaret concert. Compared with Steinlen's more engager manner, Lautrec was a sympathetic and uncritical observer of the exploited and the exploiters among the underclass, but hardly a social activist. Bruant appreciated this quality in Lautrec's work and chose him to make his cabaret posters.

Lautrec also frequented Le Divan Japonais at 75 rue des Martyrs (cat. 118; p. 39). The owner of the relatively new *café-concert* was Jehan Sarrazin, who was a former struggling olive merchant and Sunday poet, combined selling olives with his poetry to cabaret customers. Sarrazin adopted something of the affected, antiquated terms used by Rodolphe Salis. His singers, dancers, and entertainers were regularly scheduled and quite professional compared with the Le Mirliton and Chat Noir. The proprietor-poet thought of his cabaret as his "new abode" and his customers as his invited guests. He published a small book titled *Souvenirs de Montmartre et du Quatier-Latin* in which he invited "his fellow citizens, vassals, and all others, as well as their ladies, wives, or concubines, to visit him in his new abode, where they may drink heartily, amuse themselves, and ensure the eternal welfare of their souls and bodies by sampling the triply divine olive, unchallenged princess of the products of nature, served on dishes of gold and silver."[36] In Lautrec's 1892 lithograph poster advertising entertainment at the Le Divan Japonais he shows Jane Avril with Edouard Dujardin, editor of the *Revue indépendante* and co-editor of the

Revue Wagnérienne, who was an influential promoter of symbolist art and an ardent follower of Mallarmé. In the background can be seen the cropped figure of the singer Yvette Guilbert. Lautrec had became known for his interior scenes of the *cabaret artistique* as well as private, but hardly sensational, interiors of the *maison close*, offering a considerable contrast to the religious murals of Denis and Osbert, and nothing of the ideal harmony of the interior designs of Colonna, de Feure, Gaillard and Mucha. On the other hand, in the 1890s, all were influenced by the flat decorative quality of Japanese art, and like the *ukiyo-e* artists, by the variety and richness of life around them, and by the sacred and the profane.

Endnotes

[1] The model for Barrias, *La Nature se dévoilant devant la Science*, was exhibited at the Salon in 1893.

[2] Roger Gounot, *Charles Maurin 1856-1914 Essai sur le peintre et catalogue de l'exposition de 1978* (Le-Puy-en-Velay: Musée Crozatier du Puy, 1978: 12).

[3] John Rewald, *The History of Impressionism* (New York: The Museum of Modern Art, 1973: 514).

[4] The accounts of Péladan's First Salon de la Rose + Croix are based on information in Robert Pincus-Witten, *Occult Symbolism in France Joséphin Peladan and the Salons de la Rose-Croix* (New York & London: Garland Publishing, Inc., 1976: 104-6).

[5] *Catalogue du Salon de la Rose + Croix* (10 March-10 April), Paris, Galerie Durand-Ruel, 11 rue Le Peletier, 1892 :7-11. Quoted in Pincus-Witten, op. cit.: 105.

[6] Abbot Suger, "De administratione," in: *Abbot Suger on the Abbey Church of St.-Denis and its Art Treasures*. Edited, translated, and annotated by Erwin Panofsky, second edition by Gerda Panofsky-Soergel (Princeton, NJ: Princeton University Press, 1973: 63-5). One of the early publications of Abbot Suger's writings appeared in the late nineteenth century: Lecoy de la Marche, *Œuvres complètes de Suger* (Paris: Société de L'Histoire de France, Publications, no. 139, 1867). (Ed. Paris, 1886; Reprint by Georg Olms, Hildesheim, in press.)

[7] Viollet-le-Duc, M. F. Hearn, ed., *The Architectural Theory of Viollet-le-Duc: Readings and Commentary* (Boston: Massachusetts Institute of Technology, 1990: 287).

[8] Ibid.

[9] *Eugène Emmanuel Viollet-le-Duc 1814-1879*; Stuart Durant, "The Notre-Dame Murals"; and anonymous, "Le Château de Pierrefonds." (London: Architectural Design and Academy Editions, 1980: 41-7, 64-71).

[10] See part one: "The Goncourts' Legacy," in: Debora L. Silverman, *Art Nouveau in Fin-de-Siècle France. Politics, Psychology, and Style* (Berkeley, Los Angeles, London: University of California Press, 1989: 17-39).

[11] Ibid.: 28.

[12] Joris-Karl Huysmans, *Against Nature* a new translation of *À rebours* by Robert Baldick (Middlesex, England: Penguin Books Ltd. Harmondsworth, 1968: 25).

[13] Ibid.: 25.

[14] Ibid.

[15] Ibid.: Robert Baldick's introduction: 8.

[16] Ibid.: 28.

[17] Ibid.: 25

[18] Ibid.: 69

[19] H. Caillet, "Monsieur F. Khnopff's Villa," *The Studio*, vol. 57, (1912): 201-7; Pincus-Witten, op. cit.: 113. Photographs of the interior of Khnopff's studio in Nestor Eemans, Fernanad Khnopff (Anvers: de Sikkel, 1950: 8); Louis Dumont-Wilden, Fernand Khnopff, (Van Oest, Brussels, 1907: 26).

[20] Khnopff's plaster replica of the head of Hypnos was without doubt taken from or based on the original in the British Museum (probably a Roman copy of a Greek original 350-300 B.C.). It was a well-known work in the mid-nineteenth century, and a great many replicas were made of it, particularly in Naples. It was identified as Hypnos by Heinrich Brunn in 1862 (*Archälogische Zeitung*).

[21] "Mucha fixed up his new studio with Byzantine luxury. The tall, bare walls were covered with huge Chinese draperies of dark red silk, flowing from the ceiling like a heavy canopy; one end of the room was hung with pieces of richly-ornamented Turkish tent-cloth; the entrance was adorned with strips of Tibetan and Japanese embroidery; the floor was covered with Persian carpets and bear-skins; the furniture was Renaissance, baroque and Empire; there were palms ten feet high, musical instruments, stuffed birds, oriental vases, medieval statuary, church lamps, chasubles, candlesticks, ancient books, weapons, helmets and countless smaller items. To ensure that he had fresh flowers every day, he had hampers of carnations, roses, mimosa, irises or peonies sent from Nice all the year round." Jírí Mucha, *Alphonse Mucha His Life and Art by His Son Jiri Mucha* (London: Heinemann, 1966: 178).

[22] Marcel Proust, *Remembrance of Things Past*, "Swann's Way," "Swann in Love," C. K. Scott Moncrieff and Terence Kilmartin, trans., vol. 1 (New York: Vintage Books, A Division of Random House, 1982: 266).

[23] Ibid.: "The Guermantes Way," vol 11: 435.

[24] S. Tschudi Madsen, *Art Nouveau*, R. I. Christopherson, trans. (from the Norwegian), (New York, Toronto: World University Library, McGraw-Hill Book Company, 1967: 206).

[25] Arcadi Calzada i Salavedra, Jean-David Jumeau-Lafond, Pablo Jiménez Burillo, and Guillermo Solana, *Un país ideal. El paisatge simbolista a França* (Exposició, Fundació Caixa de Girona, 2006: 217-246). See also Jean-David Jumeau-Lafond, *Les Peintres de l'âme Le Symbolisme idéaliste en France* (Gent: Musée d'Ixelles, Bruxelles, SDZ Pandora, Uitgeverii Snoeck-Ducaju & Zoon, 1999. The sections on Dulac, Guilloux, Lacoste, Osbert, and Denis: 57-60; 74-5; 84-7; 115-19; 52-3).

[26] Op. cit.: Jumeau-Lafond, *Les Peintres de l'âme*: 10-6; 20-4.

[27] The following information was sent on 2 July 2007 by Willem Russell, the owner of the Charles Guilloeux landscapes: "According to Dr. Cathérine Verleysen, Museum voor Schone Kunsten, [Gent] the moon riverscape with poplars (cat. 42) could be titled *L'Allée d'eau* ['A Waterway']. There is a comparable landscape which carries the same title. As for the work formerly titled 'mirror-image landscape' (cat. 39), since this subject seems to relate to the print in *L'Estampe*, Dr. Verleysen feels it should be called *L'Inondation* ... The 'windy' landscape (cat. 40) seems to be the smaller version of a larger one that still may be in the family collection. As a title I would suggest: *paysage orageux*." Letter from Willem O. Russell, Amsterdam, 2 July 2007. Electronic consultation with Dr. Cathérine Verleysen, 16 August 2007.

[28] Electronic correspondence with Dr. Cathérine Verleysen, Museum voor Schone Kunsten, Gent, 23 August 2007.

[29] Willem Russell, the owner of *Notre Dame vue des Quais*, gave me the following information: "According to the art historian Jerôme Montcouquiol who wrote the entry of the catalogue of Galerie Mercier in Paris (where I bought this painting in 2006), this painting may belong to the series of six titled *Le Tournant de la Seine* (no. 66 to 71) exhibited at *Le Barc de Boutteville* in 1893."

[30] See reproduction of Guilloux's 1894 painting *La Seine (nocturne)* in Arcadi Calzada i Salavedra, op. cit.: 42. Dr. Cathérine Verleysen, disagrees with my Whistler analogy and feels that Guilloux's approach is more contemporary and comes from his own personal form of symbolism based on the ideas of the neo-impressionists, Les Nabis artists, and Japanese art. Her assessment reads as follows: "Je vous avoue que j'étais assez surprise de voir le lien que vous établissez entre l'œuvre de Guilloux et celle de Whistler. De mon côté, je soulignerai plus le caractère 'contemporain' de son approche esthétique: les leçons tirées des néo-impressionnistes, des Nabis, du courant japonisant, afin d'arriver à un symbolisme très personnel."

[31] Brian Reade quoted in Jack Rennert and Alain Weill, *Alphonse Mucha The Complete Posters and Panels* (Uppsala: A. Hjert & Hjert Book; and Boston: G.K. Hall & Co., 1984: 204).

[32] Bosnia and Herzegovina were then a part of Austria or the Austro-Hungarian monarchy.

[33] See plate on page 72 in *Mucha 1860-1939 peintures illustrations – affiches arts décoratifs*, Paris, Grand Palais, 1980.

[34] I am grateful to Dr. Weisberg for this information concerning the recent installation of the Fouquet boutique in the Musée Carnavalet.

[35] Gerstle Mack, *Toulouse-Lautrec* (New York: Alfred A. Knopf, 1953: 86). People who knew Lautrec were still alive, such as Yvette Guilbert, when Gerstle Mack began his interviews as part of his research for this book (first published in 1938). For example in the preface he thanks Madame Biais (Jane Avril) "for many reminiscences of Lautrec and a detailed account of her own life." He also thanks Thadée Natanson, editor of *La Revue blanche* and the artist Édouard Vuillard.

[36] Ibid.: 106-7.

The Print Culture of
Paris 1900

Gabriel P. Weisberg

When *L'Estampe Moderne* published Théophile Steinlen's lithograph of *Rue Caulaincourt* (cat. 103; p. 65) in February 1896 the editors recognized two significant aspects of the print culture of the period: first, that not all prints needed to advertise commercial products, or performers, and second, that Théophile Steinlen, a transplanted artist from Switzerland, was one of the most energetic and widely collected printmakers of the era.[1] With this lithograph, Steinlen evoked the nocturnal poetry of deserted streets by showing two displaced men, struggling against the wind on a cold night, the representatives of an underclass, unnoticed by society. The poverty he saw on the streets distressed Steinlen and he never tired of compassionately showing the effects of such misery. He was not the only artist to deal with this theme, but he used it so often and with such intensity that we can speculate that, as a transplanted artist, from a far smaller and homogeneous city, what he saw had an even more profound impact than on an artist raised in Paris. The Rue Caulaincourt, the principal street running through Montmartre, took on symbolic overtones: in the darkness of the middle of the night, men struggled to survive on this street that encapsulated the vision of Montmartre as a place where the poor congregated. Conversely, Montmartre was also becoming a center for "shocking" artistic creativity and, at the same time, the site of the Catholic Church's monument to Christian compassion – the basilica of the Sacré Coeur.[2] It was also here that Parisian print culture matured by 1900.

If Steinlen's *Rue Caulaincourt*, as well as his paintings of social unrest (cat. 103; p. 65) identified life on the streets, Eugène Grasset's powerful *Morphinomane* (cat. 37; p. 66) grappled with the drug addiction that was afflicting many during the 1890s.[3] In this image a despondent prostitute injecting herself with a pleasure-inducing intoxicant is a clear reminder to all who see her, of the dangers of drugs. Just as Steinlen used prints to draw attention to the poverty of street people, so too did Grasset use this versatile medium to address the all too prevalent problem of addiction. The social message of Morphinomane is underscored by Grasset's use of a bright yellow color and the flat, starkly outlined, decorative patterns of a Japanese print, making the work inescapably relevant in both style and content.

DETAIL   Eugène-Samuel Grasset (French, 1841-1917) (see cat. 37; p. 66)
Morphinomane [Morphine Addict], 1897
Lithograph
Jane Voorhees Zimmerli Art Museum

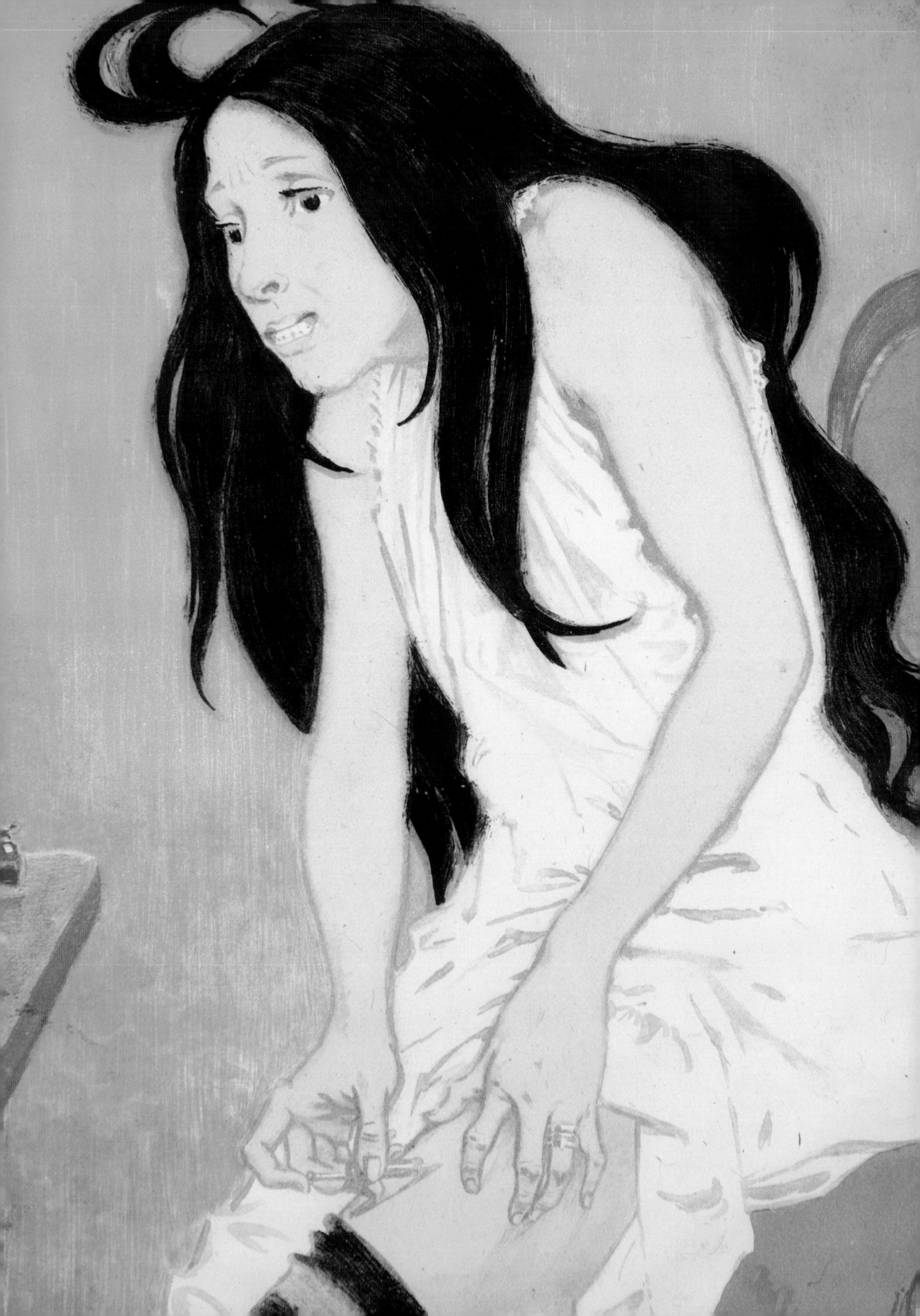

Both Grasset and Steinlen, in single printed images, demonstrated that a print culture was thriving in the Paris art world, and that this commitment was visible in books, on the walls of buildings, in newspapers, and in print shops. Because of its ubiquitous presence and low cost, print culture reached everyone, making it possible for artists to mold and influence public perceptions while also presenting fresh visual statements. Within the pages of magazines, printmakers were given great freedom to express their ideas while developing images that were inspired by the literary texts accompanying them. Seldom has this been better illustrated than in the pages of *Gil Blas Illustré*, beginning in 1891.

Gil Blas Illustré and Théophile Steinlen

The proliferation of illustrated journals in the 1890s is a well-known fact; by the time of the Exposition Universelle in 1900, printmaking and illustrated journals were remarkably numerous. New technological advances made it possible for images to be photo-mechanically reproduced, and for magazines to be published at a very low cost. As was the case with Steinlen, a single artist was often almost exclusively associated with a periodical. Steinlen, for example, produced hundreds of images for *Gil Blas Illustré* between 1891 and 1903.[4] Other artists, such as Louis Legrand, contributed to the journal as well, but few were as prolific as Steinlen. Such loyalty to one artist, thus popularizing one artistic style, proved to be an excellent strategy for building an audience for a particular magazine. Since the price of *Gil Blas Illustré* was minimal – it sold for five centimes between 1895-1896, and ten centimes from 1897 until 1899 when it sold for fifteen centimes – a reader saw the best artists illustrating topical texts by contemporary writers. This mutually beneficial arrangement between writers, illustrators, and magazines assured the creative contributors of a steady source of income while advancing their careers as leading moral commentators of their era. Steinlen used the system to his great advantage, securing not only his livelihood, but also his reputation, even into our time.

Steinlen's selection of themes reflects an awareness of reigning celebrities from the stage and popular culture, including those who had become cultural phenomena such as the American dancer, Loïe Fuller, who was mesmerizing everyone by mid-1892 (cat. 95; p. 67). While Steinlen focused on Loïe Fuller for the cover of *Gil Blas Illustré*, other artists were producing works imagining Fuller on stage. The sculptor François Rupert Carabin, for example, showed Fuller in her billowing costume enhanced by continually changing colored light effects.[5] (cat. 13; p. 68)

In the February 1892 edition of *Gil Blas Illustré*, Steinlen humorously represented another performer, Yvette Guilbert, who was a well-known singer in the nightclubs and cabarets of Montmartre, including the Moulin Rouge (cat. 94; p. 89). In *Sur la Scène* he used a chanson that Guilbert had performed on stage to suggest the possibility that an artist's creative life and fame could end in obscurity. Playing on the homonyms "scène" and "Seine," Steinlen amusingly, and also with a degree of sarcasm, suggested that a melancholy end could await a performer whose days on stage were numbered. His use of Yvette Guilbert was timely, as other artists caricatured her facial features in small plasters, such as done by the printmaker Leonetto Cappiello (cat. 10; p. 71). Likewise, after 1900, Georges d'Espagnat, maintained this fascination with her stage career in a gouache that owed a clear debt to an earlier moment in Guilbert's career in the limelight (cat. 30; p. 72).

In another print, Steinlen emphasized the mesmerizing role of Aristide Bruant who allied himself closely with the people by using street argot and slang in his performances at Montmartre cabarets (cat. 98; p. 73). Bruant jumped up on tables as well as the stage, wearing his working-class black coat, pants, boots, and often a long Communard red scarf, to demonstrate that he knew how to reach the proletariat. The fact that Steinlen illustrated a book, *Dans la Rue*, which featured Bruant and did a print of the raconteur performer for *Gil Blas Illustré* in February 1895, added to Bruant's reputation. Steinlen was seen as the artist best able to capture the personality and messages of Bruant's songs

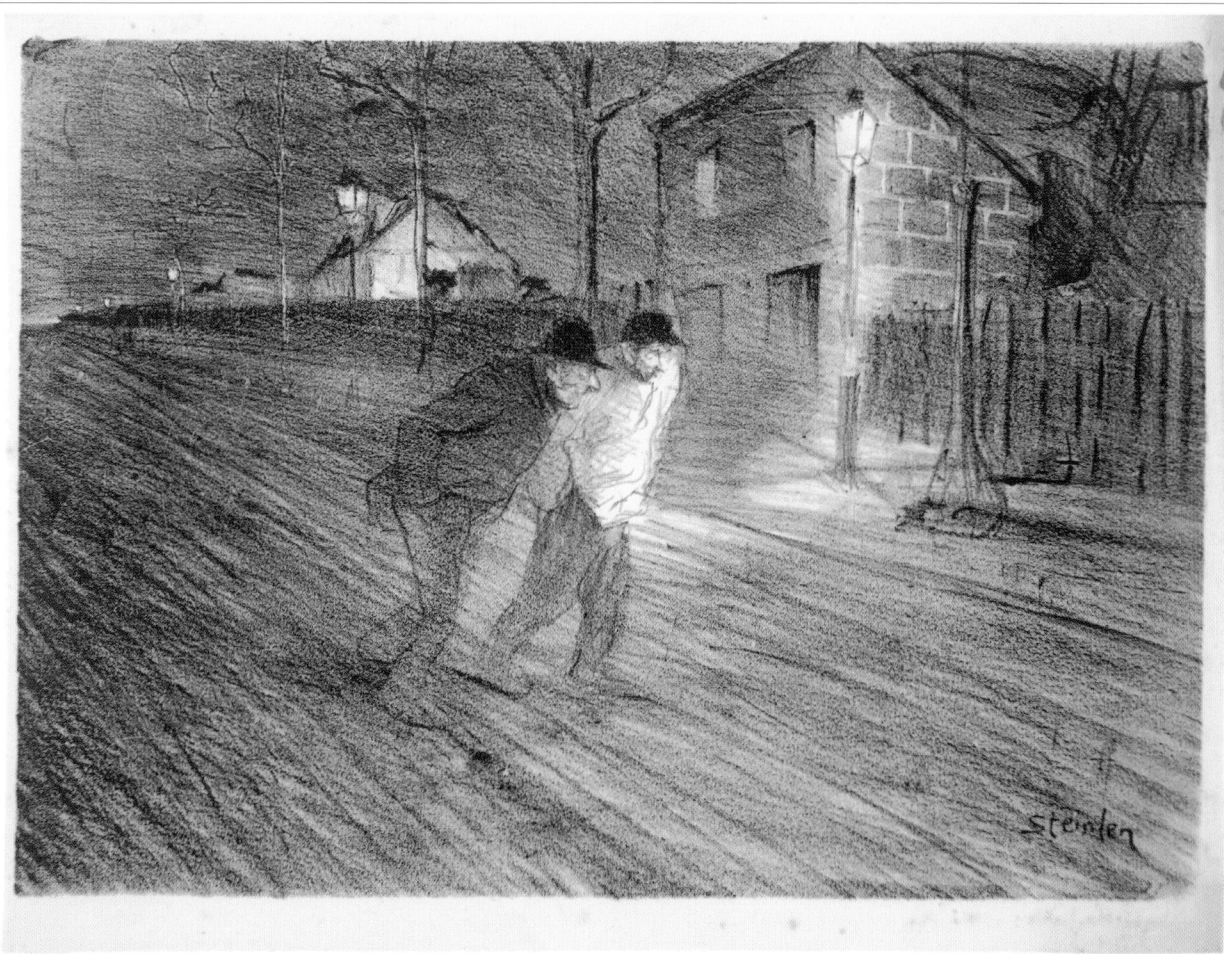

CAT. 103 Théophile-Alexandre Steinlen (Swiss, 1859-1923)

Rue Caulaincourt, 1896

Lithograph, 11 x 14 9/16 in. (27.8 x 37 cm)

Jane Voorhees Zimmerli Art Museum; Rutgers, The State University of

New Jersey; Norma B. Bartman Purchase Fund

Photograph by Jack Abraham; 1986.0354

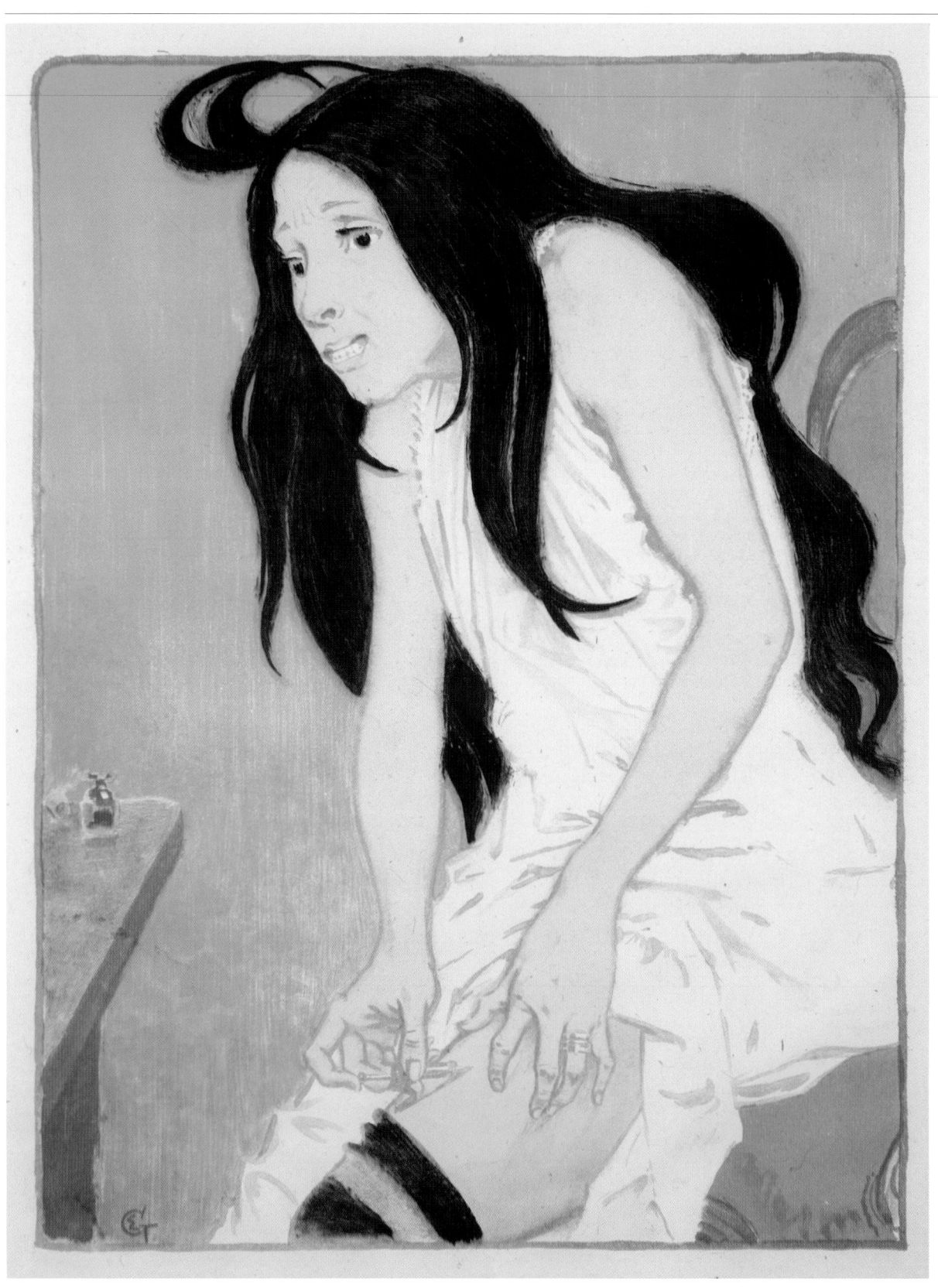

CAT. 37   Eugène-Samuel Grasset (French, 1841-1917)
Morphinomane [Morphine Addict], 1897
Lithograph, 29½ x 23⁷⁄₁₆ in. (75 x 59.5 cm)
Jane Voorhees Zimmerli Art Museum: Rutgers, The State University of
New Jersey; Friends Purchase Fund
Photograph by Jack Abraham; 77.054.001

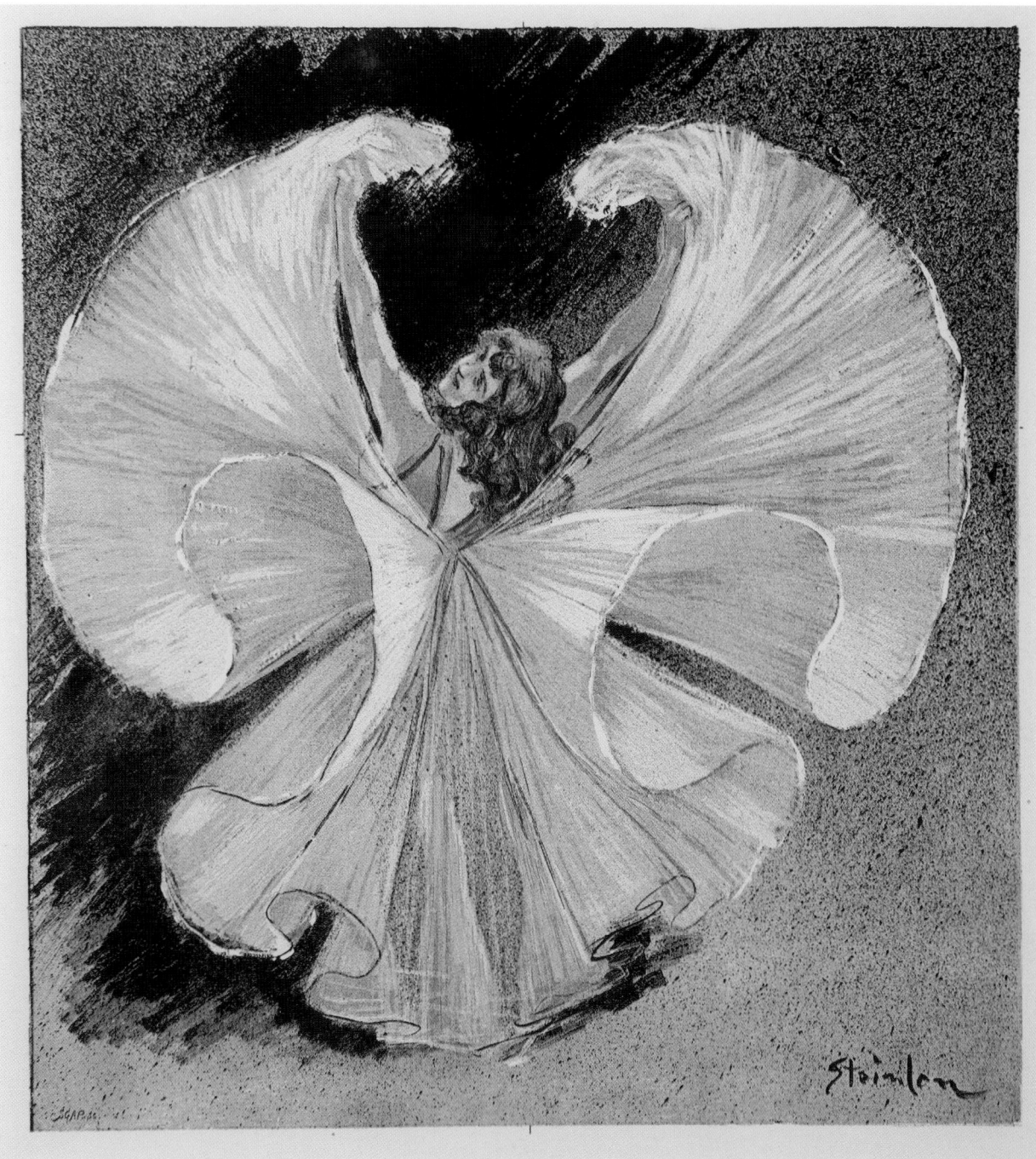

CAT. 95   Théophile-Alexandre Steinlen (Swiss, 1859-1923)
          "La Loïe Fuller aux Folies-Bergère" Cover for *Gil Blas Illustré*, no. 52,
          25 December 1892; *Gil Blas Illustré* proof, 12¾ x 10⁷⁄₁₆ in. (32.4x 26.5 cm)
          Jane Voorhees Zimmerli Art Museum; Rutgers, The State University of
          New Jersey; Gift of Marion and Allan Maitlin; Photograph by Jack Abraham
          1986.0490

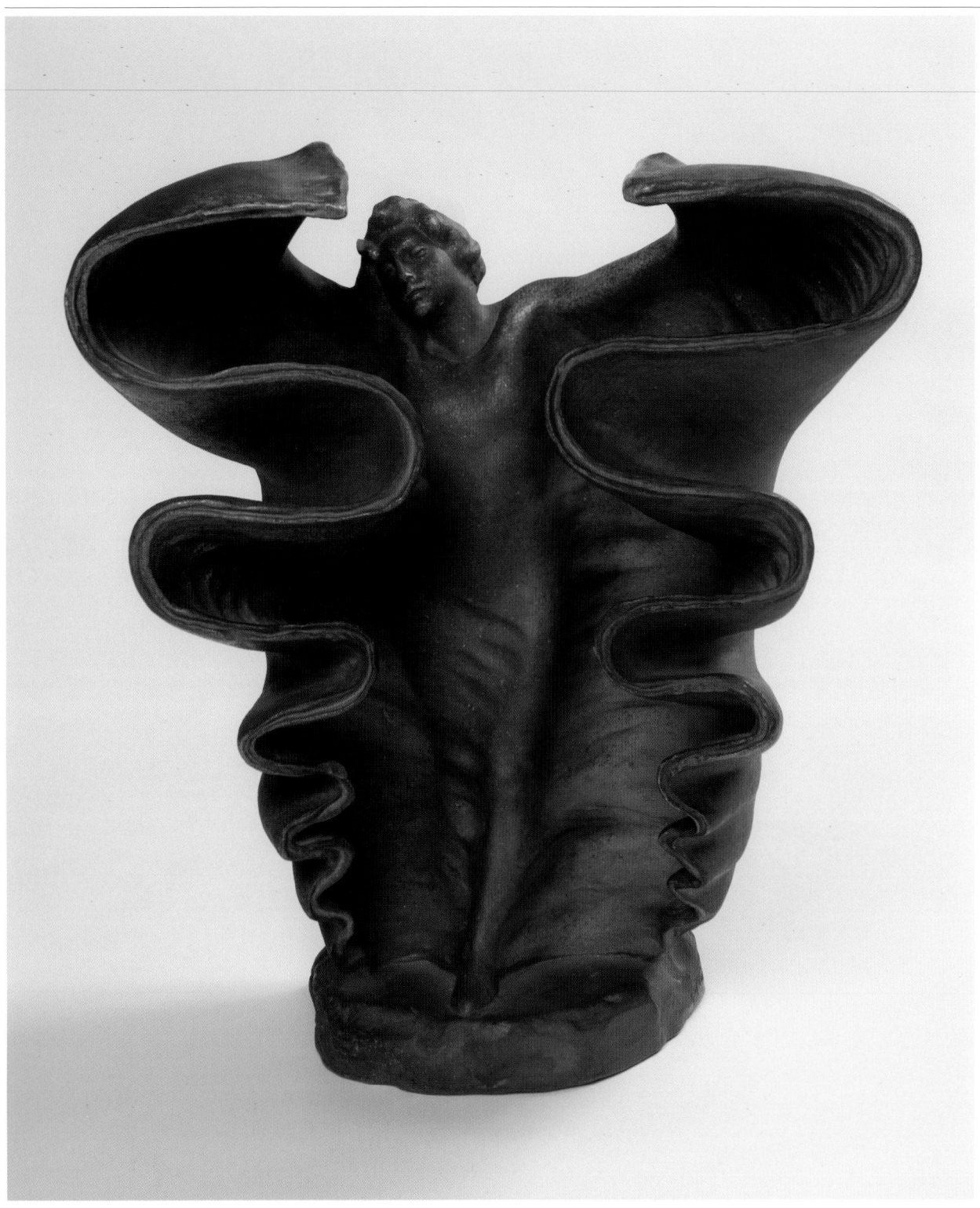

CAT. 13   François-Rupert Carabin (French, 1862-1932)
Loïe Fuller, ca. 1897-1898
Enameled stoneware, 18 x 15 3/16 x 9 in. (45.7 x 38.5 x 21.2 cm)
Jane Voorhees Zimmerli Art Museum; Rutgers, The State University of
New Jersey; Gift of Herbert D. and Ruth Schimmel
Photograph by Jack Abraham; 2000.0668

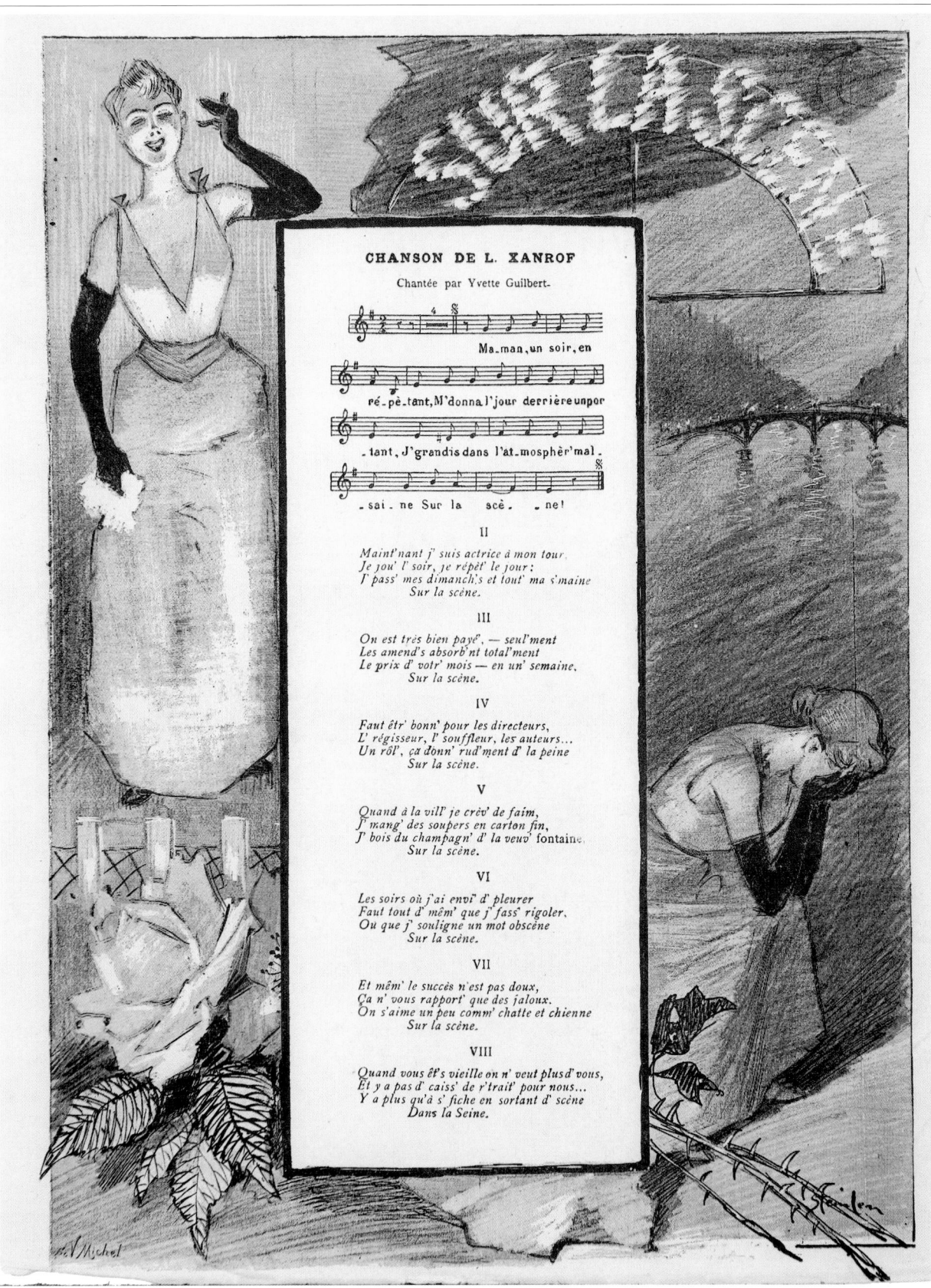

CAT. 94   Théophile-Alexandre Steinlen (Swiss, 1859-1923)

"Sur la Scène, Chanson by L. Xanrof," from *Gil Blas Illustré*,

14 February 1892, p. 8; Photo relief of page, 12¹³/₁₆ x 9¹⁵/₁₆ in. (32.5 x 25.3 cm)

Jane Voorhees Zimmerli Art Museum; Rutgers, The State University of

New Jersey; Gift of Marion and Allan Maitlin

Photograph by Jack Abraham; 1986.0558

to the public.[6] A double-sided drawing, showing a range of Bruant's gestures and facial reactions, as well as members of the audience, further revealed how closely Steinlen studied this performer for the images he used in the pages of *Gil Blas Illustré* (cat. 108; p. 74).

For the most part the illustrations that Steinlen produced for *Gil Blas Illustré* were not of actual performers on stage, but of illustrated texts – often short stories – to be printed in the same issue. In *Pygmalion* by René Maizeroy (cat. 97; p. 75) (*Gil Blas Illustré*, 29 January 1894), the artist used an imaginary performer's obsession with a mannequin to create an image that was both amusing and disturbing. The dancer, failing to bring the mannequin to life despite all manner of advances, destroys his love in a moment of extreme passion. Through this story, one that was detailed on the pages following Steinlen's cover image, symbolic and fetishistic references became apparent and Steinlen's central theme was revealed.

Steinlen also found himself illustrating short stories by the naturalist writer, Aurelien Scholl, as in his work *Ombres Parisiennes* (3 September 1893) (cat. 96; p. 76). While the image does not reference a specific episode from the text, Steinlen conveys the sense of misery and distress that accompanied the fate of any young girl (Valentine in this case) who found herself so destitute that she seriously considered becoming a prostitute in Paris. The atmosphere is haunted as Steinlen shows a young woman on her way toward oblivion; he uses his penchant for the creation of easily recognizable social types, thereby encouraging the readers of *Gil Blas Illustré* to identify with those who found themselves (or members of their family) in such a condition.

Another image, *Passe le Détroit* (19 March 1895), by the author Gabriel Mourey (cat. 99; p. 78) commented on the presence of English performers in the streets of Paris. Their enthusiasm, their unusual garments, and the presence of one figure playing the bagpipes provided amusement for onlookers. While there could be parallels with actual performers on stage (such as May Milton, for example), Steinlen revealed an interest in all types of street performers. These figures in particular brought a glimpse

of modern England, at least an England as chronicled by Gabriel Mourey in *Gil Blas Illustré*.

Other stories, such as *Un Mari* by Camille de Sainte-Croix (28 April 1895) (cat. 100; p. 79) provided Steinlen with the opportunity to comment on infidelity, mistaken identity, and the deviousness of the woman and her lover. The climax of the affair leads to one figure being arrested by the police; but the story provides several strands that suggest that the main protagonists are careful to cover up their infidelity. A battle between the two men, both seeking the woman's affections, provided Steinlen with the opportunity to suggest irony as the woman observes the struggle with a bemused expression. Once again, his ability to draw something deeper out of the text, such as the contemporary vision of women as femmes fatales, makes Steinlen's images more than mere illustrations.[7]

As a commentator on the foibles of man Steinlen was particularly taken by the story of *Une Réputation* by Henry Caen (5 May 1895) (cat. 101; p. 80) where an old woman recounted a tale of infidelity that involved her dead husband. Intent on trying to heal old wounds, the woman returned to the location where she had first met her husband and, there, dressed as an old prostitute and accompanied by her well-dressed son, hoped to relocate the love that she had lost. This sad story, about the delusions of life, and the need to bring something to closure, allowed Steinlen an opportunity to increase the range of his social types while dressing an old woman as a flirtatious fool. Working in a similar vein in his *Les Fous*, after a story by Emile Goudeau (15 December 1895) (cat. 102; p. 81), Steinlen created an allegorical image – one unusual for an artist grounded in reality – that suggested that the pursuit of fame, or money, or sensuality led to delusions and the death of the soul. It is one of the more provocative images in *Gil Blas Illustré*. The city of Paris is seen in the image of the woman as the provider of sensual love as she tries to attract young blond, or dark-haired men with strong backs who might satisfy all her needs.

Similar to Edgar Degas' fascination with how performers were created, Steinlen was drawn back to the

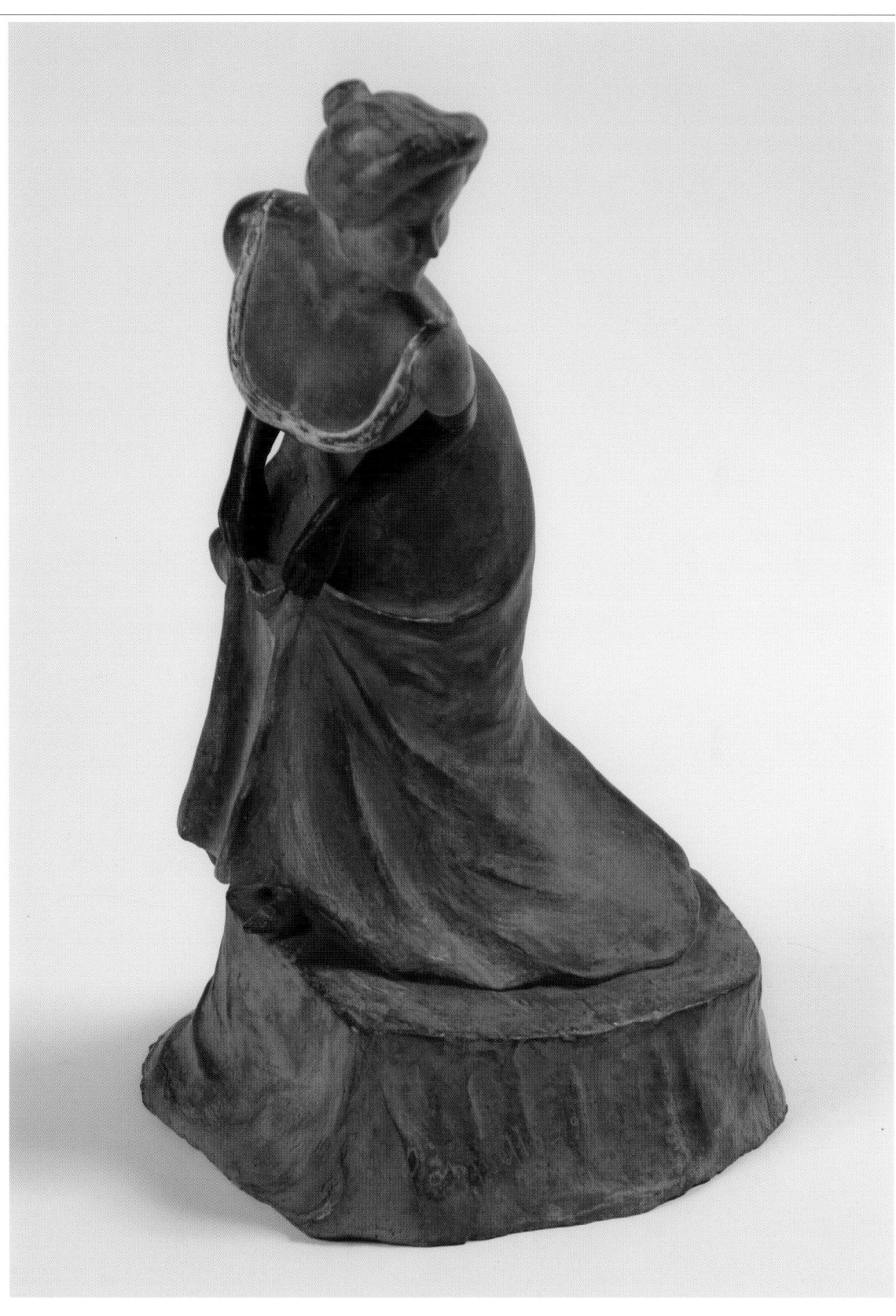

CAT. 10   Leonetto Cappiello (French, 1875-1942)
Portrait of Yvette Guilbert, 1899
Painted plaster, 13½ x 9 x 6⅞ in. (34 x 23.5 x 17.4 cm)
Jane Voorhees Zimmerli Art Museum; Rutgers, The State
University of New JerseyCarleton A. Holstrom and Mary Beth Kineke
Purchase Fund; Photograph by Jack Abraham; 2001.0976

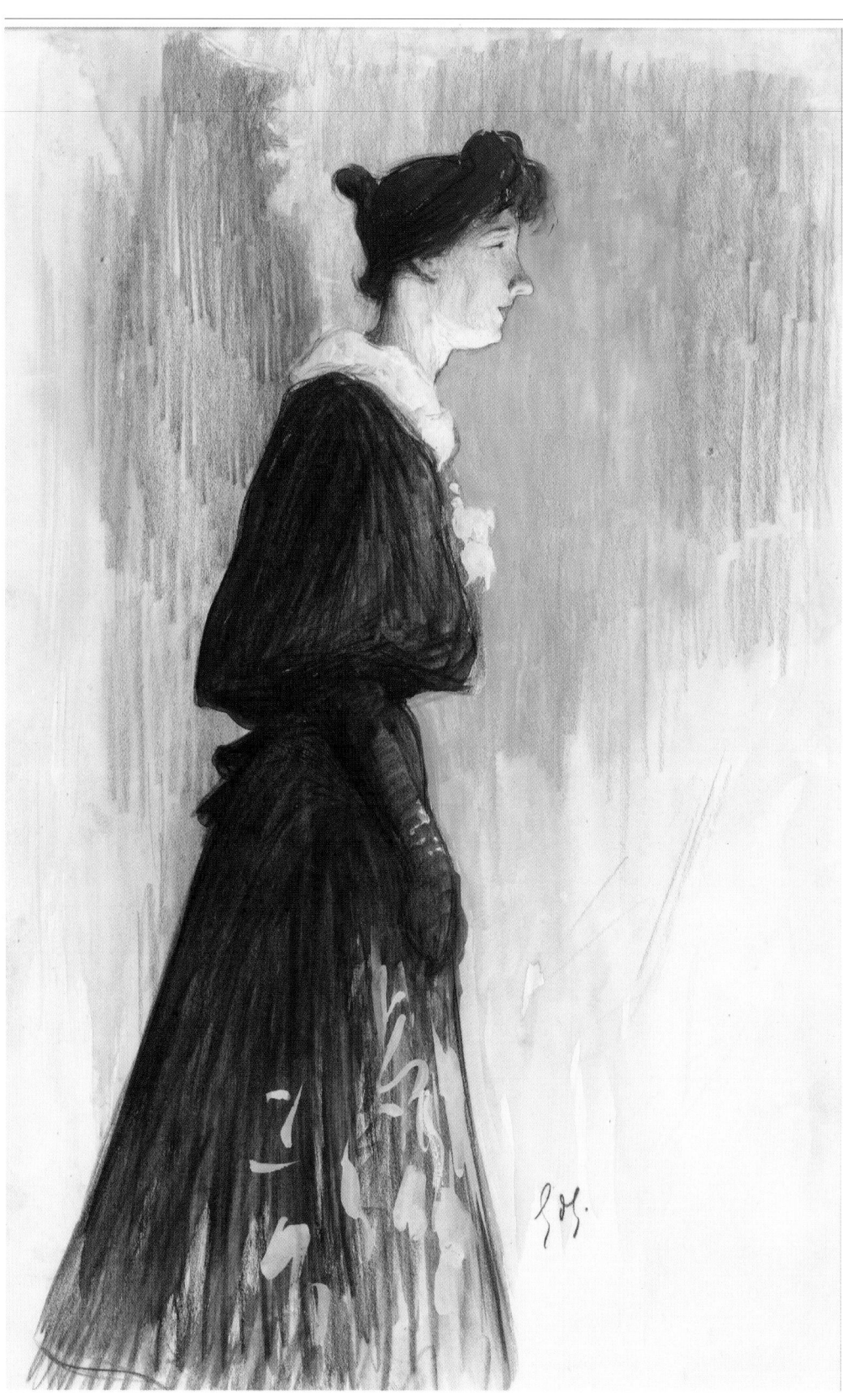

CAT. 30   Georges d'Espagnat (French, 1870-1950)
Yvette Guilbert, ca. 1900
Gouache, 22 x 16½ in. (55.9 x 41.9 cm)
Dr. Gabriel and Yvonne Weisberg Collection

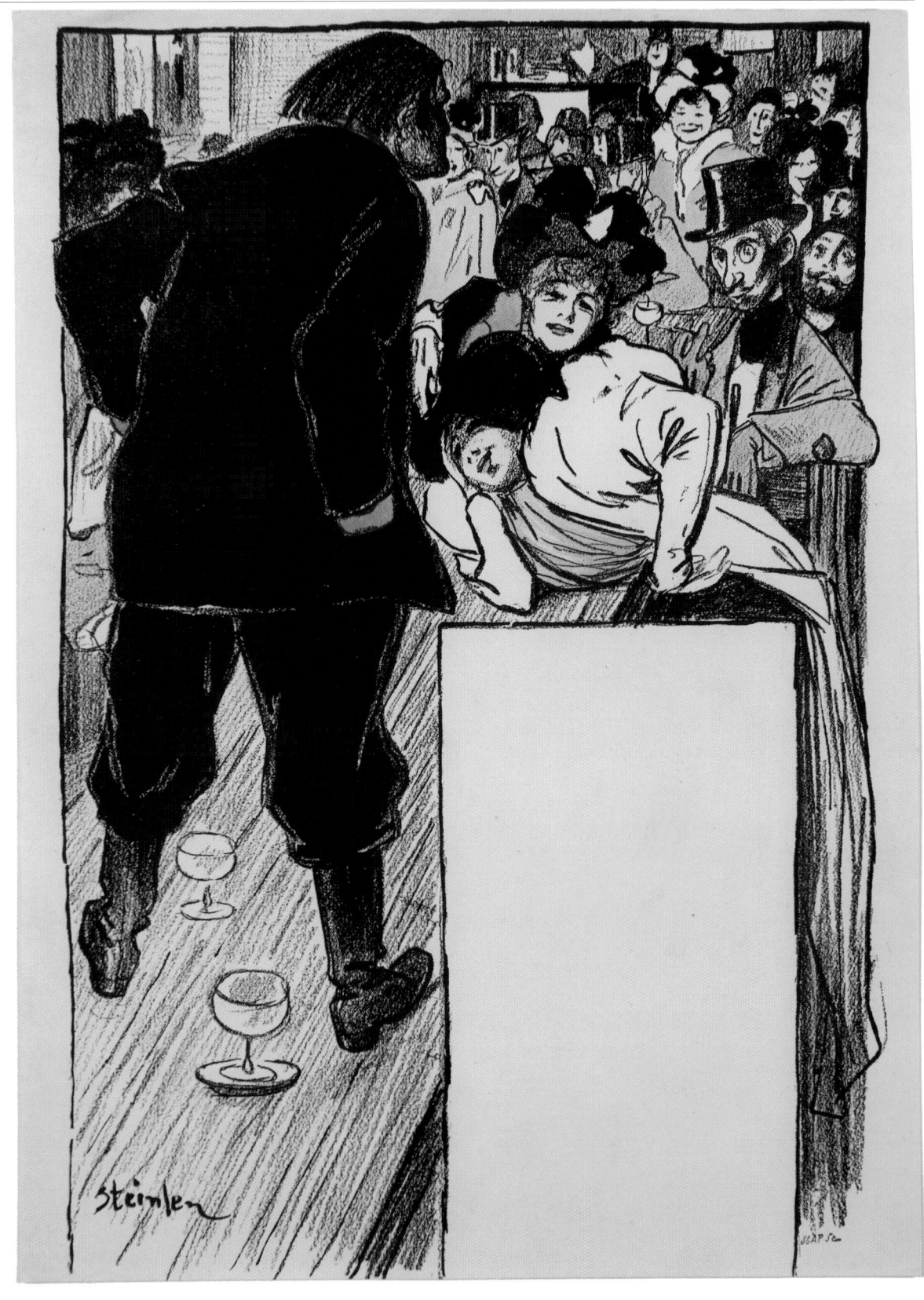

CAT. 98 Théophile-Alexandre Steinlen (Swiss, 1859-1923)
"Pièces à dire, Fin de Siècle," by Aristide Bruant, illustrated by
Steinlen for *Gil Blas Illustré*, no 8, 24 February 1895; *Gil Blas Illustré*
proof (before the letters), 13½ x 10 in. (34.5 x 25.4 cm); Jane Voorhees
Zimmerli Art Museum; Rutgers, The State University of New Jersey;
Gift of Marion and Allan Maitlin; Photo by Jack Abraham; 1986.0538

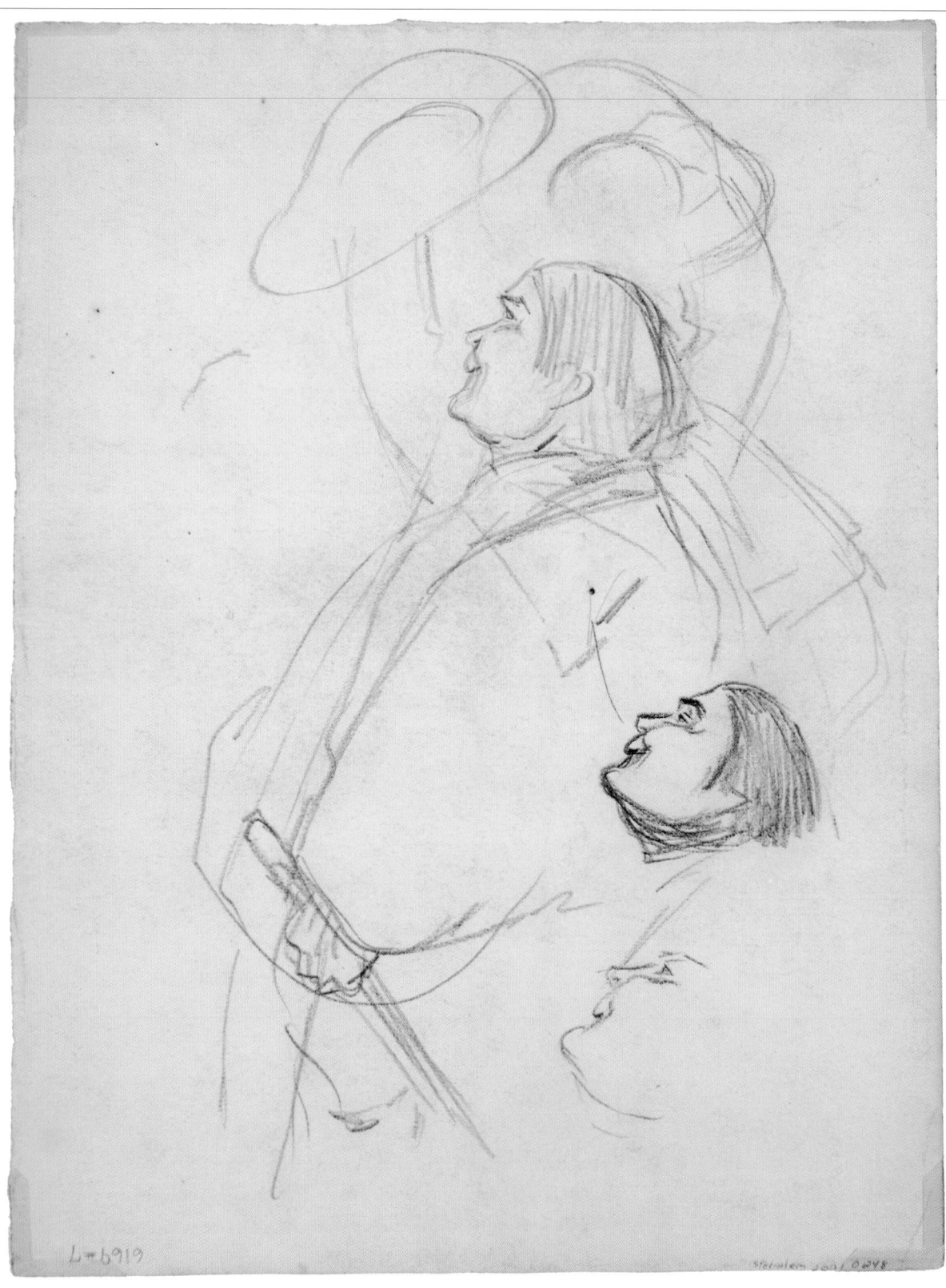

CAT. 108 Théophile-Alexandre Steinlen (Swiss, 1859-1923)
Portrait of Aristide Bruant (doublesided; see p. 58), n.d.
Pencil, 14 9/16 x 11 7/16 in. (37 x 29 cm)
Jane Voorhees Zimmerli Art Museum; Rutgers, The State University of
New Jersey; Photograph by Jack Abraham; 2001.0248

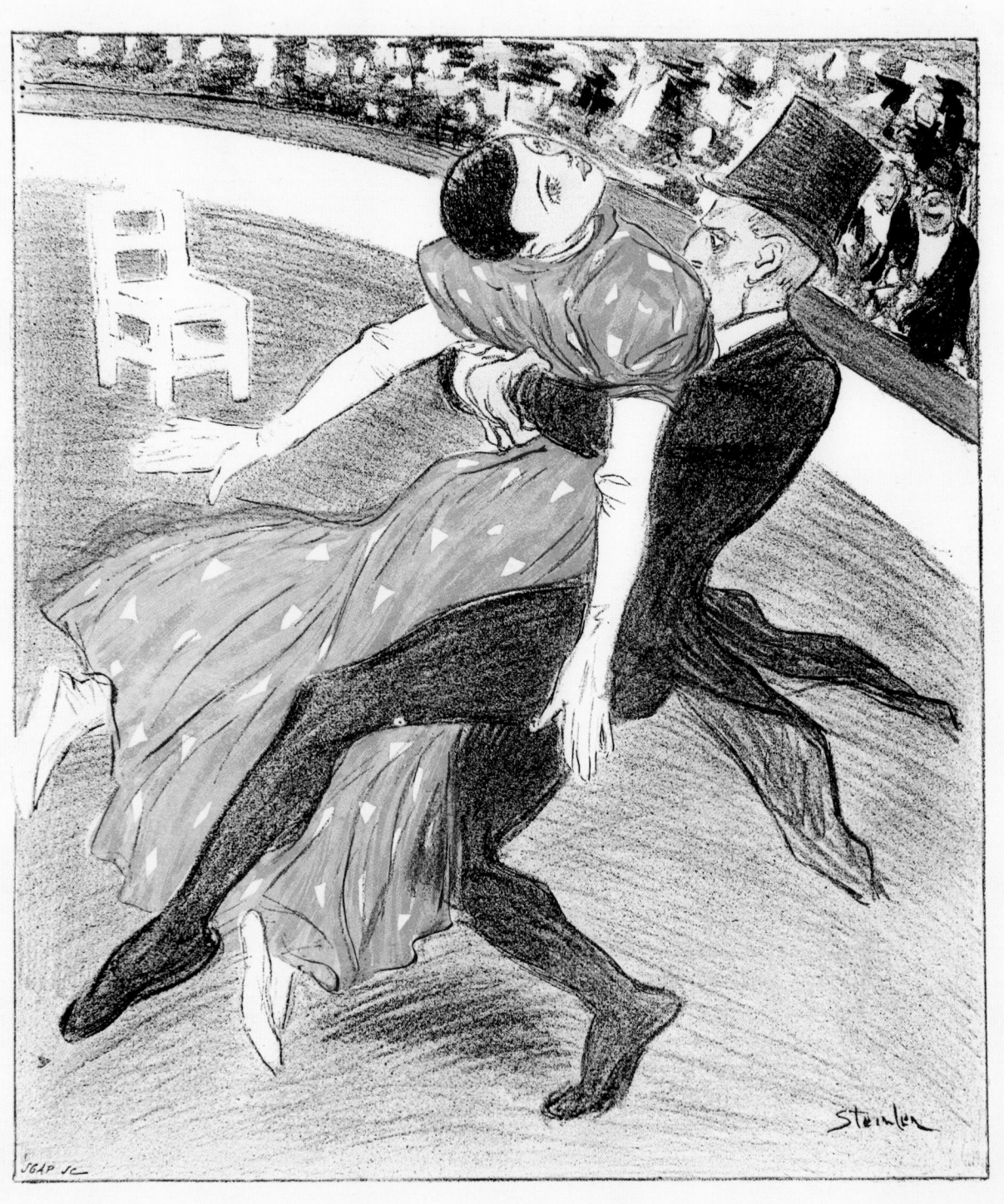

CAT. 97   Théophile-Alexandre Steinlen (Swiss, 1859-1923)
"Pygmalion," by René Maizeroy; Cover for *Gil Blas Illustré*,
29 January 1894; *Gil Blas Illustré* proof, 14 5/16 x 10 3/8 in. (36.3 x 26.3 cm)
Jane Voorhees Zimmerli Art Museum; Rutgers, The State University of
New Jersey; Gift of Marion and Allan Maitlin
Photo by Jack Abraham; 1986.0599

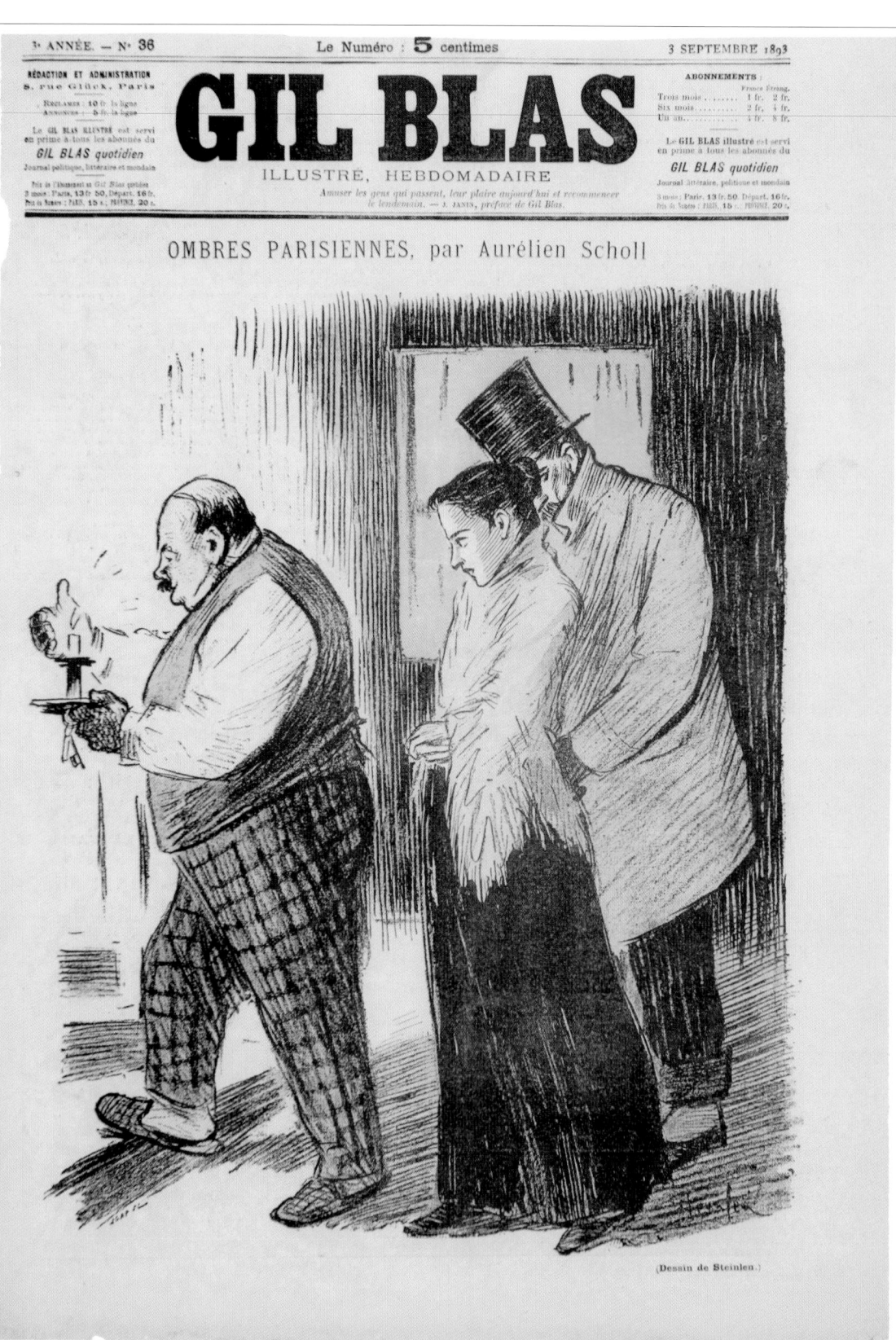

CAT. 96 Théophile-Alexandre Steinlen, (Swiss, 1859-1923)

"Ombres Parisiennes," by Aurelien Scholl; Cover for *Gil Blas Illustré*,

3 September 1893; Lithograph, 10¹³/₁₆ x 15⅜ in. (27.5 x 39 cm)

Jane Voorhees Zimmerli Art Museum; Rutgers, The State University of

New Jersey; Gift of Herbert D. and Ruth Schimmel

Photograph by Jack Abraham; 1987.0530

stage in his image of *Permutantes* by Lucien Descaves (13 November 1896) (cat. 104; p. 82). Here Steinlen examines an audition. A mother has pursued a stage director to get an audition for her daughter, but when the time comes for the performance, the pianist, who was to accompany the child, has already left for the day. The mother convinces the theatre owner that she can take the place of the pianist and the story ends well: the child gets the job. However, the irony in the story, not shown in the drawing, is that the mother will have to play in all performances for no pay. Inspired by the text, Steinlen shows the child on stage, the mother in the foreground, and the stage director seated in the audience.

Two other illustrations rely on well-advanced types that Steinlen used in numerous prints at the close of the 1890s. In one, *Les Trottins* (1 April 1898) (cat. 105; p. 83) after a short text by Jean Reibrach, the artist focused on a new class: the young errand girls who appeared on the streets of the city early in the morning on their way to work. Steinlen captures their appearance and demeanor with the same verve found in the text, which emphasizes their youth, and desire to be dressed in the most up-to-date and alluring fashion. In *L'Assistance* by naturalist writer Oscar Méténier (27 July 1900) (cat. 106; p. 84), a brief interlude drawn from street life provides the format for Steinlen. An unemployed man with no place to sleep – his girlfriend has been taken to prison – and no money in his pockets moves into the foreground of the image. His sense of dejection is captured by Steinlen who reveals that women will take care of him, including the figure at the left who is coming to his rescue, by finding lodging for him with another woman. The sense of life on the street provides the rationale for this image.

By 1900, with the Paris Exposition Universelle drawing millions to the city, there was a very well-established visual and literary tradition linked to the life of the people. Steinlen's *L'Assistance* illustration sums up the position of many in the city – they struggle to survive any way they can, often depending on the kindness of strangers to help them through the night or the day. As an artist with a message, Steinlen's images augmented the texts in *Gil Blas Illustré*, helping to make it a widely read publication grounded in well-understood eternal truths.

Consuming the Poster Revolution

When the image of Georges de Feure's 1894 *Paris-Almanach* (cat. 32; p. XX) was disseminated throughout the city, he demonstrated again how posters informed issues – either about new performers or publications or about the clear marketing strategies required to succeed. *Paris-Almanach* encapsulates all of these aspects.[8] In featuring a fashionably dressed woman strolling through the streets of Paris holding a copy of *Paris-Almanach*, de Feure gave visual presence to the new woman – the young, chic figure eager to be noticed since she was wearing the newest fashion and, hopefully attracting the men's gazes both to herself and especially to the publication she held in her hands. At the same time, de Feure created an emblematic icon of the new woman who had become a metaphor for the new Paris, just as *Paris-Almanach*, the publication, was calling attention to the temptations, sites, and performers that one could see throughout the city. Paris was embodied in the new woman, and *Paris-Almanach* was her tool, the vehicle for the seduction of the people in the city. With this poster, de Feure became a very active member of the poster revolution, a movement that involved such well-known artists as Henri de Toulouse-Lautrec and Jules Chéret.[9]

Unlike many of the poster artists, Toulouse-Lautrec's images are often linked to specific performers he knew well in Montmartre. He portrayed Aristide Bruant in his own cabaret speaking to the masses (cat. 111; p. 87) or moved to the Moulin Rouge where he immortalized such performers as Jane Avril or La Goulue (cats. 113, 110; pp. 88, 89). His posters exemplify Parisian life, transforming the performers who populated the cabarets and dance halls into icons of the capital. His design genius, encapsulating the essence of an entertainer through a distinctive pose, a type of dress, or hairstyle, makes them immediately recognizable. Often attacked during the 1890s for creating posters that failed to meet the demands of informing the public clearly, and for valuing aesthetic effects over clarity of design, Toulouse-Lautrec today represents the highest creative perfection of the poster revolution.[10]

In spite of Toulouse-Lautrec's extensive contributions, the artist who led the movement toward the

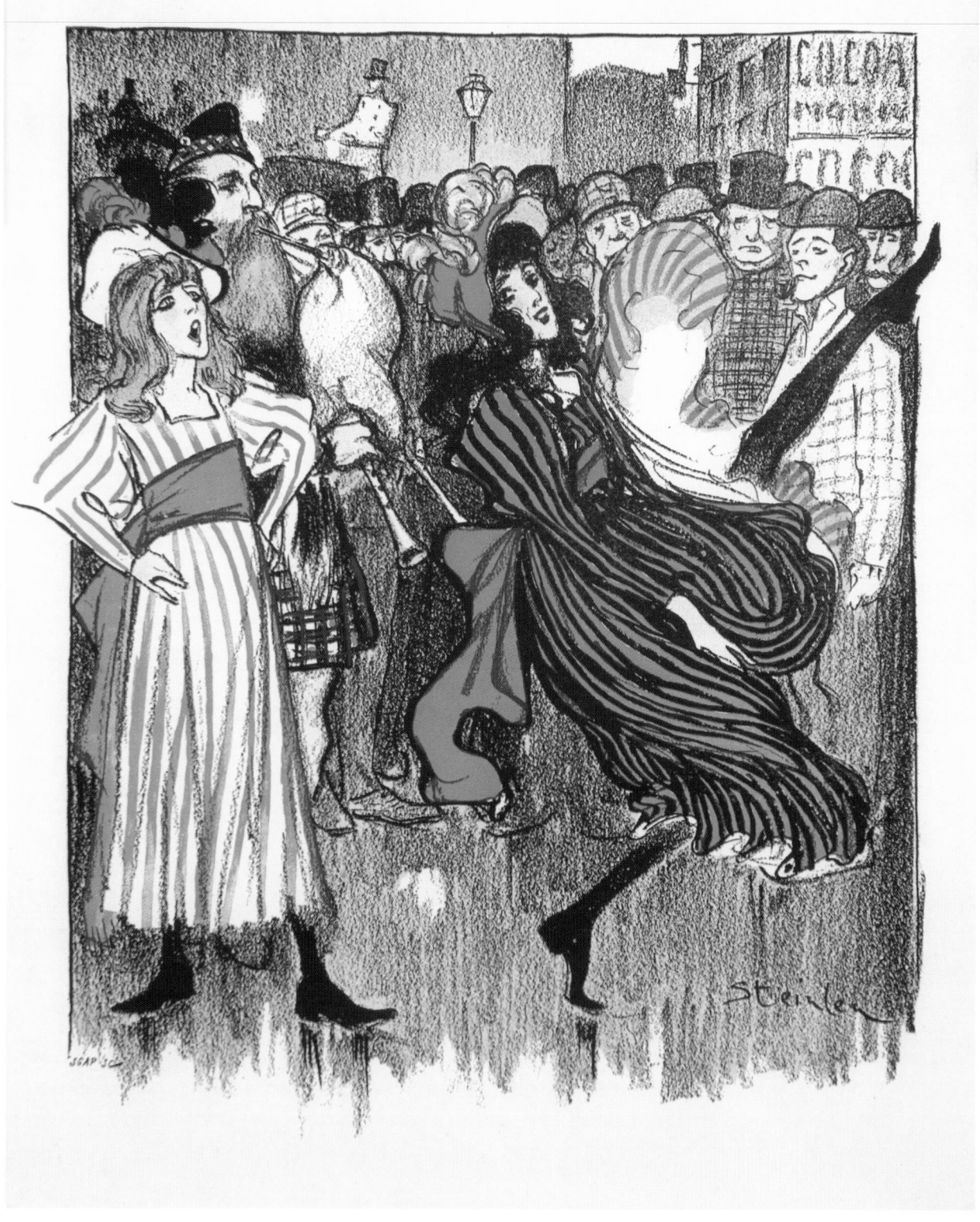

CAT. 99   Théophile-Alexandre Steinlen, (Swiss, 1859-1923)
"Passe le Détroit" by Gabriel Mourey; Cover for *Gil Blas Illustré*,
no. 10, 19 March 1895; *Gil Blas Illustré* proof, 13¹/₁₆ x 10 in. (33.2 x 25.4 cm)
Jane Voorhees Zimmerli Art Museum; Rutgers, The State University of
New Jersey; Gift of Marion and Allan Maitlin
Photograph by Jack Abraham; 1986.0592

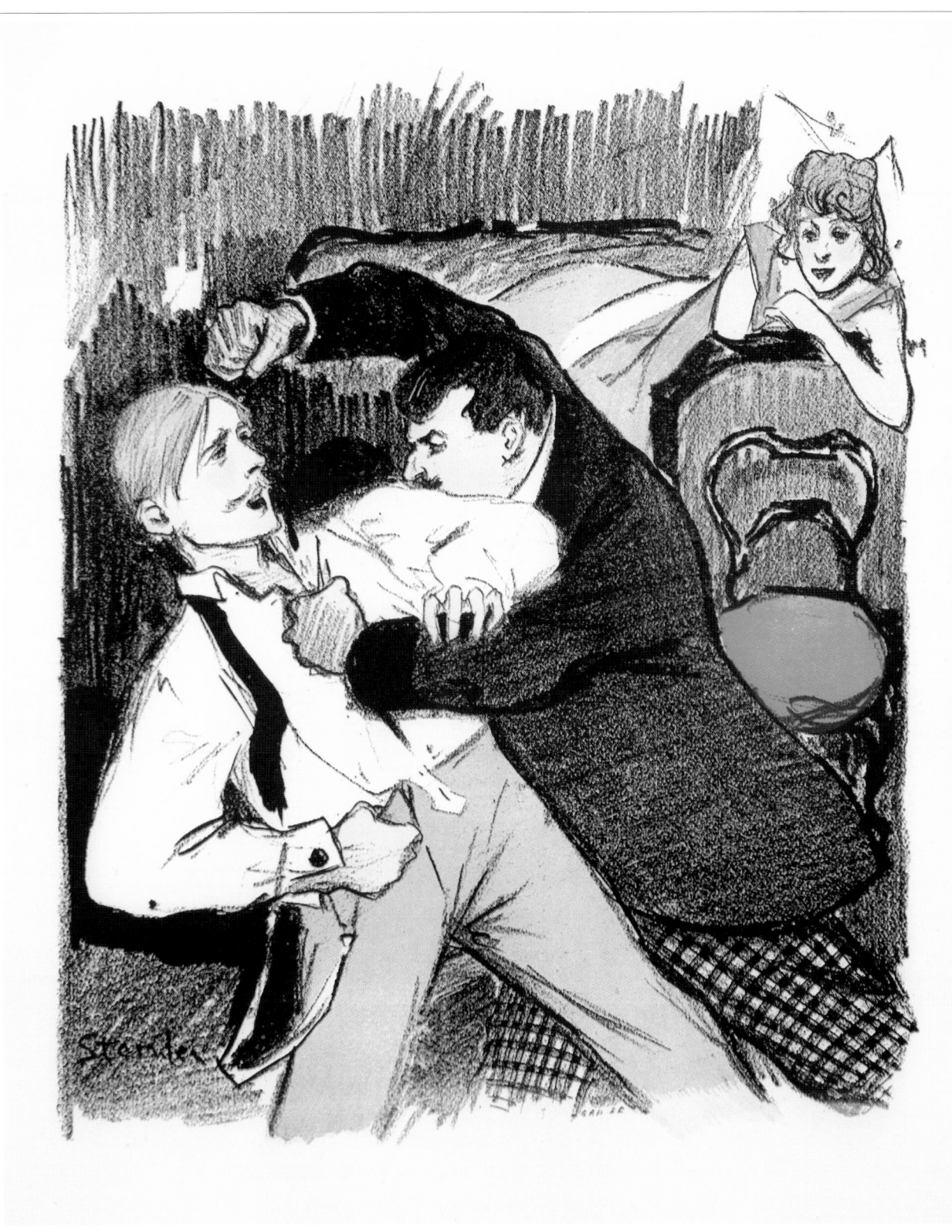

CAT. 100 Théophile-Alexandre Steinlen (Swiss, 1859-1923)
"Un Mari," by Camille de Sainte-Croix; Cover for *Gil Blas Illustré*,
no. 17, 28 April 1895; *Gil Blas Illustré* proof, 12¾ x 10⁵⁄₁₆ in. (32.4 x 26.2 cm)
Jane Voorhees Zimmerli Art Museum; Rutgers, The State University of
New Jersey; Gift of Marion and Allan Maitlin
Photograph by Jack Abraham; 1986.0592

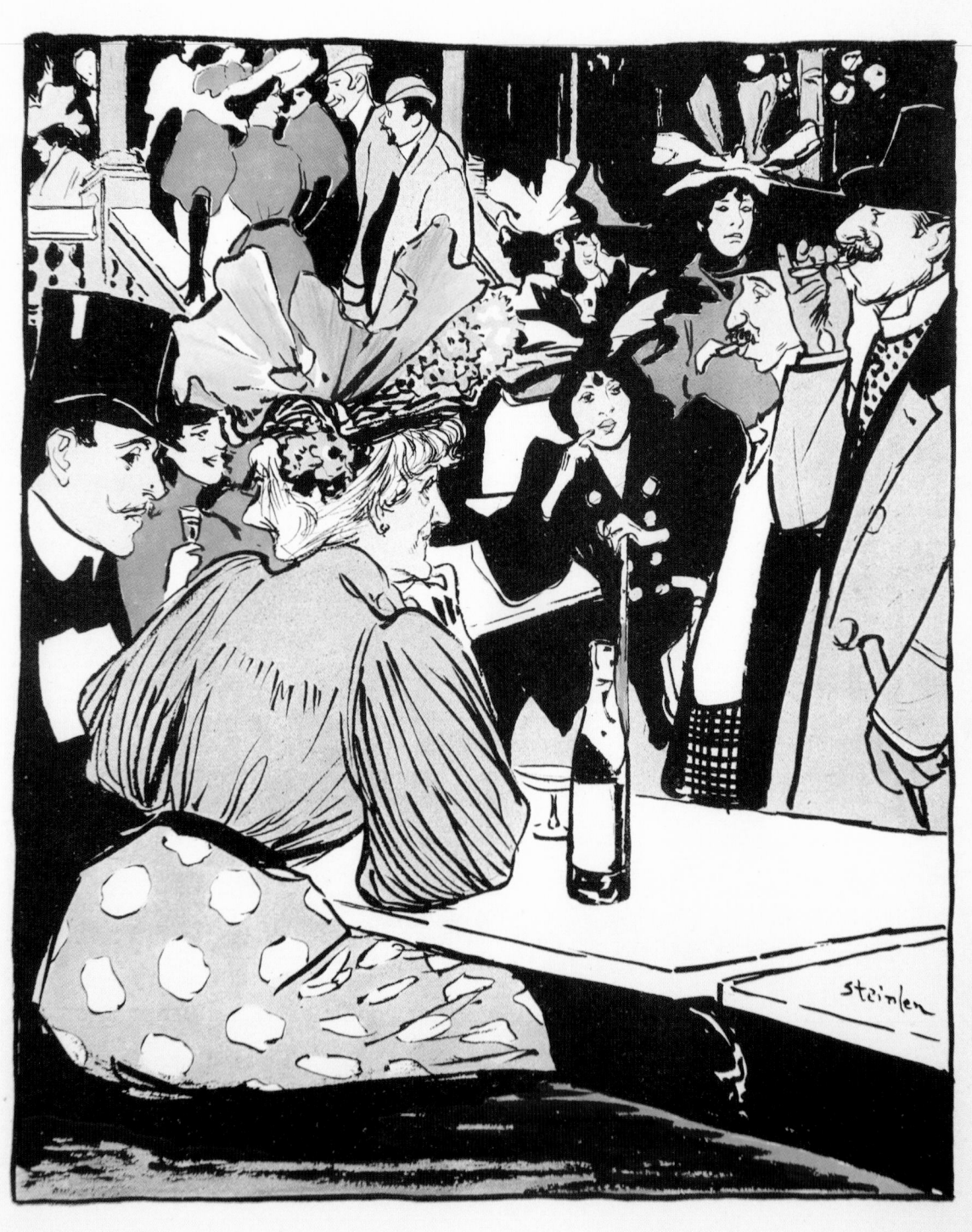

CAT. 101 Théophile-Alexandre Steinlen (Swiss, 1859-1923)
"Une Réputation" by Henry Caen. Cover for *Gil Blas Illustré*, no. 18,
5 May 1895; *Gil Blas Illustré* proof, 12¹⁵/₁₆ x 10½ in. (32.9 x 26.6 cm)
Jane Voorhees Zimmerli Art Museum; Rutgers, The State University of
New Jersey; Gift of Marion and Allan Maitlin
Photograph by Jack Abraham; 1986.0501

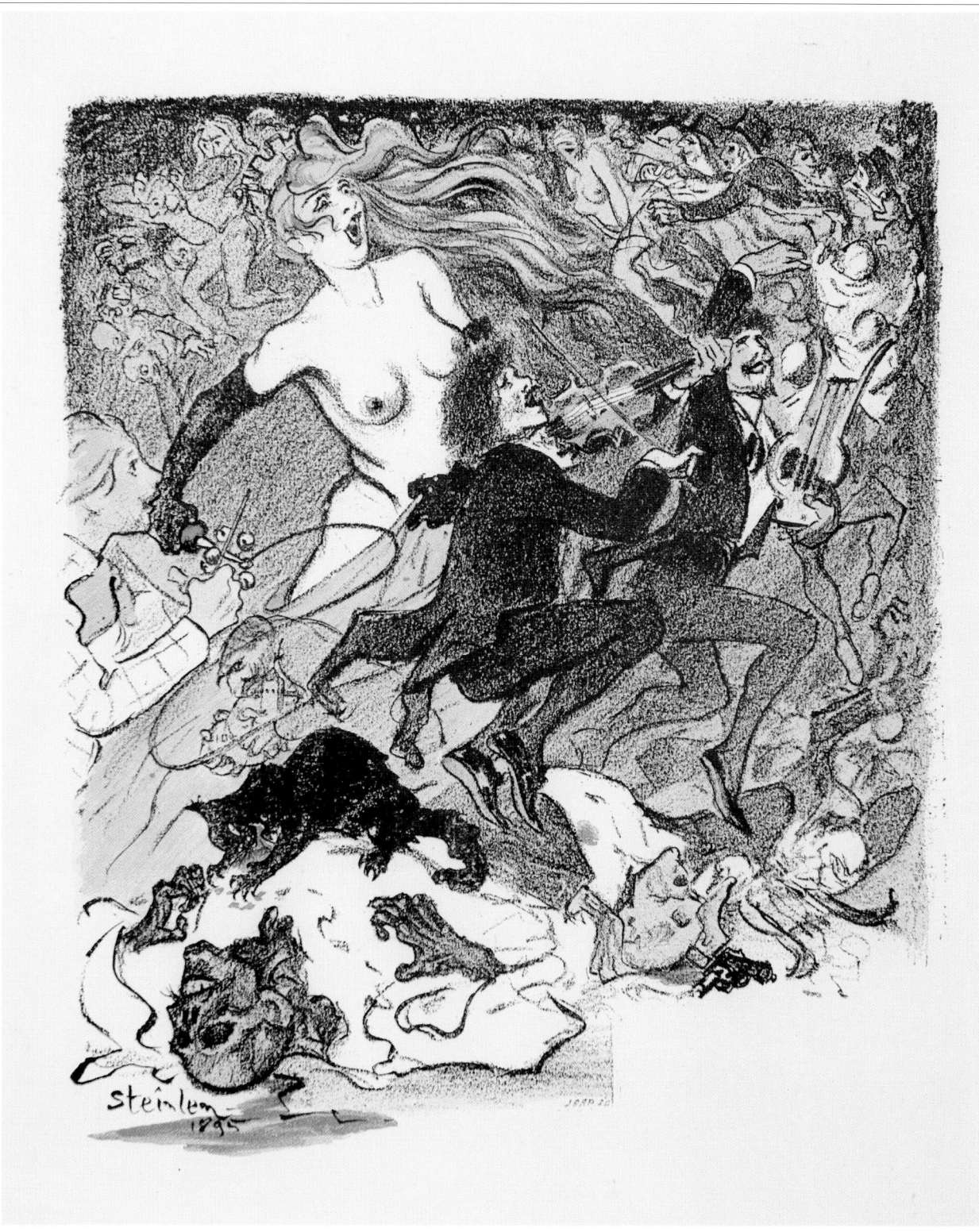

CAT. 102 Théophile-Alexandre Steinlen (Swiss, 1859-1923)
"Les Fous," by Émile Goudeau; Cover for *Gil Blas Illustré*, 15
December 1895; *Gil Blas Illustré* proof, 12⅞ x 10½ in. (32.7 x 26.7 cm)
Jane Voorhees Zimmerli Art Museum; Rutgers, The State University of
New Jersey; Gift of Marion and Allan Maitlin
Photograph by Jack Abraham; 1986.0505

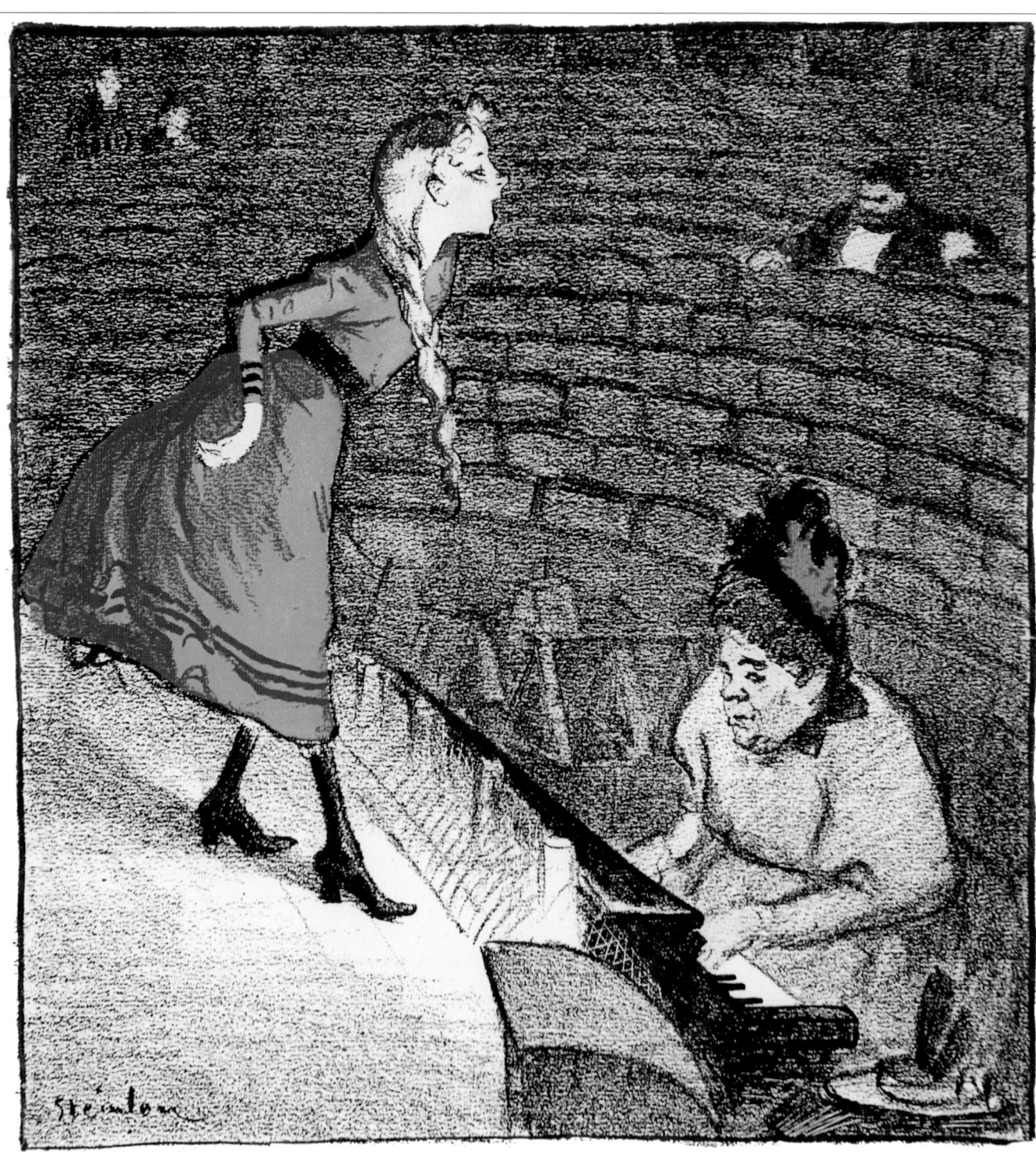

CAT. 104 Théophile-Alexandre Steinlen (Swiss, 1859-1923)
"Permutantes" by Lucien Descaves; Cover for *Gil Blas Illustré*, no. 46,
13 November 1896; *Gil Blas Illustré* proof, 12¹³/₁₆ x 9⅞ in (32.6 x 25.1 cm)
Jane Voorhees Zimmerli Art Museum; Rutgers, The State University of
New Jersey; Gift of Marion and Allan Maitlin
Photograph by Jack Abraham; 1986.0477

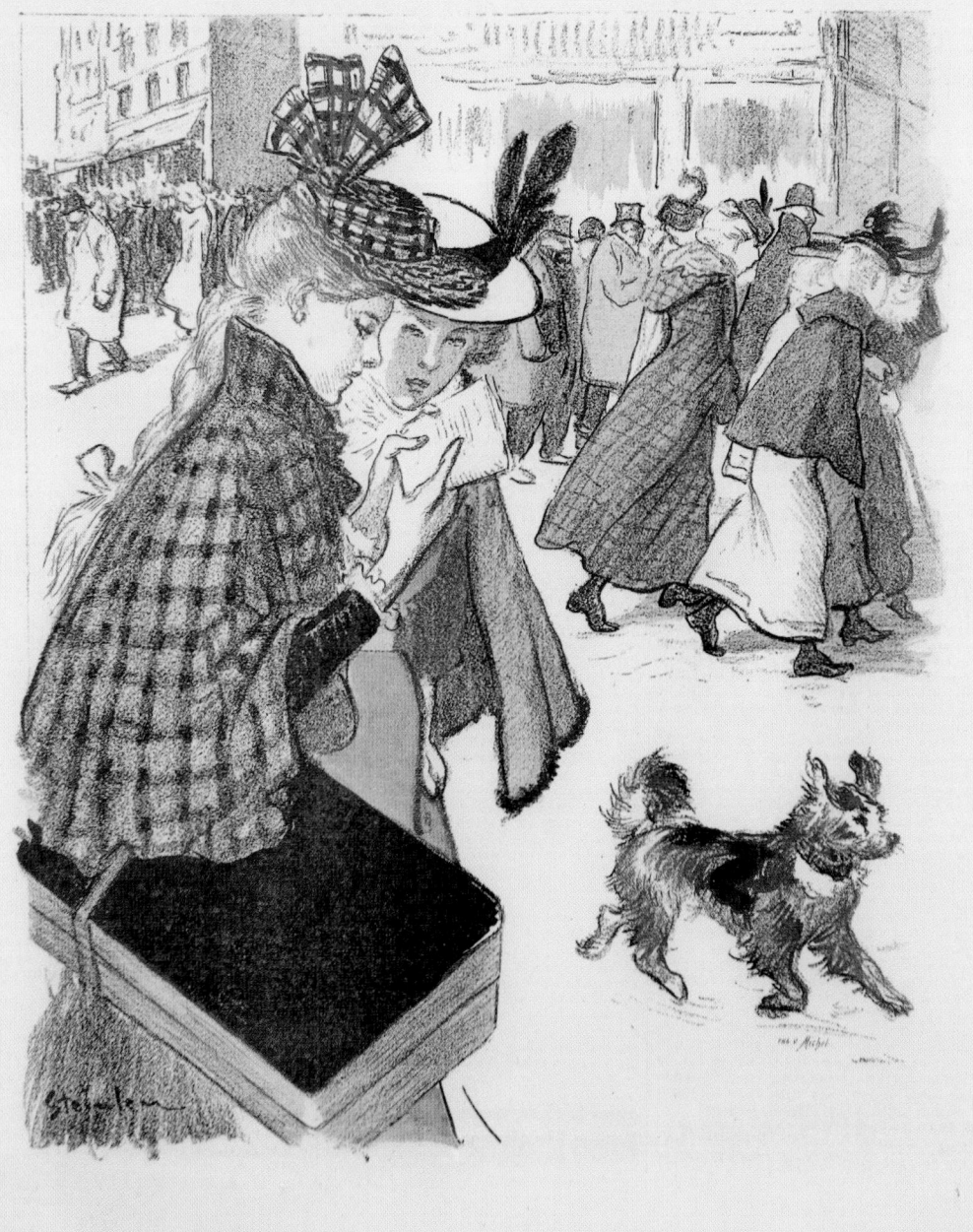

CAT. 105 Théophile-Alexandre Steinlen (Swiss, 1859-1923)
"Les Trottins," by Jean Reibrach; Cover for *Gil Blas Illustré*, no. 13,
1 April 1898; Lithograph, 14 9/16 x 10 13/16 in. (37 x 27.5 cm)
Jane Voorhees Zimmerli Art Museum; Rutgers, The State University of
New Jersey; Gift of Herbert D. and Ruth Schimmel
Photograph by Jack Abraham; 1987.0516

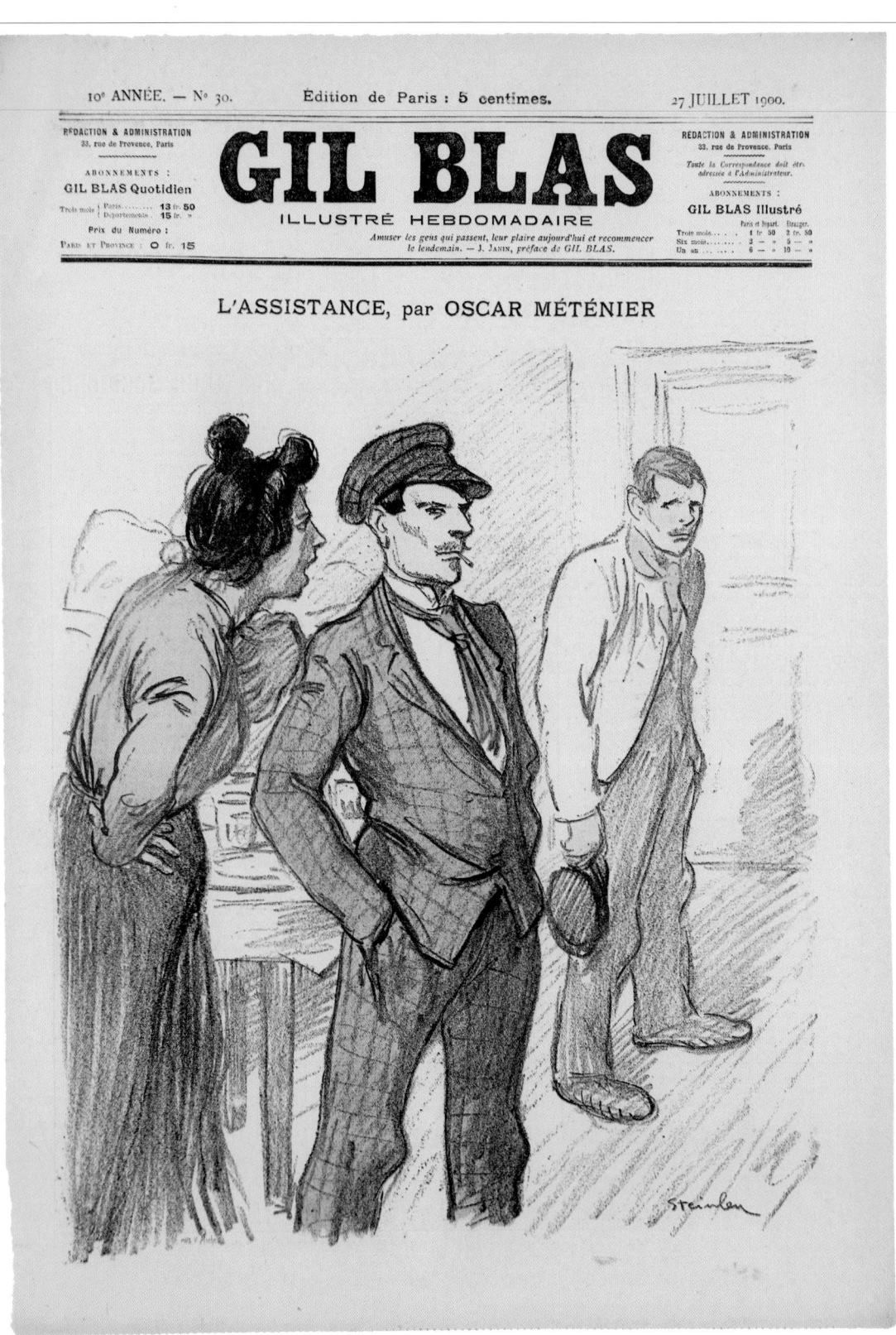

CAT. 106 Théophile-Alexandre Steinlen (Swiss, 1859-1923)
"L'Assistance" by Oscar Méténier; Cover for *Gil Blas Illustré*, no. 40,
27 July 1900; Lithograph, 15½ x 11 in. (39.3 x 28 cm)
Jane Voorhees Zimmerli Art Museum; Rutgers, The State University of
New Jersey; Gift of Herbert D. and Ruth Schimmel
Photograph by Jack Abraham; 1987.0758

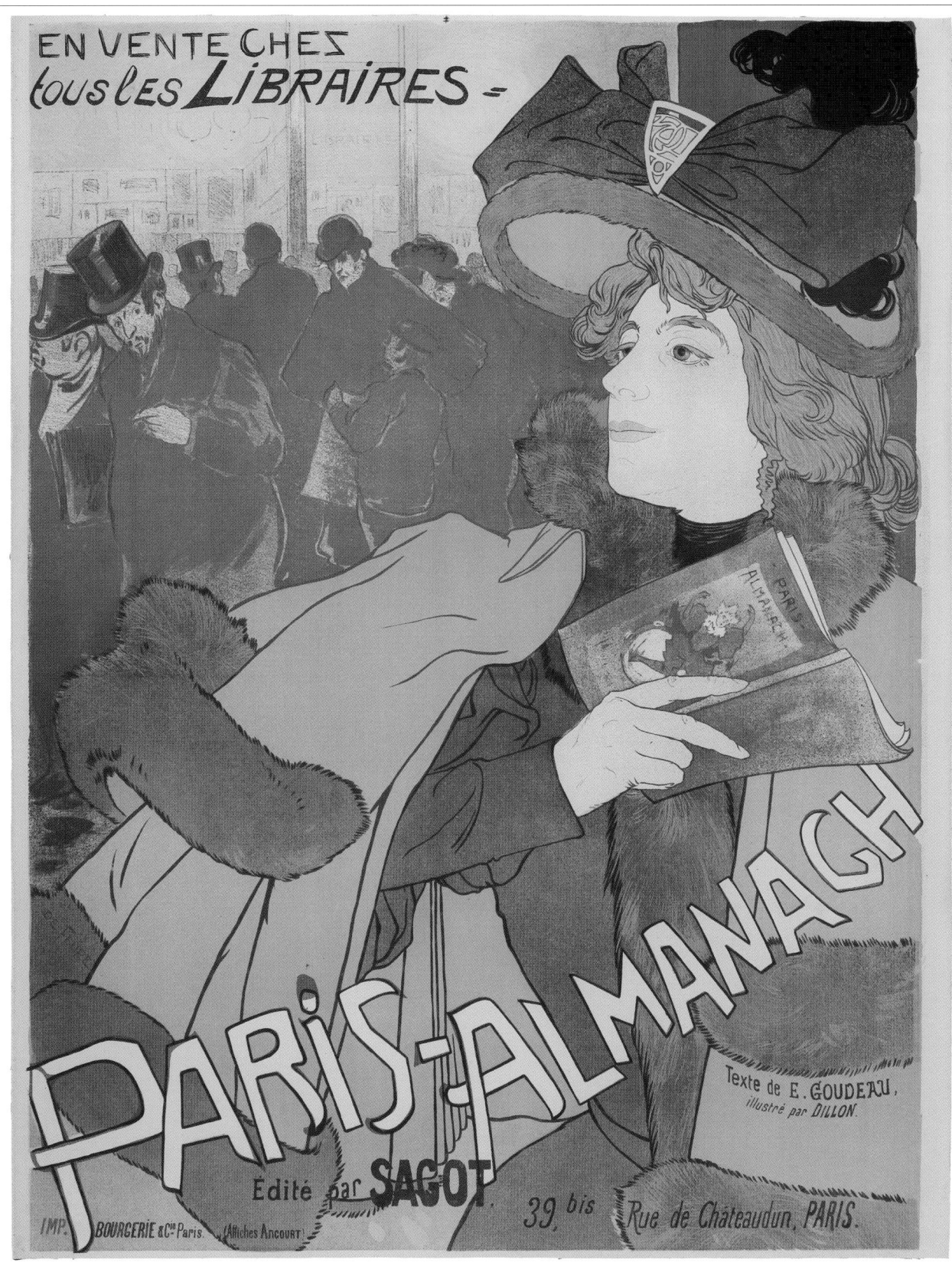

CAT. 32   Georges de Feure (French, 1868-1943)
Paris Almanach, 1894
Lithograph, 32 x 26½ in. (81.3 x 67.3 cm)
Dr. Gabriel and Yvonne Weisberg Collection

modernization of poster design, and who is now given full credit for using color for effect and mood, is Jules Chéret.[11] Chéret invented a new type of woman for his posters called *chérettes*; and they had distinctive characteristics. Chéret's floating angels exude a sense of ebullience, charm, and seduction adding to the impression of the city's perpetual effervescence as seen in the dance halls of Montmartre or in skating rinks such as the Palais de Glace. A sense of ease, enjoyment, and light-heartedness is what Chéret achieved whether he was called on to promote a new drink such as *Pippermint* (cat. 19; p. 91) or his *chérettes* were found dancing, dressed in flimsy garments.

In the *Bal au Moulin Rouge* (cat. 20; p. 89), the one image that changed the direction of posters most dramatically by 1889-1890, the *chérettes* are positioned on the backs of donkeys that move toward the red windmill – symbol of the Moulin Rouge – in the background. The poster was to suggest to potential clients that the Moulin Rouge was both a place where one could dance and see the fabled "can-can" performed. Chéret's colors created a joyful impression that combined intoxication and sensuality, qualities also present in other posters such as *Arc en Ciel* (1893) (cat. 21; p. 92) or *Jardin de Paris* (1889-1890) (cat. 22; p. 93). There can be little doubt that Chéret became as popular as he did because his women were charming visions of immediate relaxation whose presence suggested to a viewer that a given location would be similarly refreshing and novel. By 1900, when Chéret completed his large lithographs of *La Fileuse* (cat. 23; p. 94) his work had been turned into a pleasant game which transported a viewer to an imaginary realm.[12] There is nothing depressing or distressing in these visions of Parisian life. It was Chéret's viewpoint that created the lasting impression that Paris, during what came to be known as the belle époque, was a light-filled paradise where one could be easily removed from the cares of the commonplace and the sad commentaries that dominated many of the prints of others, from Steinlen to Louis Legrand.

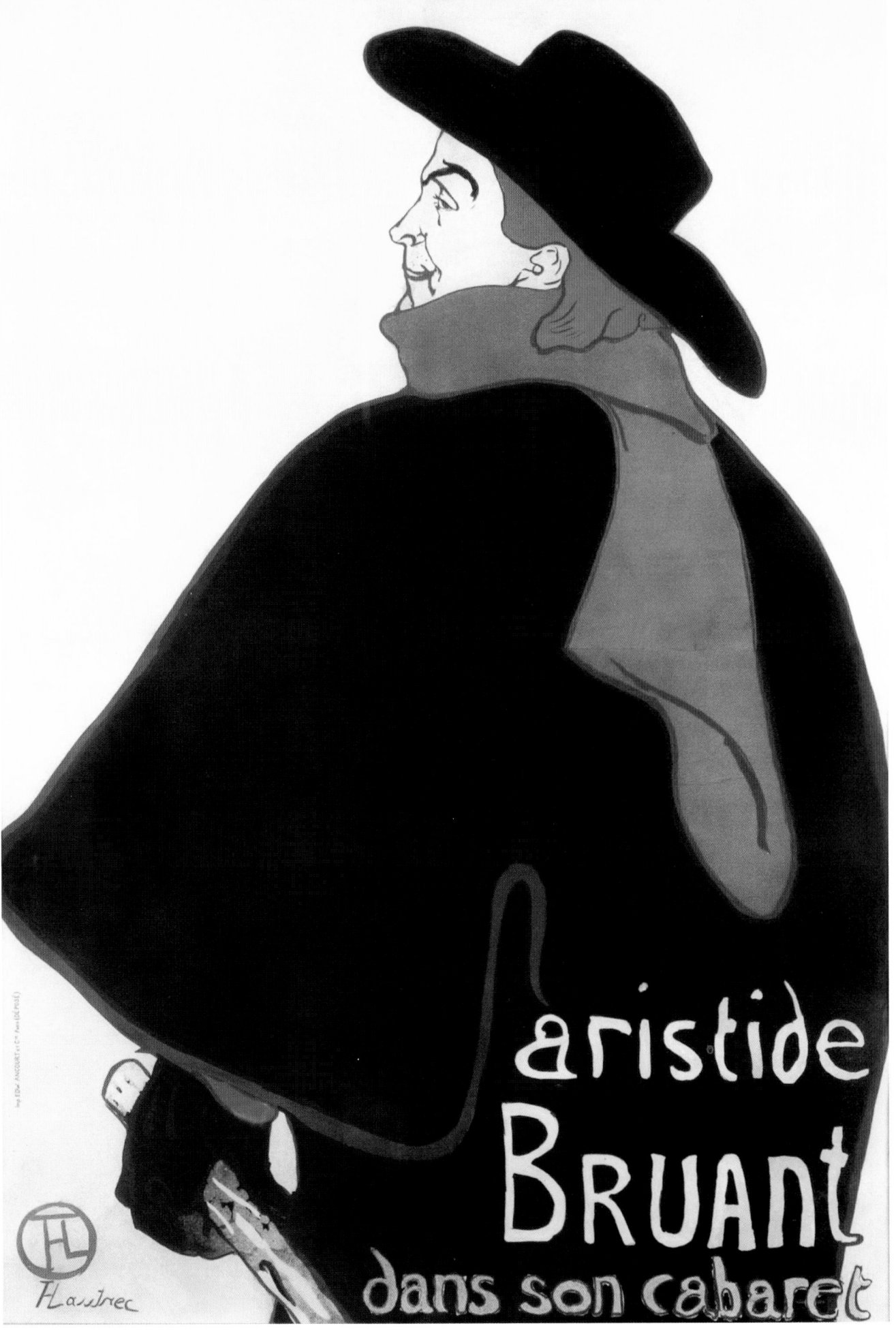

CAT. 111   Henri de Toulouse-Lautrec (French, 1864-1901)
Aristide Bruant dans son cabaret, 1893
Color lithograph, linen backed, 52 x 37 in. (132.08 x 94 cm)
Courtesy Mr. & Mrs. Clay Timon through Galerie Michael,
Beverly Hills, California

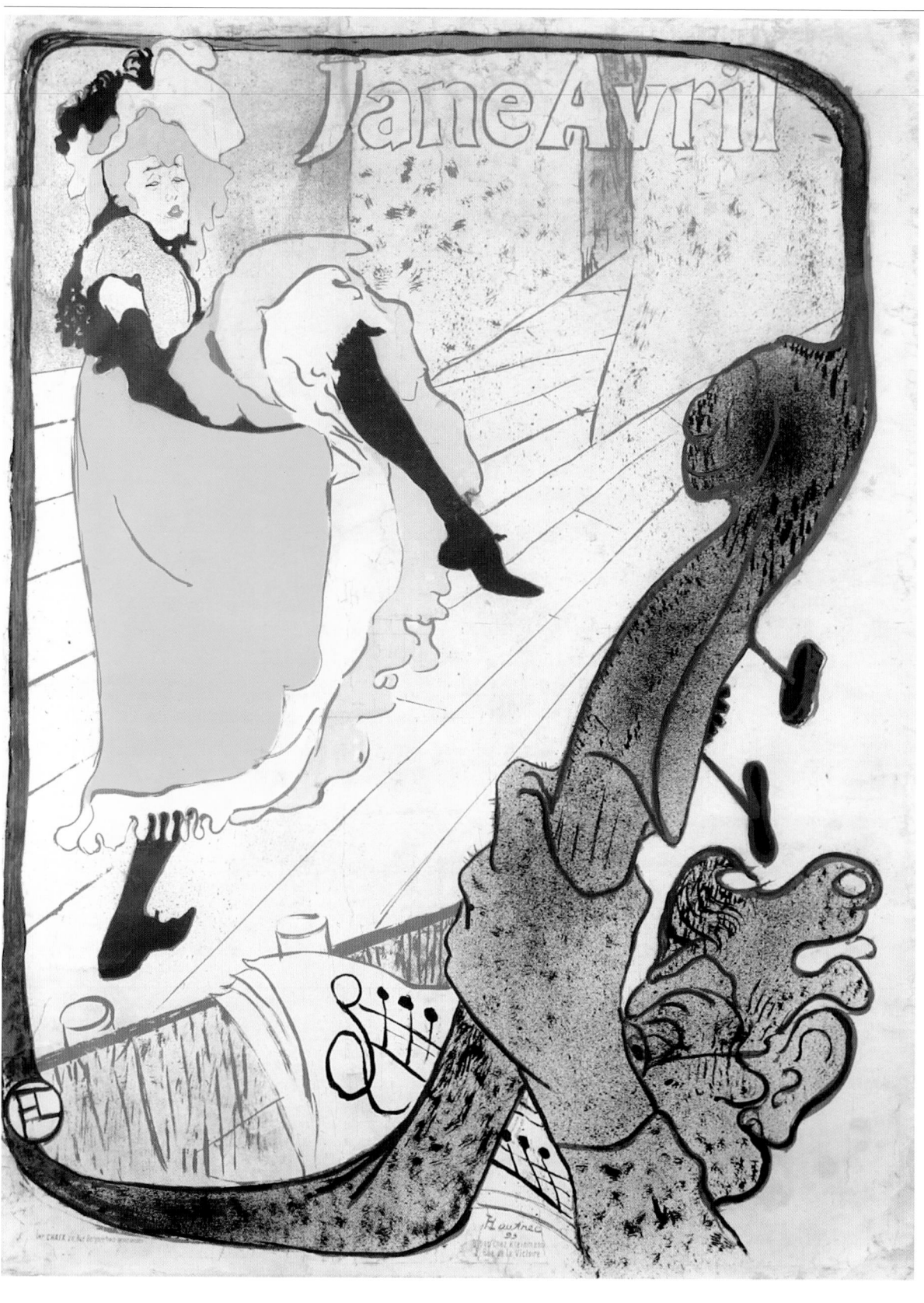

CAT. 113 Henri de Toulouse-Lautrec (French, 1864-1901)
Jane Avril, 1893
Color lithograph, 48 13/16 x 36 in. (124 x 91.5 cm)
Courtesy Katherine Kovins through Galerie Michael,
Beverly Hills, California

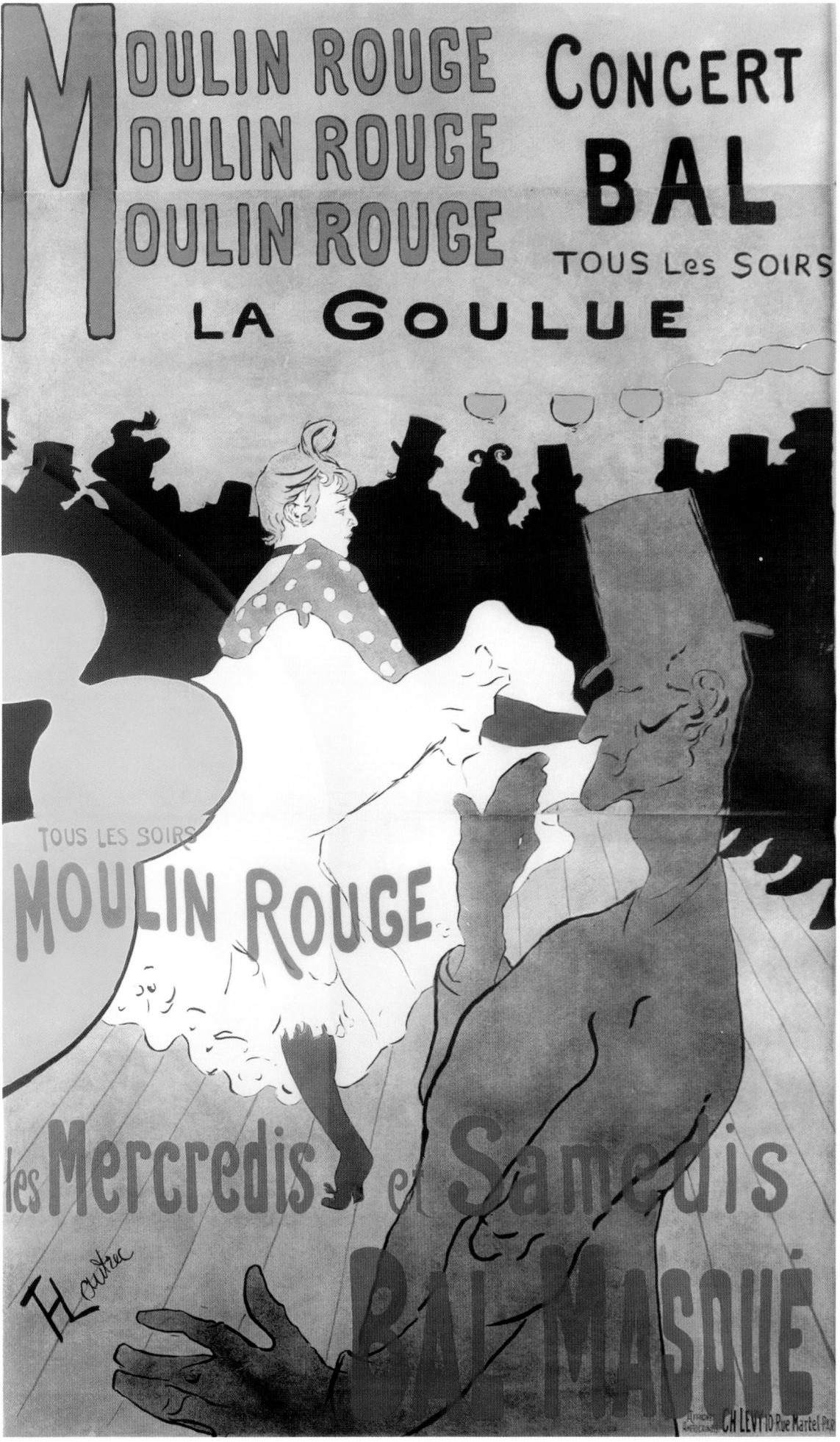

CAT. 110 Henri de Toulouse-Lautrec (French, 1964-1901)
Moulin Rouge, La Goulue, 1891
Color lithograph, linen backed
74 x 45 in. (187.96 x 114.3 cm)
Courtesy Mr. & Mrs. Clay Timon through Galerie Michael,
Beverly Hills, California

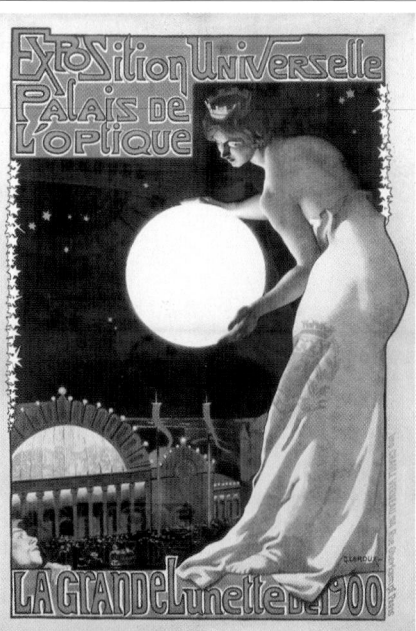

By 1900, the poster revolution dominated the print culture of the time. Often the scale of these images, such as the *Théâtre de l'Opéra Comique* (cat. 33; p. 95) proved as engaging as the image itself. To be effective, a poster had to be read from a distance and the lettering had to be clear to achieve its purpose. Other posters, such as that by Jules-Alexandre Grün, resorted to more earthy images. In order to engage the masses and insure their appearance at performances, the artist often relied on types that suggested a conspicuous sensuality (cat. 38; p. 96). Occasionally, artists created images of nude models that suggested a muse. This is the case with Georges Leroux, whose drawing of a single figure (cat. 61; p. 97) was transformed into a standing icon when he developed it as a poster. In this poster, Leroux, then only twenty-three, created a work that called attention to the Optique Pavilion at the Exposition Universelle and the new inventions which were proposed in its enclosure.[13] (fig. 25).

By 1900, the range of posters was diverse, and the availability of these images made it clear that artists had found an effective way to reach the masses while also satisfying the needs of their patrons. Art and consumerism were significantly united at this moment in history.

Independent Prints

At the same time that many printmakers were completing images for the popular press and posters, they were also doing independent prints, which they hoped would reach an increasing number of private collectors. Working in all media – etching, woodcut, lithography, photo-mechanical reproduction, among others – allowed the print culture to broaden its base. The interest from dealers and collectors such as Siegfried Bing or Julius Meier-Graefe or Ambroise Vollard, Roger-Marx and Edmond Sagot demonstrated that prints were no longer a secondary artistic medium. They had become central to artistic creativity.[14]

One artist crucial to the independent print market was Louis Legrand who had attracted attention for his controversial prints such as *Prostitution*, which had appeared in *Le Courrier Français* during the 1880s. In

FIG. 25   Georges Paul Leroux (French, 1877-1957)
         Exposition Universelle. Palais de l'Optique, 1900, Paris
         Color lithograph, 51 ³⁄₁₆ x 37 in. (130 x 94 cm)
         Les Arts Décoratifs, Musée de la Publicité, Paris
         Photograph by Laurent Sully Jaulmes. Tous droits réservés

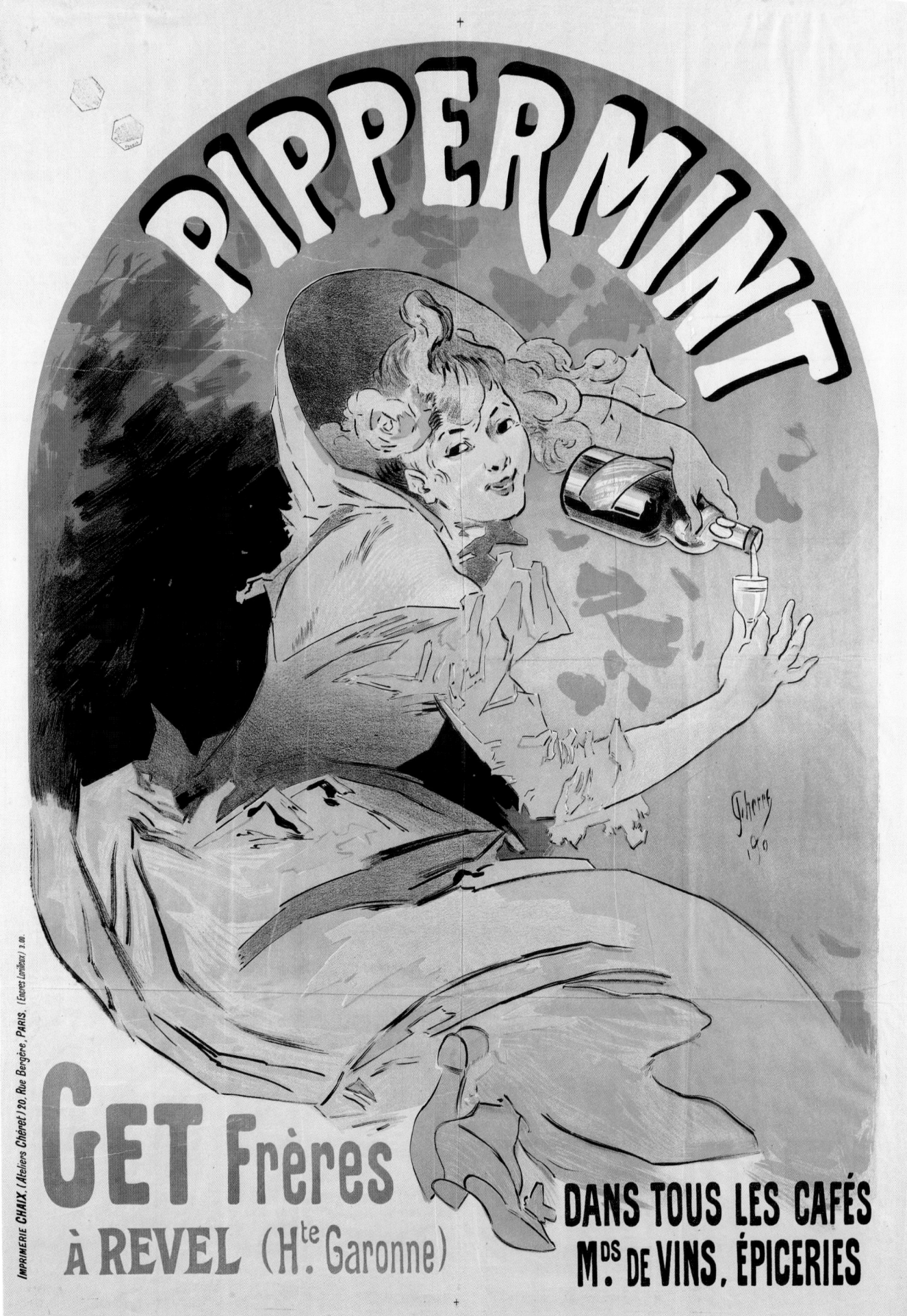

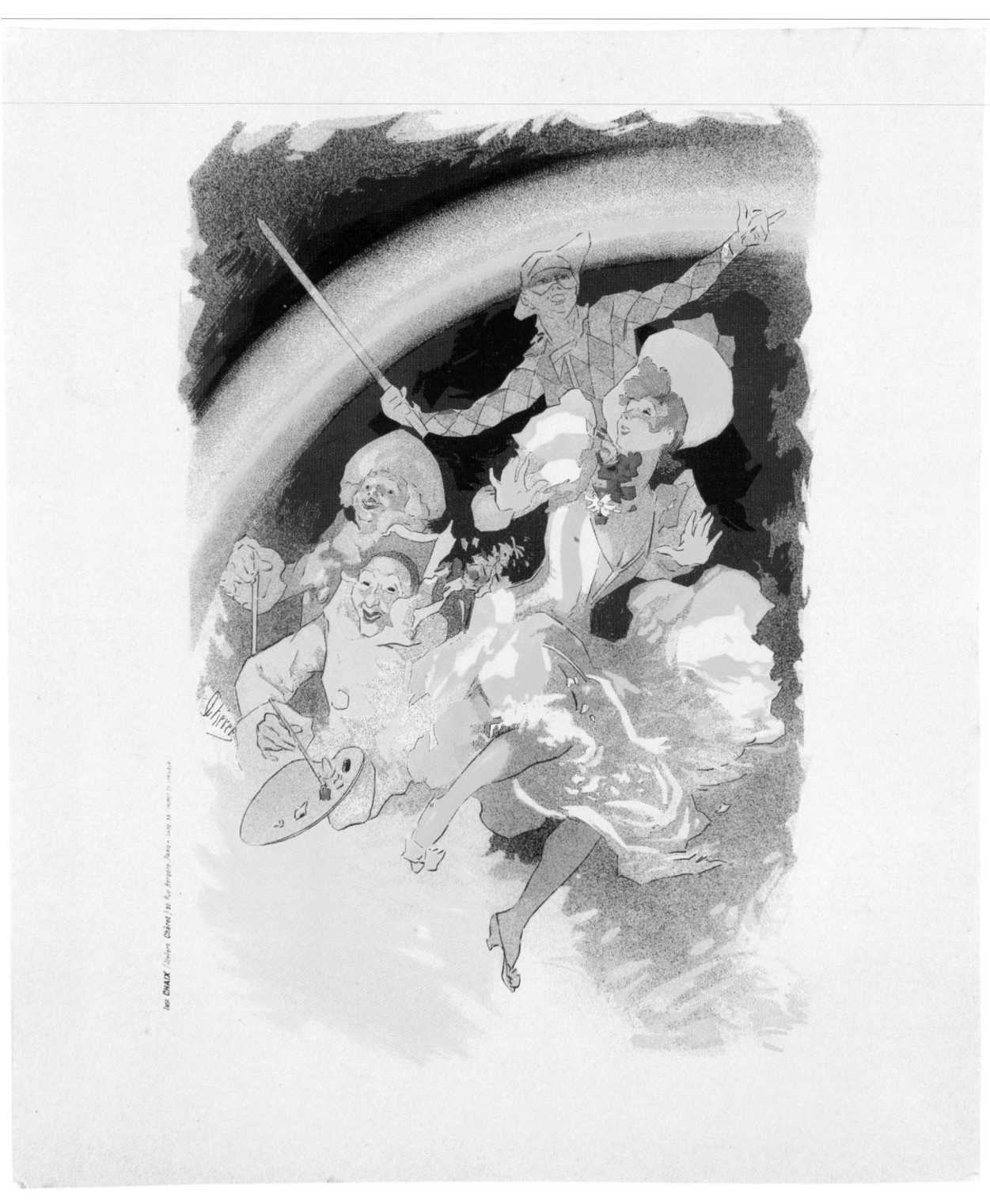

CAT. 21   Jules Chéret (French, 1836-1932)
L'arc en Ciel [The Rainbow], 1893
Lithograph, 12 ³/₁₆ x 10 ⅝ in. (31 x 27 cm)
Jane Voorhees Zimmerli Art Museum, Rutgers, The State University of
New Jersey; Gift of Herbert D. and Ruth Schimmel
Photograph by Jack Abraham; 1988.0739

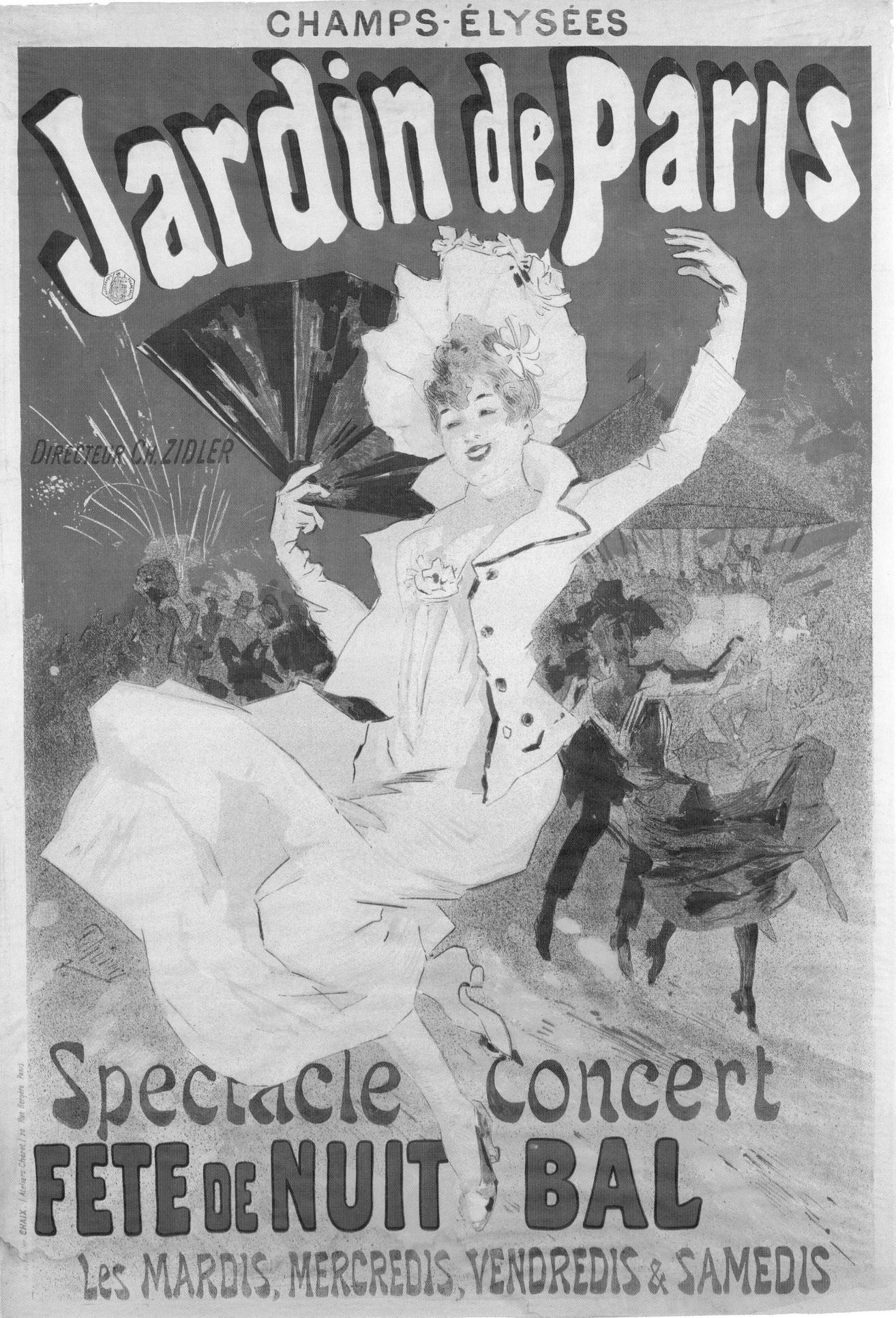

CAT. 22   Jules Chéret (French, 1836-1932)
Jardin de Paris, ca. 1895
Color lithograph, 48 x 34⅛ in. (121.92 x 86.68 cm)
Lent by The Minneapolis Institute of Arts,
Gift of Bruce B. Dayton, P.85.4

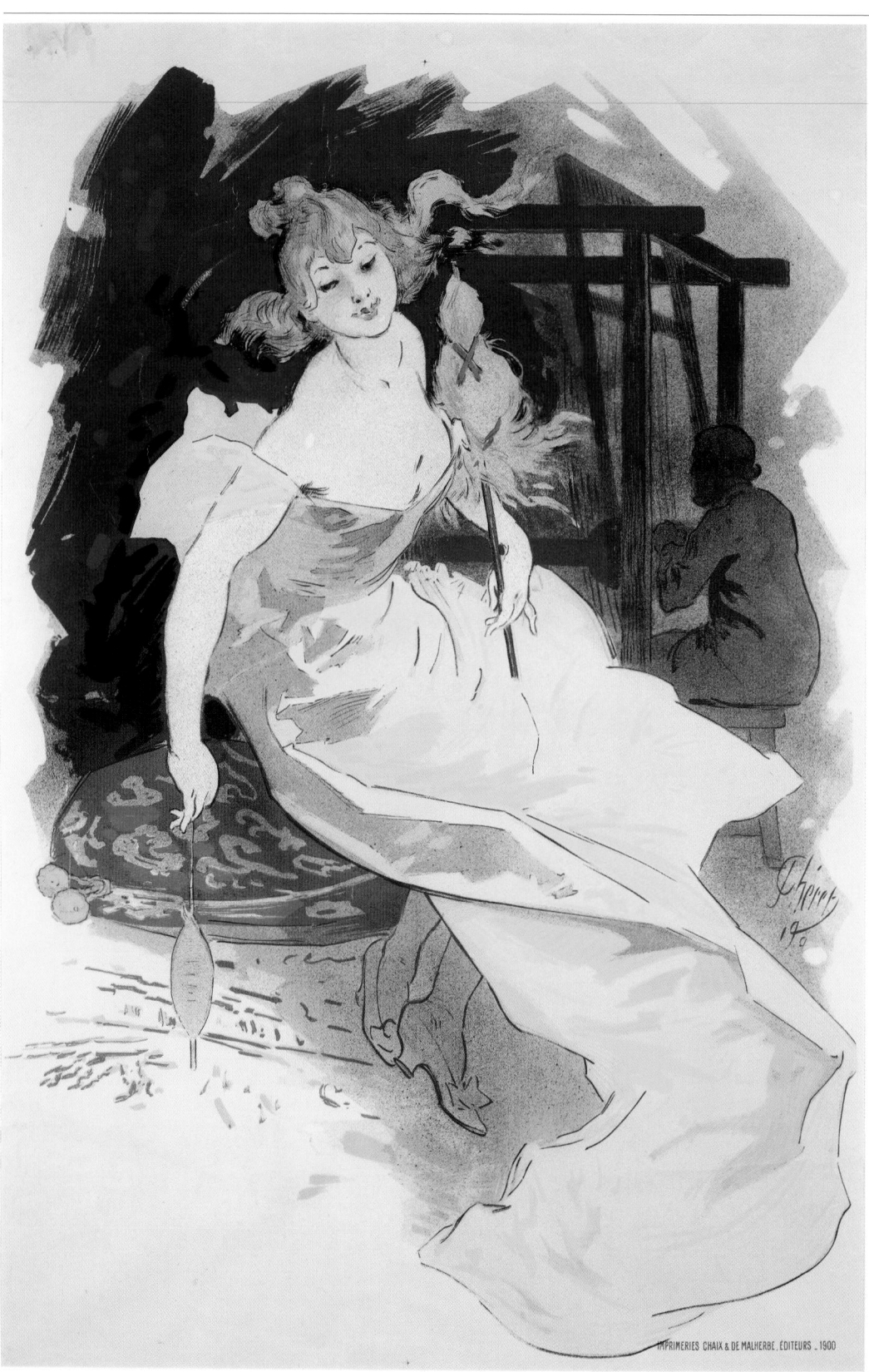

CAT. 23   Jules Chéret (French, 1836-1932)

La Fileuse [The Spinner], 1900

Color lithograph, 49 x 32½ in. (124.46 x 82.55 cm)

Lent by The Minneapolis Institute of Arts,

The Modernism Collection, gift of Norwest Bank Minnesota, P.98.33.113

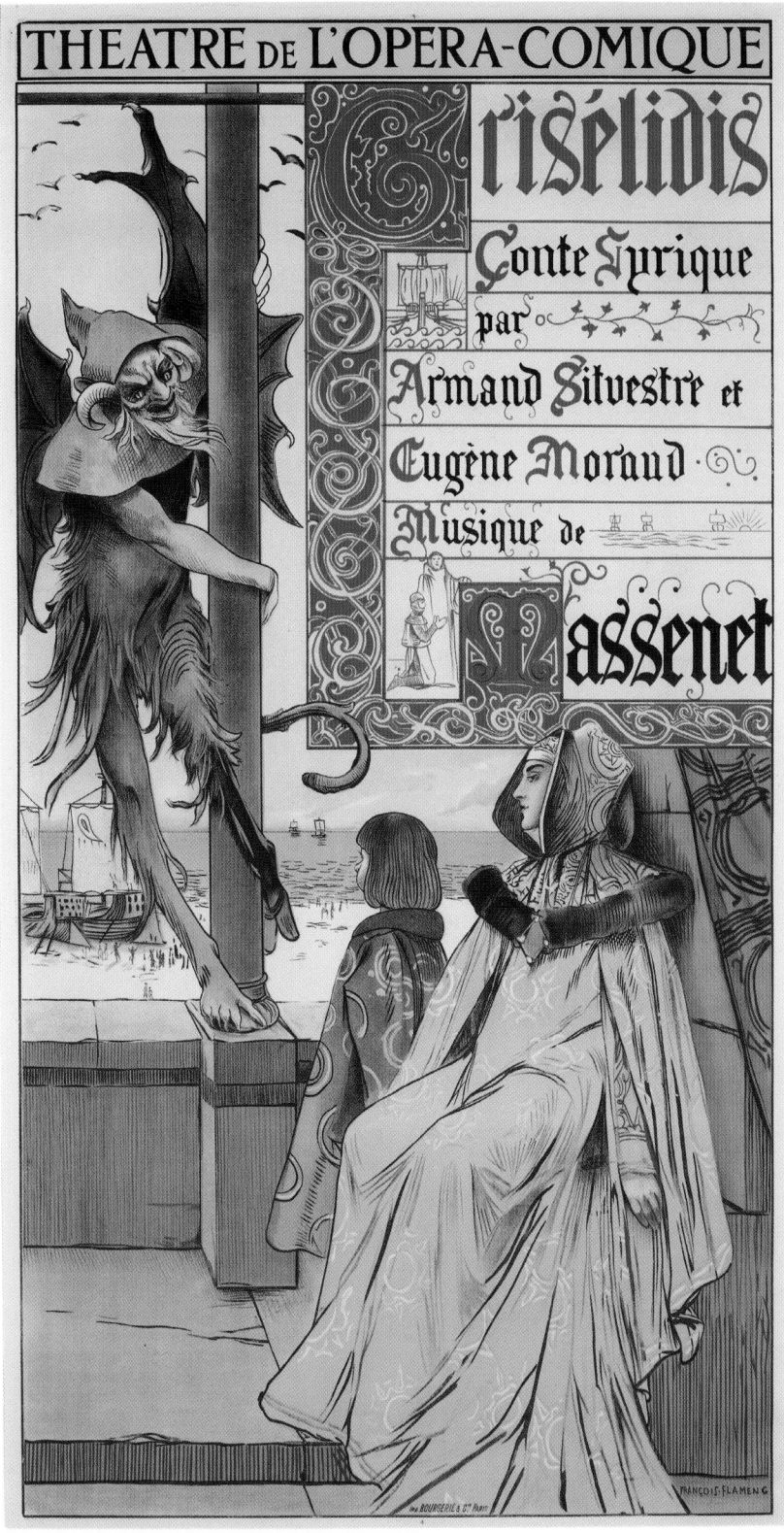

CAT. 33   François Flameng (French, 1856-1923)

Théâtre de l'Opéra-Comique: Griselidis [Griselda], ca. 1900

Color lithograph, 52⅜ x 27⅞ in. (133.03 x 70.8 cm)

Lent by The Minneapolis Institute of Arts,

Gift of funds from John E. Andrus III, 2003.213.3

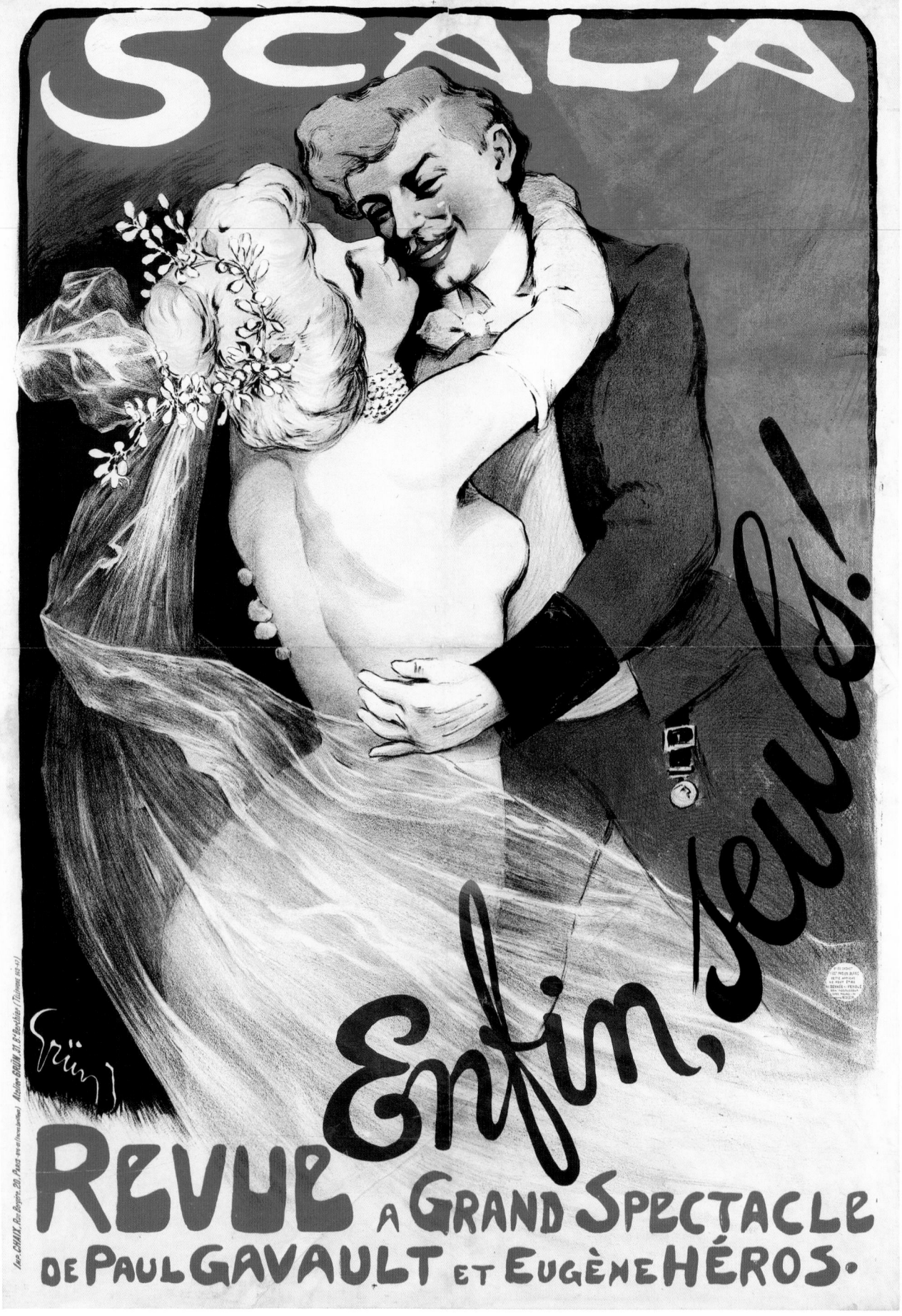

CAT. 38   Jules-Alexandre Grün (French, 1868-1934)
Enfin Seuls! [At Last Alone!], n.d.
Color lithograph mounted on linen, 46⅜ x 32½ in. (117.79 x 82.55 cm)
Lent by The Minneapolis Institute of Arts
Gift of Marguerite and Russell Cowles, P.79.82.6

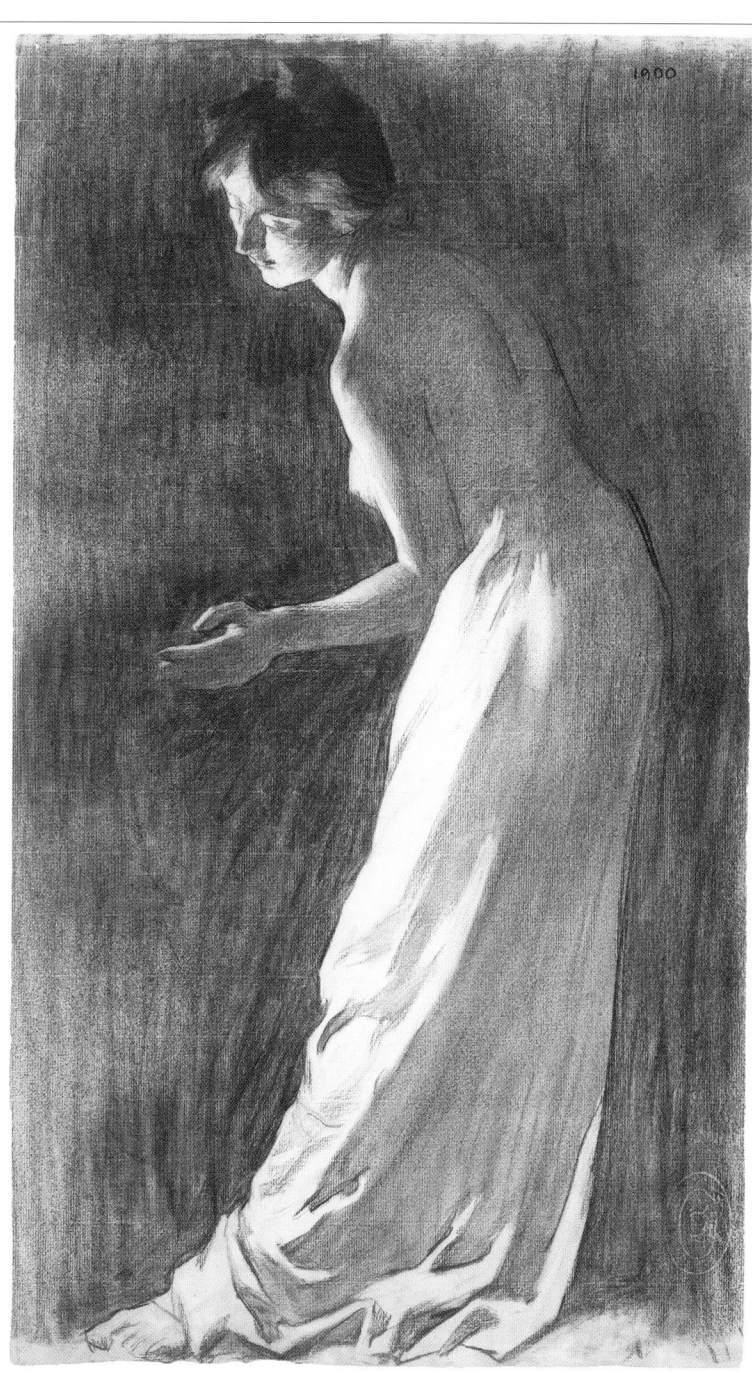

CAT. 61   Georges Leroux (French, 1877-1957)

Optique Pavilion Paris World Fair, 1900

Drawing, 24½ x 14 in. (62.2 x 35.6 cm)

Dr. Gabriel and Yvonne Weisberg Collection

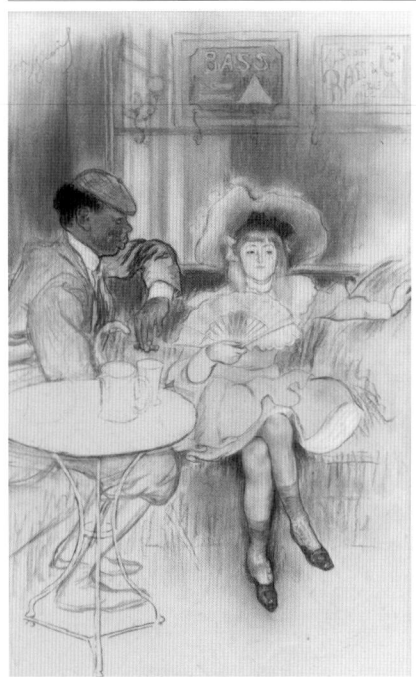

his prints for this journal and his independent prints, Legrand was promoting the right of printmakers to be creative, but also to tackle unusual or even problematic themes – even those themes that might offend a timid public.[15] This attitude was maintained in his etchings, where he was caught up in the debates surrounding alcohol and its effects on people. In *Gin*, (cat. 57) a young woman is sprawled on the street, collapsing from intoxication. Effects of prostitution haunted Legrand, as much as the fear of infection or disease, which made his print of a *Woman in Bed with Death* (1895) (cat. 58; p. 100) an etching influenced by the specter of contagion that dominated the end-of-the-century art world. Even in his prints picturing dance performances, Legrand injected a level of disquiet in regard to the true meaning of his otherwise benign subjects; male figures hovering in the background or simply female guardians watching over the young girls. The little vignette at the bottom of the print of a woman sipping a drink gives the impression that the young child visualized above her (cat. 56; p. 101) is about to enter a world where her innocence might be corrupted. This atmosphere comes full circle in Legrand's later image of *Au Bar* (cat. 60; p. 102) (fig. 26). Here a tantalizing young child, a vision of sophisticated innocence, is prostituting herself at a bar accompanied by a debonair black man who could either be her lover or her procurer. Whatever the final meaning, Legrand's prints create a symbolic iconography, establishing that etching could be used provocatively to challenge other media.[16]

Like Louis Legrand, Hermann-Paul was also a printmaker with a strong social inclination. Whether he did prints for journals, or in the early twentieth century completed devastating woodcuts that caricatured World War I, the artist was a force in the print world.[17] Individual lithographs reveal the presence of women attending art exhibitions, and becoming a very lively force in the art world, both as patrons and collectors (cat. 44; p. 104) during the 1890s. He also showed people moving about the city, missing the *Omnibus* (cat. 45; p. 105) and being stranded on the sidewalk, as in a lithograph from 1900.

FIG. 26   Louis Legrand (French, 1863-1951)
Au Bar [At the Bar]
Drawing, 35 x 23.5 cm
Russell Collection, Amsterdam

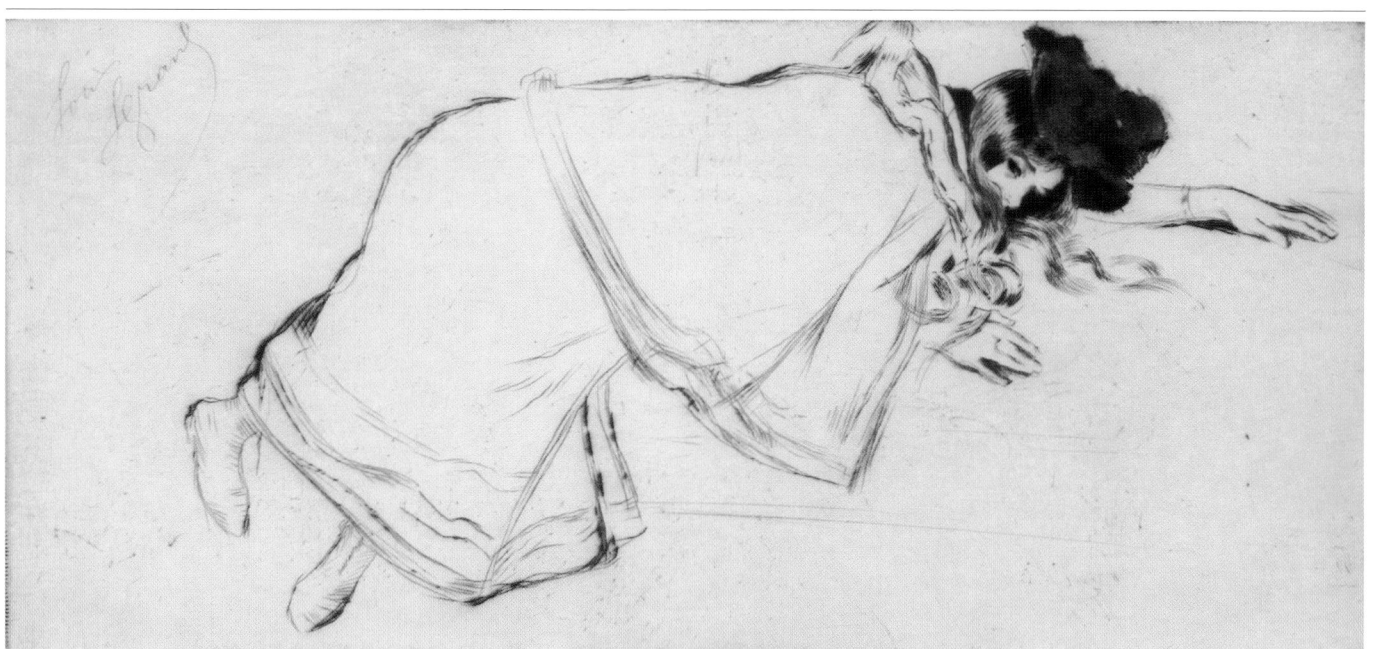

CAT. 57   Louis Legrand (French, 1863-1951)

Gin, 1894

Drypoint, 12⅛ x 18⅜ in. (30.8 x 46.6 cm)

Jane Voorhees Zimmerli Art Museum; Rutgers, The State University of
New Jersey; Gift of Reese and Marilyn Arnold Palley

Photograph by Jack Abraham; 1991.0302

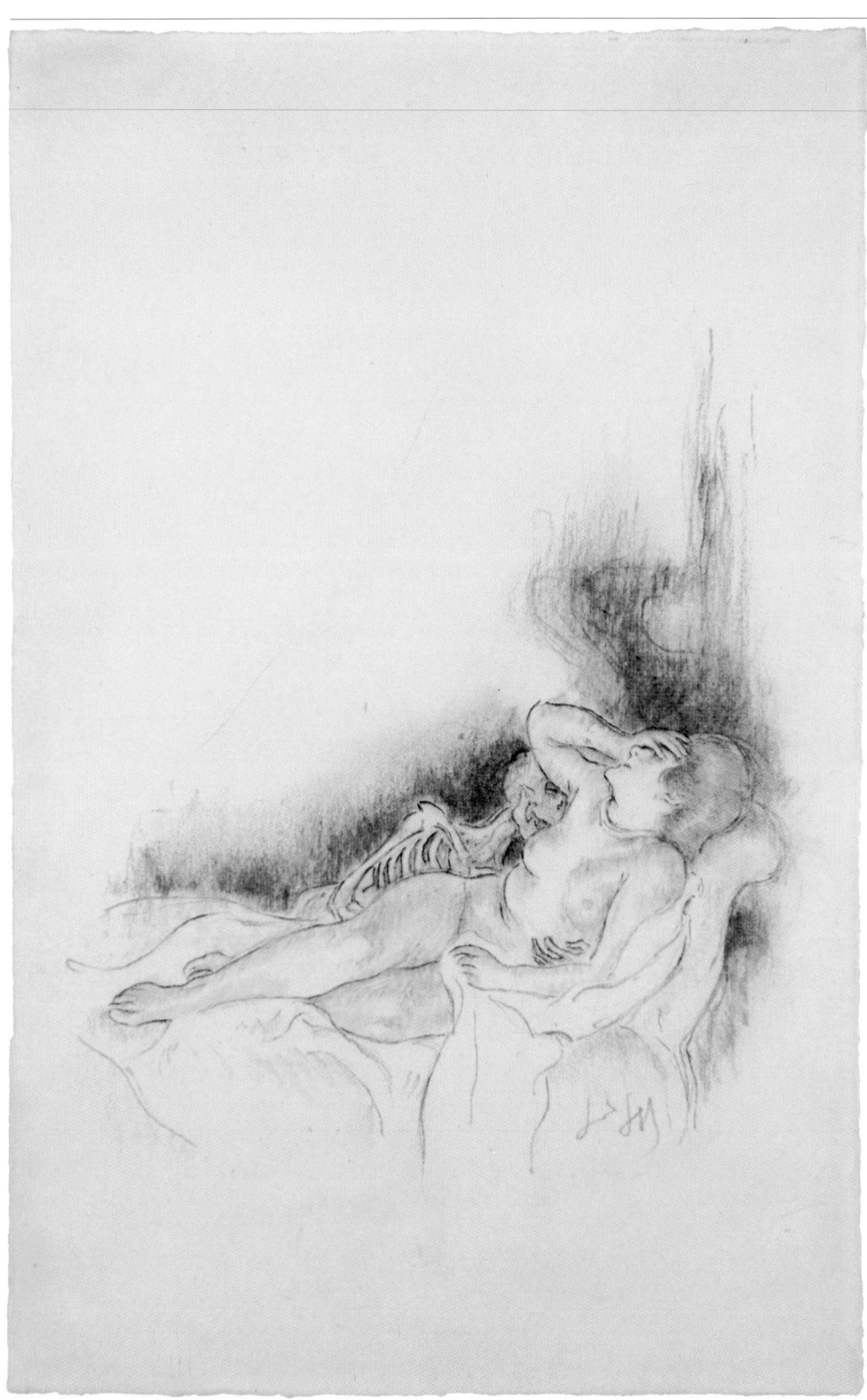

CAT. 58   Louis Legrand (French, 1863-1951)
Woman in Bed with Death, ca. 1895
Black and colored chalks, 12⅜ x 8¹/₁₆ in. (31.5 x 20.5 cm)
Jane Voorhees Zimmerli Art Museum, Rutgers, The State University of
New Jersey; David A. and Mildred H. Morse Art Acquisition Fund
Photograph by Jack Abraham; 1986.0418

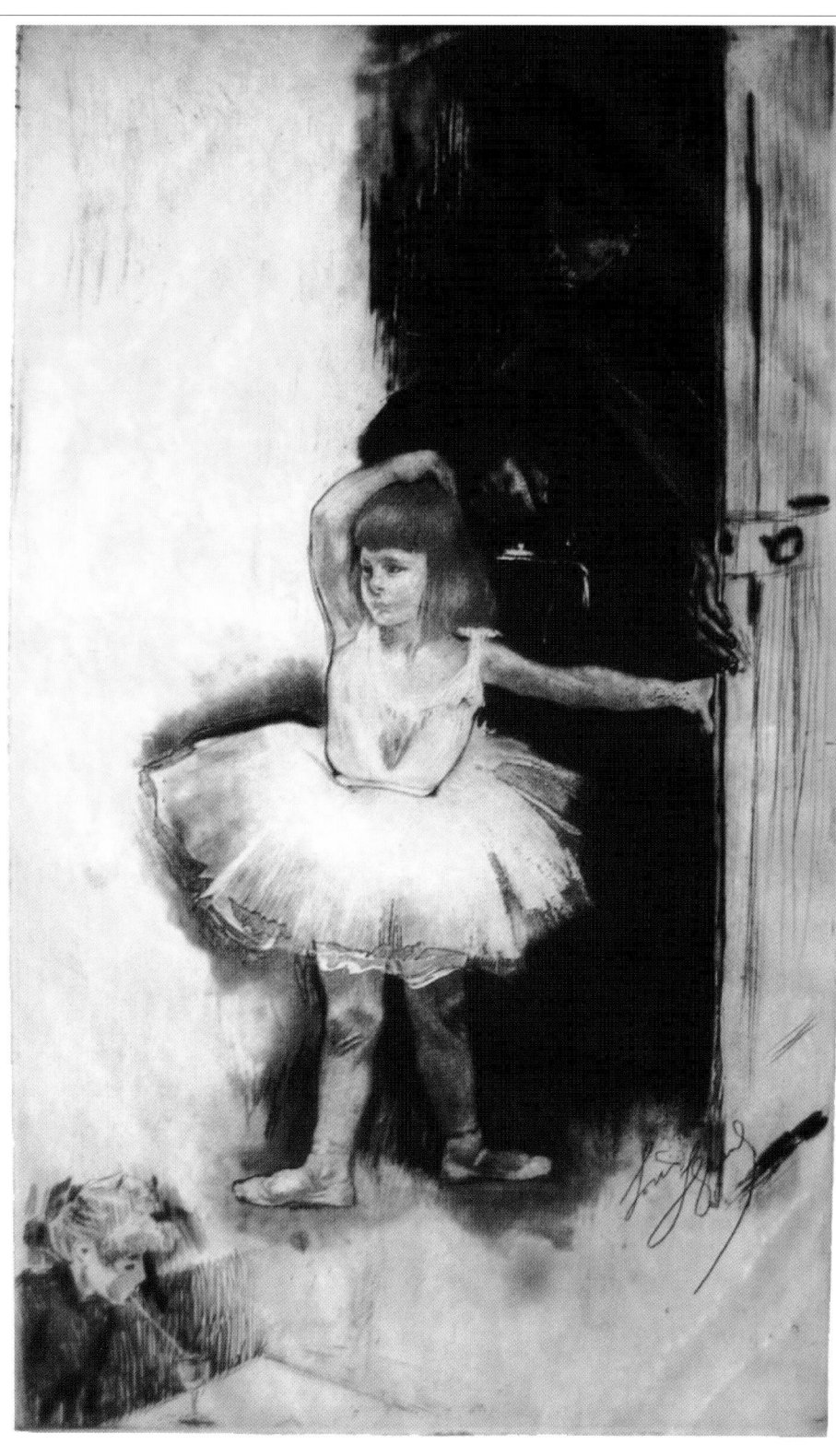

CAT. 56   Louis Legrand (French, 1863-1951)
First Lesson, Little Ballerinas, 1893
Aquatint and etching, 19¾ x 12⅞ in. (50.2 x 32 cm)
Jane Voorhees Zimmerli Art Museum; Rutgers, The State University of
New Jersey; David A. and Mildred H. Morse Art Acquisition Fund
Photograph by Jack Abraham; 1986.0418

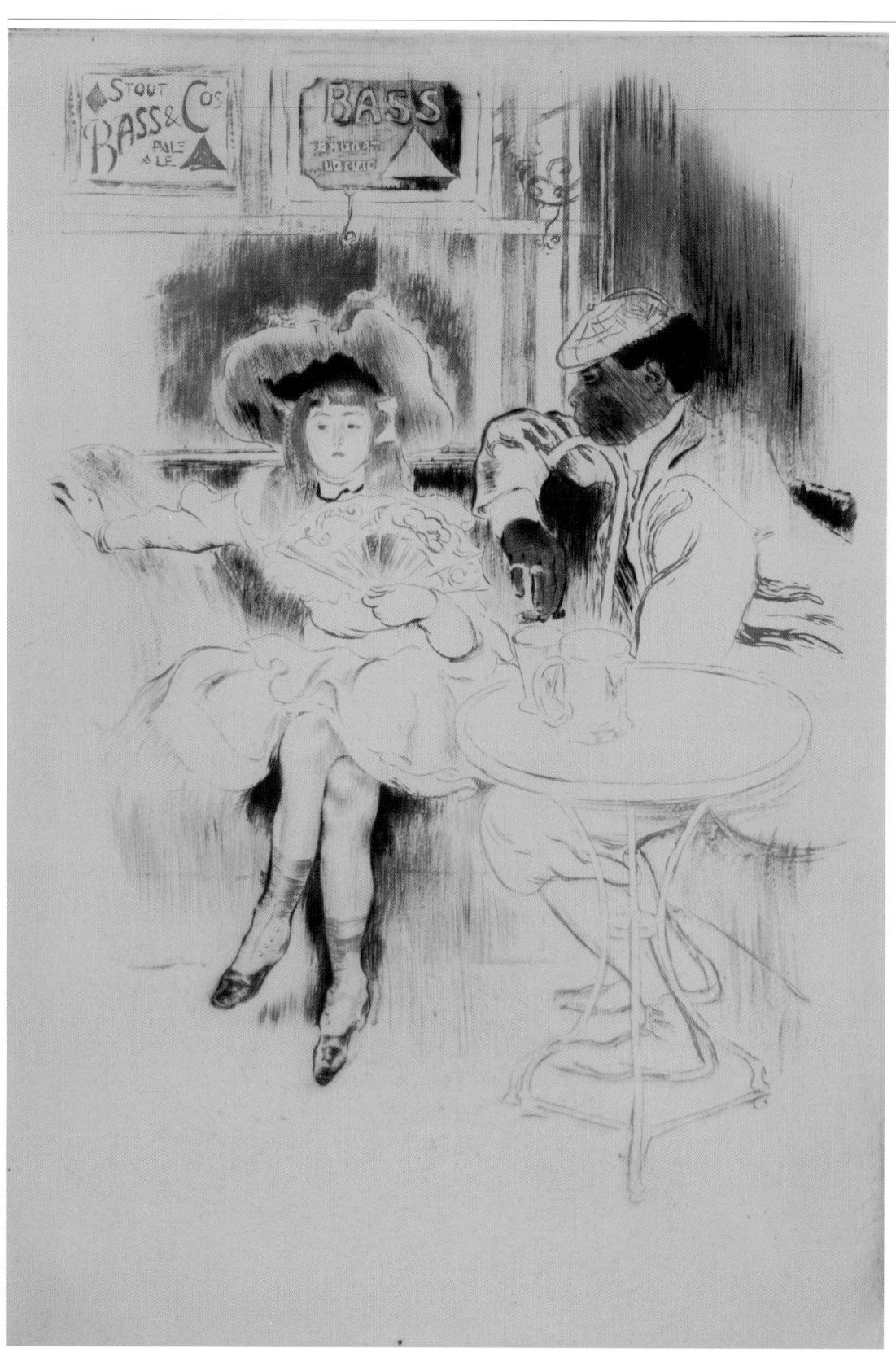

CAT. 60   Louis Legrand (French, 1863-1951)
Au Bar, 1908
Etching and drypoint, 21 13/16 x 13 3/4 in. (55.4 x 35 cm)
Jane Voorhees Zimmerli Art Museum; Rutgers, The State University of
New Jersey; Gift of Reese and Marilyn Arnold Palley
Photograph by Jack Abraham; 1991.0441.001

He too was caught up in topical issues that often subtly revealed the increasing roles of women in modern life.

As muse of the visual arts, "the new woman" also attracted the Belgian artist Armand Rassenfosse whose *L'Art Indépendant* suggested that the new art — with an international inflection — was found in group shows outside the Salon. Women were encouraged to attend these exhibitions as reiterated in this print (cat. 86; p. 106). As women found their own voices, the images of them evolved from passive, rather lost figures strolling along the quays, as in Armand Point's drawing of 1895 (cat. 85; p. 107), to strong creative icons. These changes, in reading the images iconographically, further demonstrate the importance of the print culture in suggesting changing societal patterns.

Paris as Muse

Behind the emergence of a diverse print culture were the changes taking place in Paris itself. It was the city that dominated the moods of many creators. While the achievements of the past were noted at the Exposition Universelle of 1900, many pavilions pointed the way toward the future with new creations in photography, in light, and, unfortunately, in military equipment. Although millions came to the World's Fair, it was the city itself that haunted and mesmerized artists and tourists alike.

Among those who saw the city in a new way was Henri Rivière. Whether drawing parallels between views of the Eiffel Tower and views of Japan's Mount Fuji, or portraying a rain drenched *Isle des Cygnes* (cats. 91, 92; p. 108) as a mysterious environment, his lithographs and watercolors venerated certain sites in the city. In a series of eight lithographs sold in 1900 for seventy-five francs, Rivière immortalized locations that were unusual and historic.[18] Similar to the painter Charles Guilloux, Rivière found that certain locations evoked a sense of mystery. He initiated a romance between the people of Paris, the visitors who came to the city, and the urban environment that gave an added dimension of meaning to his prints. By 1900, it was Paris itself that was the muse; the city was to become a continually reinvented source for artists, writers, and dramatists. And it was this life of Paris that Rivière extolled in his lithographs.

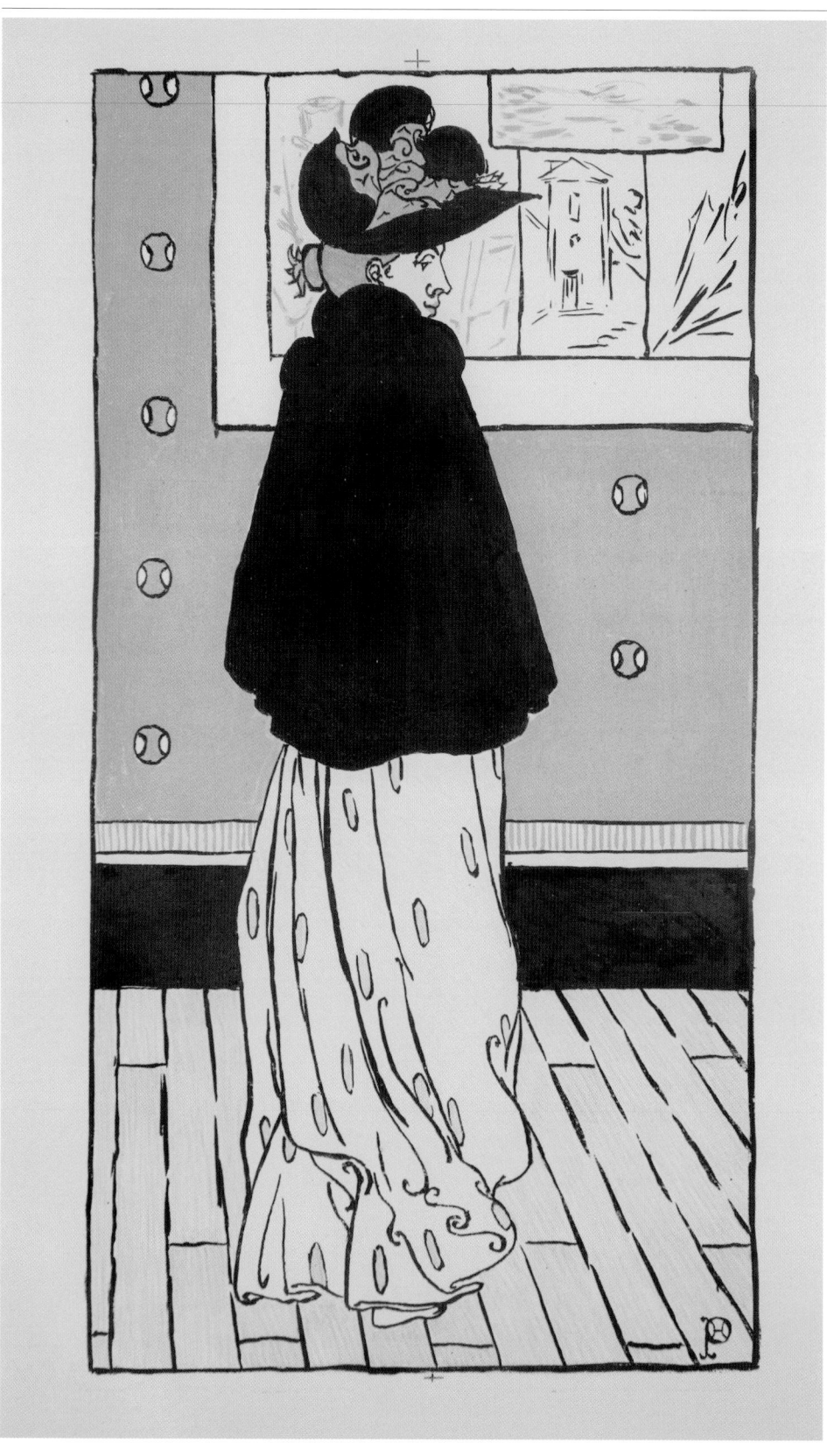

CAT. 44   Hermann-Paul (French, 1864-1940)

Au Salon de peinture [At the Painting Salon], 1891

Lithograph, 18¼ x 9¹³⁄₁₆ in. (46.3 x 24.9 cm)

Jane Voorhees Zimmerli Art Museum; Rutgers, The State University of

New Jersey; Herbert Littman Purchase Fund

Photograph by Jack Abraham; 84.047.075

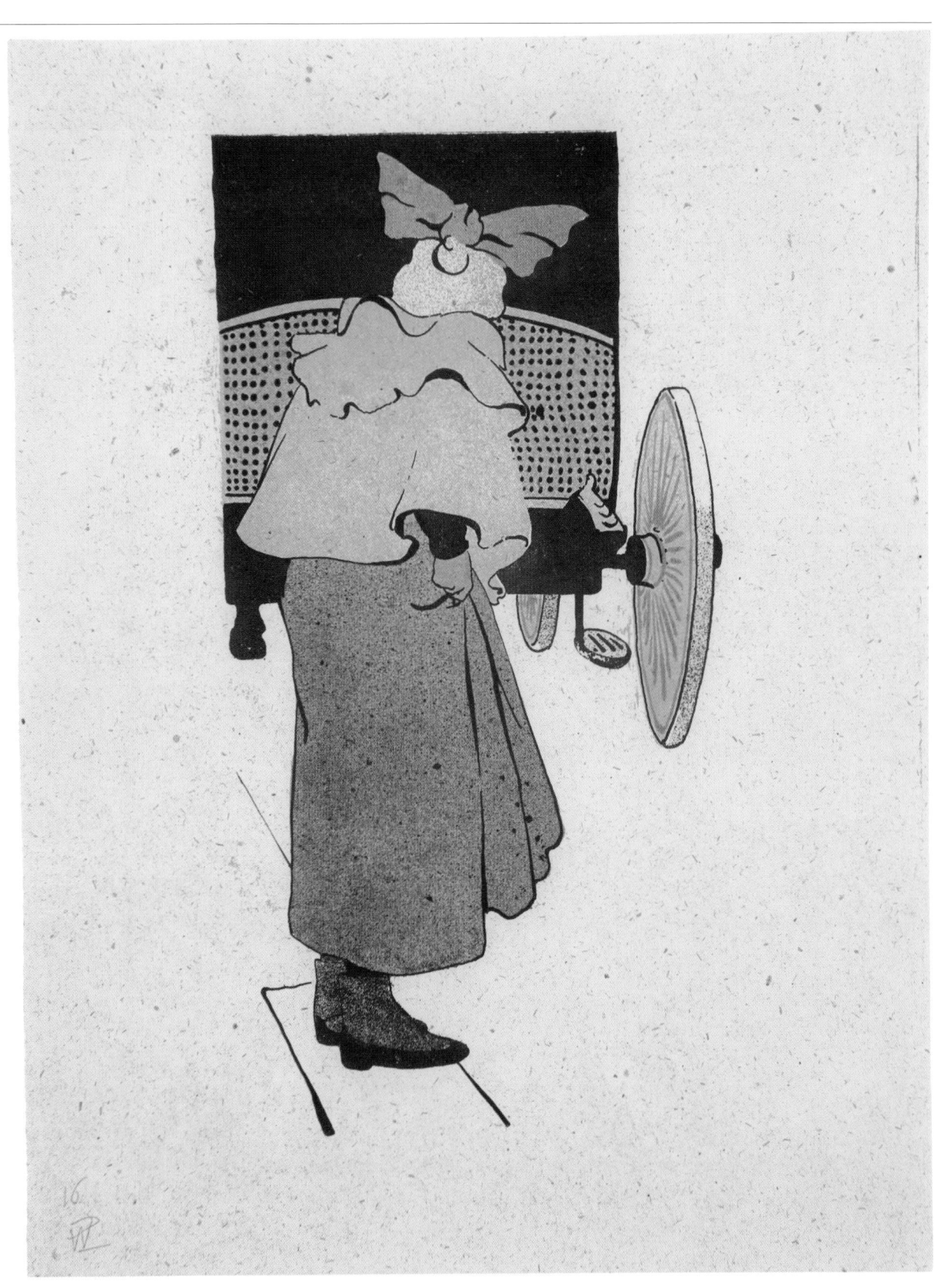

CAT. 45   Hermann-Paul (French, 1864-1940)
The Omnibus, n.d.
Lithograph, 12 ¹³/₁₆ x 9¾ in. (32.6 x 24.8 cm)
Jane Voorhees Zimmerli Art Museum; Rutgers, The State University of
New Jersey; Regina Best Heldrich Art Acquisition Fund
Photograph by Jack Abraham; 2001.0469

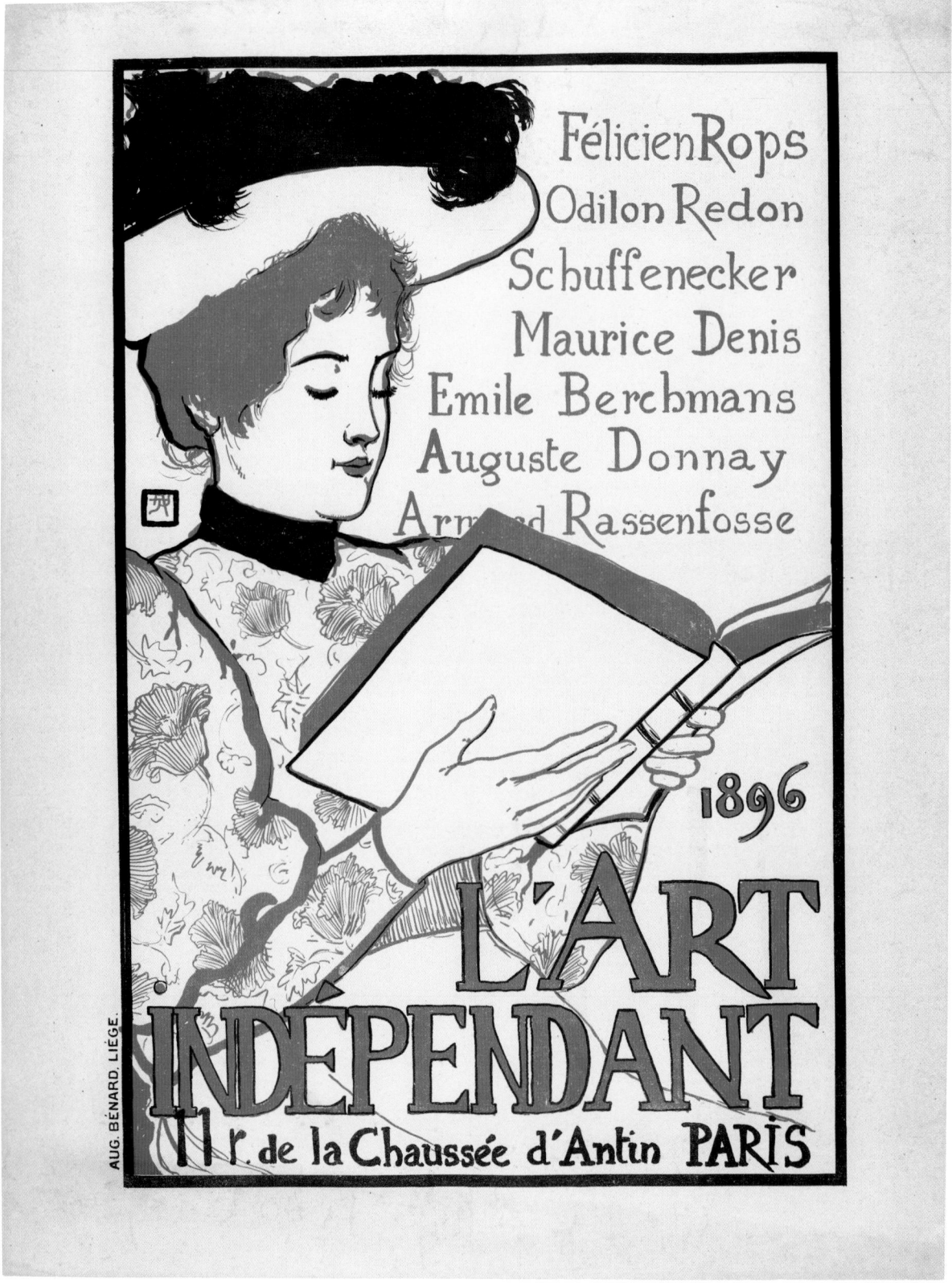

CAT. 86   Armand Rassenfosse (Belgian, 1862-1934)

L'Art Indépendant, 1896

Color lithograph, 24½ x 16¹⁵⁄₁₆ in. (62.23 x 43.02 cm)

Lent by The Minneapolis Institute of Arts, The Modernism Collection

Gift of Norwest Bank Minnesota, P.98.33.110

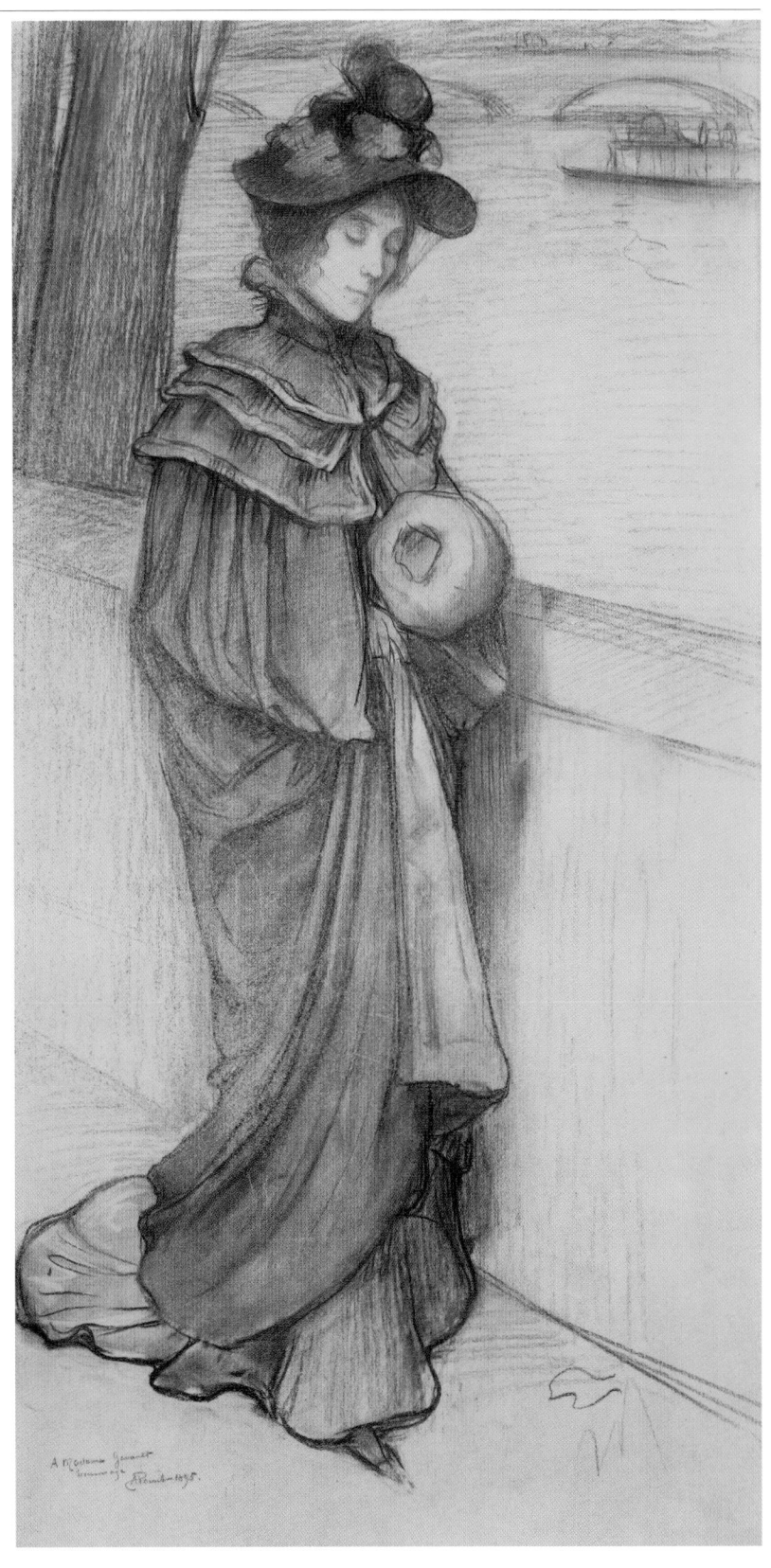

CAT. 85   Armand Point (French, 1861-1932)
Lady on the Banks of the Seine, 1895
Color pencil drawing, 15¾ x 9⁷⁄₁₆ in. (40 x 24 cm)
Russell Collection, Amsterdam

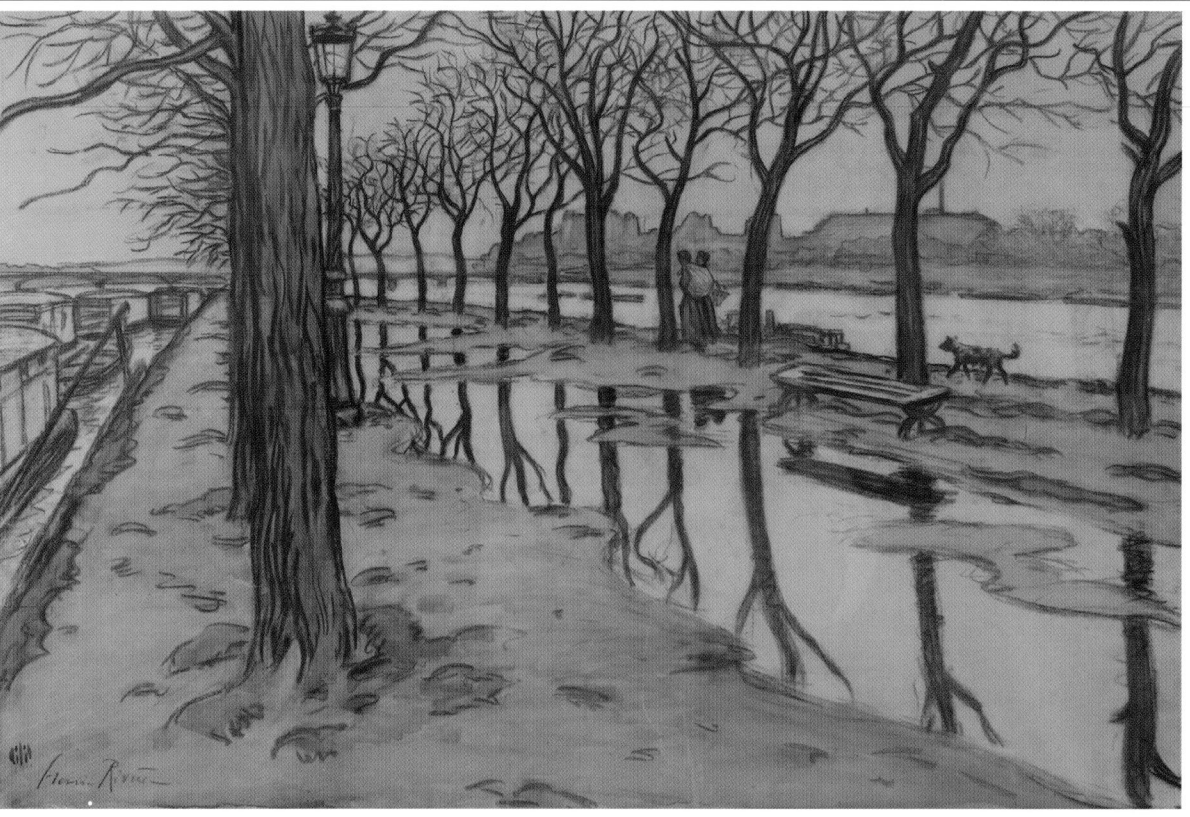

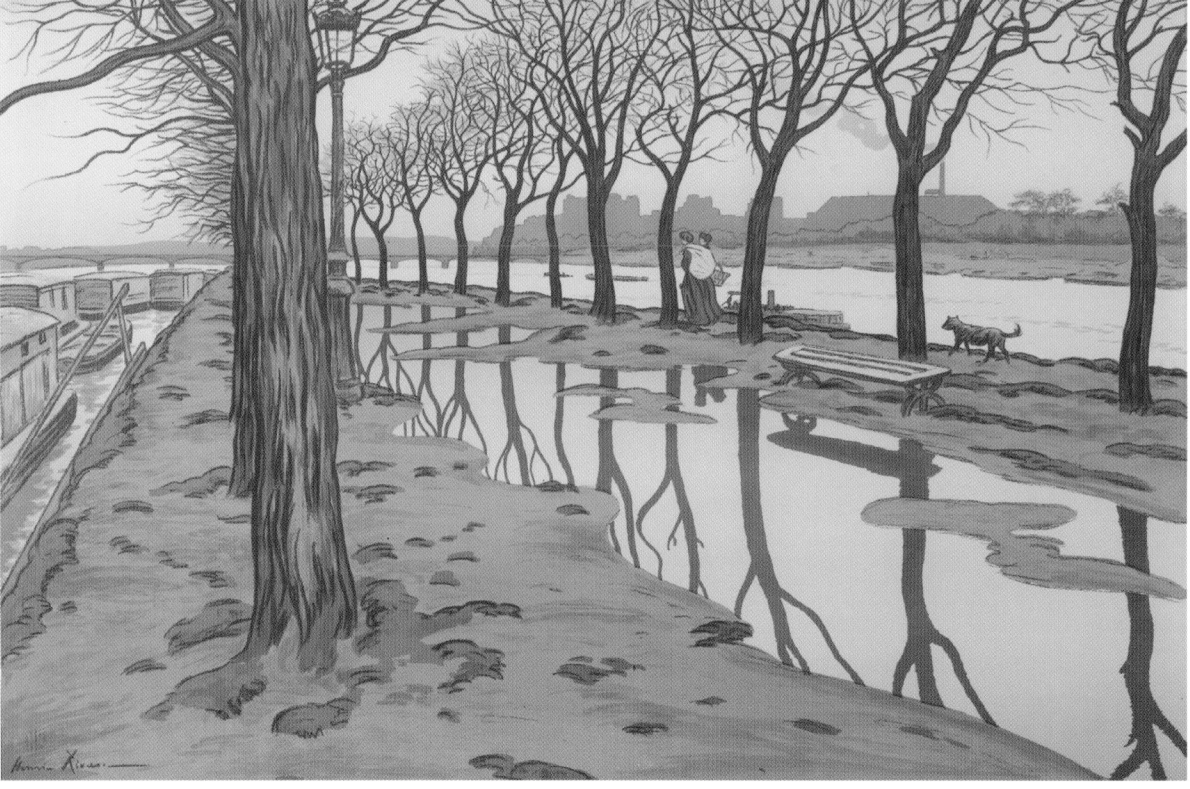

CAT. 91 Henri Rivière (French, 1864-1951)
L'Isle des cygnes, ca. 1900
Crayon and watercolor, 20¹¹/₁₆ x 32 in. (52.5 x 82 cm)
Russell Collection, Amsterdam

CAT. 92 Henri Rivière (French, 1864-1951)
L'Isle des cygnes, 1900
Color lithograph, 20¹¹/₁₆ x 32¼ in. (82 x 52.5 cm)
Russell Collection, Amsterdam

Endnotes

1 E. de Crauzat, *L'Oeuvre Gravé et Lithographié de Steinlen* (Paris: Société de Propagation des Livres d'Art, 1913, 57: 171). Crauzat noted that this print was in many private collections at the time.

2 Bibliothèque Nationale (exh. cat.), *Théophile Alexandre Steinlen*, May-June 1953, commenting on the rise in estimation of his work; also see Gabriel P. Weisberg, ed., *Montmartre and the Making of Mass Culture* (New Brunswick: Rutgers University Press, 2001).

3 Elizabeth Menon, *Evil by Design: The Making and Marketing of the Femme Fatale* (Champaign-Urbana: University of Illinois Press, 2006). Also see her article "Decadent Addictions: Tobacco, Alcohol, Popular Culture and Café Society," in: Laurinda Dixon, ed., *In Sickness and in Health, Disease as Metaphor in Art and Popular Wisdom* (Newark: University of Delaware Press, 2004).

4 Crauzat, op. cit.: 182-195 for a listing of these works.

5 On Loïe Fuller see *Loïe Fuller, Danseuse de l'Art Nouveau* (exh. cat.), (Nancy: Musée des Beaux-Arts, and Musée de l'École de Nancy, 2002).

6 Steinlen's illustrations for *Dans la Rue* revealed a careful examination and use of the sayings and slogans used by Aristide Bruant in performances.

7 Menon, op. cit.: the sections on the femme fatale.

8 Ian Millman, *Georges de Feure: Maître du Symbolisme et de L'Art Nouveau* (Paris: ACR, 1992).

9 Phillip Dennis Cate, André Mellerio, and Sinclair Hitchings, *The Color Revolution: Color Lithography in France, 1890-1900* (Salt Lake City: Peregrine Smith, Inc., and Rutgers University, 1978). Also see Richard Thomson, Phillip Dennis Cate and Mary Weaver Chapin, *Toulouse-Lautrec and Montmartre* (Washington, D.C.: National Gallery of Art, 2006).

10 There were critical attacks against Lautrec at the time of his earliest posters. He was, however, protected by leading writers from the avant-garde including Roger Marx and Thadée Natanson. See Roger Marx, "Lautrec et Maurin," in: *Le Voltaire* (1 February 1893): 1; Thadée Natanson, "Oeuvres de M. de Toulouse–Lautrec," *La Revue Blanche* (February 1893): 146.

11 See Jules Chéret, *La Naissance de l'Affiche Moderne (1866-1886)* (exh. CAT.), 15 October-30 November 1994 (Chaumont: La Maison du livre et de l'Affiche, 1994).

12 See *Inventaire du Fonds Français après 1800*, Paris: Bibliothèque Nationale 4 (1949): 506, number 796 where it is noted that Chéret prepared two decorative panels linked to this theme.

13 Information on George Leroux is limited but thanks to Christine Bethenod we now have located the drawing for his very rare poster completed in 1900.

14 On Roger Marx's support of prints, crucial to the time, see Catherine Meneux in *Roger Marx un critique aux côtés de Gallé, Monet, Rodin, Gauguin...*, Musée des Beaux-Arts, Nancy and Musée de l'École de Nancy (May-August 2006) and the review of this exhibition by Gabriel P. Weisberg, *Nineteenth Century Art Worldwide* 6, issue 1 (Spring 2007).

15 On this debate, see Gabriel P. Weisberg, "Louis Legrand's Battle over Prostitution: The Uneasy Censoring of *Le Courrier Français*," *Art Journal*, 51 (Spring, 1992): 45-50.

16 On Legrand see E. Ramiro, *Louis Legrand, Peintre-Graveur, catalogue de son oeuvre gravé et lithographié*, Paris 1896 and Victor Arwas and Veronique Arwas, Louis Legrand, *Catalogue Raisonné* (London: Papadakis, 2006).

17 See Mathieu Varille, *Hermann-Paul, Peintre-Graveur (1864-1940)*, Lyon, 1941; on his World War I images, see his "Calendrier de la Guerre, 1914-1917" preserved in the Cabinet des Estampes, Bibliothèque nationale, Paris.

18 Evidence of the availability of the series is found in a four-page advertising brochure that called attention to the *Estampes décoratives en couleurs du peintre Henri Rivière* including the collection of eight lithographs titled *Paysages parisiens*. For reference to this document, see the boxes on Henri Rivière in the Musée d'Orsay Documentation.

Pirated Posters: International Print Politics and The Graphic Art of Maurice Biais

Sarah Sik

For the more than fifty million visitors to the Exposition Universelle et Internationale de Paris 1900,[1] the sights at the fairgrounds epitomized both the optimistic hopes and sublimated fears that characterized the belle époque – the period of European peace and comparative prosperity between the conclusion of the Franco-Prussian War (1871) and the declaration of the First World War (1914). On one hand a visitor to the fair could peruse the private pavilion of art nouveau presented by the Parisian dealer Siegfried Bing, tucked in a corner of the Esplanade des Invalides.[2] On the other hand, the visitor could warily – or approvingly – observe presiding over the Seine the militaristic pavilion of the French arms producer Schneider & Co., with its metallic shell and long-barreled armaments an ominous harbinger of the catastrophic conflicts to come. While the exposition outwardly confirmed the conciliatory tones tenuously espoused by the self-identified "civilized" nations of the world, the intense nationalistic and capitalistic interests that would culminate in the First World War did not cease to simmer beneath the formal cordiality.

Both excitement and anxiety had accompanied the fin de siècle, which culminated in 1900 in the grand meeting of nations for cultural and commercial competition in Paris, fittingly the city that would later be deemed by the German literary critic Walter Benjamin as "the capital of the nineteenth century."[3] For locals and visitors alike, the city was a maze of seductive spectacles, an exciting cosmopolitan landscape ablaze with images vying for attention. Kiosks touted an endless supply of illustrated journals, large-scale color posters advertised the latest theatrical productions and sensational cabaret acts, and fine art prints graced the windows and walls of dealers' galleries. Not only was the city figuratively alight with the printed image, but colorful advertisements also literally provided dazzling screens for the lighted kiosks that dotted the evening cityscape.[4] While Jules Chéret is credited with arriving at the first phenomenally successful formula for advertising the city's businesses and pleasure domes, it is the younger artist Henri de Toulouse-Lautrec whose work is often identified as the conspicuous popping cork at the beginning of the fin-de-siècle print explosion.[5]

DETAIL: Maurice Biais (French, 1875-1926) (detail, see cat. 9; p. 116)
Tuff Tuff, 1902
Lithograph
Dr. Gabriel and Yvonne Weisberg Collection

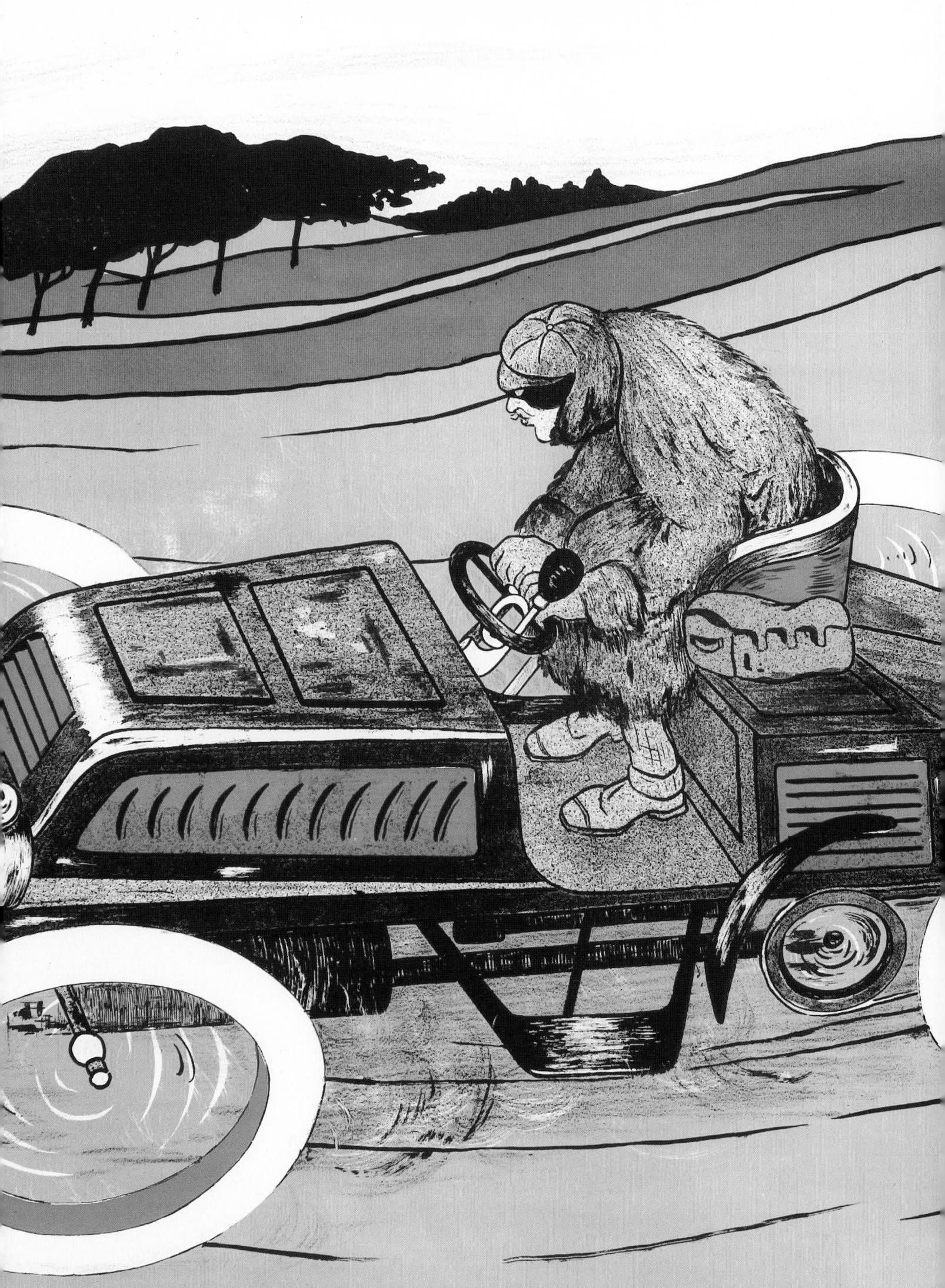

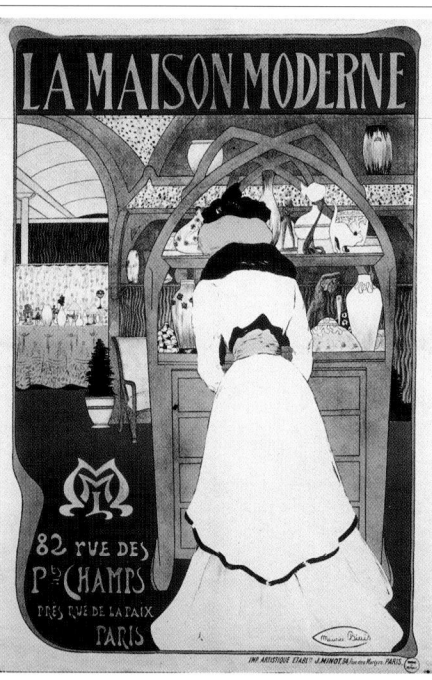

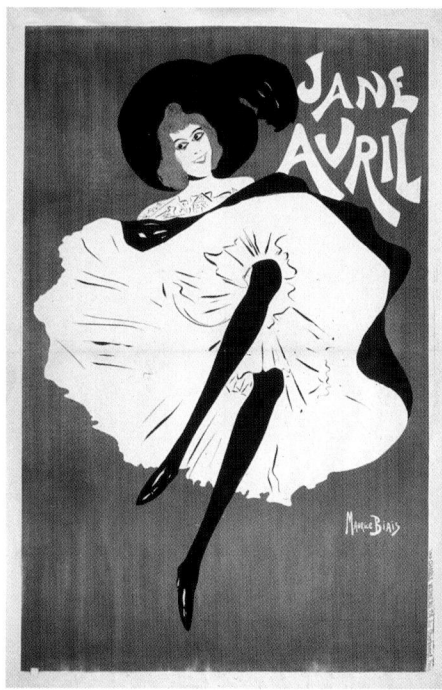

This essay, however, will not be devoted to an examination of the legacies of Chéret and Toulouse-Lautrec, but will rather take as a case study one of Lautrec's contemporaries – the little-known graphic artist Maurice Biais (1872-1926)[6] – to examine fundamental issues concerning the printmaker's art in what Walter Benjamin would famously identify as the "age of mechanical reproduction."[7] The tensions between commercial and artistic prints, between manipulatory and revelatory images were not the only distinctions that interested avant-garde artists of the fin de siècle. As discussed by Weisberg, there was also a pronounced tension between social commitment and lofty aesthetic pursuits, and, as will be discussed in this essay, between originality and appropriation. Of the images that have come to symbolize Paris at the turn of the century, one of the most enigmatic is a poster produced by Biais for the design firm La Maison Moderne (fig. 27). One of only two posters known to have been commissioned by the German art critic Julies Meier-Graefe to promote his new entrepreneurial venture, the image of a fashionable woman gazing at decorative objects offered by the firm is visually striking yet does not yield easily to interpretation. The most compelling art historical speculation[8] has suggested that the female visitor to the shop is a Montmartrian performer and close friend of Toulouse-Lautrec, the dancer Jane Avril, whom Biais married in 1911.[9] Biais had designed a publicity poster for Avril as early as 1898 (fig. 28), and was clearly on close terms with her again in 1902, when the French journal *Le Sourire* published an image of her from an album Biais had underway.[10] Avril had furthermore developed a reputation as a discriminating connoisseur, particularly through her well-known association with such major Parisian figures as the art critics Theodore de Wyzewa and Arsène Alexandre, as well as the poet Edouard Dujardin and the artist Toulouse-Lautrec. When Lautrec was commissioned to design the cover for the inaugural portfolio of the major printmaking endeavor *L'Estampe originale* (fig. 29; p. 114), it was in fact his friend Avril whom he selected as a symbol of the knowledgeable modern collector as well as a celebrity endorser of the project. It thus stands to reason,

FIG. 27   Maurice Biais (French, 1875-1926)
La Maison Moderne, ca. 1900
Color lithograph, 44⅞ x 30½ in. (114 x 78.5 cm)
Les Arts Décoratifs, Musée des Arts décoratifs, Paris
Photo by Laurent Sully Jaulmes. Tous droits réservés

FIG. 28   Maurice Biais (French, 1875-1926)
Jane Avril, 1898
Color lithograph, 47¼ x 32 ½ in. (120 x 80.5 cm)
Les Arts Décoratifs, Musée des Arts décoratifs, Paris
Photo by Laurent Sully Jaulmes. Tous droits réservés

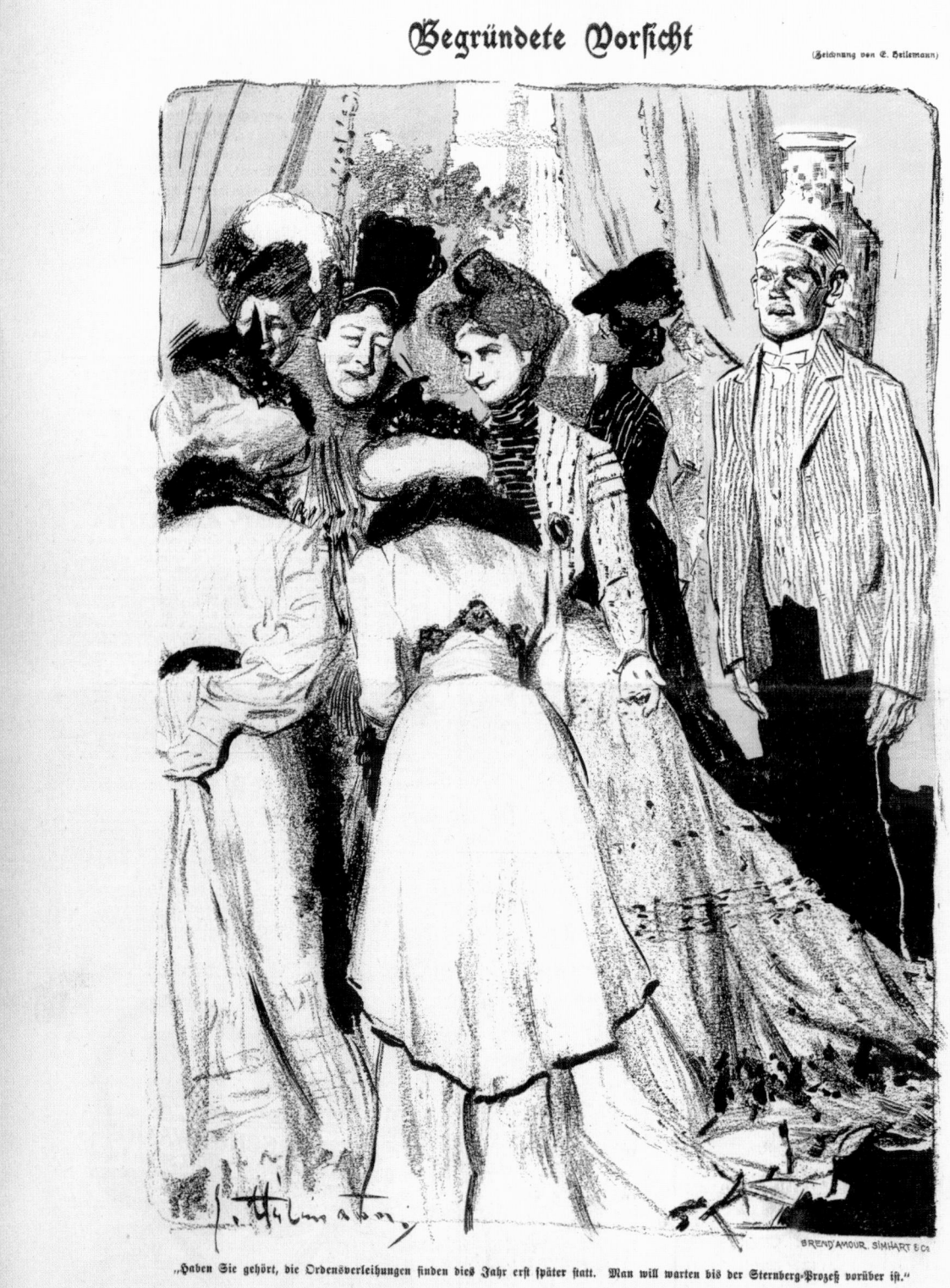

CAT. 43   Ernst Heilemann (German, 1870-?)
"Bergründete Vorsicht" ["Established Caution"], in:
Simplicissimus, vol. 5, no. 41 (1900), p. 332
Special Collections and Rare Books, University of Minnesota,
Minneapolis, Minnesota

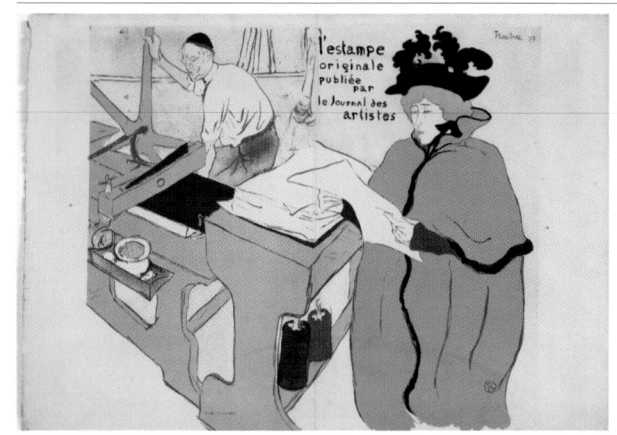

given Avril's known intimacy with Biais and the weight of her appeal as a celebrity connoisseur, that hers is the identity of the fashionable woman in the poster for La Maison Moderne. While I do not wish to preclude this interpretation as a possible valence of the finished poster, the print must also be examined under the light of new research that has revealed the German source from which Biais directly copied the figure – the satirical magazine *Simplicissimus* (cat. 43; p. 113).[11]

When the German art critic, Meier-Graefe, opened the design firm La Maison Moderne in the fall of 1899,[12] he aimed to realize in the heart of Paris a set of business and artistic ideals that he had espoused as the editor of a series of significant journals. Ever keen to unite theory with practice, as editor of the Parisian design journal *L'Art décoratif* he published a call to action in the spring of 1899 that he answered himself only months later. "Enough rhetoric" the anonymous writer, possibly Meier-Graefe himself, opined. "After a hundred books and a thousand articles, we won't be any further than we are today. A single work, an example will do more to get things moving than torrents of ink."[13] With money inherited from his recently deceased father, Meier-Graefe threw his energies into the development and promotion of such an emporium devoted to the production of goods for the modern home and fashionable modern life. Having served as an adviser to Siegfried Bing (1838-1905), Meier-Graefe had been well positioned to observe closely the successes and failures with which Bing met as he attempted to introduce a markedly international vision of art nouveau to the Parisian public. The critical response to Bing's first salon of art nouveau in 1895 had been in many instances quite reactionary and chauvinistic, taking exception with Bing's incorporation of designs from an expansive roster of European and American artists.[14] "Nothing had ever before seemed so strange to Parisians as the Bing Salon of the early days" an anonymous critic recalled in 1900. "Yet nevertheless there were wonderful things…But it was not French. Bing became convinced that he had to approach the French in a French way."[15]

FIG. 29   Henri de Toulouse-Lautrec (French, 1864-1901)

Wraparound cover for the portfolio *L'Estampe originale*, 1893

Lithograph, 22⅞ x 32¾ in. (58.23 x 83.36 cm)

The Museum of Modern Art/Licensed by SCALA/Art Resource, New York

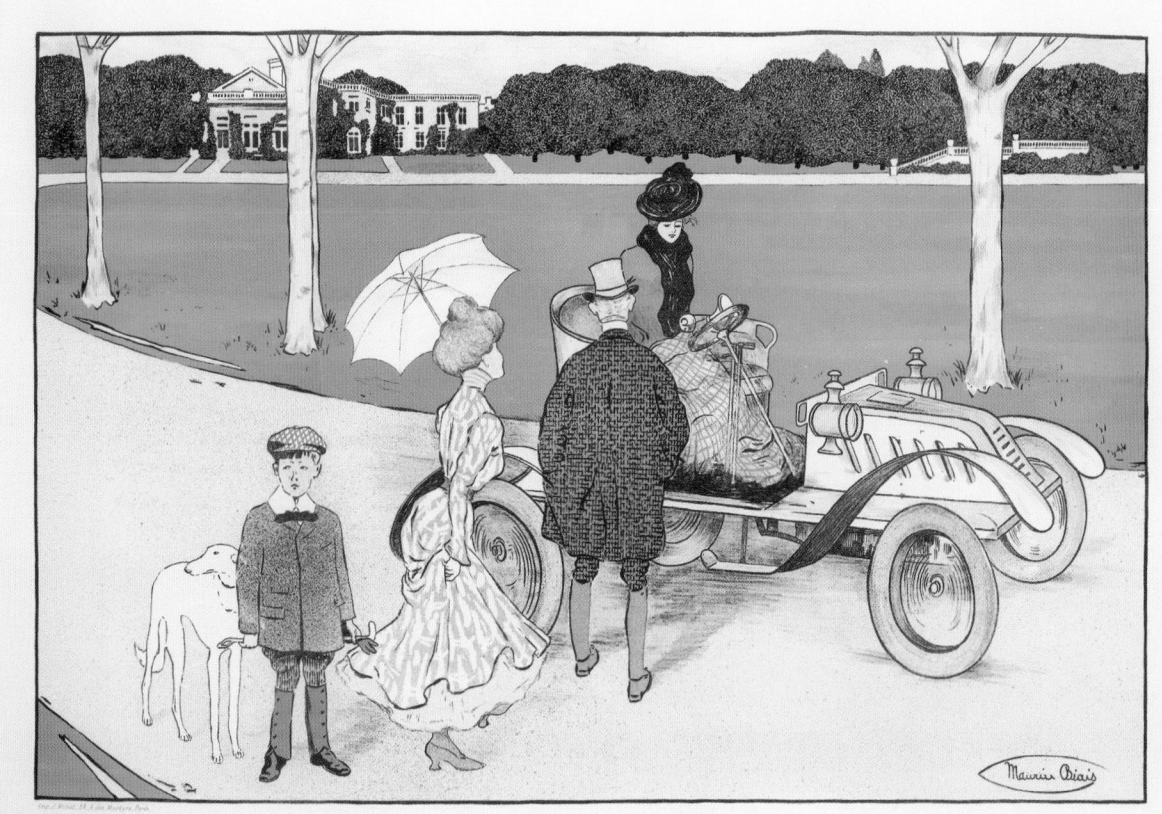

CAT. 7   Maurice Biais (French, 1875-1926)
         In the Park, ca. 1900
         Lithograph, 26½ x 33½ in. (67.3 x 85.1 cm)
         Dr. Gabriel and Yvonne Weisberg Collection

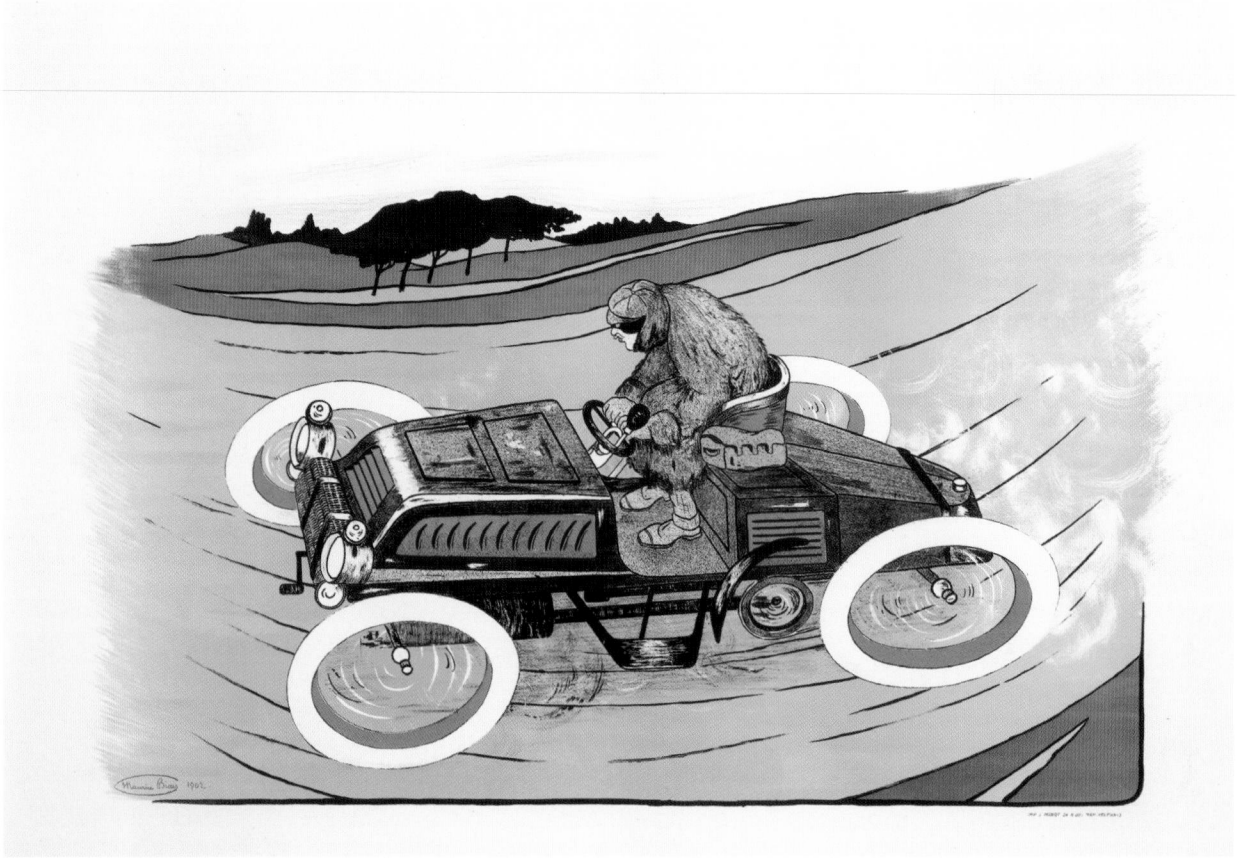

CAT. 9   Maurice Biais (French, 1875-1926)
Tuff Tuff, 1902
Lithograph, 26½ x 33½ in. (67.3 x 85.1 cm)
Dr. Gabriel and Yvonne Weisberg Collection

In her succinct study *Modernism and the Decorative Arts in France: Art Nouveau to Le Corbusier*, Nancy Troy argues that by the time Meier-Graefe opened La Maison Moderne, Bing had indeed begun to recalibrate his marketing philosophy, featuring designs at the L'Art Nouveau Bing pavilion for the 1900 Paris Exposition Universelle that were notably French in their neo-rococo sensibilities. At La Maison Moderne, however, both the citizens and guests of Paris in 1900 were offered a much different vision of modern design – one that shared greater aesthetic similarities with the linear *Jugendstil* designs exhibited in the German and Austrian pavilions at the Exposition Universelle than with the florid styles adopted by Bing's stable of designers. And, in fact it was Meier-Graefe himself who in an 1899 article for *Dekorative Kunst* first distinguished between "floral" and "linear" tendencies in art nouveau.[16] In founding his own design firm, Meier-Graefe was additionally strongly influenced by his admiration of the organization of the Vereinigten Wekstätten für Kunst im Handwerk in Munich (the United Workshops for Art in Craft).[17] At La Maison Moderne, Meier-Graefe thus adopted not only the starker *Jugendstil* aesthetic in the shop front and interior displays commissioned from the Belgian designer Henry Van de Velde, but was also committed to the social ideals of the Kunstgewerbe [Arts and Crafts] movement – to increase the common man's access to quality designs through efficient production.[18] La Maison Moderne was described in the pages of *Dekorative Kunst* as an effort for designers and artisans to band together to pursue the goal of sustainable design and efficient production.[19] "The artist gives exclusive rights for production to the firm and receives a portion of the selling price – which he helps to determine – for each object sold," a Parisian correspondent reported in *Dekorative Kunst*. "Moreover, advertising will not remain limited to this single store, but there will be many more agents, in France and abroad; this too breaks with the tradition of Parisian dealers, whose desire for fame means that the objects they sell can only be seen in their own establishments."[20]

Given Meier-Graefe's express desire to support modern design as a viable profession as well as his tireless efforts to promote modernism in both the visual and applied arts, what might we make of his decision to endorse blatant plagiarism from a contemporary foreign source in one of a small number of posters commissioned to advertise his venture? In the same year Meier-Graefe opened La Maison Moderne, as editor of *L'Art décoratif* he had published opinions calling for "revolution in the customary practices of the industry, which protect the pecuniary interests of the artist poorly and his moral interests not al all."[21] As the editor of *Dekorative Kunst* and the French-language edition *L'Art décoratif*, until his resignation from the posts in 1899 when he turned his attentions fully to the opening and operations of La Maison Moderne, it seems highly unlikely that Meier-Graefe would not have possessed a contemporary visual vocabulary sufficient to identify the copied image. Indeed as an art critic and ambitious historian of modern art, Meier-Graefe specifically evinced his familiarity with contemporary German artists on a number of occasions, even going so far as to characterize the forms of two *Simplicissimus* artists, Rudolf Wilke and Bruno Paul, as unique and as identifiable as "their handwriting."[22]

For Biais's part, the "borrowing" utilized in the construction of the poster for La Maison Moderne is an early example of what would become a pronounced creative habit, as he raided the pages of both *Simplicissimus* and *Jugend* in search of forms to insert into designs he signed with his own name.[23] Was Biais simply lazy, unskilled, and uncreative? Such an explanation is, of course, possible, but seems highly unlikely, particularly given Meier-Graefe's support of him. How then, might we understand his prolific pilfering from German sources? How might we understand Meier-Graefe's approval of it? One possible explanation can be derived through interpreting Biais's work within a broader discourse concerning originality, authorship, and coherence in modern art.[24] Particularly in the case of the poster for La Maison Moderne, the "borrowing" must also be considered in light of the pronounced tensions between national and international viewpoints among the promoters of art nouveau as the movement coalesced.

While an editor at the highbrow cultural journal *Pan*, the young and ambitious Meier-Graefe had butted heads repeatedly with members of the Berlin PAN Society (which produced the journal) over the question of whether the publication would promote modern art in general or would foster exclusively the development of German art. Meier-Graefe's staunchest opponent at PAN was Eberhard von Bodenhausen, who locked horns with Meier-Graefe over the question of whether Toulouse-Laturec's print *Mademoiselle Marcelle Lender* (c. 1895), which Meier-Graefe had already secured from the artist, would be included in an upcoming edition of the journal.[25] Hoping that he might cajole Bodenhausen into realizing the limiting nature of his nationalist views, Meier-Graefe wrote to him from London concerning the objections that had been raised by another committee member, Wilhelm Weigand. "You win the bet about Lautrec, right, I've always considered Weigand to be a philistine," Meier-Graefe wrote. "With him it's got nothing to do with national feeling, it's just simple narrowmindedness."[26] As Catherine Krahmer has succinctly pointed out in addressing this exchange, for Bodenhausen "national feeling" was sacrosanct.[27] A month prior to Meier-Graefe's letter to Bodenhausen, Alfred Lichtwark had similarly opined in the pages of *Pan*:

> We Germans were the first to put into practice the idea of a National Service for the defence [sic] of the country. Now we should realize that this applies also to the cultural field. Even in times of peace there exists a silent but frightening fight between nations.... If we want art, it has to be German art, art that has meaning in Germany, not English or French art, that has meaning in those countries.[28]

Krahmer underscores that Bodenhausen privately expressed his well-known concurrence with Lichtwark's views, explicitly stating his sentiments in a letter. "I can tell you now that, generally speaking, one of my priorities is to cut down the cost of our foreign representatives, whom I consider to be worthless," he wrote to Lichtwark. "The main issue should be this: PAN is on national ground and has as its aim the development and encouragement of the art of our country. That is to say, we have to put the emphasis on German art and never mix it with foreign art."[29] While the Toulouse-Lautrec print was ultimately published by *Pan* in October of 1895, the schism the conflict had revealed amongst the editorial staff and the members of the PAN Society led to the resignation of Meier-Graefe and two of his colleagues, Otto Julius Bierbaum and Richard Dehmal, who had served as literary editors.[30]

Meier-Graefe retreated to Paris, where he wrote art criticism for German journals[31] and served as an adviser to Bing, before embarking upon his more ambitious projects as editor of *Dekorative Kunst* and *L'Art décoratif* and as proprietor of La Maison Moderne. In Paris, however, Meier-Graefe met with the opposing critique, and, according to historian Robert Jensen, La Maison Moderne quickly "came under fire as a German import and a threat to French cultural traditions," particularly as he clearly "intended to model his business after the Munich and Viennese *Werkstätten*.[32] From the outset, both Bing and Meier-Graefe were committed to international design and to the support of the designer and craftsman. In the essay "Wohin treiben wir?" ["Where are we drifting?"], which opened the first issue of Meier-Graefe's journal *Dekorative Kunst*, Bing argued that national identity was not as important as "the necessity in the creation of a commodity, to create the fundamental nature of the thing in such a way as to respect the means of manufacture."[33] Given his irritation over having been told by the Germans that he was not German enough only to relocate to Paris, where his close friend Bing was criticized for not being French enough, it seems possible that the witty and erudite Meier-Graefe overcame his desire to protect the rights of designers long enough to commission a type of in-joke to promote his shop. The poster at once represents the contributions of the Belgian designer Van de Velde as well as the satirical printmaking found in the pages of *Simplicissimus*, all parading under the guise of French connoisseurship. Truly only extremely knowledgeable and cosmopolitan viewers would have appreciated the visual joke – those

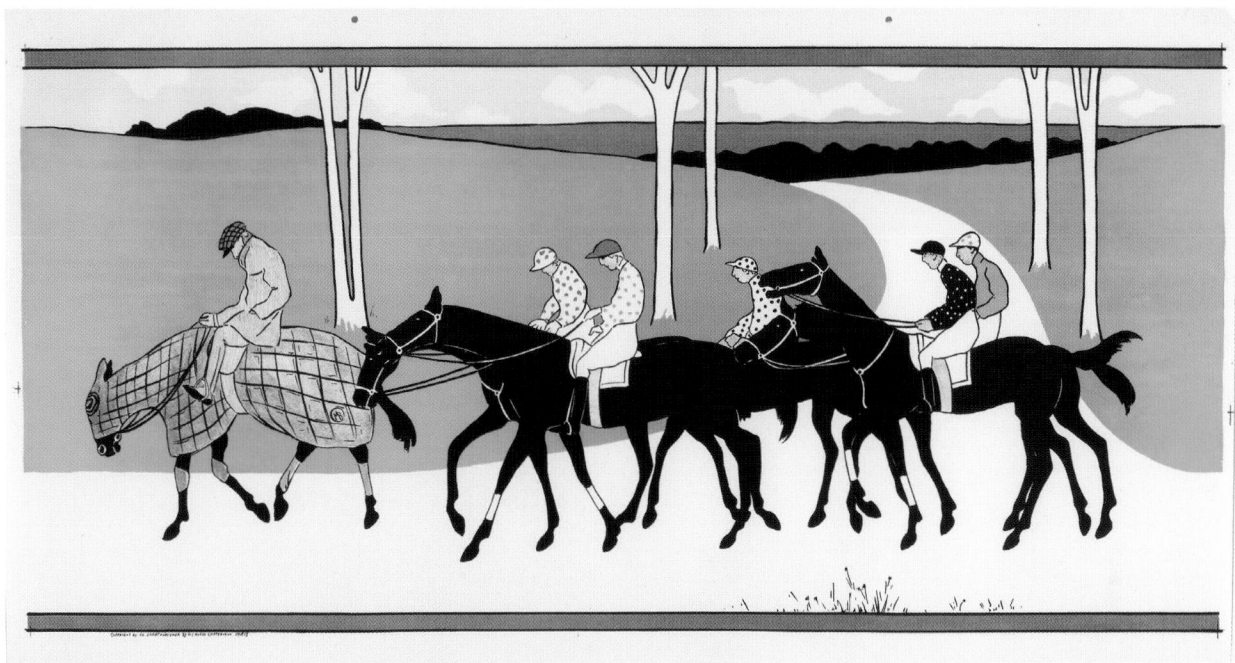

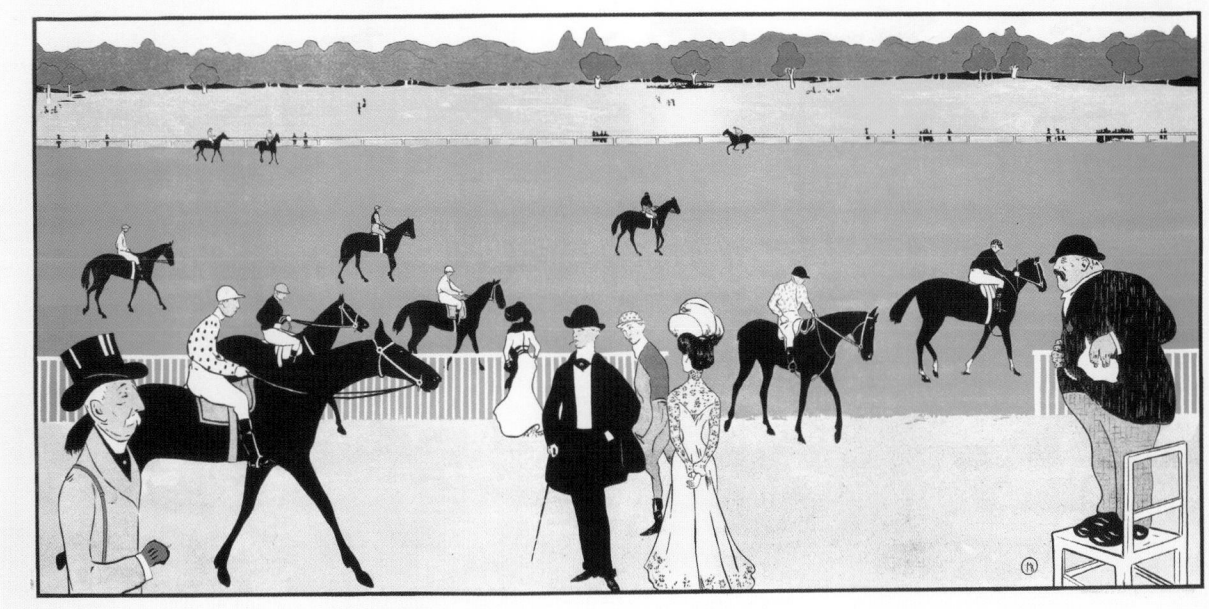

CAT. 6   Maurice Biais (French, 1875-1926)
Back from the Race, ca. 1900
Lithograph, 26½ x 46 in. (67.3 x 116.8 cm)
Dr. Gabriel and Yvonne Weisberg Collection

CAT. 8   Maurice Biais (French, 1875-1926)
The Race Track, ca. 1900
Lithograph, 20½ x 41⅞ in. (52.1 x 106.4 cm)
Dr. Gabriel and Yvonne Weisberg Collection

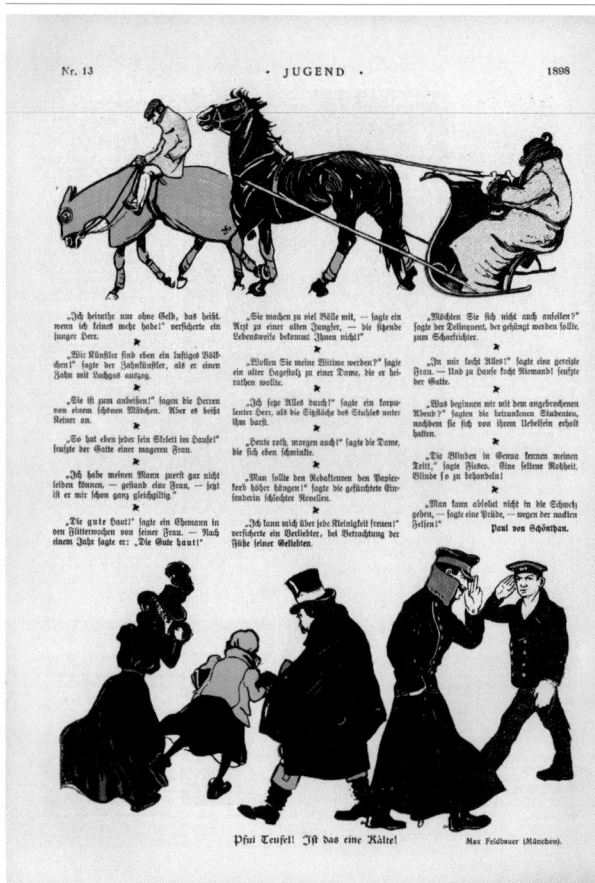

viewers most open to the vision of international modern art carried out by Meier-Graefe at La Maison Moderne.

Simplicissimus, the journal from which Biais pirated the central figure used in the production of the poster for La Maison Moderne, appeared in Munich in 1897, only months before Meier-Graefe founded *Dekorative Kunst* in the same German city, likewise addressing a German-speaking audience. When Meier-Graefe assessed *Simplicissimus* in his study of the development of modern art, he characterized both *Simplicissimus* and its Munich contemporary *Jugend* as "weekly papers, anything but conservative in tone, and intended for popular consumption."[34] Both journals, however, quickly joined the ranks of avant-garde infamy – *Jugend* for its moral license, and *Simplicissimus* for its liberal political and social views. Of the latter, the Russian novelist, Leo Tolstoy, remarked: "For the historian of the 22nd and 23rd centuries who describes the 19th century, *Simplicissimus* will be the most valuable source, enabling him to become familiar not only with the state of our present-day society, but also to test the credibility of all other sources."[35]

From its inception, tangible ties had existed between *Simplicissimus* and Paris. In fact the nascent ideas for founding the journal, ironically, appear to have stemmed from the fallout over a set of forged paintings. The rascally writer, Willy Grétor, claimed that although he had indeed sold the suspect paintings to the future publisher of *Simplicissimus*, Albert Langen, he had more than made amends for his transgression by proposing to Langen the idea to publish a satirical journal modeled on the Parisian weekly *Gil Blas Illustré*.[36] As a result of lawsuits swiftly brought against *Simplicissimus* for offenses to the State in a now infamous "Palestine" issue, Langen had sought refuge in Paris, while the cartoonist for the issue Theodore Heine, and the contributor of the offending verse, Frank Wedekind, were sentenced to six- and seven-month prison terms respectively. From 1898, when the affair erupted, until 1903, Langen lived as a political refugee in Paris.[37] Consequently, the publisher of *Simplicissimus*, who would obviously have been intimately aware of the content of the journal from which Biais sourced material, was in Paris at precisely the period in which Biais's pirating was most

FIG. 30   Max Feldbauer
   "Pfui Teufel! Ist das enie kälte" ["Pfui Devil! It's a Cold One!"]
   Jugend, vol. 3, no. 13 (26 March 1898)
   Special Collections and Rare Books, University of Minnesota,
   Minneapolis, Minnesota

prolific. Whether this flagrant and highly visible plagiarism led to lawsuits is an aspect of research that remains to be pursued. It is evident that copyright protection was a particularly pointed concern for the Reichstag as it attempted to protect its products of export.[37] Yet given the thorn in the side *Simplicissimus* constituted for the German establishment, it seems highly unlikely that the Reichstag would have been concerned explicitly with protecting the specific journal's rights against unauthorized reproduction.[38]

In the summer of 1901, Maurice Biais arrived in New York City,[39] to participate in the only known exhibition devoted to his prints. The exhibition of seventy lithographs was held at the Max Williams Gallery on Fifth Avenue, near Thirty-seventh Street. Included in the exhibition is a poster entitled *Les Bookmaker*, which the reviewer of the show for the *New York Times* described as "a skit on the habitués of the race course, male and female." The description fits a known lithograph by Biais that has been entitled, *The Race Track*, 1900 (cat. 8; p. 119). The reviewer of the show perceptively remarked that Biais's work in some instances "causes one to recall some of the caricaturists for Munich 'Jugend.'"[40] If this is indeed the poster that was exhibited, a number of the figures far more than "recall" forms from *Jugend*. In fact, two of the forms in this poster are direct copies of caricatures first published in *Jugend* (cat. 122, p. 122; cat. 87, p. 124) while an additional pair of forms is lifted from the pages of *Simplicissimus* (cat. 90; p. 126 and cat. 84; p. 127). Similarly the description of a print entitled *Champs de Course*, which the *New York Times* reviewer suggests could be transposed effectively into a design for a wall paper, fits a known Biais print that has until this point been identified as *Back from the Race*, 1900 (cat. 6; p. 119). Whether or not this was indeed the print exhibited in New York, it can be established that Biais again drew the key figures from two issues of *Jugend* – copying the lead horse and rider from a cartoon commenting on the cold March weather of 1898 (fig. 30) and the riders "Mr. Flipp, Mr. Stop, Mr. Gin, Mr. Smart und Mr. Blaff" with their horses, from a small cartoon by H. Pampel (fig. 31).

The two German journals upon which Biais is known to have drawn constituted something of a political

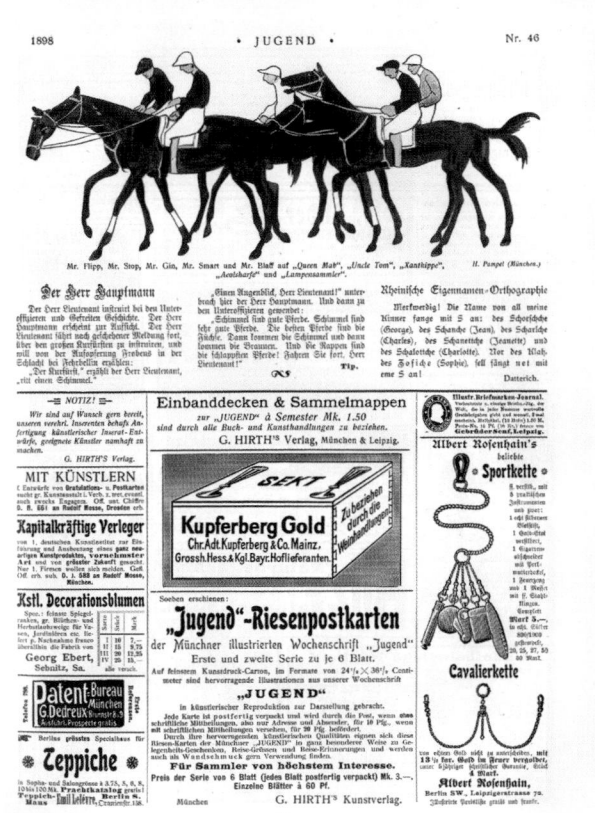

FIG. 31   H. Pampel
"Mr. Flipp, Mr. Stop, Mr. Gin, Mr. Smart und Mr. Blaff"
Jugend, vol. 3, no. 46 (12 November 1898)
Special Collections and Rare Books, University of Minnesota, Minneapolis, Minnesota

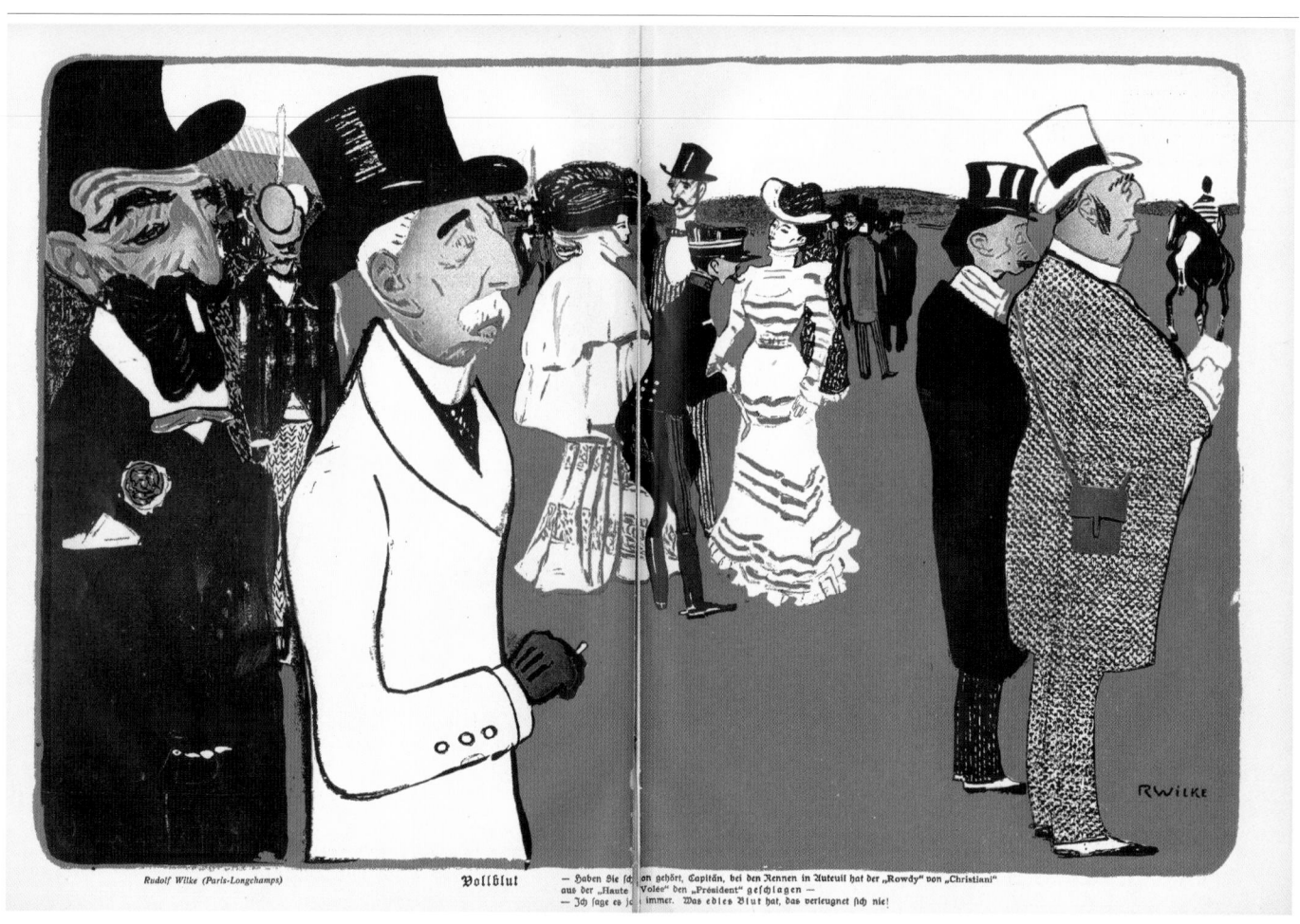

Rudolf Wilke (Paris-Longchamps)

Vollblut

— Haben Sie schon gehört, Capitän, bei den Rennen in Auteuil hat der „Rowdy" von „Christiani" aus der „Haute Volée" den „Président" geschlagen —
— Ich sage es ja immer. Was edles Blut hat, das verleugnet sich nie!

CAT. 122 Rudolf Wilke (German, 1873-1908)

"Vollblut" ["Thoroughbred"], in: *Jugend*, vol. 4, number 28 (8 July 1899),
pp. 446-7, two-page illustration. Special Collections and Rare Books,
University of Minnesota, Minneapolis, Minnesota

lightening rod in Germany, currents not unobserved by those outside the country. Liberal sympathizers realized the effectiveness of exposing social injustices through the use of bitter humor, satire, and exaggeration. The dramatist Gerhardt Hauptmann, for one, characterized *Simplicissimus* as the "sharpest and most ruthless satirical force in Germany."[42] Not surprisingly, the sardonic wit of the caricaturists who contributed to these publications was considered by conservative critics to be among the worst offenders of the avant-garde press. "The *Simplicissimus* German has become a type, as has the morally loose *Jugend* type," the Catholic *Augsburger Postzeitung* lamented in 1912, "and both these types are represented in thousands among the so-called educated elite of the Empire."[43] The publications from which Biais drew thus both created well-known "types," a cultural shorthand that was associated explicitly by conservative critics with degenerate and depraved upstarts. Unlike *Pan*, which was pitched to erudite art lovers, *Simplicissimus*, which appeared in April of 1896, was geared toward a middle-class readership.[44] While *Pan* had endeavored to encourage the middle class to elevate their tastes to those of refined connoisseurs,[45] *Simplicissimus* chose as its mascot a growling crimson bulldog with a broken collar restraint, symbolizing the brute power and pugnacious potential of the " 'volk' spirit" of the lower classes.[46] In Germany, a conservative censorial obsession quickly arose over what the drawings in *Simplicissimus* and journals of its ilk "meant." As Ann Taylor Allen comments in her study *Satire and Society in Wilhelmine Germany*, "Many contemporary observers noted, with approval or with anger, that *Simplicissimus* provided a vocabulary of protest for the previously passive and inarticulate."[47] These forms, of course, were rarely threatening in and of themselves, but accrued meaning only when viewed in context, with their accompanying captions. Taylor Allen argues that it was "socially committed" artists in Europe and America who modeled their work upon *Simplicissimus*,[48] yet this seems not to have been Biais's goal. In raiding the pages of *Sim-plicissimus* and *Jugend*, Biais is not known in any instances to have copied complete images. Rather he selected sometimes as many as two or three sources to work together into a new visual pastiche. By changing the contexts of the images, and always altering the caption or more often eliminating it entirely, Biais effectively depoliticized these images and reconfigured them for a design context – turning caustic social satire into something deemed appropriate for the decoration of country manors.[49]

Biais's piracy must also be considered, however, within the context of the revival of the original print in the 1890s. Both in the artistic as well as popular arenas, printmaking enjoyed a flowering in this period. Yet advancements in photomechanical printing led artists and critics to question the value of the original artistic print in relation to the mechanically reproduced image. An archetypal example of a printmaker's concern with this issue is found in the print *Vitrioleuse*, contributed by Eugène Grasset to the sixth album of *L'Estampe originale*. In the print, Grasset combined the two extremes – filling in each color with stencils applied by hand onto a photorelief outline. Meier-Graefe also would have been particularly cognizant of the distinction between fine art prints and mass-produced journal illustrations, particularly as he had left PAN over such a print when several members of the PAN Society had radically divergent visions for resuscitating the print as an original art form.[50] J.A. Clarke furthermore has analyzed Meier-Graefe's efforts to distinguish the portfolio of prints by Edvard Munch that he commissioned from the "commercialism associated with the journal trade in order, ironically, to sell them."[51]

While *Simplicissimus* was most infamous for its political pugnacity, Taylor Allen observes that it was also an important forum for "artistic and intellectual innovation"[52] and characterizes it as "a conspicuous advocate of artistic innovation."[53] While *Simplicissimus* was well known for its pacifistic, anti-clerical, and anti-monarchical stances, Allen argues, the publication ultimately "stood much less for a single cause, much more for the freedom of the

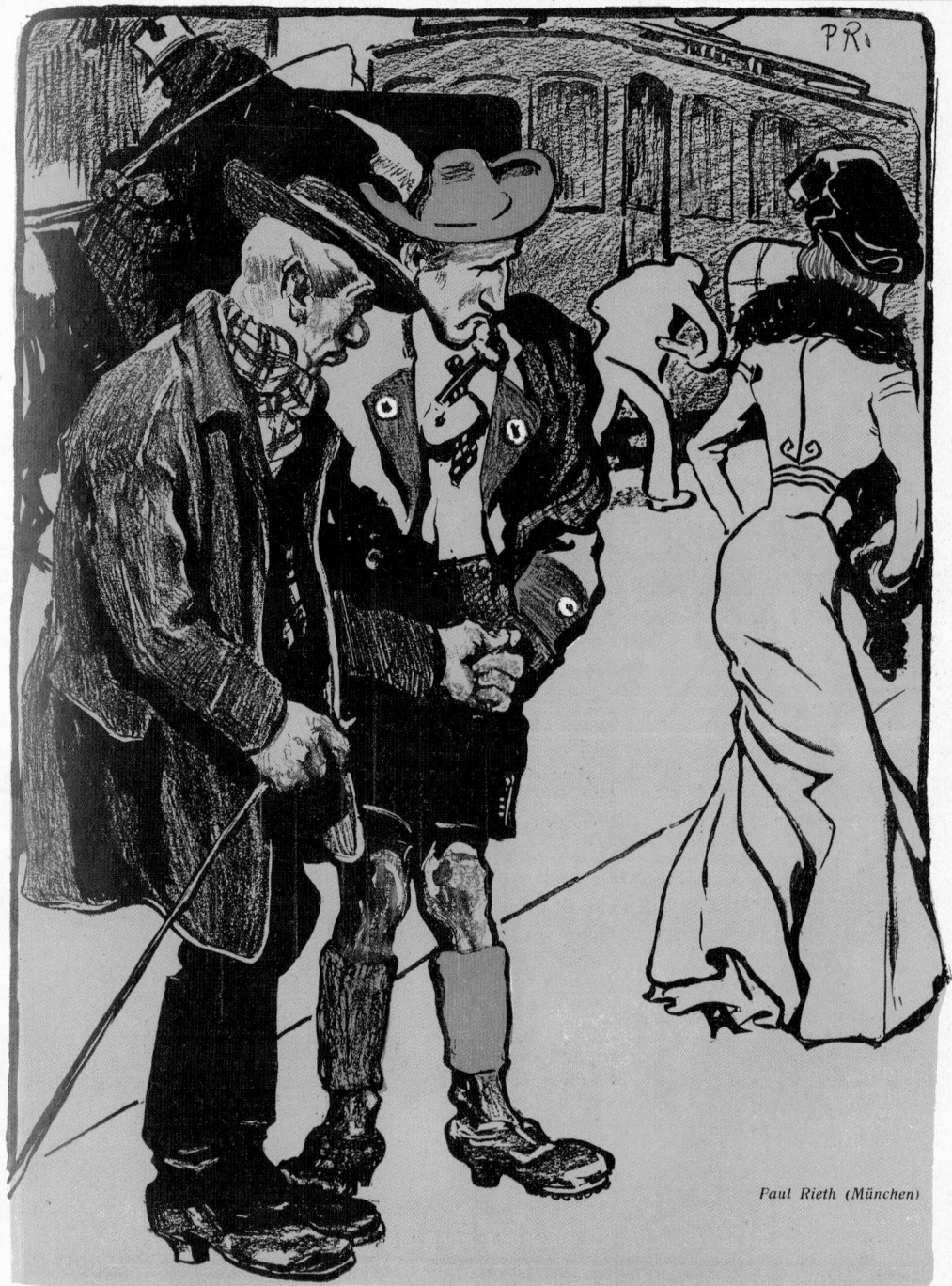

CAT. 90   Paul Rieth (German, 1871-1925)
"Wespentaille" ["Wasp Waist"], in: *Jugend*, vol. 5, number 31
(30 July 1900), p. 523
Special Collections and Rare Books, University of Minnesota,
Minneapolis, Minnesota

individual to express his own personality and view-point."[54] In addressing the publications in his tome on modern art, Meier-Graefe similarly mused, "Unlike 'Pan' they had no artistic programme and no didactic aim; neither had they any abstract ideal to defend. They initiated an attack, but against whom or what was not clear."[55] The forms Biais drew from the pages of *Simplicissimus* and *Jugend* led to posters that could hardly be defined as original, at least in the legal sense, but remain provocative for their subversion of the stability of meaning imbedded in forms and words, as his finished posters typically no longer "stood" for anything coherent.

Thought as intellectual property was a key point of legal theory of the nineteenth century and has remained such to this day, garnering the additional attention of critical theorists in the twentieth century.[56] The international implications of the shrinking geopolitical map led many nations to recognize at the end of the nineteenth century the need for legal protection for individual creators as well as national economies. Indeed with the specific meeting of minds and commercial interests at the Paris Exposition Universelle of 1900, the issue would have been particularly fraught.[57] Biais's work, especially within the light of the support given by Meier-Graefe, can thus be read as a provocative jab not only at emerging legal definitions of plagiarism and appropriation but also at artistic prejudice for originality and creativity over selection and juxtaposition. While the fin de siècle is broadly known as the age of socially committed illustrations, colorful advertising posters, and artistically meritorious *belles épreuves*, an examination of the work of Biais and the patronage of Meier-Graefe reveals additional political and intellectual dimensions to the print culture of 1900 that raised questions of individual versus collective rights to intellectual property, stable versus pliable meaning, social versus artistic prerogatives of art, and national styles versus international medleys.

Endnotes

[1] The Bureau International des Expositions cites the number of visitors to the *Exposition Universelle et Internationale de Paris 1900* as 50,860,801 <http://www.bie-paris.org/main/index.php?p=-34&m2=111>.

[2] Karine Lacquemant, "The Bing Art Nouveau Pavilion at the World's Fair of 1900: 'New Art from Old,'" in: *The Origins of L'Art Nouveau: the Bing Empire*. Gabriel P. Weisberg, Edwin Becker, and Évelyne Possémé, eds. (Amsterdam: Van Gogh Museum; Paris: Musée des arts décoratifs; Antwerp: Mercatorfonds, 2004: 191).

[3] Walter Benjamin, *The Arcades Project* (Cambridge: Belknap Press, 1999: 3-26).

[4] For an illustration of this see: *Le Courrier français*, 15.11 (13 March 1898): 9.

[5] Phillip Dennis Cate and Sinclair Hamilton Hitchings, *The Color Revolution: Color Lithography in France 1890-1900* (Salt Lake City: Peregrine Smith, Inc., 1978: 3, 12-13, 17).

[6] Dates of birth and death gathered from Biais's death certificate. Research courtesy of Gabriel P. and Yvonne M.L. Weisberg.

[7] Walter Benjamin, *Illuminations*, H. Arendt, ed. (London: Fontana/Collins, 1973: 219-53).

[8] Gabriel P. Weisberg, "The Urban Mirror: Contrasts in the Vision of Existence in the Modern City," in: *Paris and the Countryside: Modern Life in Late-19th-Century France* (Portland: Portland Museum of Art, 2006: 1-2).

[9] Maurice Biais and Jeanne Beaudon (the legal name of Jane Avril) were married on 7 June 1911 in Jouy-en-Josas. Marriage certificate, Le Maire Conseiller Général des Yvelines, Ville de Jouy-en-Josas. Research courtesy of Gabriel P. and Yvonne M.L. Weisberg.

[10] *Le Sourire*, 4.33 (24 May 1902).

[11] This essay presents a small portion of a larger project investigating both the dancer Jane Avril and the artist Maurice Biais. Research has been generously supported through a Grant-in-Aid of Research, Artistry, and Scholarship granted by the Office of the Dean of the Graduate School, University of Minnesota, to Dr. Gabriel P. Weisberg, for whom Ms. Sik served as a research assistant.

und enden Gott weiß wie . . . Nur Ihre Frau . . . Verzeihen Sie, aber das ist ja gar nicht interessant und . . . nicht einmal witzig."

„Komisch! Sie wollten also, daß es nicht meine eheliche Frau, sondern irgend eine Fremde sein sollte! Ach, meine Damen, meine Damen! Wenn Sie schon jetzt so denken, wie wird es erst dann sein, wenn Sie einmal verheiratet sind?"

Die jungen Mädchen wurden verlegen und schwiegen. Sie machten gelangweilte, finstere Gesichter und begannen enttäuscht zu gähnen.

Während des Abendessens aßen sie nichts, rollten Brotkügelchen und schwiegen.

„Nein, das ist sogar . . . unpassend!" hielt es eine von ihnen nicht länger aus. „Wozu brauchten Sie es denn zu erzählen, wenn das Ende so war? Es ist nichts Schönes an dieser Erzählung . . . Sogar sonderbar!"

„Sie fingen so verlockend an und plötzlich . . ." jetzte ihre Freundin hinzu. „Sie haben sich bloß über uns lustig gemacht . . ."

„Nun, nun, nun . . . es war ja nur ein Scherz . . ." sagte der Oberst. „Seien Sie nicht böse, meine Damen, ich habe nur Spaß gemacht. Es war nicht meine Frau, sondern die Frau des Verwalters . . ."

„Ja?!"

Die jungen Mädchen wurden plötzlich wieder lustig, ihre Augen funkelten . . . Sie rückten näher zum Oberst heran, schenkten ihm Wein ein und überschütteten ihn mit Fragen. Die Langeweile verschwand. Auch das Abendessen verschwand bald, da die jungen Damen mit großem Appetit zu essen begannen.

Wir Volk

Das Volk, das Volk spielt jetzt in Tele-
   grammen
Auch eine Rolle, als Staffage bloß;
Nur vor der Welt erscheinen wir zusammen,
Sonst sagt man gerne von dem Pack sich los.

Man hegt den Wunsch, in England zu
   gefallen
Und macht sich nun mal gerne angenehm.
Hier eignet sich der Samtbegriff von allen
Als Volk, als Ziffer, Kopfzahl sehr bequem.

Sonst gelten wohl nur, die behende tänzeln,
Grimassen schneidend vor dem hohen Thron,
Die mit gebog'nen Rücken rumschwänzeln
Als Reinextrakt der deutschen Nation.

Die Herren mögen sich zu unserm Spotte
Nach Gnaden drängen, hastend im Gewühl,
Wir vaterlands-gesinnungslose Rotte,
Wir haben für die Ehre kein Gefühl.

Wir bitten, sich geneigtest zu bequemen,
Auf uns Gemeine ohne Ordenstern
Auch in Depeschen nicht Bezug zu nehmen,
Wir steh'n einander ja unendlich fern.

Peter Schlemihl

Lieber Simplicissimus!

Herr X wurde zum „Hofschornsteinfegermeister" ernannt. Viele Wochen nach diesem freudigen Ereignis trifft ihn ein alter Freund, der auch zugleich sein Sangesbruder ist, auf der Straße. „Sieh, Fritze — lebst de noch? Ich gratuliere auch! Aber man sieht dich ja gar nicht mehr? Weshalb bist de denn so lange nich im Verein gewesen?" „Ach, weißt du, Conrad, die Gesellschaft da wird mir doch, offen gesagt, ein wenig zu gemischt." Erstaunen malt sich auf des Alten Zügen: „Ja, aber Fritze, du kannst doch nich verlangen, daß da bloß Schornsteinfegers drin sind?"

Ein braver Vater

(Zeichnung von F. von Reznicek)

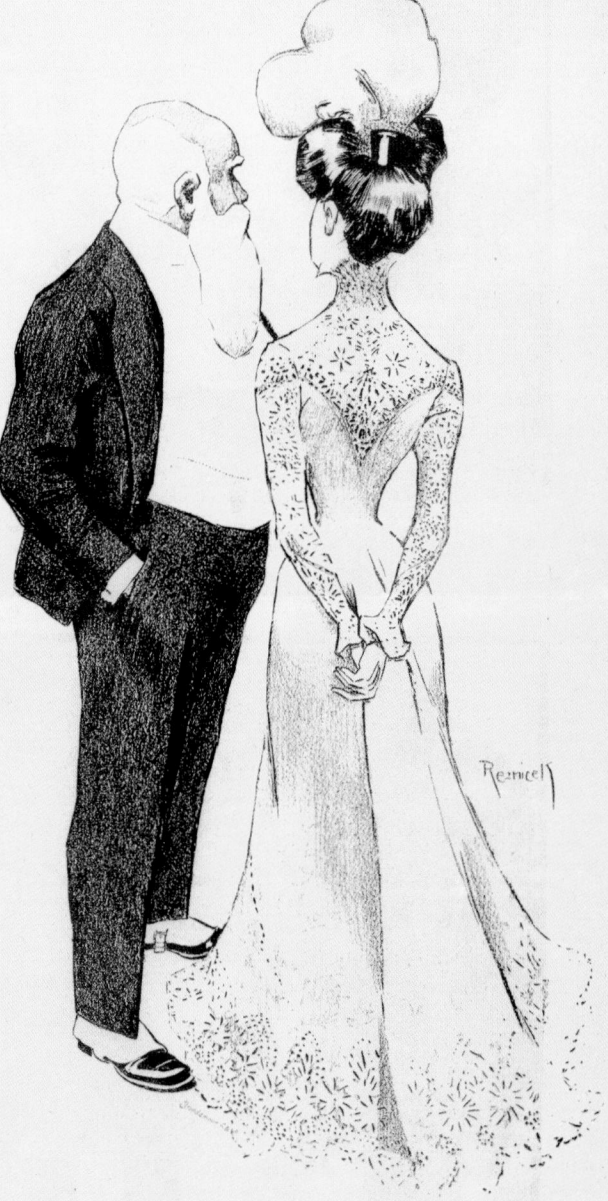

Reznicek

„Wie alt sind Ihre Kinder, Baron?" — „Man muß sich vor ihnen schon genieren."

CAT. 88 Ferdinand Freiherr von Reznicek (Austrian, 1868–1909)
"Ein braver vater" ["A Fine Father"], in:
Simplicissimus, vol. 5, no. 10 (1900), p. 79
Special Collections and Rare Books, University of Minnesota,
Minneapolis, Minnesota

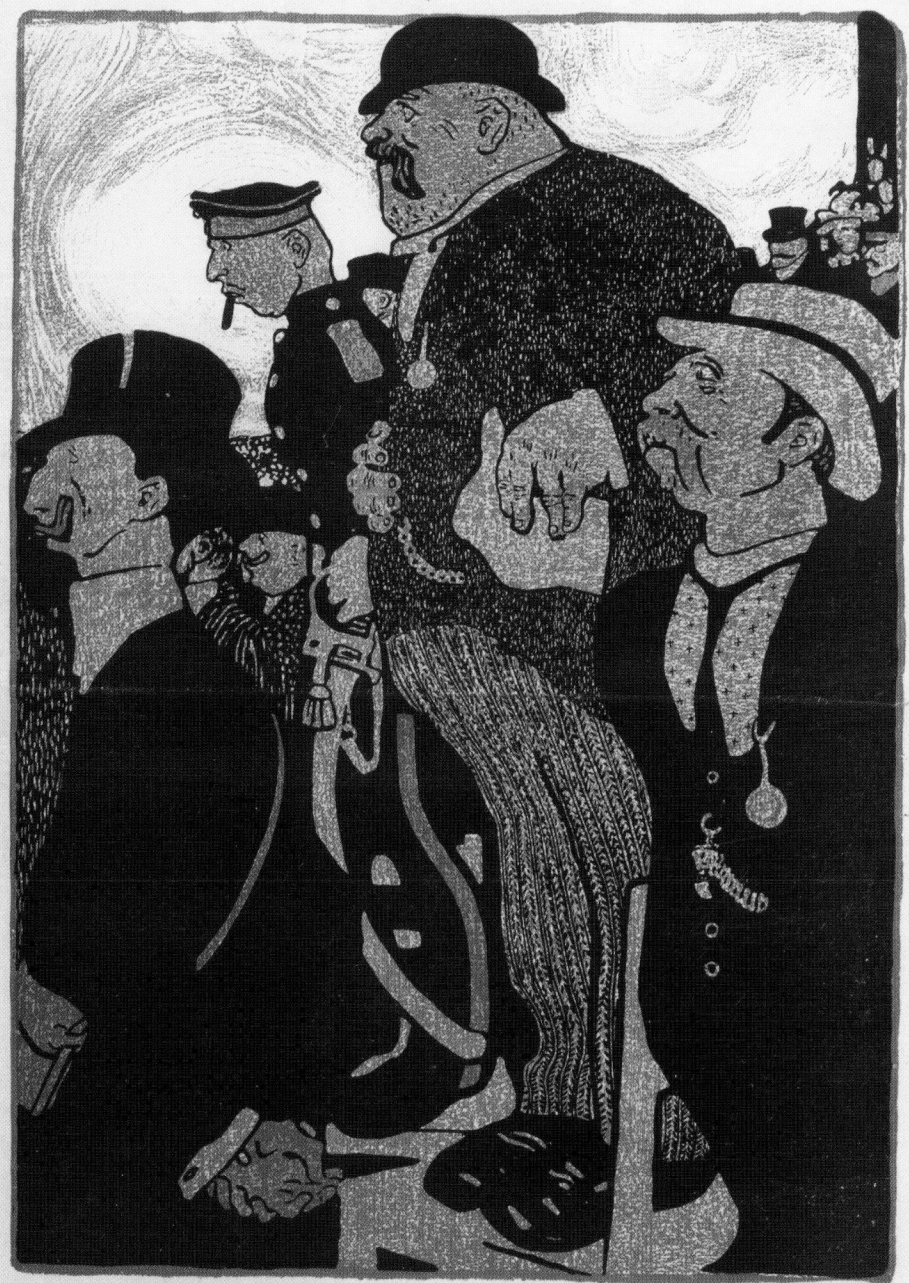

CAT. 84   Bruno Paul (German 1874-1968)
"Der Münchner beim Rennen" ["A Munich Citizen at the Races"], in:
Simplicissimus, vol. 5, no. 14 (14 May 1900)
Special Collections and Rare Books, University of Minnesota,
Minneapolis, Minnesota

[12] Nancy Troy, *Modernism and the Decorative Arts in France: Art Nouveau to Le Corbusier* (New Haven; London: Yale University Press, 1991: 45).

[13] "Art industriel," *L'Art décoratif* 1 (March 1899): 254. Cited in: Ibid.

[14] Perhaps the most infamous of these reviews was written by Arsène Alexandre for *Le Figaro*. Appearing on 28 December 1895, the review opined: "All this is confused, incoherent, almost unhealthy. All this is one moment too sloppy and the next too proper, either something diseased coming from a man who doesn't know his *métier*, or a caricature of English art. It all smacks of the vicious Englishman, the Jewess addicted to morphine, or the cunning Belgian, or a good mixture of those three poisons." Cited in: Ibid.: 26.

[15] "Der Bing'sche Pavillon l'Art Nouveau auf der Weltausstellung," *Dekorative Kunst* 3 (1900): 490-92. Cited in: Ibid.: 32.

[16] Julius Meier-Graefe, "Floral-Linear," *Dekorative Kunst* 4 (1899): 169. Citied in: Kathryn Bloom Hiesinger, ed., *Art Nouveau in Munich: Masters of Jugendstil from the Stadtmuseum, Munich, and other Public and Private Collections* (Philadelphia: Philadelphia Museum of Art and Prestel Verlag, Munich: 1988: 19).

[17] Robert Jensen, *Marketing Modernism in Fin-de-Siècle Europe* (Princeton: Princeton University Press, 1994: 241); Troy, op. cit. : 45.

[18] Jenson, ibid.: 242.

[19] Troy, op. cit.: 43.

[20] "Korrespondenzen: Paris," *Dekorative Kunst* 2 (1899): 215. Cited in: Ibid.: 44.

[21] "Chronique," *L'Art décoratif* 1 (February 1899): 250. Cited in: Ibid.: 43.

[22] Julius Meier-Graefe, *Modern Art: Being a Contribution to a New System of Aesthetics* (London: W. Heinemann; New York: G.P. Putnam's Sons, 1908: 321). Meier-Graefe was well able to distinguish among the hands that contributed to *Simplicissimus* and *Jugend*. In his study *Modern Art*, Meier-Graefe wrote: "The richness of effect they [Paul and Wilke] get with three or four colours, a skilful use of overprint, dots, squares &c., is amazing. Wilke is the most distinguished of the two, the Whistler of this little noisy world. Paul prefers the bold surface, which he cloisonnés with fresh tones, but Wilke attempts more discreet charms." Ibid.: 322. In an October 1896 article for *The Studio*, concerning recent designs in continental bookbinding, Meier-Graefe also addressed directly two of the German artists working in Munich, commenting: "Germany possesses only two artists engaged in book work – Th. Heine and Otto Eckmann, both of Munich. The former sent a very amusing drawing for the cover of a German translation of *Demi-Vierges* (A. Langen, Munich); and the latter displayed covers for various books published by S. Fischer, of Berlin, including *Vome Weibe* (the design for which reminds one of Walter Crane), *Eine glückliche Ehe, Maria*, &c. Eckmann has lately designed a cover for the firm of Bruckman, of Munich, and is at present employed on a set of bindings for *editions de luxe*, which give one an excellent idea of his fine gifts." A. J. Meier-Graefe, "Some Recent Continental Bookbindings," *Studio* 9 (October 1896): 38.

[23] It should be remarked that Biais signed his posters in two forms—one including a circle around his name. It is not, as of yet, clear if the circle is a significant distinguishing mark.

[24] It should be noted that in the 1884 catalogue of the annual exhibition of the *Arts Incohérents* a curious reference is made to a Maurice Blais. While the spelling of the last name is different and Biais himself would have been only twelve at the time, it is not entirely impossible that the reference is to him. *Catalogue Illustré de l'Exposition des Arts Incohérents* (Paris: E. Bernard et cie, 1884: 29).

[25] For a detailed account of the affair see: Catherine Krahmer, "Pan and Toulouse-Lautrec," *Print Quarterly* 10.4 (December 1993): 392-7.

[26] Cited in: Ibid.: 395.

[27] Ibid.

[28] *Pan* 1.2 (June 1895): 99-100. Cited in: Ibid.: 396.

[29] Bodenhausen to Lichtwark (16 July 1895), Kunsthalle, Hamburg, Lichtwark-Archiv. Cited in: Ibid.

[30] Robert Jensen, *Marketing Modernism in Fin-de-Siècle Europe* (Princeton: Princeton University Press, 1994: 237).

[31] Meier-Graefe contributed to *Die Zukunft* and *Das Atelier*. Ibid.: 242.

[32] Ibid.: 241.

[33] Cited in: Ibid.

[34] Meier-Graefe, *Modern Art*. op. cit.: 317.

[36] Cited in: Robert Justin Goldstein, *Censorship of Political Caricature in Nineteenth-Century France* (Kent; London: The Kent State University Press, 1989: 10).

[36] Ann Taylor Allen, *Satire and Society in Wilhelmine Germany: Kladderadatsch & Simplicissimus, 1891-1914* (Lexington, KY: University Press of Kentucky, 1984: 35).

[37] Ibid.: 39, 41.

[38] Both Germany and France were among the ten signatory nations of the first Berne Convention for the Protection of Literary and Artistic Works, which was ratified on 9 September 1886, and eligible for enforcement on 5 December 1887. *Guide to the Berne Convention for the Protection of Literary and Artistic Works (Paris Act, 1971)* (Geneva: World Intellectual Property Organization, 1978: 6). For the history of the Berne Convention see also: *The Berne Convention for the Protection of Literary and Artistic Works, from 1886 to 1986* (Geneva: International Bureau of Intellectual Property, 1986).

[39] It should be noted that it remains a possibility that Biais secured permission for the images he copied.

[40] "The Man in the Street," *New York Times* (2 June 1901): SM1.

[41] "A Poster Artist: Maurice Biais at the New Gallery of Williams," *New York Times* (19 October 1901): 9.

[42] Cited in: Goldstein, op. cit.: 10.

[43] (15 March 1912). Cited in: Taylor Allen, op. cit.: 226.

[44] Ibid.: 3, 34.

[45] Kenworth Moffett, *Meier-Graefe as Art Critic* (Munchen: Prestel-Verlag, 1973: 15).

[46] S. Heller, "Late, Great *Simplicissimus*," *Print* 33 (September 1979): 36.

[47] Taylor Allen, op. cit.: 226.

[48] Ibid.: 228.

[49] A *New York Times* review of Biais's 1901 exhibition at the Max Williams gallery comments: "the taste for owning posters [in France] is on the increase, and especially country houses are apt to be decorated with them." "A Poster Artist," op. cit.: 9.

[50] Catherine Krahmer argues that a founding initiative of the PAN Society, which published the journal, was to revive the art of printmaking. Krahmer, op. cit.: 392.

[51] J.A. Clarke, "Munch, Liebermann, and the question of etched 'reproductions,'" *Visual Resources* 16.1 (2000): 28.

[52] Taylor Allen, op. cit.: 43.

[53] Ibid.: 44.

[54] Ibid.: 35.

[55] Meier-Graefe, *Modern Art*, op. cit.: 316-17.

[56] For critical discussion of the role of the author see especially: Roland Barthes, "The Death of the Author" (1968) and Michel Foucault, "What is an Author" (1969).

[57] Copyright protection and compliance with the trade agreements was also a heated point of contention between Germany and the United States following Germany's participation in the Louisiana Purchase Exposition. See: "We Get German Brains for Free," *New York Times* (16 March 1905): 2.

Paris 1900:
Art Nouveau Ceramics

Elizabeth J. Fowler

In the nineteenth century, Paris held five great exhibitions: 1855, 1867, 1878, 1889, and 1900. The last exhibition, held in 1900, was both a celebration of the achievements of the nineteenth century and an optimistic celebration of the progress and modernity of the new century. In the arts, this exhibition is best remembered for art nouveau, the "modern style" seen in both architecture and the decorative arts. Beginning in Belgium, in the early 1890s, the movement spread to France and eventually to other countries such as Germany, Austria, Scotland, Italy, as well as several Scandinavian and Eastern European countries. The Exposition Universelle (1900) celebrated the achievements of those working in this new style and brought their accomplishments to the attention of a wider public, especially those that rode the new *métro* and experienced firsthand Hector Guimard's art nouveau stations.

Art nouveau, which literally means "new art," was the first truly international movement in the decorative arts. Based on principles established by the English Arts and Crafts movement, art nouveau was a separate movement that also sought to reform the decorative arts. The proponents and practitioners of the movement advocated for newness and originality, a return to quality craftsmanship, and looked to other cultures, especially Japan, for aesthetic inspiration.[1] Many identify art nouveau solely by one of its dominant stylistic motifs – the whiplash curve – and this does appear quite frequently in furniture, prints, and fabric design. In ceramics, however, art nouveau manifested itself in a search for new forms, new glazes, and the ability to create a unique expression in a very traditional medium.

There were three major types of French art nouveau ceramics: those that were inspired by Chinese and Japanese forms, glazes, and techniques, such as China's Song Dynasty porcelains or the *wabi sabi* aesthetic of Japanese tea wares.[2] Some of these were used in Asian art to create an entirely new aesthetic while others employed a more literal interpretation of East Asian art, as seen in the interest in slithering creatures such as lizards, like those on Lachenal's *Lizard Vase* (ca. 1895-1900) (cat. 53; p. 144) or

DETAIL   Edmond Lachenal (French, 1855-1930) (see cat. 53; p. 144)

Lizard Vase, ca. 1895-1900

Earthenware

Jason Jacques Inc.

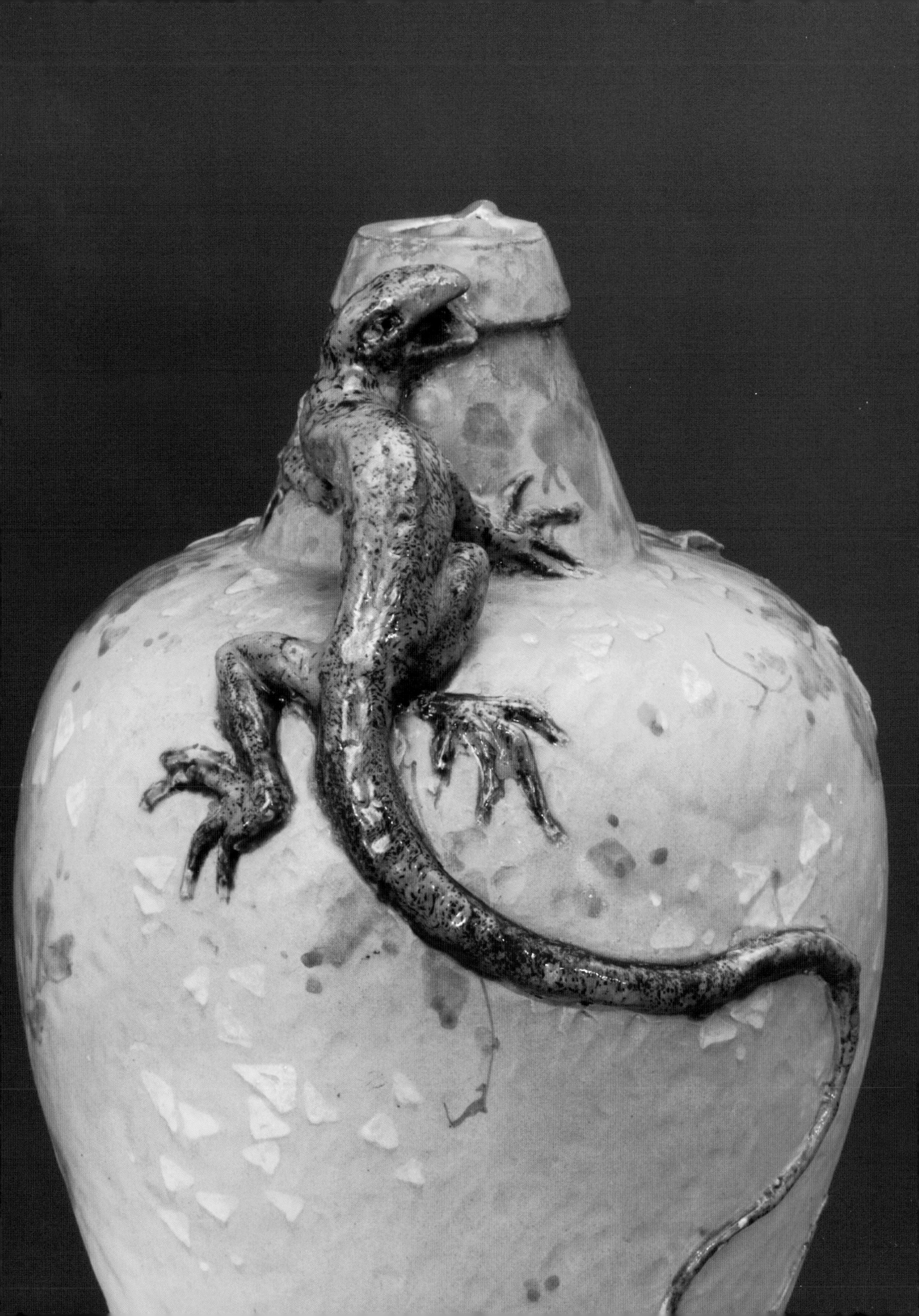

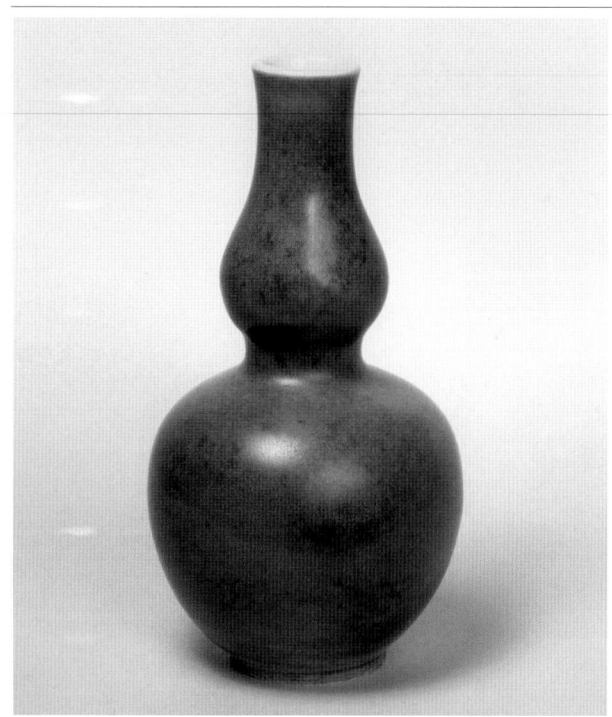

the menacing dragon that perches atop the lip of Eduard Stellmacher's *Amphora Eastern Dragon Vase* of 1899 (cat. 109; p. 11).[3] The second type of wares were those that were, to use a twentieth-century term, "ceramic sculpture." These forms were not based on vessels or functional objects, but were instead three-dimensional sculptures in clay, primarily based on figural forms. Given the interests of art nouveau ceramists and their connections with symbolist artists, such as Auguste Rodin and Paul Gauguin, it is not surprising that many of symbolists motifs and conceits appear in these works. The third group is the porcelains that displayed typical art nouveau motifs, such as those produced by Bing and Grøndahl, Royal Copenhagen, and Sèvres, which are not represented in this show. The division between these groupings, however, is not absolute as there was tremendous overlap between them.

The true art nouveau ceramist worked either in a designated "art pottery," either an independent entity of a branch of a firm or company or were independent artists who ran their own studios. Sèvres and Haviland & Co.'s contribution to art nouveau was less in the pieces it produced than in the artists they trained: Taxile Doat and Albert Dammouse spent time working at Sèvres as did Ernest Chaplet, who also worked at Haviland & Cie (Haviland & Co. after 1891), as did Auguste Delaherche. These three men, Ernest Chaplet, Auguste Delaherche, and Pierre Adrien Dalpayrat, were the three leading art potters in France, closely followed by other quality artists such as Edmond Lachenal, Clement Massier, and the Carriès school, centered around the ceramist Jean Carriès.

Ernest Chaplet began his career as a porcelain painter at Sèvres in 1848; he was hired by Haviland & Cie. in 1875; and he established his own studio in 1885.[4] While at Haviland in the early 1880s, he rediscovered the secret of the Chinese *sang de bœuf* (oxblood) glaze, for which he would receive recognition at the 1889 Paris Exposition, and by the 1890s, the beginning of the art nouveau period, he was already an established potter known for his simple forms and experimental glazes.[5] Although art nouveau is often linked with *Japonisime*, or the interest in the art and culture of Japan, Chaplet also looked back to perhaps the

FIG. 32   *Vase*, from Jingdezhen, China, 1700-1800
Porcelain with streaked *flambé* glaze, 4 x 7½ in. (10.2 x 19.2 cm)
©Victoria and Albert Museum, London, Salting Bequest

world's greatest ceramists, the Chinese. The Chinese developed extremely delicate and refined stoneware and porcelains with innovative glazes, including the *sang de bœuf* glaze, which were developed during the Song Dynasty (960-1279) but produced well into the modern period (fig. 32). In 1899, Chaplet, using the *sang de bœuf* glaze he had rediscovered in France, in the early 1880s, created a delicate and innovate porcelain vessel.[6]

Two other French ceramists who were also interested in innovative glazes were Taxile Doat and Pierre Adrien Dalpayrat. Doat worked at Sèvres from 1877 to 1905, mainly producing historical revival styles rendered in the *pâte-sur-pâte* technique.[7] His art nouveau wares – those that demonstrated his interest in innovation and originality – were produced in his own atelier. Doat's *Blood Gourd Vase* from 1907 also employs the *sang de bœuf* glaze, but instead of Chaplet's simple form, Doat applies it to the body of a naturalistically rendered gourd, complete with bulbous green warts (cat. 28; p. 145). Dalpayrat's *Gourd* from 1900, is, as the name suggests, also in the form of a gourd, although slightly larger than Doat's piece (cat. 25; p. 139). Instead of firing the ware in an anaerobic environment, Dalpayrat introduced oxygen into the kiln, which allowed for the creation of glazes streaked with blue and green, or what is known as *flambé*, an attempt to imitate the blue and reddish purple of the Chinese Jun glaze.[8] Dalpayrat became so well known for his glazes that the term "*rouge Dalpayrat*" or "Dalpayrat red" was coined to describe his typical glaze; an example of this "Dalpayrat red" can also be seen in his *Teapot* from 1898, which was exhibited at the 1900 exposition (cat. 24; p. 147).[9] Two other examples of the *flambé* glaze can be seen in the *Petit Vase* of 1900, produced by Sèvres, and the *Genie Bottle*, produced in 1895 by Edmond Lachenal (cats. 54 and 93; pp. 148 and 149).

Jean Carriès was another well-known art nouveau artist who actually trained as a sculptor before turning to stoneware in the late 1880s.[10] Carriès' *Laughing Man Mask* from 1891, one of his sculptural pieces, resembles a Japanese Noh mask, except that it represents the wrinkled, mustached, and bearded face of a European man

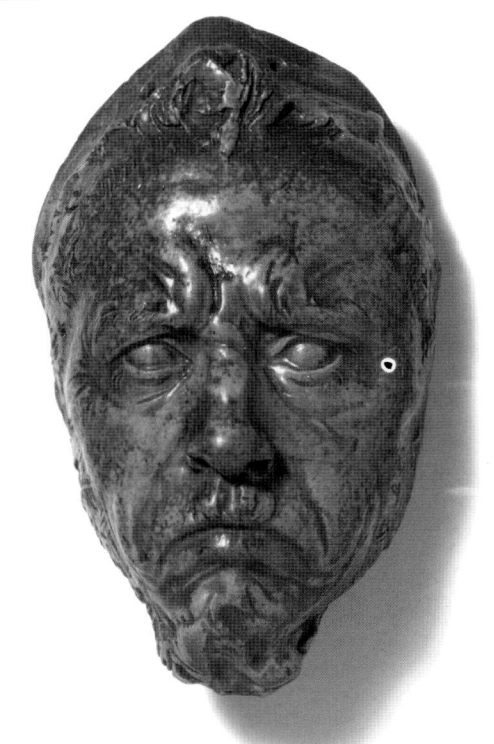

FIG. 33 Jean Joseph Marie Carriès (French, 1855-1894)
Mask, 1890-1892
Salt-glazed stoneware, 10 x 9 ¹/₅ x 6 ²/₉ in. (25.6 x 25.4 x 15.8 cm)
©Victoria and Albert Museum, London
Given by Prince Antoine Bibesco and Mons. Paul Morand

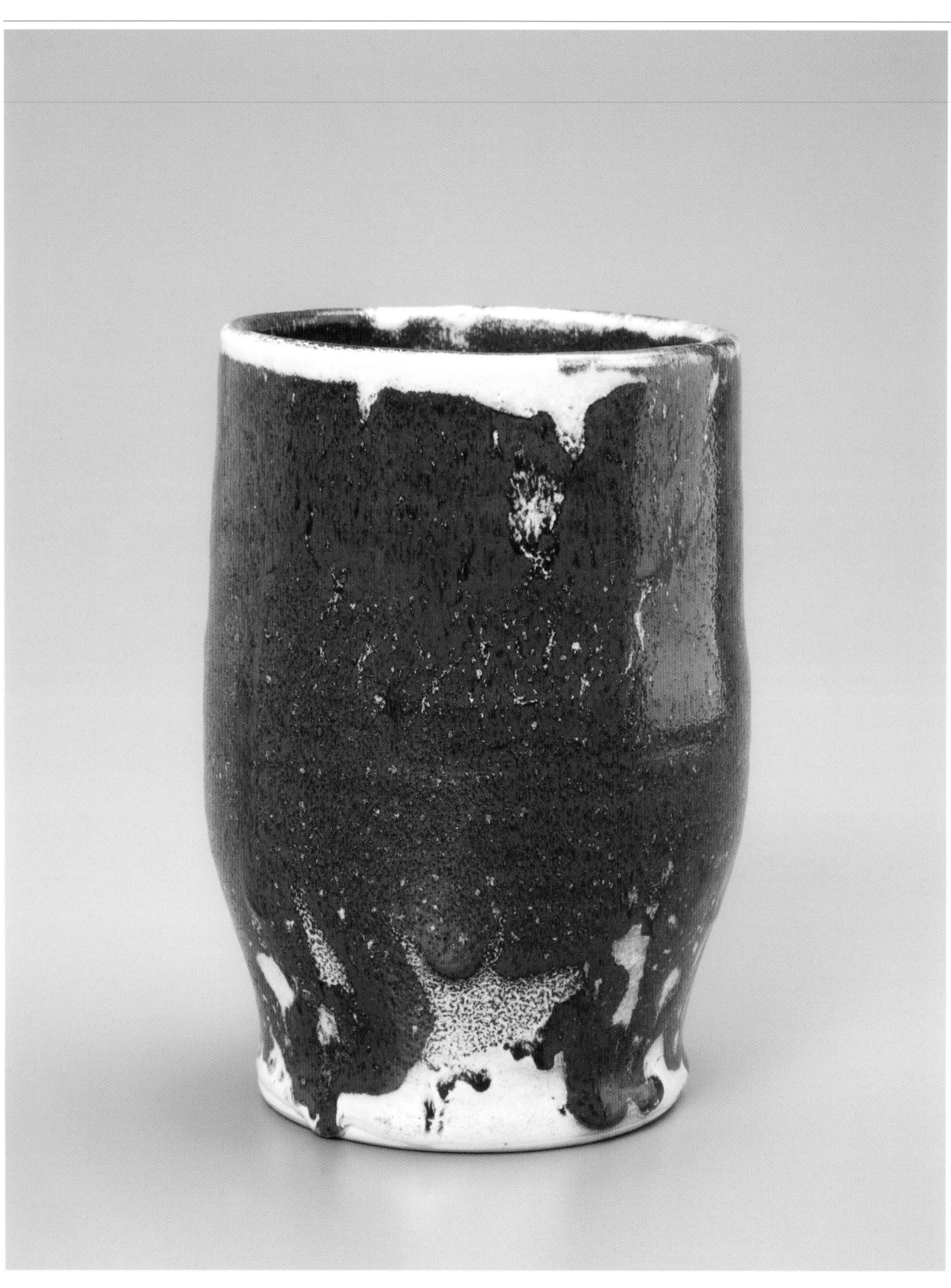

CAT. 18   Ernest Chaplet (French, 1835-1909)
Studio Vase, 1899
Porcelain, 7 x 5 in. (17.8 x 12.7 cm)
Jason Jacques Inc.

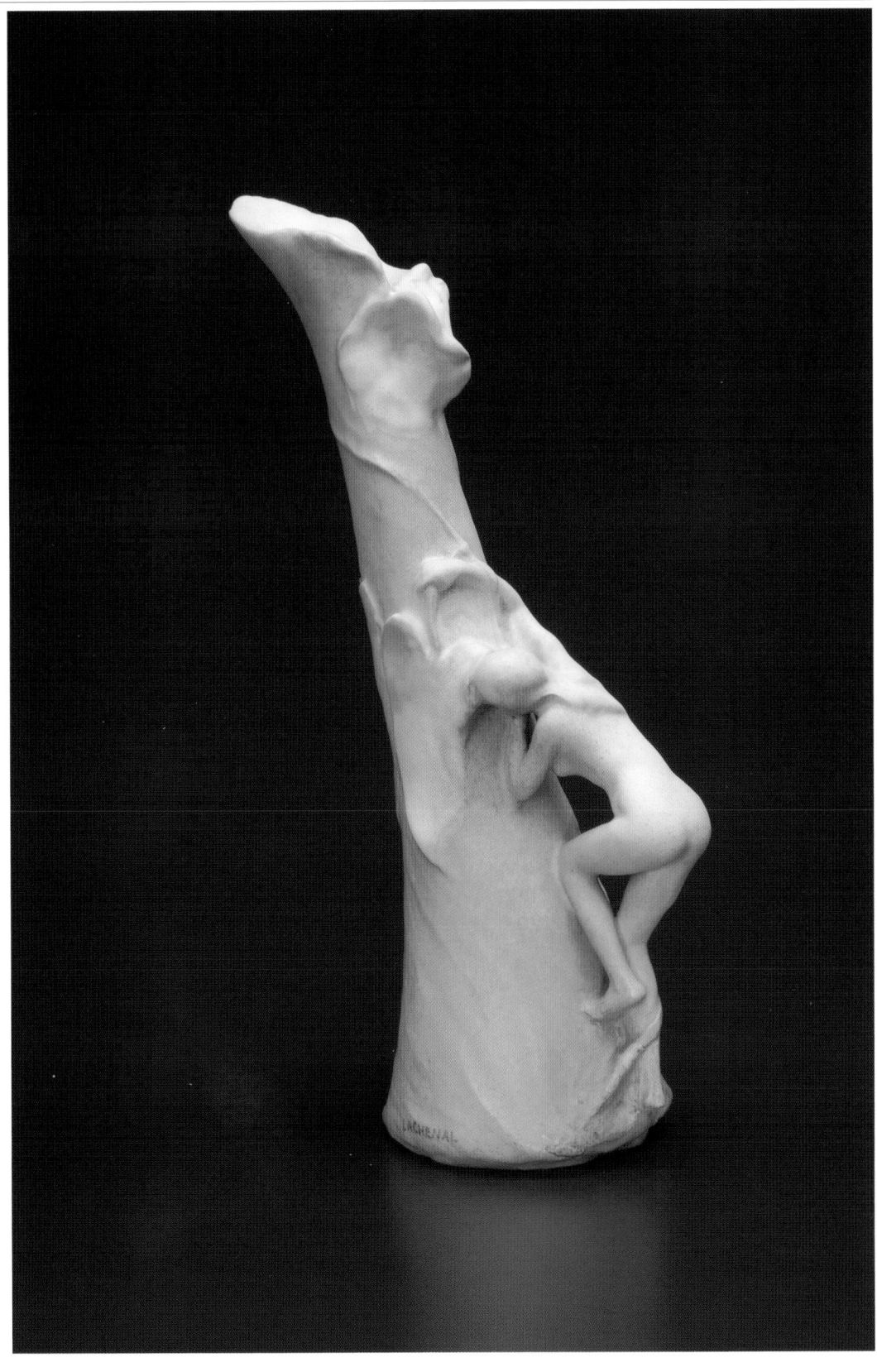

CAT. 34   Agnes de Frumerie for Lachenal (Swedish, 1869-1937)
Nymph and Lily Vase, 1897
Earthenware, 14 x 8 x 4½ in. (35.6 x 20.32 x 11.43 cm)
Jason Jacques Inc.

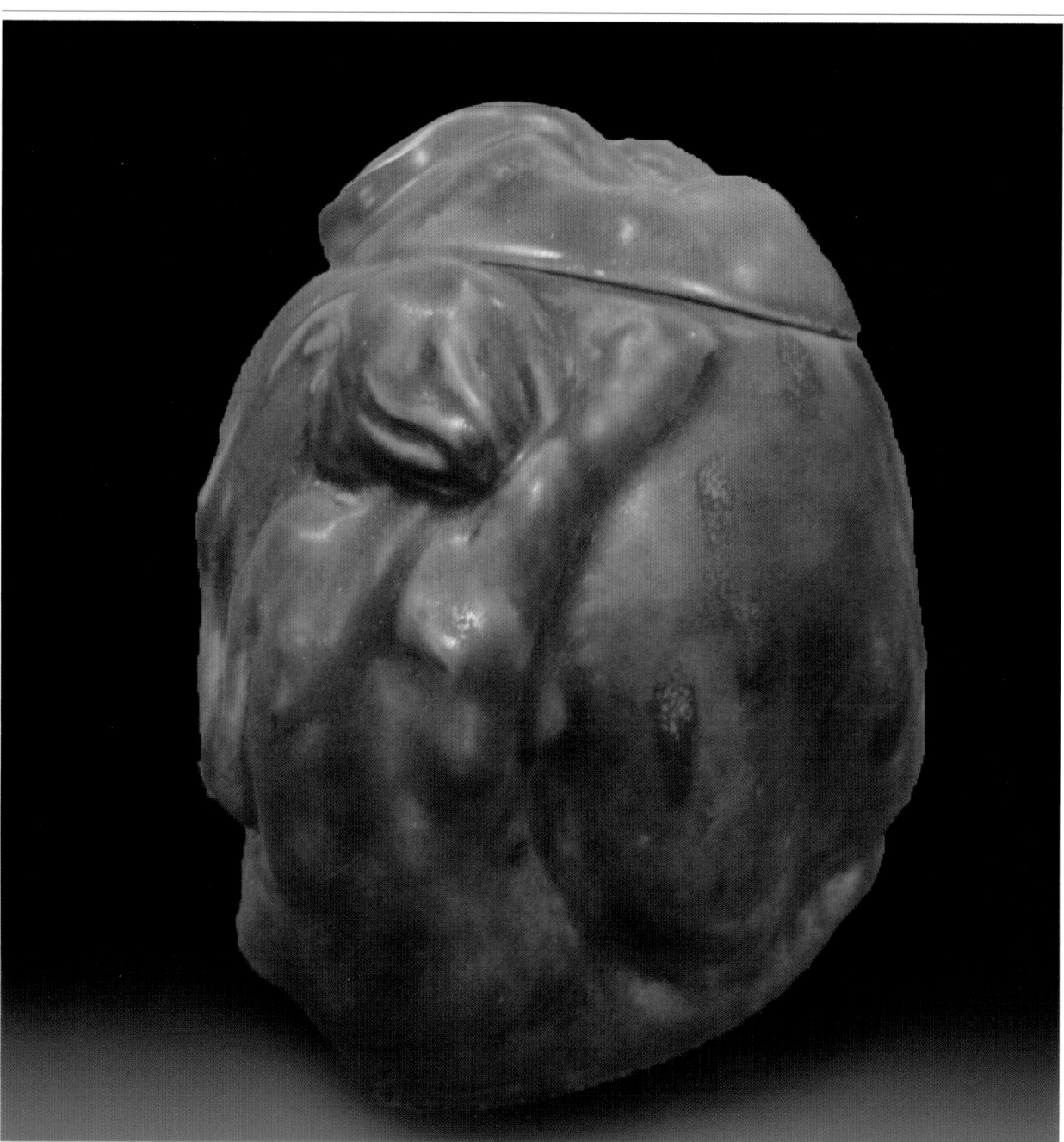

CAT. 12   François-Rupert Carabin (French, 1862-1932)
Woman with Gourd, 1894-1895
Enameled stoneware, 6 x 6½ x 4 in. (15 x 15 x 10 cm)
Jane Voorhees Zimmerli Art Museum

that would fit seamlessly into the groupings of masked figures in a James Ensor's painting, the famous Belgian symbolist (cat. 16; p. 143). Although Carriès died in 1894, his influence was still felt in 1900: he was still recognized as an important leader in his medium and he had dedicated followers, such as Paul Jeanneney and Émile Grittel, known as the Carriès school. Jeanneney's *Double Gourd Vase* of 1900 is a double-gourd form, like the eighteenth-century porcelain vase from Jingdezhen, China, but combines this form with the *wabi sabi* aesthetic found in Japanese stoneware, which Jenneney and Carriès both collected. (cat. 52; p. 146) [11] The dripping glaze and the irregularity of the vessel form, dented in several places, indicate the aesthetic link with Japan. Georges Hoentschel, another member of the Carriès school, was an interior designer who sometimes also worked as a pottery designer. He wrote an article about Carriès that was published in 1900 in the influential French journal *Art et Décoration*, which reproduces a photograph of two of Carriès masks, one of which is either the piece in this show or a very similar version, and other examples of both his figural and nonfigural work in clay. [12] Another Carriès mask in the collection of the Victoria and Albert Museum in London, shows another male figure rendered in similar naturalistic detail, except this time with a pouty frown (fig. 33; p. 133).

Other popular themes in art nouveau ceramics are floral motifs and the combination of flowers and the female form, known in symbolist circles as the *femme fleur*. One such piece, the 1897 vase designed by Swedish sculptor Agnes de Frumerie and executed in clay by Edmond Lachenal, represents a woman climbing the side of the vase surrounded by white lilies (cat. 34; p. 135). This piece suggests a functional form, but the emphasis is more on the interplay between the woman and the flower instead of on the vessel, which serves primarily as a background setting. The whiteness of the glaze suggests the female form as a type of blossom, but there are tendrils – one wrapped around her right leg and one she grasps with her right hand – that also suggest the figure as a blossom in corporeal form. As art historian Elizabeth Menon has demonstrated, this type of imagery was very

popular in France during the nineteenth century. [13] There are two layers of meaning in this vase: the first is the symbolism of the white lily; the second is the representation of the woman as a flower. The white lily is associated with purity and the Virgin Mary in a Christian context, and seems to suggest the innocence and goodness of the woman on the vase. Lachenal also made use of white flowers set against a mint green background in another piece in this exhibition, the 1899 *Floral Vase* (cat. 55; p. 138).

The woman-as-flower, however, could have more sinister implications, as developed by Charles-Pierre Baudelaire's work *Les Fleurs du mal*, first published in 1857, suggesting the link between women and nature, raw sexuality, and feminine desire. [14] It is uncertain whether de Frumerie, given her gender, intended these latter interpretations, but contemporary audiences may have interpreted it in this manner nonetheless. A variant of the woman-as-flower theme, the woman-as-fruit, or *femmes-fruits*, is suggested by another ceramic sculpture in the exhibition done in 1894-1895 by François-Rupert Carabin. His *Woman with Gourd* links the female form with this fruit in much the same way as de Frumerie (cat. 12). Like other Carabin works in a variety of media, there are subtle sexual overtones in this piece as the sleeping woman presses her nude body into the fleshy surface of the gourd. While gourds were a popular form in East Asian art and were embraced by French art nouveau artists, none resonate with symbolist meaning in quite the same manner as Carabin's *femme-fruit*. [15]

One of the largest displays for viewing French art nouveau ceramics was the Sèvres Manufactory section of the French palace located on the Esplanade des Invalides. The Sèvres Manufactory, established in 1740, in Vincennes, France, is still in existence today. While their reputation primarily rests on their eighteenth- and nineteenth-century porcelains produced in a rococo or neo-classical style, they were not immune to the aesthetic innovations of art nouveau. [16] Under the directorship of Alexandre Sandier (1897-1916), Sèvres would produce wares that were increasingly inventive, especially in stoneware. [17] Marie-Noëlle Pinot de Villechenon, a curator at

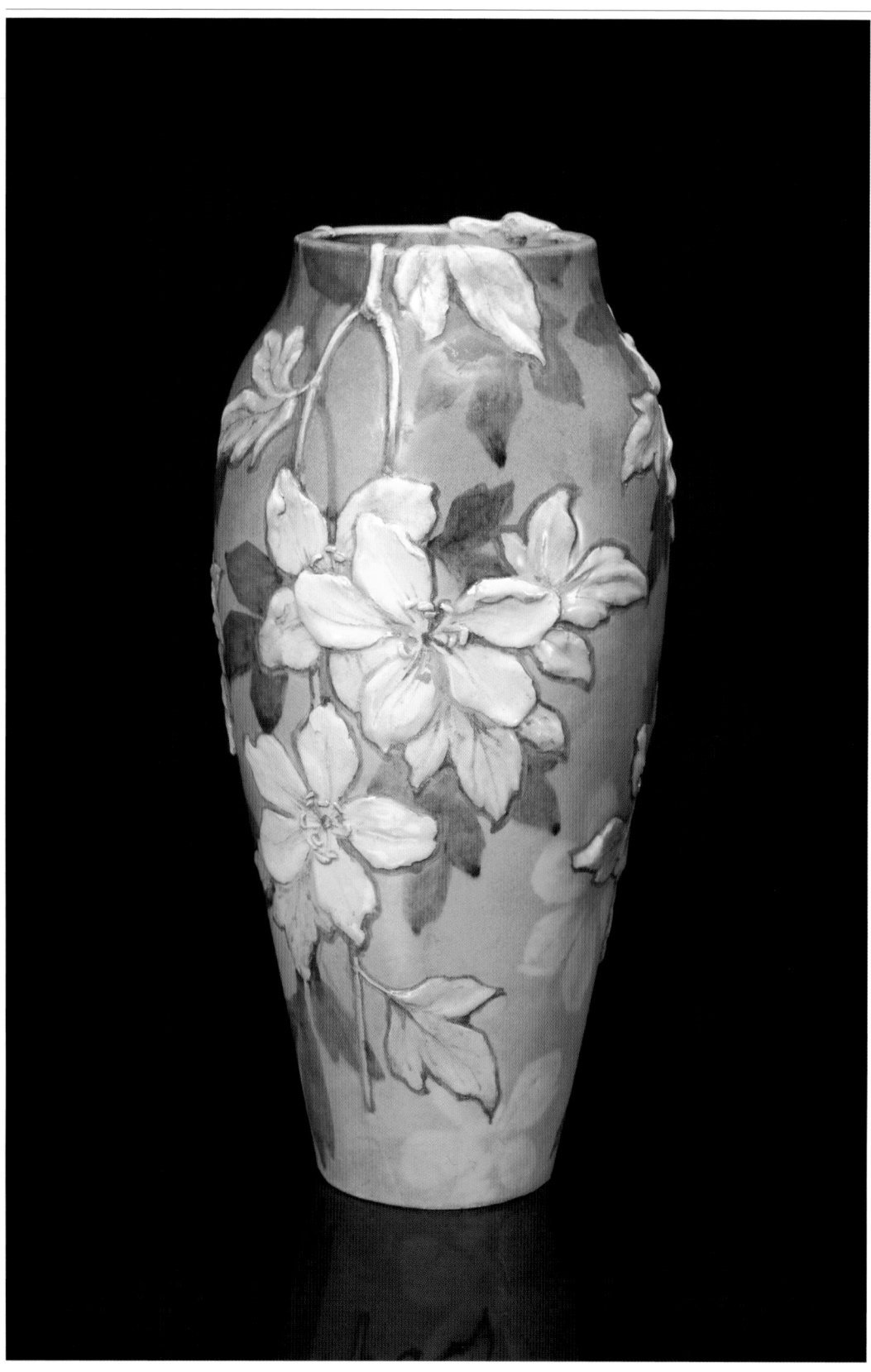

CAT. 55 Edmond Lachenal (French, 1855-1930)
Floral Vase, ca. 1899
Matte and glossy glazed earthenware, 16 x 18½ in. (40.6 x 47 cm)
Laurie and David Weiner Collection

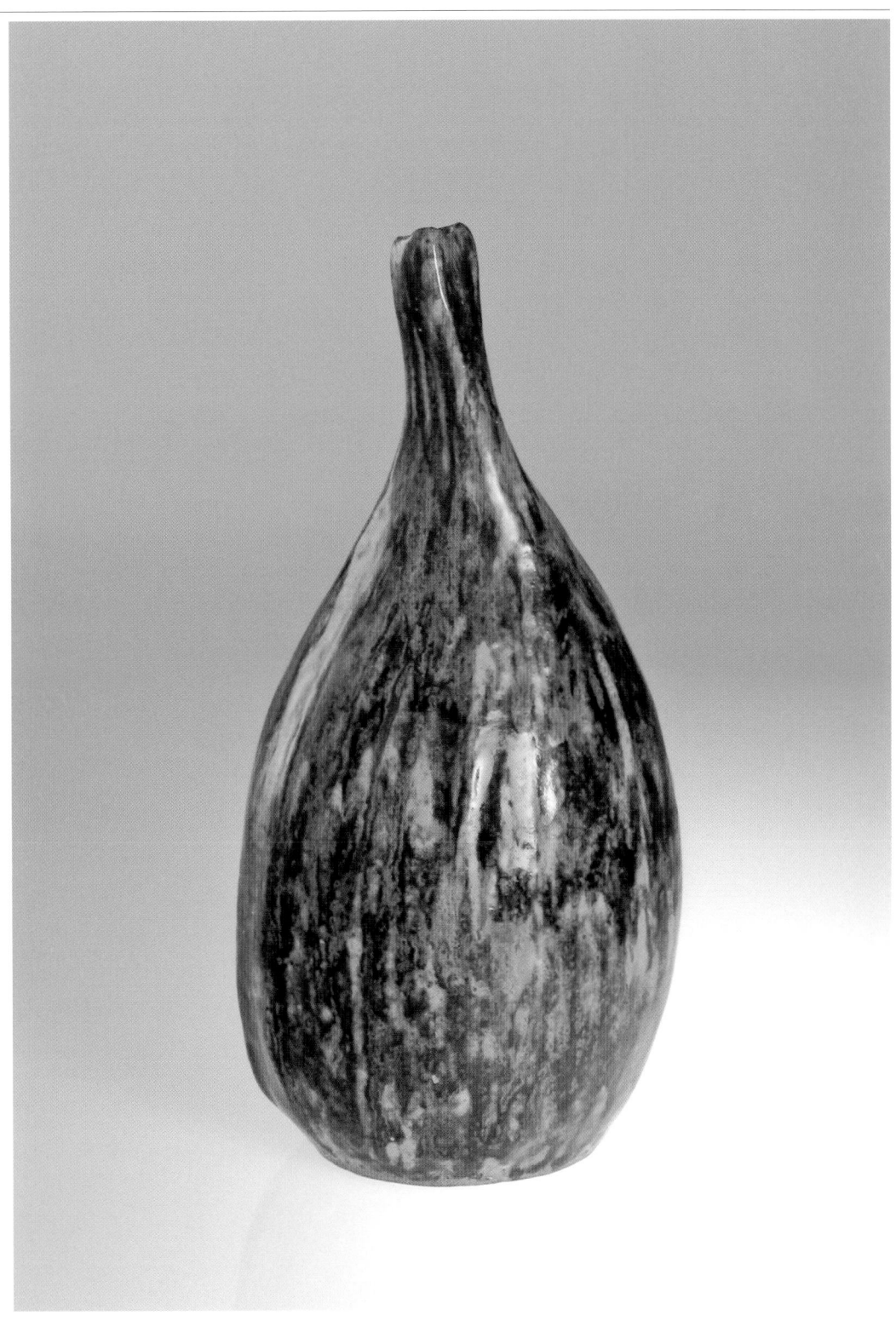

CAT. 25   Adrien Pierre Dalpayrat (French, 1844-1910)
Gourd, 1900
Stoneware, 8¾ x 6½ in. (22.2 x 16.5 cm)
Eunice and Herbert Shatzman Collection

the Sèvres Museum, felt that their porcelains were not the best art nouveau creations:

> [a]ctually, the adoption of the Art Nouveau style by Sèvres was not wholly convincing. The simple, restrained shapes imposed on porcelain did not lend themselves happily to the fantastic, sometimes frenzied, forms of decoration so suited to contemporary works in wood, glass, or metal. Only stoneware allowed more freedom.[18]

One piece in this show, the previously mentioned *Petit Vase* done in 1900, illustrates that many of Sèvres porcelains, especially those that employed a *flambé* glaze, were still extremely high-quality creations (cat. 93; p. 149).

Sèvres also exhibited many small sculptures in porcelain biscuit at the 1900 Exposition Universelle. One of these sets, titled *Jeu de l'écharpe* [Play of the Scarf] was a series of several small female figurines dancing, holding torches, or playing musical instruments.[19] The "scarf dance" was associated with the American dancer Loïe Fuller (fig. 34), who had her own pavilion at the 1900 exposition and who is also represented in another piece in this show by Carabin. His work, done in 1897-1898 and simply titled *Loïe Fuller*, represents a much more dynamic representation of Fuller dancing (cat. 13; p. 68). The Sèvres piece, designed by Agathon Léonard, suggests some flowing art nouveau curves, but Carabin's piece represents Fuller in a chrysalis of undulating, tense movement. Fuller's dances were seen as a living embodiment of art nouveau and Carabin's work, much more than the Sèvres pieces, directly communicates her energy and elegance.

In closing, it is clear when examining these ceramic wares that art nouveau produced much more than objects adorned with vines, tendrils, and whiplash curves. It was an international movement that sought to revitalize the decorative arts and educate both artists and designers about the expressive possibilities of various media. The movement also embraced the Wagnerian ideal of the *Gesamtkunstwerk*, a "total work of art," where a variety of media would co-exist harmoniously in a single, united space. The wares in this show, many of which were a tour de force in the ceramic medium, were intended to be displayed in a sensitively designed art nouveau interior. Without understanding their intended context, the pieces themselves function only as independent objects; as art nouveau objects, however, it is important to remember how they would have been marketed and displayed in 1900. One of the icons of the art nouveau movement, the advertising poster done by Maurice Biais in 1897-1898 for La Maison Moderne shop, perfectly illustrates this point. (fig. 27; p. 112) Here we see a well-dressed woman in the interior of La Maison Moderne closely examining their art nouveau wares. She is standing in front of a large cabinet filled with ceramic vessels; two ceramic vases are also exhibited in a niche along the back wall. Each piece is designed as an independent objet d'art, but in this poster we see how in this Parisian shop interior they become part of the larger *Gesamtkunstwerk*.

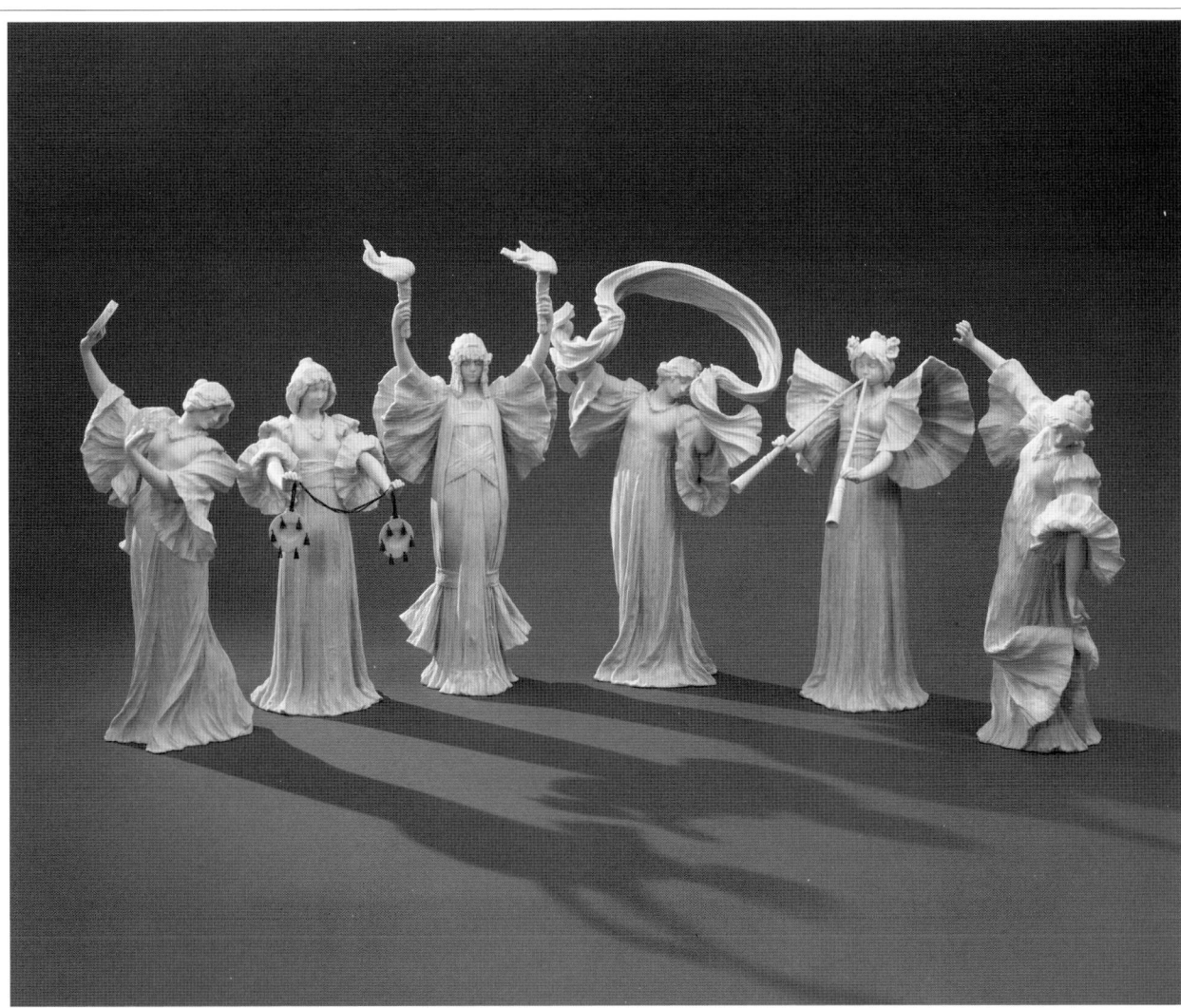

Endnotes

[1] For additional information on the international art nouveau movement, see the 2000 exhibition catalogue *Art Nouveau, 1890-1914*. Paul Greenhalgh, ed. (London: Victoria and Albert Publications, 2002).

[2] *Wabi sabi* is a difficult term to translate into English. A good working definition is by Andrew Juniper in his book *Wabi Sabi: The Japanese Art of Impermanence* (Boston: Tuttle Publishing, 2003: 1-2). He states: "[w]abi sabi embodies the Zen nihilist cosmic view and seeks beauty in the imperfections found as all things, in a constant state of flux, evolve from nothing and devolve back to nothing. Within this perpetual movement nature leaves arbitrary tracks for us to contemplate, and it is these random flaws and irregularities that offer a model for the modest and humble wabi sabi expression of beauty."

[3] Amphora was founded in 1892 in what is today the Czech Republic. This piece, while not made in France, bears an impressed "Paris 1900" mark, which means that it was made for the Exposition Universelle.

[4] Claire Cass. "Ernest Chaplet," in *Masterpieces of French Art Pottery, 1885-1910* (New York: Jason Jacques: n.p.).

[5] Ibid.

[6] The most complete source of information on Chaplet remains Jean d'Albis's book *Ernest Chaplet: 1835-1909* (Paris: Les Presses de la Connaissance, 1976).

[7] Cass, op. cit. "Taxile Doat," n.p.

[8] Contemporary critics writing about the Paris 1900 exhibition will use both the term *flammé(e)* (*une flammé* is a blaze) and *flambé(e)* (*une flambée* is a flame) when describing this particular glaze; *flambé* is the more established term, but their similar spellings and meanings explain the co-existence of the two terms even today. *Sang de bœuf* and *flambé* glazes are both copper oxides: when fired in an aerobic (oxygen-rich) kiln, the glaze will fire red; when fired in an anaerobic (reduction) kiln, the glaze will fire blue and/or green. See *Materials and Techniques in the Decorative Arts: An Illustrated Dictionary*, Lucy Trench, ed. (Chicago: University of Chicago Press, 2000: 169, 311, 426). The Jun glaze, like the copper red *sang de boeuf*, was developed in China during the Song Dynasty (960-1279). According to Marie-Noëlle Pinot de Villechenon, a curator at the Sèvres Museum, the *flambé* (she uses the term *flammé*) glaze was first discovered in France at Sèvres in 1845 and was perfected by Georges Vogt in the 1880s. See *Sèvres: Porcelain From the Sèvres Museum, 1740 to the Present Day* (London: Lund Humphries Publishers, 1997: 102-3).

[9] A photograph of the teapot appears in Alexandre Sandier's essay "La Céramique à l'Exposition." *Art et Décoration*, no. 9 (January-June 1901): 62.

[10] Cass, op. cit. "Jean Carriès," n.p.

[11] Ibid.: "Paul Jeanneney," n.p.

[12] A. M. Georges Hoentschel, "Notes sur Carriès." *Art et Décoration*, no. 7 (January-June 1900): 64-73.

[13] Elizabeth K. Menon, "Les Fleurs du mal," in: *Evil By Design* (Urbana and Chicago: University of Illinois Press, 2006, 127-63).

[14] Ibid.: 145-63.

[15] Additional information on Carabin and his interpretation of female forms can be found in Sarah Sik's dissertation, titled "Satire and Sadism: François-Rupert Carabin and the Symbolist Treatment of the Female Form in Fin-de-siècle France." University of Minnesota, expected date of completion in 2009.

[16] For a history of the Sèvres Manufactory, see Pinot de Villechenon, op. cit.

[17] Historian Pilippe Julian explains that at the Sèvres exhibition in 1900, visitors could "observe the clash between the heavy Neo-Rococo style of official art (mainly articles produced for the embassies and vases presented to visiting monarchs) and Art Nouveau, which was represented by a whole series of vases inspired by the *grisaille* designs of the porcelain factory of Copenhagen": 110.

[18] Pinot de Villechenon, op. cit.: 106.

[19] A period source that discusses the production of these wares in detail is E. Baumgart's essay "La Manufacture Nationale de Sèvres en 1900: Les Biscuits." *Art et Décoration*, no. 7 (January-June 1900): 139-47. In this article, there are also several photographs of various dancers of the *Jeu de l'écharpe* series.

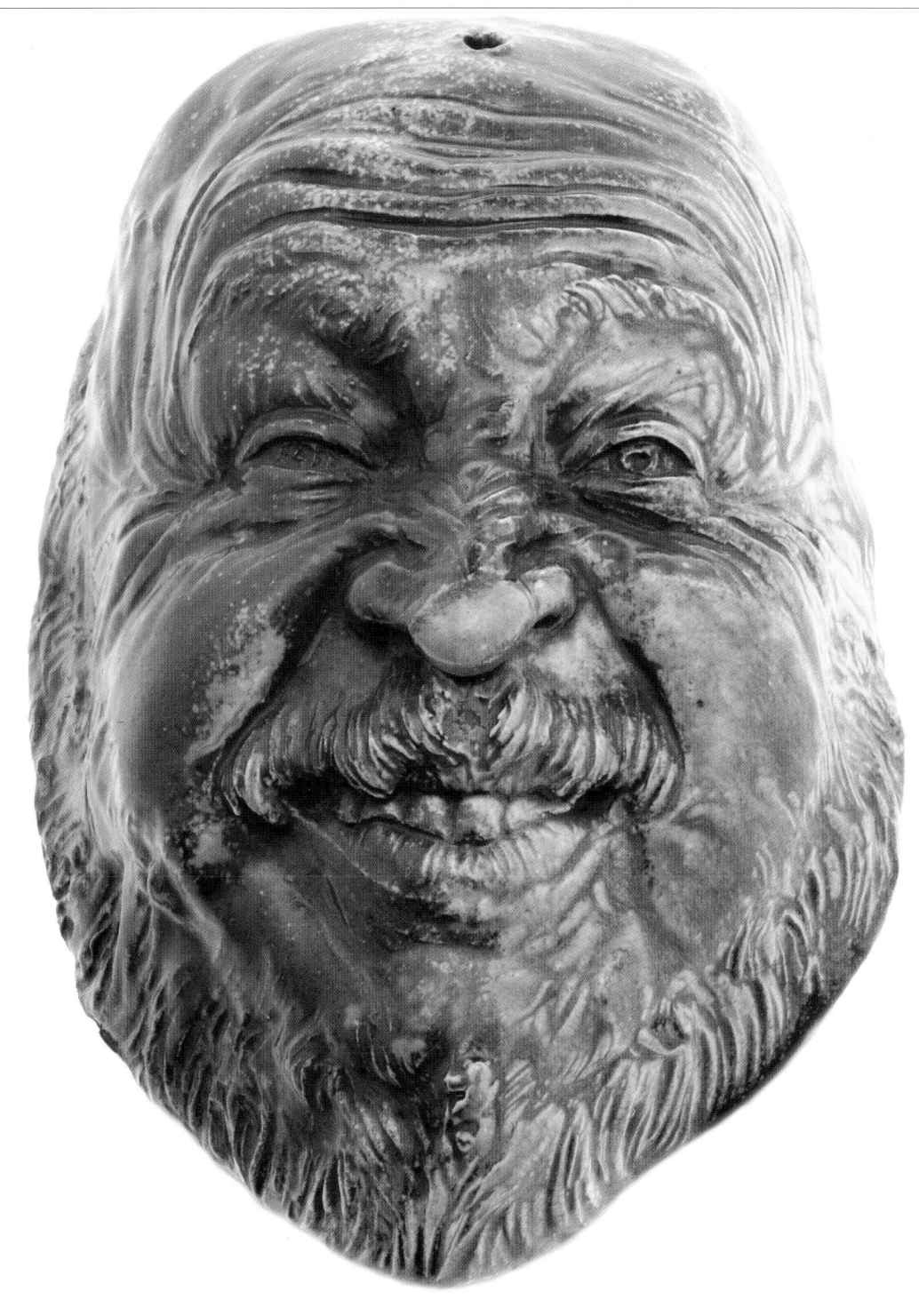

CAT. 16   Jean Joseph Marie Carriès (French, 1855-1894)
Laughing Man Mask, 1891
Stoneware, 8¾ x 6 in. (22.2 x 15.2 cm)
Mark Tyson Collection

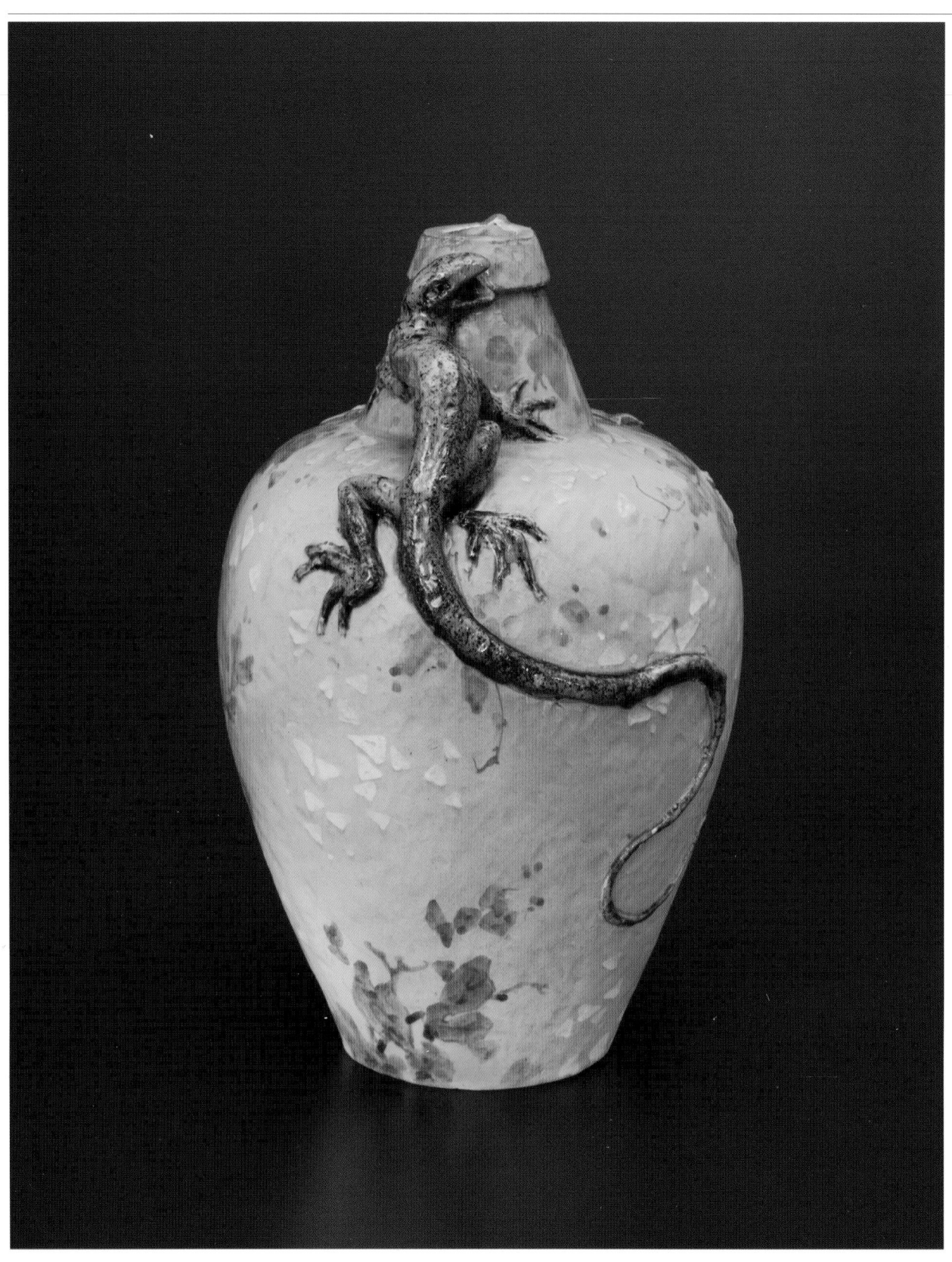

CAT. 53   Edmond Lachenal (French, 1855-1930)
Lizard Vase, ca. 1895-1900
Earthenware, 11¼ x 6¾ in. (28.6 x 17.1 cm)
Jason Jacques Inc.

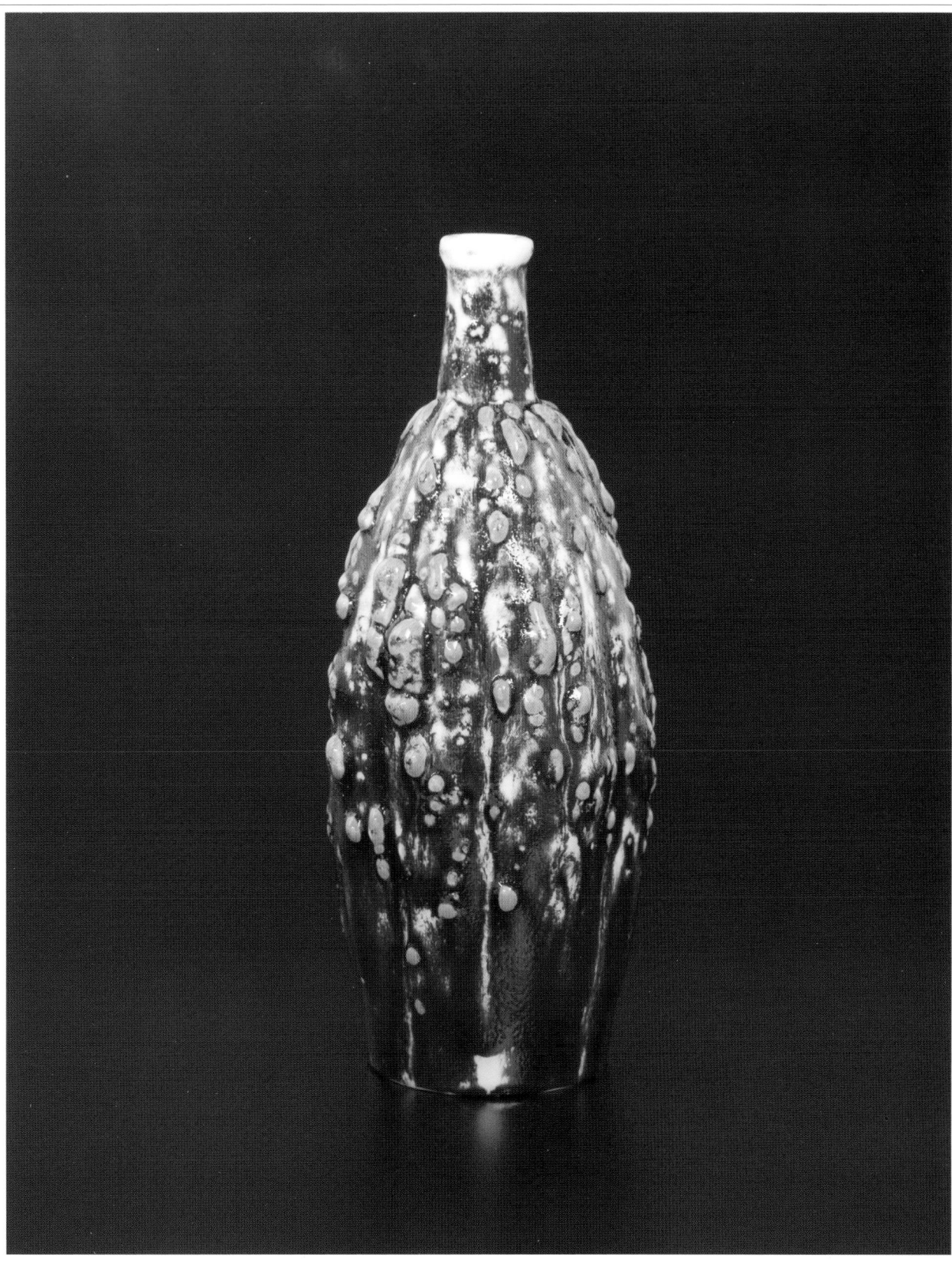

CAT. 28   Taxile Maximin Doat (French, 1851-1939)
Blood Gourd, 1907
Porcelaneous stoneware, 8 x 3½ in. (20.3 x 8.9 cm)
Private Collection

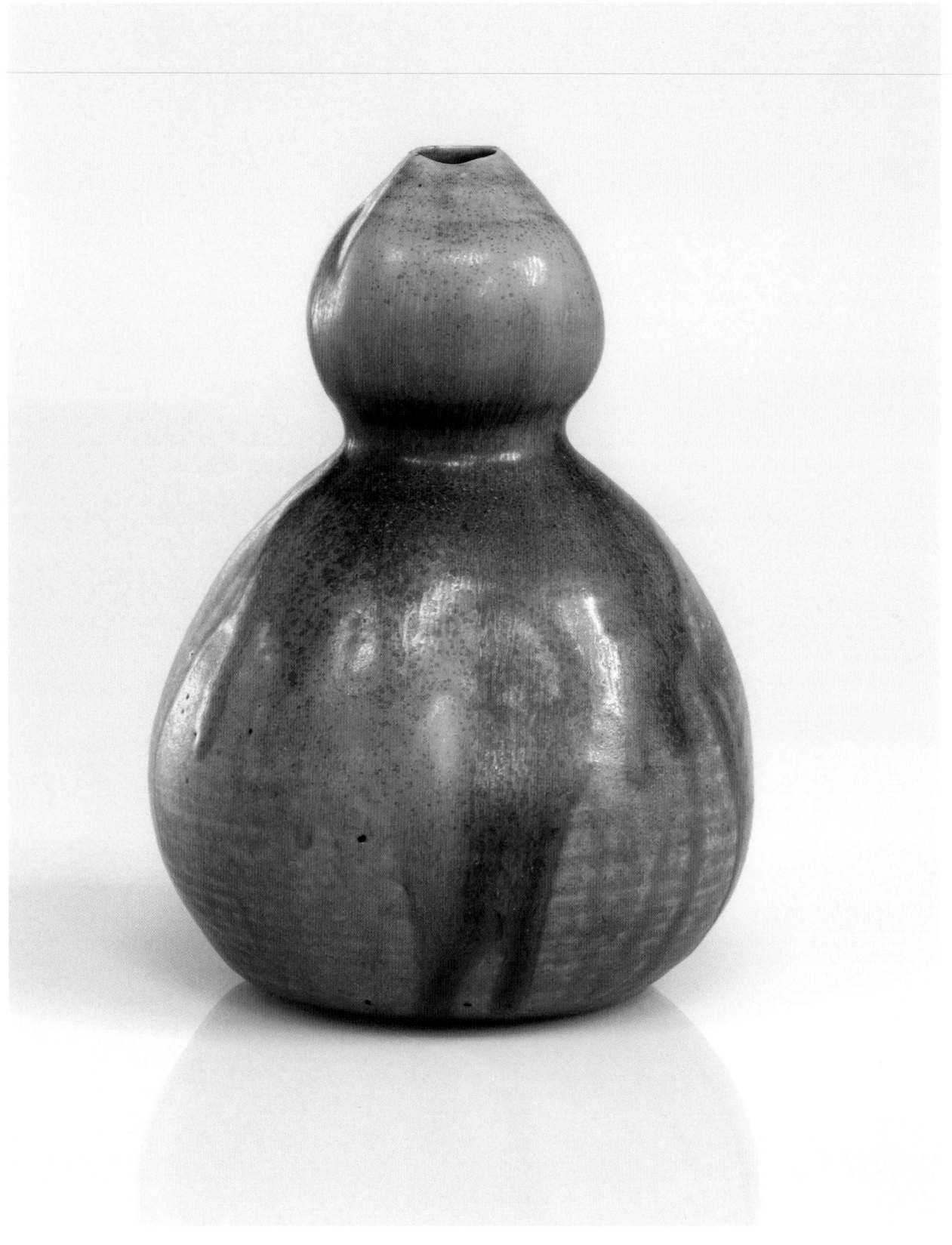

CAT. 52 Paul Jeanneney (French, ca. 1861-ca. 1920)
Double Gourd, 1900
Stoneware, 9½ in. (24.1 cm)
Mark Tyson Collection

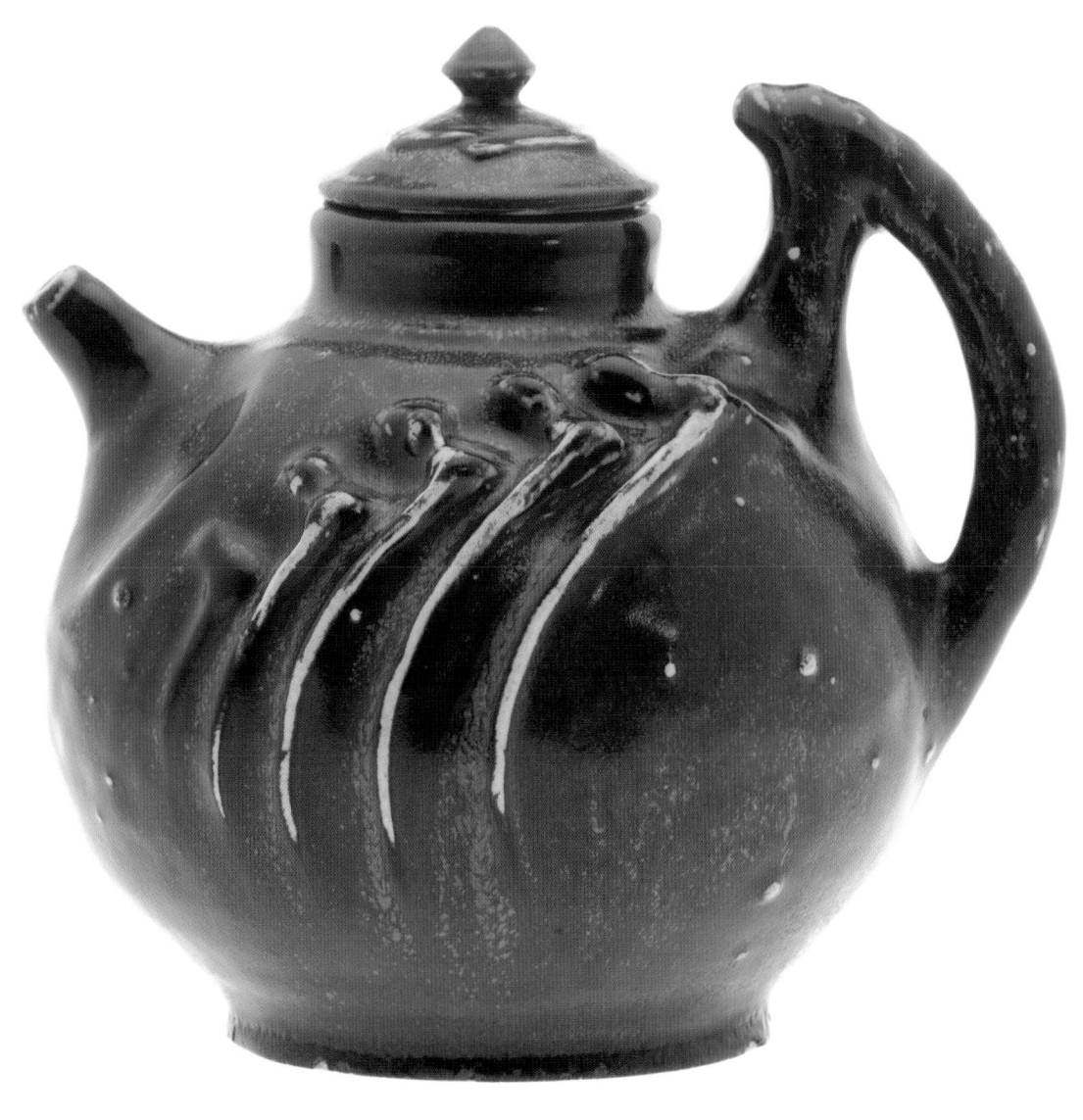

CAT. 24   Adrien Pierre Dalpayrat (French, 1844-1910)
Teapot, 1899
Porcelaneous stoneware, 8¾ x 7½ in. (22.2 x 19.1 cm)
Jason Jacques Inc.

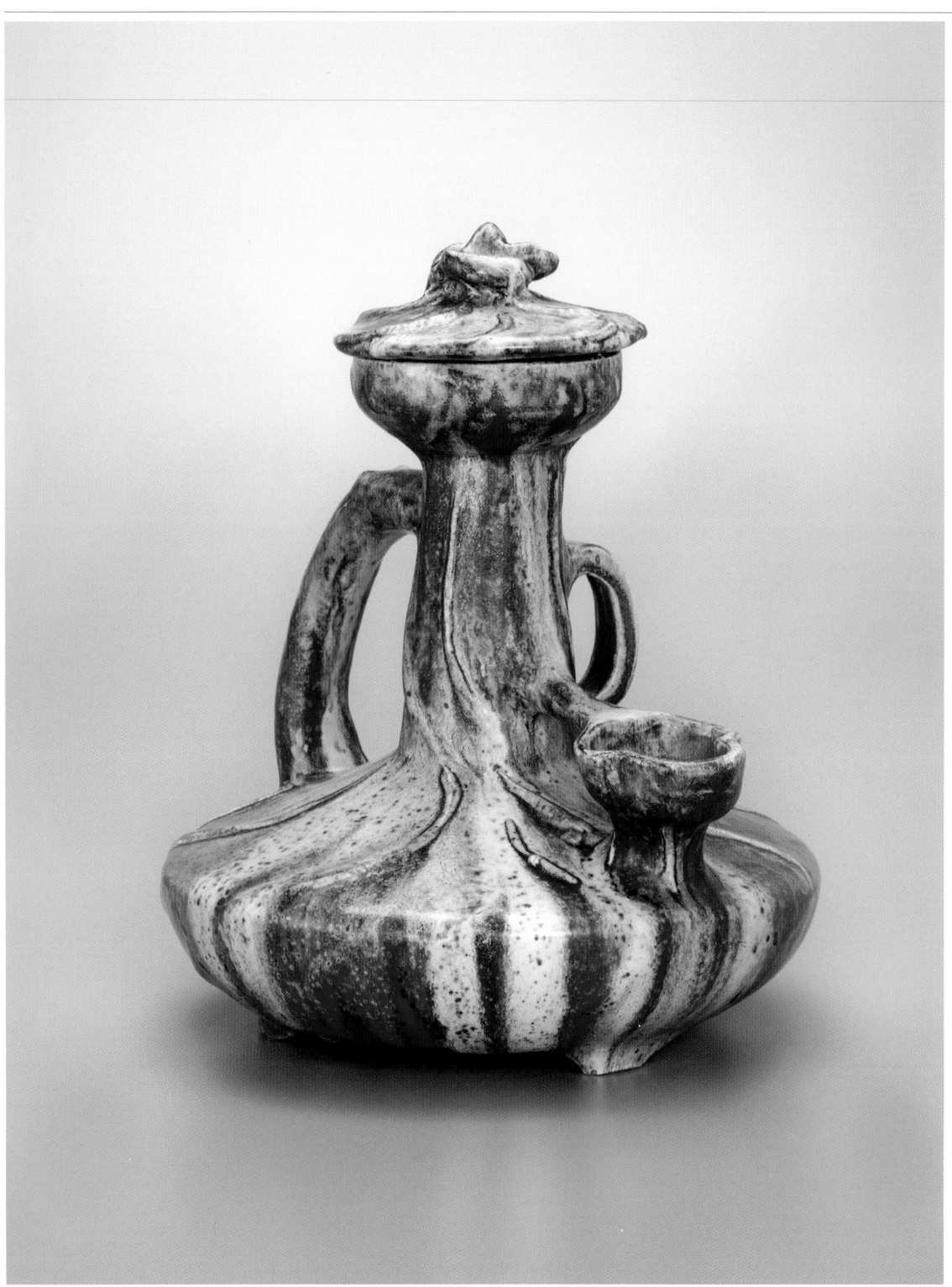

CAT. 54   Edmond Lachenal (French, 1855-1930)
Genie Bottle, 1895
Stoneware, 12¾ x 11¾ in. (32.4 x 29.8 cm)
Jason Jacques Inc.

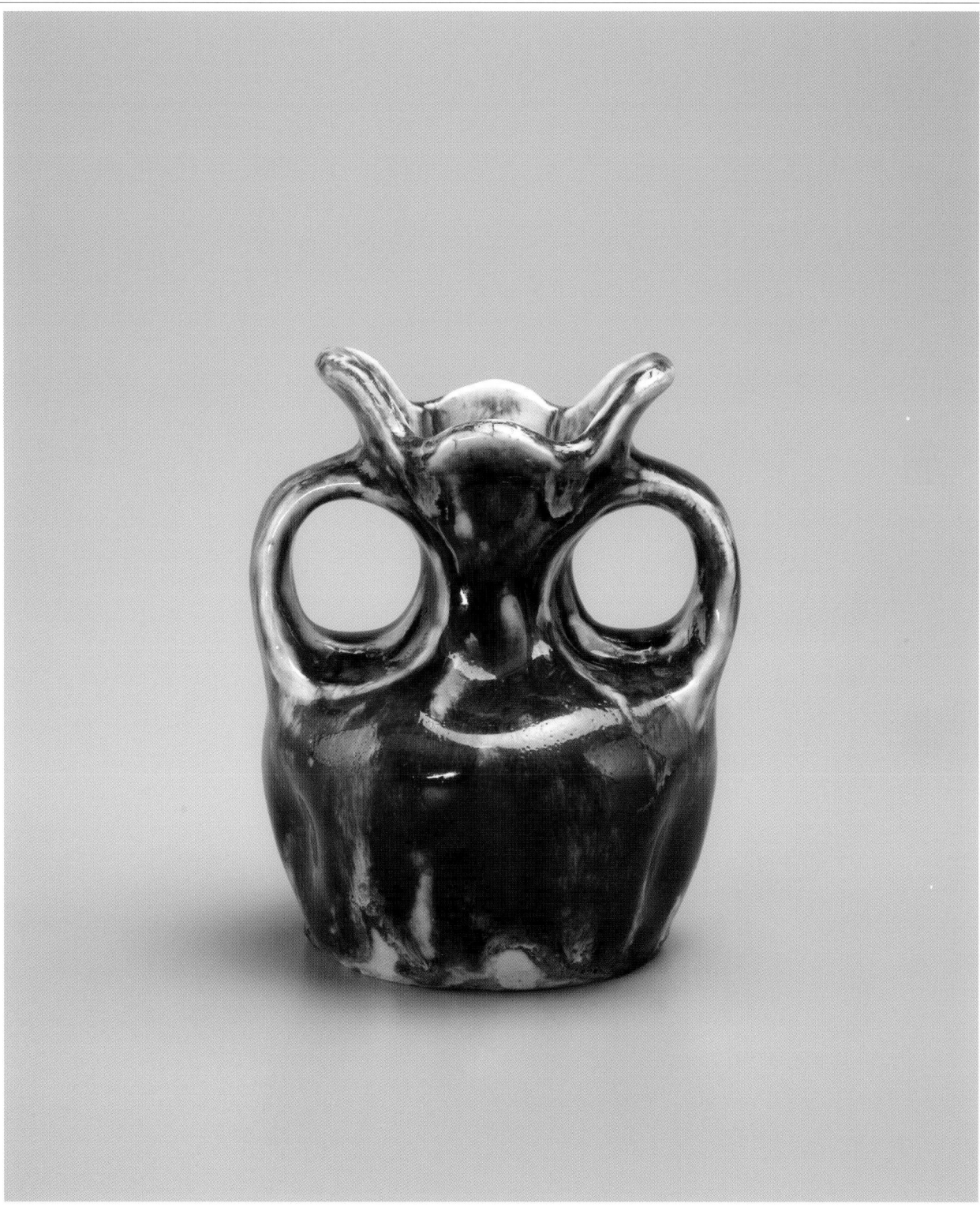

CAT. 93 Sèvres Porcelain Manufactory
Petit Vase, 1900
Porcelain, 4½ x 4 in. (11.4 x 10.2 cm)
Jason Jacques Inc.

Paris 1900

Lenders to the Exhibition

Mr. J. Raj K. Dhawan

Jason Jacques Inc.

Ms. Katherine Kovins

Galerie Michael, Beverly Hills, California

The Minneapolis Institute of Arts

Special Collections and Rare Books,
University of Minnesota

University of Oklahoma Libraries

Mr. Willem O. Russell

Mr. Howard Singer

Mr. & Mrs. Clay Timon

Wadsworth Atheneum Museum of Art

Dr. Gabriel and Yvonne Weisberg

The Jane Voorhees Zimmerli Art Museum

Paris 1900

Exhibition Checklist

1. Louis Anquetin (French, 1861-1932)
   City Scene, ca. 1905
   Oil on canvas, 25¼ x 32 in. (64.13 x 81.28 cm)
   Jane Voorhees Zimmerli Art Museum

2. *Art & Décoration*, vol. 2, 1900
   Special Collections and Rare Books,
   University of Minnesota, Minneapolis, Minnesota

3. Ernest Barrias (French, 1841-1905)
   La Nature se dévoilant devant la Science [Nature
   Unveiling Herself Before Science], ca. 1899
   Bronze, signed "E. Barrias" on top of base. Seal on
   side of base indicates edition by "Susse Frères Editeurs
   Paris." Stamped "P" below the seal.
   17 x 8 x 4 in. (43.2 x 20.3 x 10.2 cm)
   Private Collection

4. Jean Béraud (French, 1849-1935)
   Paris Street Scene, ca. 1910
   Oil on canvas, 9½ x 15 in. (24.13 x 38.1 cm)
   Wadsworth Atheneum Museum of Art, Hartford,
   Connecticut. Bequest of Genevieve Harlow Goodwin

5. Émile Bertrand (French)
   Cendrillon [Cinderella], 1899
   Color lithograph, 31 x 23¼ in. (78.74 x 59.06 cm)
   Lent by The Minneapolis Institute of Arts, The
   Modernism Collection, gift of Norwest Bank
   Minnesota, P.98.33.85

6. Maurice Biais (French, 1875-1926)
   Back from the Race, ca. 1900
   Lithograph, 26½ x 46 in. (67.3 x 116.8 cm)
   Dr. Gabriel and Yvonne Weisberg Collection

7. Maurice Biais (French, 1875-1926)
   In the Park, ca. 1900
   Lithograph, 26½ x 33½ in. (67.3 x 85.1 cm)
   Dr. Gabriel and Yvonne Weisberg Collection

8. Maurice Biais (French, 1875-1926)
The Race Track, ca. 1900
Lithograph, 20½ x 41⅞ in. (52.1 x 106.4 cm)
Dr. Gabriel and Yvonne Weisberg Collection

9. Maurice Biais (French, 1875-1926)
Tuff Tuff, 1902
Lithograph, 26½ x 33½ in. (67.3 x 85.1 cm)
Dr. Gabriel and Yvonne Weisberg Collection

10. Leonetto Cappiello (French, 1875-1942)
Portrait of Yvette Guilbert, 1899
Painted plaster, 13½ x 9 x 6⅞ in. (34 x 23.5 x 17.4 cm)
Jane Voorhees Zimmerli Art Museum

11. Leonetto Cappiello (French, 1875-1942)
L'Assiette au Beurre, 8 November 1902
12½ x 9¾ in. (31.82 x 24.81 cm)
Special Collections and Rare Books,
University of Minnesota, Minneapolis, Minnesota

12. François-Rupert Carabin (French, 1862-1932)
Woman with Gourd, 1894-1895
Enameled stoneware, 6 x 6½ x 4 in. (15 x 15 x 10 cm)
Jane Voorhees Zimmerli Art Museum

13. François-Rupert Carabin (French, 1862-1932)
Loïe Fuller, ca. 1897-1898
Enameled stoneware
18 x 15³⁄₁₆ x 9 in. (45.7 x 38.5 x 21.2 cm)
Jane Voorhees Zimmerli Art Museum

14. François-Rupert Carabin (French, 1862-1932)
Nude Sleeping Woman, ca. 1900
Wax, 7³⁄₁₆ x 3⁷⁄₁₆ x 1³⁄₁₆ in. (18.2 x 8.7 x 3 cm)
Jane Voorhees Zimmerli Art Museum

15. Eugène Carrière (French, 1849-1906)
Jean-René and Lucie Carrière, ca. 1898-1900
Oil on canvas, 18¼ x 15¹⁄₁₆ in. (46.35 x 39.67 cm)
Wadsworth Atheneum Museum of Art, Hartford,
Connecticut. Gift of Ivan Loiseau

16. Jean Joseph Marie Carriès (French, 1855-1894)
Laughing Man Mask, 1891
Stoneware, 8¾ x 6 in. (22.2 x 15.2 cm)
Mark Tyson Collection

17. Frederic-Auguste Cazals (French, 1865-1941)
Cover of *La Plume Littéraire, Artistique et Sociale*,
no. 163, 1 February 1896. The cover illustration shows
a reclining man, in contemporary dress, smoking a
cigarette while resting under the statue of a faun.
This issue dedicated to the work of the poet Paul Verlaine
with illustrations after Cazals. 9¹³⁄₁₆ x 7 in. (24.8 x 17.8 cm)
Russell Collection, Amsterdam

18. Ernest Chaplet (French, 1835-1909)
Studio Vase, 1899
Porcelain, 7 x 5 in. (17.8 x 12.7 cm)
Jason Jacques Inc.

19. Jules Chéret (French, 1836-1932)
Pippermint, 1890
Color lithograph, 48 x 34⅝ in. (123.19 x 87.95 cm)
Lent by The Minneapolis Institute of Arts, Gift of Bruce B.
Dayton, P.85.6

20. Jules Chéret (French, 1836-1932)
Bal au Moulin Rouge, 1892
Color lithograph, 50¼ x 35¼ in. (127.6 x 89.5 cm)
Lent by The Minneapolis Institute of Arts, The Modernism
Collection, gift of Norwest Bank Minnesota, P.98.33.1

21. Jules Chéret (French, 1836-1932)
L'Arc en Ciel [The Rainbow], 1893
Lithograph, 12³⁄₁₆ x 10⅝ in. (31 x 27 cm)
Jane Voorhees Zimmerli Art Museum

22. Jules Chéret (French, 1836-1932)
Jardin de Paris, ca. 1895
Color lithograph, 48 x 34⅛ in. (121.92 x 86.68 cm)
Lent by The Minneapolis Institute of Arts,
Gift of Bruce B. Dayton, P.85.4

23. Jules Chéret (French, 1836-1932)
La Fileuse [The Spinner], 1900
Color lithograph, 49 x 32½ in. (124.46 x 82.55 cm)
Lent by The Minneapolis Institute of Arts, The
Modernism Collection, gift of Norwest Bank
Minnesota, P.98.33.113

24. Adrien Pierre Dalpayrat (French, 1844-1910)
Teapot, 1899
Porcelaneous stoneware, 8¾ x 7½ in. (22.2 x 19.1 cm)
Jason Jacques Inc.

25. Adrien Pierre Dalpayrat (French, 1844-1910)
Gourd, 1900
Stoneware, 8¾ x 6½ in. (22.2 x 16.5 cm)
Eunice and Herbert Shatzman Collection

26. Henri-Adolphe-Auguste Deglane (French, 1855-1931)
and Albert-Félix-Théophile Thomas (French,
1847-1907), architects
Grand Palais, Paris, Exposition Universelle, 1900
Photographic reproduction
L'architecture & la sculpture à l'Exposition de 1900,
series I. Paris, A. Guerinet, 1904
15¾ x 12½ in. (40.09 x 31.82 cm)
Architecture Collections, University of Oklahoma
Libraries

27. Maurice Denis (French, 1870-1943)
Avril, after 1894 (1907?)
Drawing, ink wash heightened with white on paper,
diam. 7¼ in. (18.5 cm)
Russell Collection, Amsterdam

28. Taxile Maximin Doat (French, 1851-1939)
Blood Gourd, 1907
Porcelaneous stoneware, 8 x 3½ in. (20.3 x 8.9 cm)
Private Collection

29. Gustave Eiffel (French architect and engineer,
1832-1923)
La Tour Eiffel en 1900. Paris, 1902
Photographs of Eiffel Tower, and map of the area
indicating what can be seen from the top of the tower.
10.23 x 12.59 x 1.18 in. (26 x 32 x 3 cm)
History of Science Collections, University of
Oklahoma Libraries

30. Georges d'Espagnat (French, 1870-1950)
Yvette Guilbert, ca. 1900
Gouache, 22 x 16½ in. (55.9 x 41.9 cm)
Dr. Gabriel and Yvonne Weisberg Collection

31. *L'Estampe moderne*, vol. 2
Special Collections and Rare Books, University of
Minnesota, Minneapolis, Minnesota

32. Georges de Feure (French, 1868-1943)
Paris Almanach, 1894
Lithograph, 32 x 26½ in. (81.3 x 67.3 cm)
Dr. Gabriel and Yvonne Weisberg Collection

33. François Flameng (French, 1856-1923)
Théâtre de l'Opéra-Comique: Griselidis [Griselda], ca. 1900
Color lithograph, 52⅜ x 27⅞ in. (133.03 x 70.8 cm)
Lent by The Minneapolis Institute of Arts, Gift of funds
from John E. Andrus III, 2003.213.3

34. Agnes de Frumerie for Lachenal (Swedish, 1869-1937)
Nymph and Lily Vase, 1897
Earthenware, 14 x 8 x 4½ in. (35.6 x 20.32 x 11.43 cm)
Jason Jacques Inc.

35. Andhré des Gashons (French, 1871-1951)
La Plume Littéraire, Artistique et Sociale, no. 159, 15
December 1895. Issue concerning the Salon des Cent
with a cover design and illustrations by Andhré des
Gashons. The cover illustration shows a woman in a
long gown, holding a book in her right hand and a
flower in her left, standing in a park-like landscape.
The towers of a medieval castle can be seen in the
distance. The composition is within an architectural
frame with pointed arch. 9⅞ x 7³⁄₁₆ in. (25.1 x 18.3 cm)
Russell Collection, Amsterdam

36. Eugène-Samuel Grasset (French, 1841-1917)
La Plume Littéraire, Artistique et Sociale, no. 148,
15 June 1895. Cover design showing the
personifications of the "arts" and "literature."
A male figure on the left holds a palette and stretched
canvas in his right hand and brushes in his left. A
female figure on the right, representing literature,
writes with a quill pen and holds a book in her left hand.
9⅞ x 7³⁄₁₆ in. (25.1 x 18.3 cm)
Russell Collection, Amsterdam

37. Eugène-Samuel Grasset (French, 1841-1917)
Morphinomane [Morphine Addict], 1897
Lithograph, 29½ x 23⁷⁄₁₆ in. (75 x 59.5 cm)
Jane Voorhees Zimmerli Art Museum

38. Jules-Alexandre Grün (French, 1868-1934)
Enfin Seuls! [At Last Alone!], n.d.
Color lithograph mounted on linen
46⅜ x 32 in. (117.79 x 82.55 cm)
Lent by The Minneapolis Institute of Arts,
Gift of Marguerite and Russell Cowles, P.79.82.6

39. Charles Guilloux (French, 1866-1946)
L'Inondation, ca.1892
Oil on paper laid down on board
9⁷⁄₁₆ x 13 in. (24 x 33 cm)
Russell Collection, Amsterdam

40. Charles Guilloux (French, 1866-1946)
Paysage orageux [Stormy Landscape], ca.1892-1895
Oil on canvas, 10⅝ x 13¾ in. (27 x 35 cm)
Russell Collection, Amsterdam

41. Charles Guilloux (French, 1866-1946)
Notre Dame vue des Quais, 1894
Oil on board, 9¹³⁄₁₆ x 13 in. (25 x 33 cm)
Russell Collection, Amsterdam

42. Charles Guilloux (French, 1866-1946)
L'Allée d'eau [The Waterway], 1895
Oil on board, 17¹¹⁄₁₆ x 23⁷⁄₁₆ in. (45 x 59.5 cm)
Russell Collection, Amsterdam

43. Ernst Heilemann (German,1870- ?)
"Bergründete Vorsicht" ["Established Caution"], in:
Simplicissimus, vol. 5, no. 41 (1900), p. 332
15 x 11 in. (38.17 x 28 cm)
Special Collections and Rare Books, University of
Minnesota, Minneapolis, Minnesota

44. Hermann-Paul (French, 1864-1940)
Au Salon de peinture [At the Painting Salon], 1891
Lithograph, 18¼ x 9¹³⁄₁₆ in. (46.3 x 24.9 cm)
Jane Voorhees Zimmerli Art Museum

45. Hermann-Paul (French, 1864-1940)
The Omnibus, n.d.
Lithograph, 12¹³⁄₁₆ x 9¾ in. (32.6 x 24.8 cm)
Jane Voorhees Zimmerli Art Museum

46. Andō Hiroshige (Japanese, 1797-1858)
Carp: "A Compendium of Fish," 1832
Color woodblock print, 9⅞ x 14¼ in. (25.08 x 36.19 cm)
Private Collection

47. Andō Hiroshige (Japanese, 1797-1858)
Numazu: "Fifty-three stages of the Tokaidō" series, 1832-1834
Color woodblock print, 8⅞ x 13⅝ in. (22.54 x 34.73 cm)
Private Collection

48. Andō Hiroshige (Japanese, 1797-1858)
Yui: "Fifty-three stages of the Tōkaidō" series, 1832-1834
Color woodblock print, 9 x 13⅞ in. (22.86 x 35.24 cm)
Private Collection

49. Andō Hiroshige (Japanese, 1797-1858)
The Pine Forest of Mio in Suruga Province: "Thirty-six
Views of Mount Fuji" series, 1858
Color woodblock print, 13⅜ x 8¾ in. (33.97 x 22.23 cm)
Private Collection

50. *Le Japon Artistique*, no. 32 (December 1890)
"Vue du Foujiyama par Hokusai" in: "Les paysagistes
Japonais" article by Gustave Geffroy (French,
1855-1926). Also included (but not within Geffroy's
article), a color plate of *Jeune Couple* by Suzuki
Harunobu (Japanese, 1724-1770).
13 x 9⅝ in. (33 x 24.4 cm)
Dr. Gabriel and Yvonne Weisberg Collection

51. *Le Japon Artistique*, no. 24 (April 1890)
Title page for "Le Théâtre Japonais" article by
A. Lequeux. Also included (but not within
Lequeux's article), an entry on Andō Hiroshige's
landscapes. 13 x 9⅝ in. (33 x 24.4 cm)
Dr. Gabriel and Yvonne Weisberg Collection

52. Paul Jeanneney (French, ca. 1861-ca. 1920)
Double Gourd, 1900
Stoneware, h. 9½ in. (24.1 cm)
Mark Tyson Collection

53. Edmond Lachenal (French, 1855-1930)
Lizard Vase, ca. 1895-1900
Earthenware, 11¼ x 6¾ in. (28.6 x 17.1 cm)
Jason Jacques Inc.

54. Edmond Lachenal (French, 1855-1930)
Genie Bottle, 1895
Stoneware, 12¾ x 11¾ in. (32.4 x 29.8 cm)
Private Collection

55. Edmond Lachenal (French, 1855-1930)
Floral Vase, ca. 1899
Matte and glossy glazed earthenware
16 x 18½ in. (40.6 x 47 cm)
Laurie and David Weiner Collection

56. Louis Legrand (French, 1863-1951)
First Lesson, Little Ballerinas, 1893
Aquatint and etching, 19¾ x 12⅝ in. (50.2 x 32 cm)
Jane Voorhees Zimmerli Art Museum

57. Louis Legrand (French, 1863-1951)
Gin, 1894
Drypoint, 12⅛ x 18⅜ in. (30.8 x 46.6 cm)
Jane Voorhees Zimmerli Art Museum

58. Louis Legrand (French, 1863-1951)
Woman in Bed with Death, ca. 1895
Black and colored chalks, 12⅜ x 8 1/16 in. (31.5 x 20.5 cm)
Jane Voorhees Zimmerli Art Museum

59. Louis Legrand (French, 1863-1951)
A Dancer, ca. 1896
Oil on canvas, 27³/₁₆ x 26 in. (69 x 66 cm)
Russell Collection, Amsterdam

60. Louis Legrand (French, 1863-1951)
Au Bar, 1908
Etching and drypoint, 21¹³/₁₆ x 13¾ in. (55.4 x 35 cm)
Jane Voorhees Zimmerli Art Museum

61. Georges Leroux (French, 1877-1957)
Optique Pavilion Paris World Fair, 1900
Drawing, 24½ x 14 in. (62.2 x 35.6 cm)
Dr. Gabriel and Yvonne Weisberg Collection

62. Louis Majorelle (French, 1859-1926)
*Mantel Clock with Carved Decorations of Foliage and
Seedheads*, ca. 1900
Wood with bronze front and pendulum
15¾ x 7 x 4¼ in. (40 x 17.8 x 10.8 cm)
Howard Singer Collection, New York

63. Charles Maurin (French, 1856-1914)
Chasteté, ca. 1893
Oil on canvas, 25 3/16 x 31 11/16 in. (64 x 80.5 cm)
Russell Collection, Amsterdam

64. Charles Maurin (French, 1856-1914)
Young Woman Combing Her Hair, ca. 1895
Crayon, 15 1/4 x 10 3/4 in. (38.7 x 27.3 cm)
Jane Voorhees Zimmerli Art Museum

65. Alphonse Mucha (Czech, 1860-1939)
Bernhardt American Tour, 1895
Color lithograph on linen
78 1/4 x 29 1/4 in. (198.8 x 74.3 cm)
Courtesy J. Raj K. Dhawan through Galerie Michael,
Beverly Hills, California

66. Alphonse Mucha (Czech, 1860-1939)
Figaro Illustré, vol. 7, 1896
Boussod, Valadon & Cie, Éditeurs, Paris, 1896
Illustrations by artists other than Mucha include:
Toulouse-Lautrec, Metivet, Lucien Doucet, Jean
Béraud, Lucius Rossi, Henri Boutet, Gustave Doré,
Richard Goubie, Albert Guillaume, Auguste Vimar,
and others. 16 1/2 x 12 1/2 in. (41.91 x 31.75 cm)
Courtesy J. Raj K. Dhawan

67. Alphonse Mucha (Czech, 1860-1939)
La Plume, no. 194, May 1897
A woman with red hair wearing a long gown,
perhaps the muse of poetry, leans against the
mythological winged horse Pegasus. In her right
hand she holds one of the feathers from the wing of
the creature. Cover for a special issue on the salons.
Color lithograph, 10 1/4 x 7 1/16 in. (26 x 18 cm)
Courtesy J. Raj K. Dhawan

68. Alphonse Mucha (Czech, 1860-1939)
Edmond Rostand (French, 1868-1918)
La Samaritaine, Evangile en trois tableaux en vers. 1897
Title page illustrated with a color lithograph based
on Mucha's poster for Sarah Bernhardt's production
of the play. 7 1/2 x 9 1/2 in. (19.05 x 24.13 cm)
Imprimerie F. Champenois, 1897
Courtesy J. Raj K. Dhawan

69. Alphonse Mucha (Czech, 1860-1939)
Sarah Bernhardt, La Plume, 1897
Colored lithograph, 23 x 16 in. (58.42 x 40.64 cm)
Courtesy J. Raj K. Dhawan through Galerie Michael,
Beverly Hills, California

70. Alphonse Mucha (Czech, 1860-1939)
Sarah Bernhardt, La Plume, 1897
Lithograph (proof), 25 3/4 x 18 in. (65.4 x 45.7 cm)
Courtesy J. Raj K. Dhawan through Galerie Michael,
Beverly Hills, California

71. Alphonse Mucha (Czech, 1860-1939)
Chansons d'aieules
A book of songs sung by Madame Amel from the
Comédie Française, published in Paris, in 1897 or 1898
Book with color lithographs
13 x 9 7/8 in. (33 x 25 cm)
Courtesy J. Raj K. Dhawan

72. Alphonse Mucha (Czech, 1860-1939)
Cocorico, magazine cover, no. 1, first year,
31 December 1898
Lithograph
Printer: Paul Boutigny
11 13/16 x 9 1/16 in. (31 x 24 cm)
Courtesy J. Raj K. Dhawan

73. Alphonse Mucha (Czech, 1860-1939)
Job, 1898
Color lithograph on paper mounted on linen
58 13/16 x 37 11/16 in. (149.35 x 100.84 cm)
Courtesy J. Raj K. Dhawan

74. Alphonse Mucha (Czech, 1860-1939)
Portrait of Sarah Bernhardt, 1898
Charcoal on paper, 18 11/16 x 21 5/8 in. (55 x 47.5 cm)
Russell Collection, Amsterdam

75. Alphonse Mucha (Czech, 1860-1939)
Cocorico, magazine cover, no. 4, second year,
15 February 1899
Lithograph on metallic paper
11 13/16 x 9 1/16 in. (31 x 24 cm)
Courtesy J. Raj K. Dhawan

76. Alphonse Mucha (Czech, 1860-1939)
Cover for *Le Pater*
Illustrated book with Mucha's reflections upon man's
divine place in the universe. Champenois, Henri
Piazza & Cie., Paris, 1899
13 x 10 in. (33 x 25.4 cm)
Courtesy J. Raj K. Dhawan

77. Alphonse Mucha (Czech, 1860-1939)
Paul Rouaix (French, b. 1850-?)
Dictionnaire des Arts Décoratifs, 1900
Cover for vol. 1
Montgredien et Cie, Librarie Illustée, Paris
9⅝ x 5⅞ in. (24 x 15 cm)
Courtesy J. Raj K. Dhawan

78. Alphonse Mucha (Czech, 1860-1939)
Cover of the Exposition Universelle Bosnian
booklet. Lithograph was also used for the menu of
the official banquet of the 1900 Exposition
Universelle. 9⁷⁄₁₆ x 7¹⁄₁₆ in. (24 x 18 cm)
Courtesy J. Raj K. Dhawan

79. Alphonse Mucha (Czech, 1860-1939)
Le Mois Littéraire et Pittoresque, December 1902
Cover of periodical (also issued as color postcard)
Monochrome lithograph
10 x 6¾ in. (25.4 x 17 cm)
Courtesy J. Raj K. Dhawan

80. Alphonse Mucha (Czech, 1860-1939)
Cover for the Christmas issue of *Paris Illustré*,
December 1903. Lithograph used for cover of
the 1900 Exposition Universelle Bosnian booklet and
the menu of the official 1900 Exposition banquet.
15½ x 12½ in. (39.37 x 31.75 cm)
Courtesy J. Raj K. Dhawan

81. Alphonse Mucha (Czech, 1860-1939)
Christian Brinton, (American, 1870-1942)
"Alfonse Mucha and the New Mysticism"
Seven illustrations by Mucha, in: *The Century
Magazine*, vol. 69 no. 2, December 1904
Courtesy J. Raj K. Dhawan

82. Alphonse Mucha (Czech, 1860-1939)
L'Habitation Pratique, 1908
Cover of periodical (lithograph)
Librarie de la "Construction Moderne," Paris
15³⁄₁₆ x 12⁵⁄₁₆ in. (38.99 x 32 cm)
The female figure in the center of the composition is
taken from a photograph of a model in Mucha's large
photographic archive. The model, surrounded by
laurel leaves, is posed in front of a large ionic capital.
Courtesy J. Raj K. Dhawan

83. Alphonse Osbert (French, 1857-1939)
Crepuscule du Soir, ca. 1900
Oil on panel, 14⅜ x 22¹⁄₁₆ in. (36.5 x 56 cm)
Russell Collection, Amsterdam

84. Bruno Paul (German 1874-1968)
"Der Münchner beim Rennen" ["A Munich Citizen
at the Races"], in: *Simplicissimus*, vol. 5, no. 14
(14 May 1900). 15 x 11 in. (38.17 x 28 cm)
Special Collections and Rare Books,
University of Minnesota, Minneapolis, Minnesota

85. Armand Point (French, 1861-1932)
Lady on the Banks of the Seine, 1895
Color pencil drawing, 15¾ x 9⁷⁄₁₆ in. (40 x 24 cm)
Russell Collection, Amsterdam

86. Armand Rassenfosse (Belgian, 1862-1934)
L'Art Indépendant, 1896
Color lithograph, 24½ x 16¹⁵⁄₁₆ in. (62.23 x 43.02 cm)
Lent by The Minneapolis Institute of Arts, The
Modernism Collection, gift of Norwest Bank
Minnesota, P.98.33.110

87. *La Revue illustrée*, 1 February 1901
Special Collections and Rare Books, University of
Minnesota, Minneapolis, Minnesota

88. Ferdinand Freiherr von Reznicek
(Austrian, 1868-1909)
"Ein braver vater" ["A Fine Father"], in:
Simplicissimus, vol. 5, no. 10 (1900), p. 79
15 x 11 in. (38.17 x 28 cm)
Special Collections and Rare Books,
University of Minnesota, Minneapolis, Minnesota

89. Louis Rhead (American, 1857-1926)
La Plume Littéraire, Artistique et Sociale, no. 310,
15 March 1902. Cover design shows a woman in a
long gown decorated with a floral pattern sharpening
a quill pen. An inkwell and books are seen on the
table behind her. An oil lamp hangs above the table.
10⅜ x 7½ in. (26.5 x 9cm)
Russell Collection, Amsterdam

90. Paul Rieth (German, 1871-1925)
"Wespentaille" ["Wasp Waist"], in: *Jugend*, vol. 5,
number 31 (30 July 1900), p. 523
11¾ x 8¾ in. (29.91 x 22.27 cm)
Special Collections and Rare Books, University
of Minnesota, Minneapolis, Minnesota

91. Henri Rivière (French, 1864-1951)
L'Isle des cygnes, ca. 1900
Crayon and watercolor, 20¹¹⁄₁₆ x 32¼ in. (52.5 x 82 cm)
Russell Collection, Amsterdam

92. Henri Rivière (French, 1864-1951)
L'Isle des cygnes, 1900
Color lithograph, 32¼ x 20¹¹⁄₁₆ in. (82 x 52.5 cm)
Russell Collection, Amsterdam

93. Sèvres Porcelain Manufactory
Petit Vase, 1900
Porcelain, 4½ x 4 in. (11.4 x 10.2 cm)
Jason Jacques Inc.

94. Théophile-Alexandre Steinlen (Swiss, 1859-1923)
"Sur la Scène, Chanson by L. Xanrof," from *Gil Blas
Illustré*, 14 February 1892, p. 8
Photo relief of page, 12¹³⁄₁₆ x 9¹⁵⁄₁₆ in. (32.5 x 25.3 cm)
Jane Voorhees Zimmerli Art Museum

95. Théophile-Alexandre Steinlen (Swiss, 1859-1923)
"La Loïe Fuller aux Folies-Bergère"
Cover for *Gil Blas Illustré*, no. 52, 25 December 1892
Gil Blas Illustré proof, 12¾ x 10⁷⁄₁₆ in. (32.4 x 26.5 cm)
Jane Voorhees Zimmerli Art Museum

96. Théophile-Alexandre Steinlen, (Swiss, 1859-1923)
"Ombres Parisiennes," by Aurelien Scholl
Cover for *Gil Blas Illustré*, 3 September 1893
Lithograph, 10¹³⁄₁₆ x 15⅜ in. (27.5 x 39 cm)
Jane Voorhees Zimmerli Art Museum

97. Théophile-Alexandre Steinlen (Swiss, 1859-1923)
"Pygmalion," by René Maizeroy
Cover for *Gil Blas Illustré*, 29 January 1894
Gil Blas Illustré proof, 14⁵⁄₁₆ x 10⅜ in. (36.3 x 26.3 cm)
Jane Voorhees Zimmerli Art Museum

98. Théophile-Alexandre Steinlen (Swiss, 1859-1923)
"Pièces à dire, Fin de Siècle," by Aristide Bruant, an
extract from *Dans la Rue*, the second volume of songs
and monologues by Aristide Bruant, illustrated by
Steinlen for *Gil Blas Illustré*, no. 8, 24 February 1895
Gil Blas Illustré proof (before the letters), 13½ x 10 in.
(34.5 x 25.4 cm) Jane Voorhees Zimmerli Art Museum

99. Théophile-Alexandre Steinlen, (Swiss, 1859-1923)
"Passe le Détroit" by Gabriel Mourey
Cover for *Gil Blas Illustré*, no. 10, 19 March 1895
Gil Blas Illustré proof, 11 x 9⅝ in. (33.2 x 25.4 cm)
Jane Voorhees Zimmerli Art Museum

100. Théophile-Alexandre Steinlen (Swiss, 1859-1923)
"Un Mari," by Camille de Sainte-Croix
Cover for *Gil Blas Illustré*, no. 17, 28 April 1895
Gil Blas Illustré proof, 12¾ x 10⁵⁄₁₆ in. (32.4 x 26.2 cm)
Jane Voorhees Zimmerli Art Museum

101. Théophile-Alexandre Steinlen (Swiss, 1859-1923)
"Une Réputation" by Henry Caen
Cover for *Gil Blas Illustré*, no. 18, 5 May 1895
Gil Blas Illustré proof, 12¹⁵⁄₁₆ x 10½ in. (32.9 x 26.6 cm)
Jane Voorhees Zimmerli Art Museum

102. Théophile-Alexandre Steinlen (Swiss, 1859-1923)
"Les Fous," by Émile Goudeau
Cover for *Gil Blas Illustré*, 15 December 1895
Gil Blas Illustré proof, 12⅞ x 10½ in. (32.7 x 26.7 cm)
Jane Voorhees Zimmerli Art Museum

103. Théophile-Alexandre Steinlen (Swiss, 1859-1923)
Rue Caulaincourt, 1896
Lithograph, 11 x 14⁹/₁₆ in. (27.8 x 37 cm)
Jane Voorhees Zimmerli Art Museum

104. Théophile-Alexandre Steinlen (Swiss, 1859-1923)
"Permutantes" by Lucien Descaves
Cover for *Gil Blas Illustré*, no. 46, 13 November 1896
Gil Blas Illustré proof, 12¹³/₁₆ x 9⅞ in (32.6 x 25.1 cm)
Jane Voorhees Zimmerli Art Museum

105. Théophile-Alexandre Steinlen (Swiss, 1859-1923)
"Les Trottins," by Jean Reibrach
Cover for *Gil Blas Illustré*, no. 13, 1 April 1898
Lithograph, 14⁹/₁₆ x 10¹³/₁₆ in. (37 x 27.5 cm)
Jane Voorhees Zimmerli Art Museum

106. Théophile-Alexandre Steinlen (Swiss, 1859-1923)
"L'Assistance" by Oscar Méténier
Cover for *Gil Blas Illustré*, no. 40, 27 July 1900
Lithograph, 15½ x 11 in. (39.3 x 28 cm)
Jane Voorhees Zimmerli Art Museum

107. Théophile-Alexandre Steinlen (Swiss, 1859-1923)
La Marche du Peuple, before 1923
Oil on canvas, 23½ x 16⁹/₁₆ in. (59.69 x 42.06 cm)
Wadsworth Atheneum Museum of Art, Hartford,
Connecticut. The Ella Gallup Sumner and Mary
Catlin Sumner Collection Fund

108. Théophile-Alexandre Steinlen (Swiss, 1859-1923)
Portrait of Aristide Bruant (doublesided), n.d.
Pencil, 14⁹/₁₆ x 11⁷/₁₆ in. (37 x 29 cm)
Jane Voorhees Zimmerli Art Museum

109. Eduard Stellmacher (German, 1868-?)
Amphora Eastern Dragon Vase, 1899
Earthenware, 17 x 13 in. (43.2 x 33 cm)
Jason Jacques Inc.

110. Henri de Toulouse-Lautrec (French, 1864-1901)
Moulin Rouge, La Goulue, 1891
Color lithograph, linen backed
74 x 45 in. (187.96 x 114.3 cm)
Courtesy Mr. & Mrs. Clay Timon through Galerie
Michael, Beverly Hills, California

111. Henri de Toulouse-Lautrec (French, 1864-1901)
Aristide Bruant dans son cabaret, 1893
Color lithograph, linen backed, 52 x 37 in. (132.08 x 94 cm)
Courtesy Mr. & Mrs. Clay Timon through Galerie
Michael, Beverly Hills, California

112. Henri de Toulouse-Lautrec (French, 1864-1901)
Aux Variétés, Mademoiselle Lender et Brasseur, 1893
Lithograph (second state), 15 x 11 in. (38.1 x 27.94 cm)
Original lettering removed and new text added, designed
by Lautrec: 'Est elle grasse? Oui/Est elle ici?/oui oui
oui!!!/C'est vous!!!!!!' Oklahoma City Museum of Art,
Purchase from the Mr. and Mrs. Erich P. Frank
Collection, 1967.002

113. Henri de Toulouse-Lautrec (French, 1864-1901)
Jane Avril, 1893
Color lithograph, 48¹³/₁₆ x 36 in. (124 x 91.5 cm)
Courtesy Katherine Kovins through Galerie Michael,
Beverly Hills, California

114. Henri de Toulouse-Lautrec (French, 1864-1901)
Sheet music for *Ta bouche*, 1893
Lithograph with color applied with stencils
10⅝ x 13⁹/₁₆ in. (27 x 34.4 cm)
Jane Voorhees Zimmerli Art Museum

115. Henri de Toulouse-Lautrec (French, 1864-1901)
Sheet music for *Eros Vanné*, 1894
Lithograph, 10¹¹/₁₆ x 13⅝ in. (27.1 x 34.6 cm)
Jane Voorhees Zimmerli Art Museum

116. Henri de Toulouse-Lautrec (French, 1864-1901)
La Chatelaine ou 'Le Tocsin'
[The Chatelaine, or 'Le Tocsin'] 1895
Lithograph, 25⁹/₁₆ x 19¾ in. (65 x 50.1 cm)
Jane Voorhees Zimmerli Art Museum

117. Henri de Toulouse-Lautrec (French, 1864-1901)
Irish American Bar, Rue Royale, The Chap Book, 1895
Color lithograph on wove paper,
15 x 23 in. (38.1 x 58.42 cm)
Courtesy Mr. & Mrs. Clay Timon through Galerie
Michael, Beverly Hills, California

118. Henri de Toulouse-Lautrec (French, 1864-1901)
Divan Japonais, 1896
Color lithograph, 11 x 8 in. (27.94 x 20.32 cm)
Courtesy J. Raj K. Dhawan

119. Henri de Toulouse-Lautrec (French, 1864-1901)
Ambassadeurs: Aristide Bruant dans son Cabaret, 1906
Photomechanical, 13¾ x 10¹/₁₆ in. (35 x 25.5 cm)
Jane Voorhees Zimmerli Art Museum

120. Eugène-Emmanuel Viollet-le-Duc (French, 1814-1879)
Designs for murals in the St. Denis Chapel of Notre-
Dame, Paris. Restoration work began 1845 and was
completed 1864. *Dessins inédits de Viollet-le-Duc*,
vol. I. Paris : A. Guérinet, [18— ?-1902]
15½ x 11¾ in. (39.46 x 29.91 cm)
Architecture Collections, University of Oklahoma
Libraries

121. Eugène-Emmanuel Viollet-le-Duc (French, 1814-1879)
Designs for mural decorations in the Château de
Pierrefonds. Restoration work began 1857 and
continued until Viollet-le-Duc's death in 1879.
Dessins inédits de Viollet-le-Duc, vol. II. Paris : A.
Guérinet, [18— ? 1902]
15½ x 11¾ in. (39.46 x 29.91 cm)
Architecture Collections, University of Oklahoma
Libraries

122. Rudolf Wilke (German, 1873-1908)
"Vollblut" ["Thoroughbred"], in: *Jugend*, vol. 4,
no. 28 (8 July 1899), pp. 446-7, two-page
illustration. 11¾ x 17¾ in. (29.91 x 45.18 cm)
Special Collections and Rare Books,
University of Minnesota, Minneapolis, Minnesota

123. Adolphe Willette (French, 1857-1926)
Girl on a Swing, 1900
Watercolor on cardstock, 11 x 9 in. (27.94 x 22.86 cm)
Courtesy J. Raj K. Dhawan

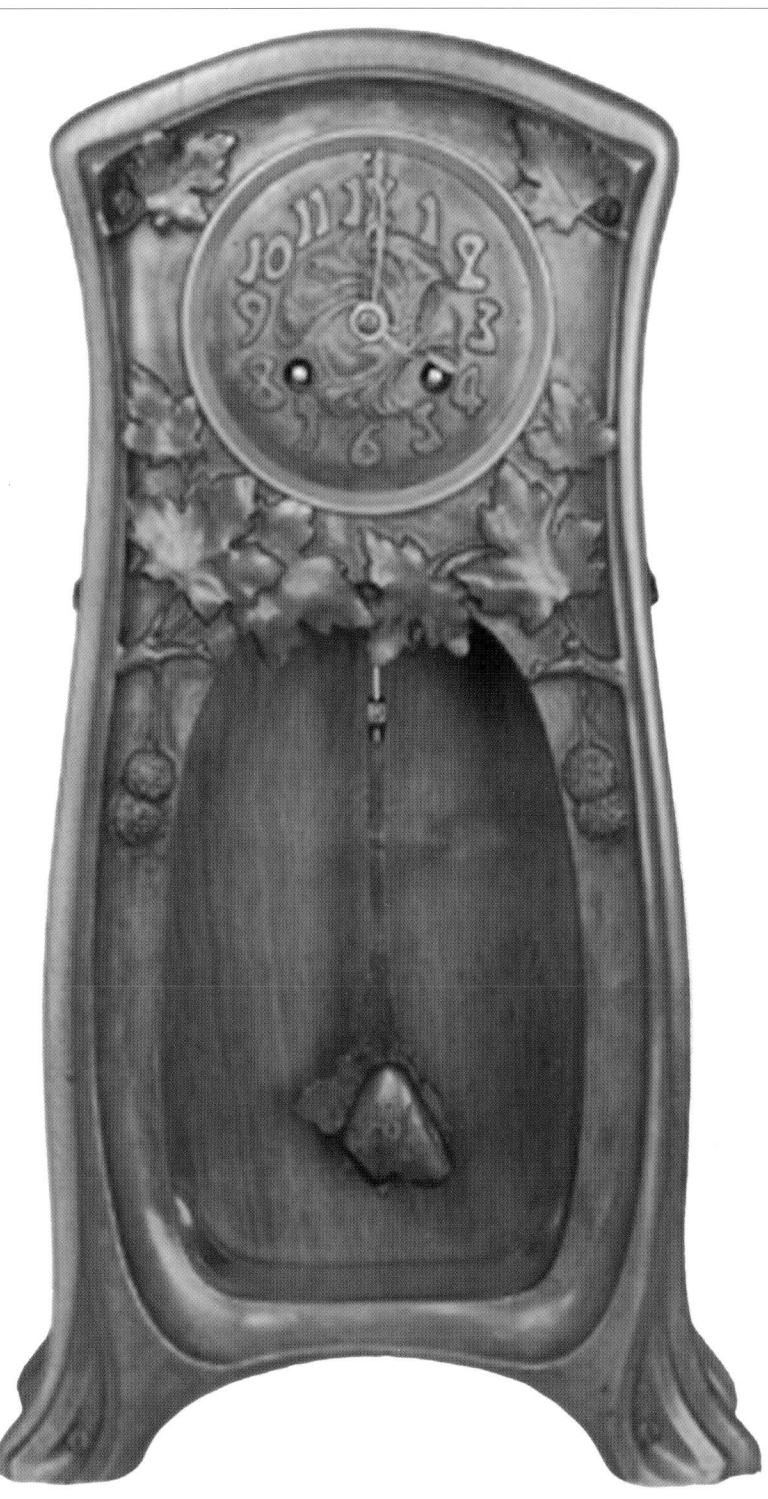

CAT. 62   Louis Majorelle (French, 1859-1926)
MantelClock with Carved Decorations of Foliage and Seedheads, ca. 1900
Wood with bronze front and pendulum,
15¾ x 7 x 4¼ in. (40 x 17.8 x 10.8 cm)
Howard Singer Collection, New York

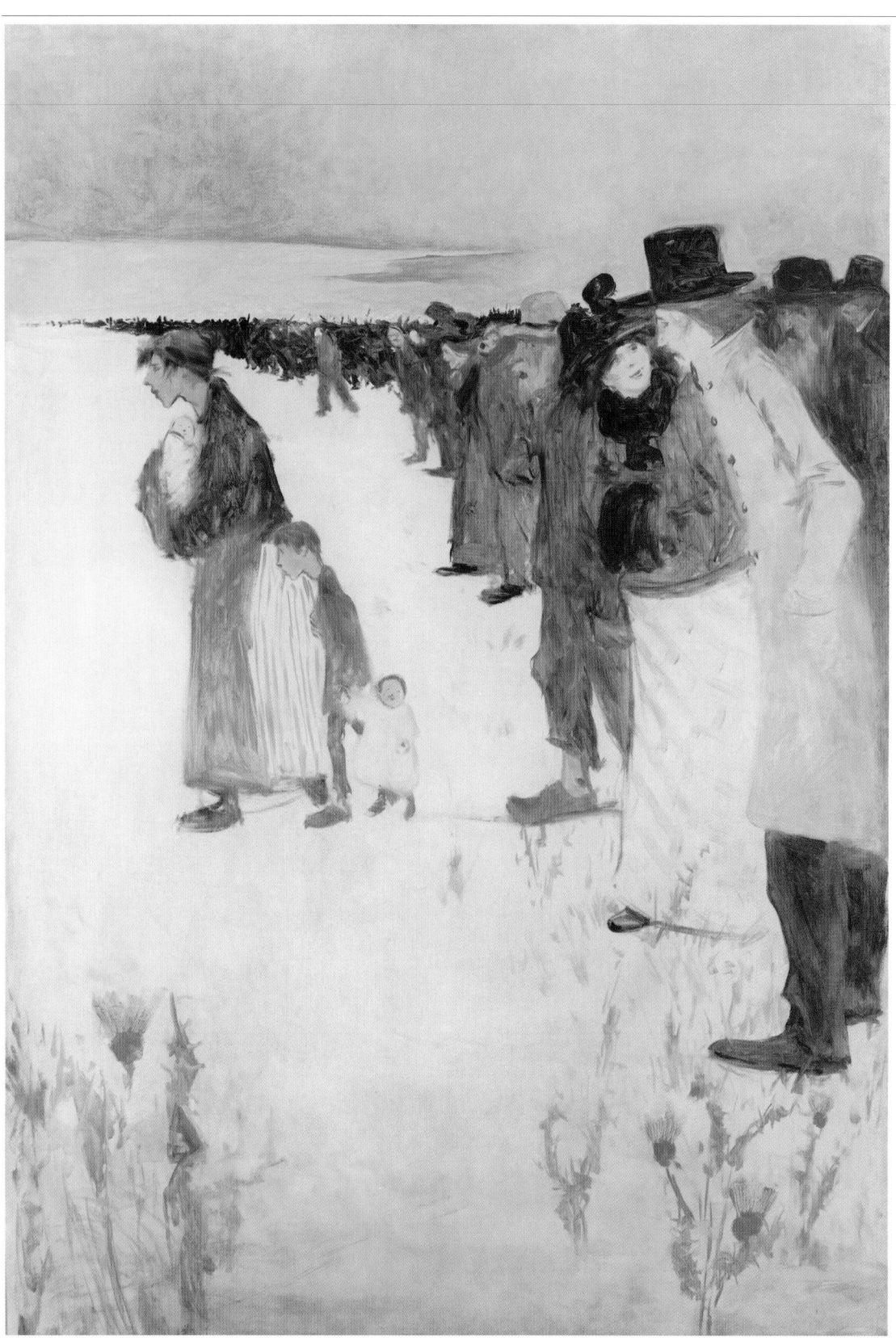

CAT. 107 Théophile-Alexandre Steinlen (Swiss, 1859-1923)
La Marche du Peuple, before 1923
Oil on canvas, 23½ x 16⁹⁄₁₆ in. (59.69 x 42.06 cm)
Wadsworth Atheneum Museum of Art, Hartford, Connecticut.
The Ella Gallup Sumner and Mary Catlin Sumner Collection Fund

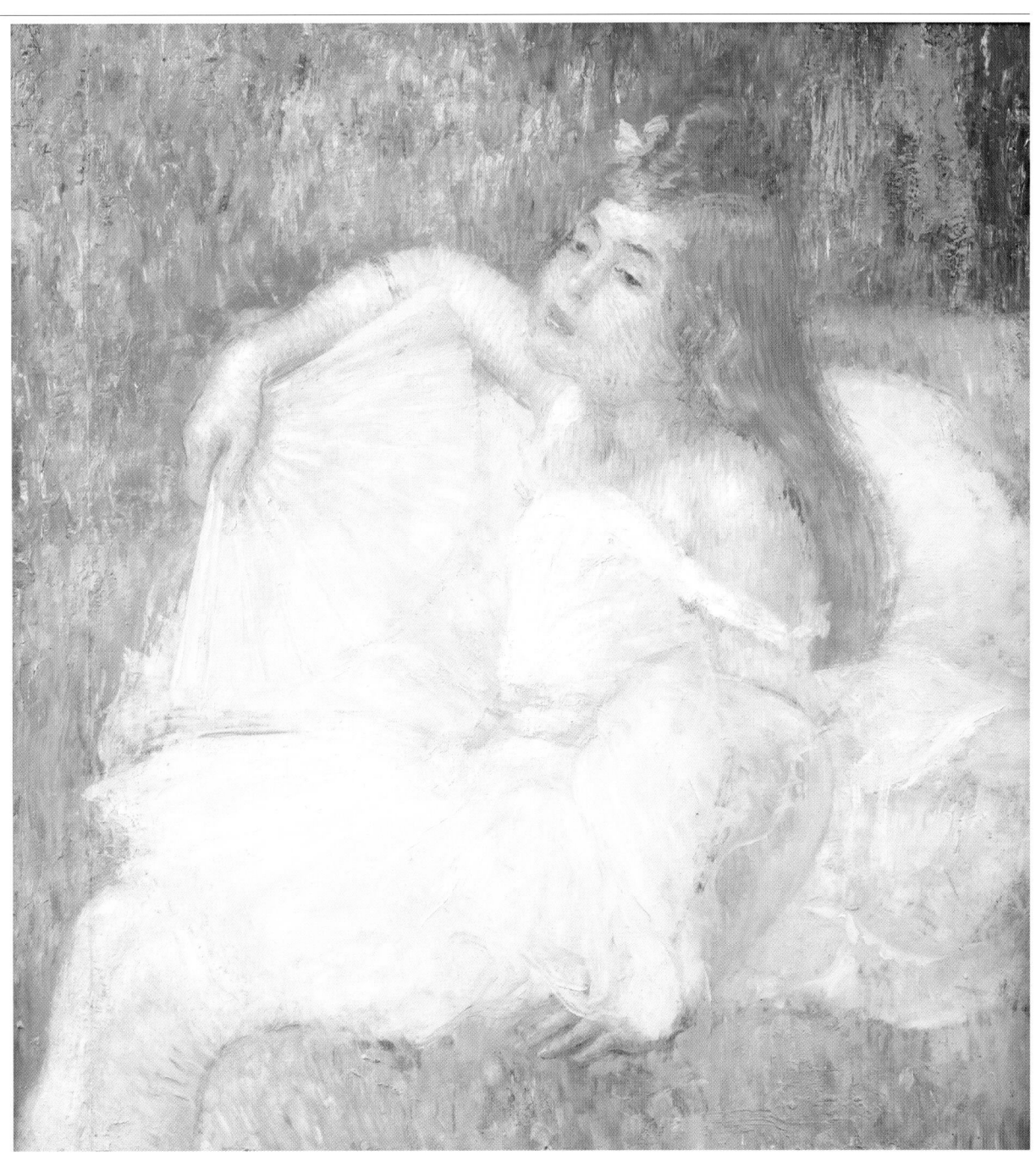

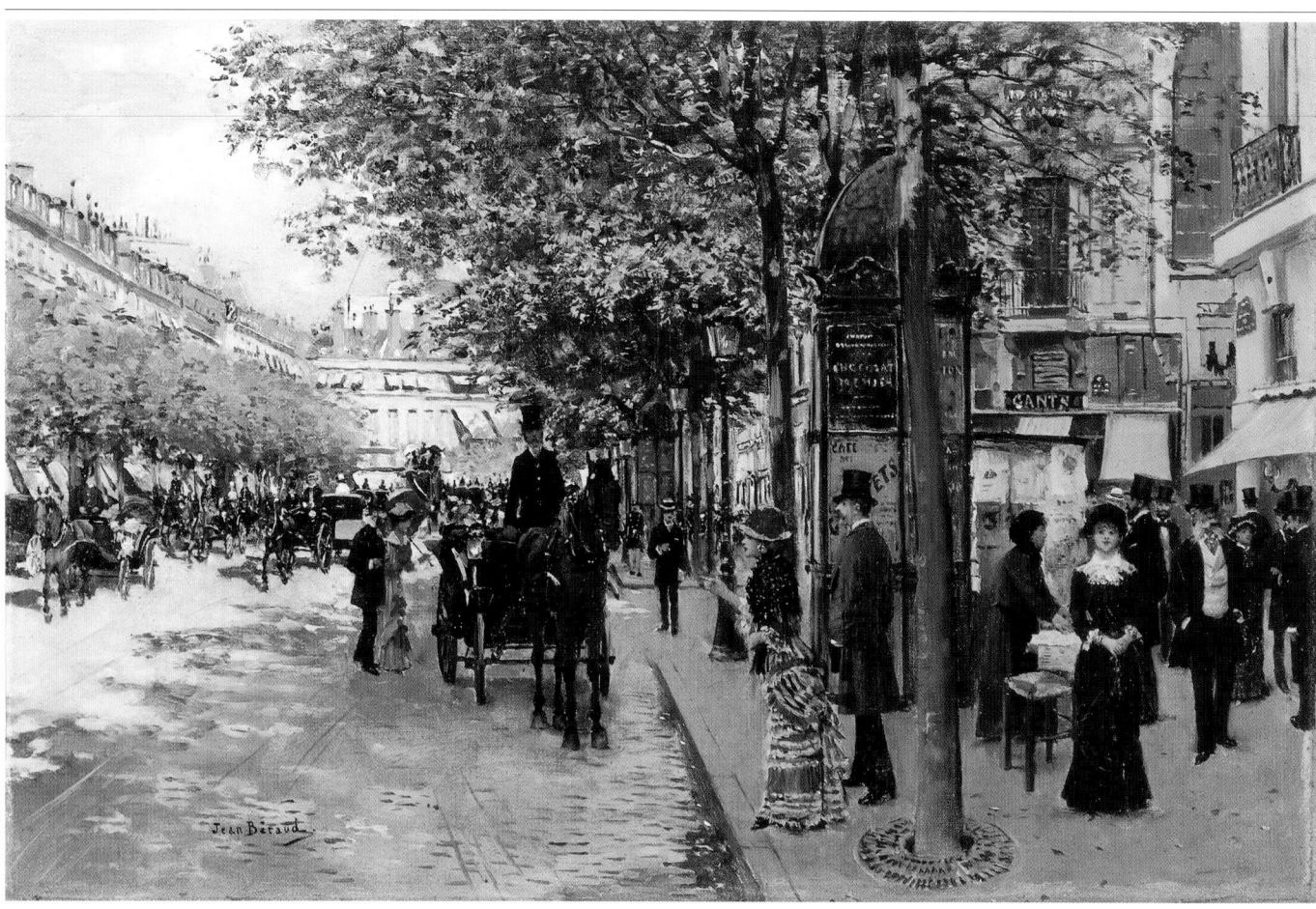

CAT. 4   Jean Béraud (French, 1849-1935)

Paris Street Scene, ca. 1910

Oil on canvas, 9½ x 15 in. (24.13 x 38.1 cm)

Wadsworth Atheneum Museum of Art, Hartford, Connecticut.

Bequest of Genevieve Harlow Goodwin

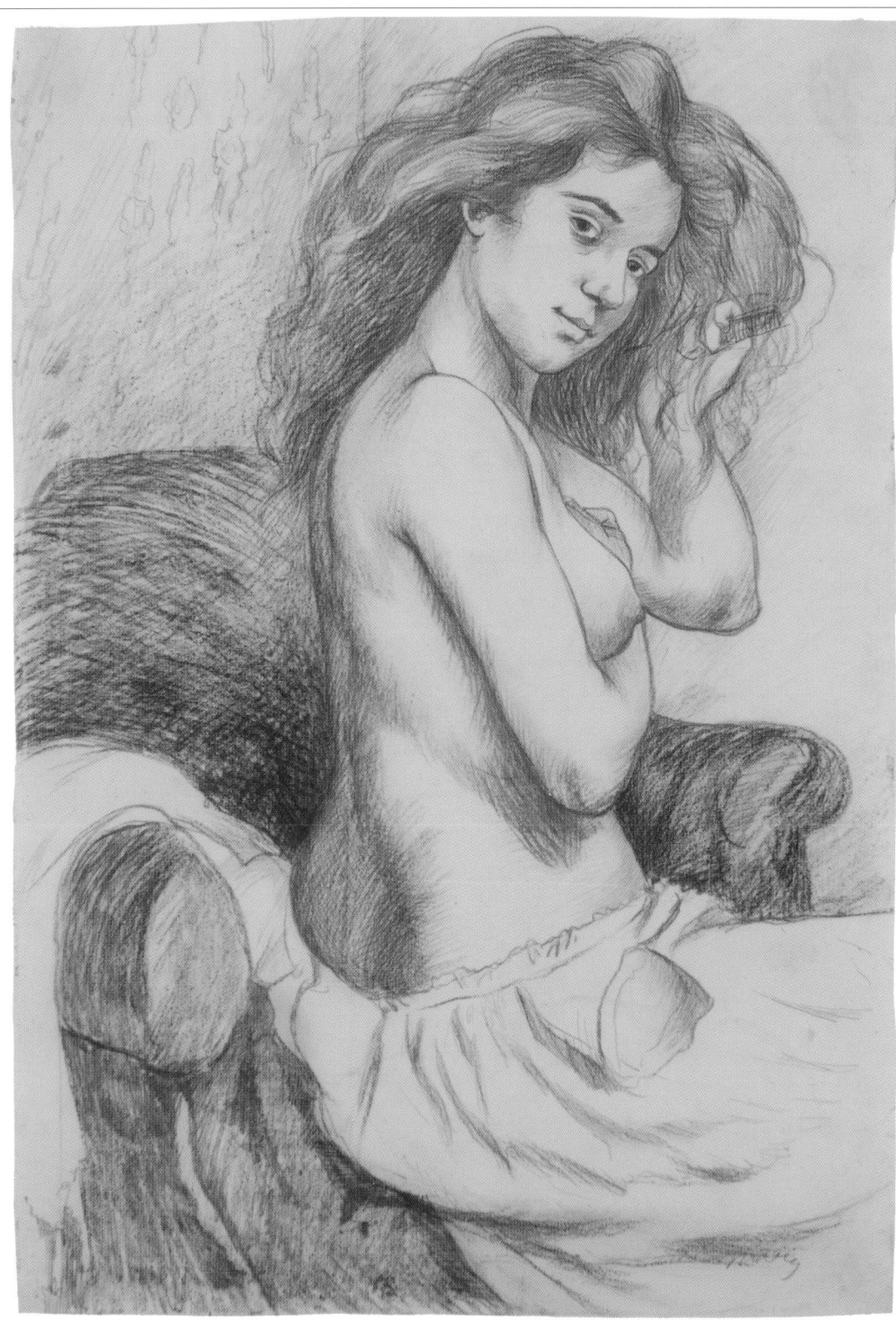

CAT. 64   Charles Maurin (French, 1856-1914)
Young Woman Combing Her Hair, ca. 1895
Crayon, 15¼ x 10¾ in. (38.7 x 27.3 cm)
Jane Voorhees Zimmerli Art Museum; Rutgers, The State University of
New Jersey; David A. and Mildred H. Morse Art Acquisition Fund
Photograph by Jack Abraham; 84.007.005

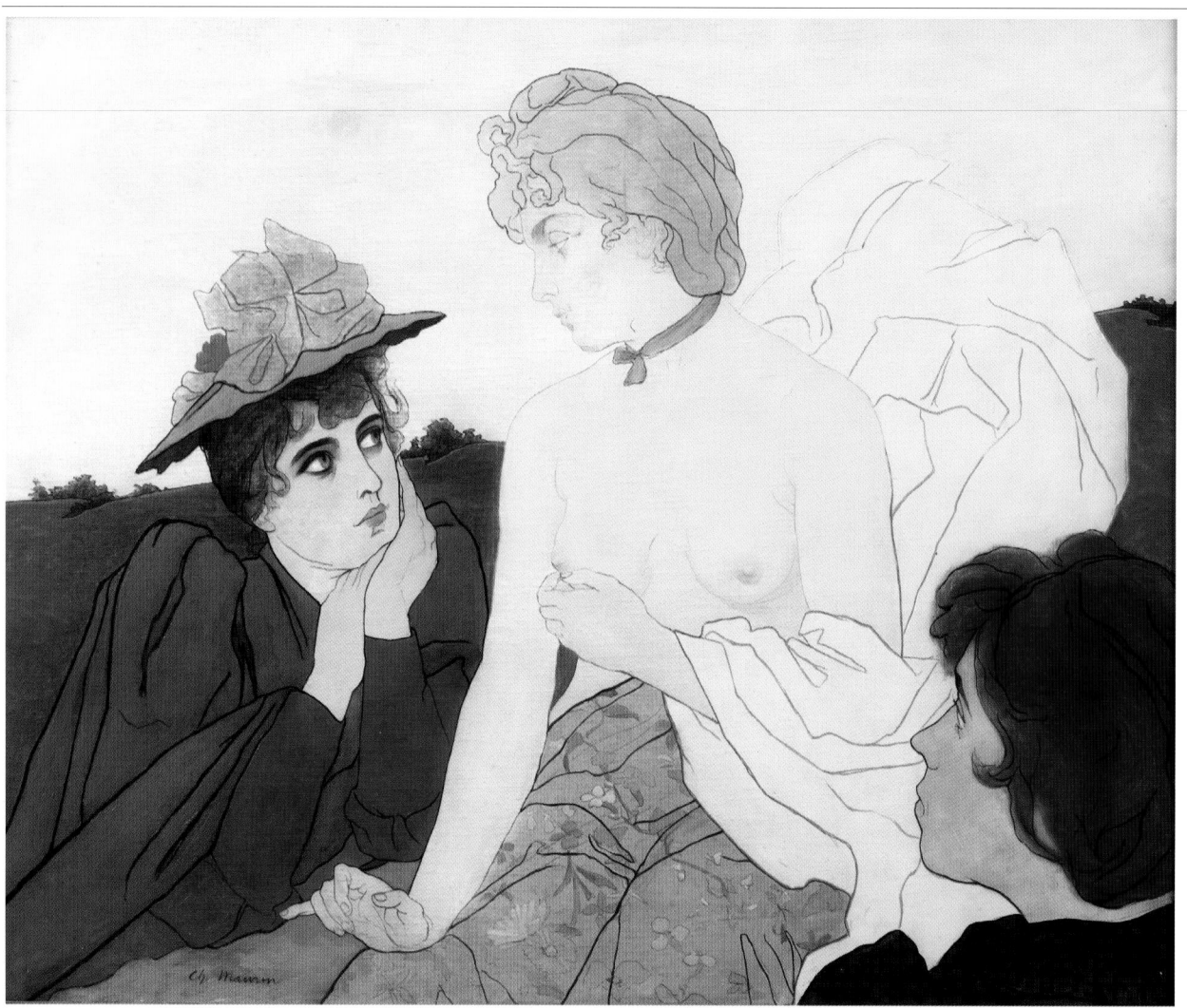

CAT. 63   Charles Maurin (French, 1856-1914)

Chasteté, ca. 1893

Oil on canvas, 25 ³⁄₁₆ x 31 ¹¹⁄₁₆ in. (64 x 80.5 cm)

Russell Collection, Amsterdam

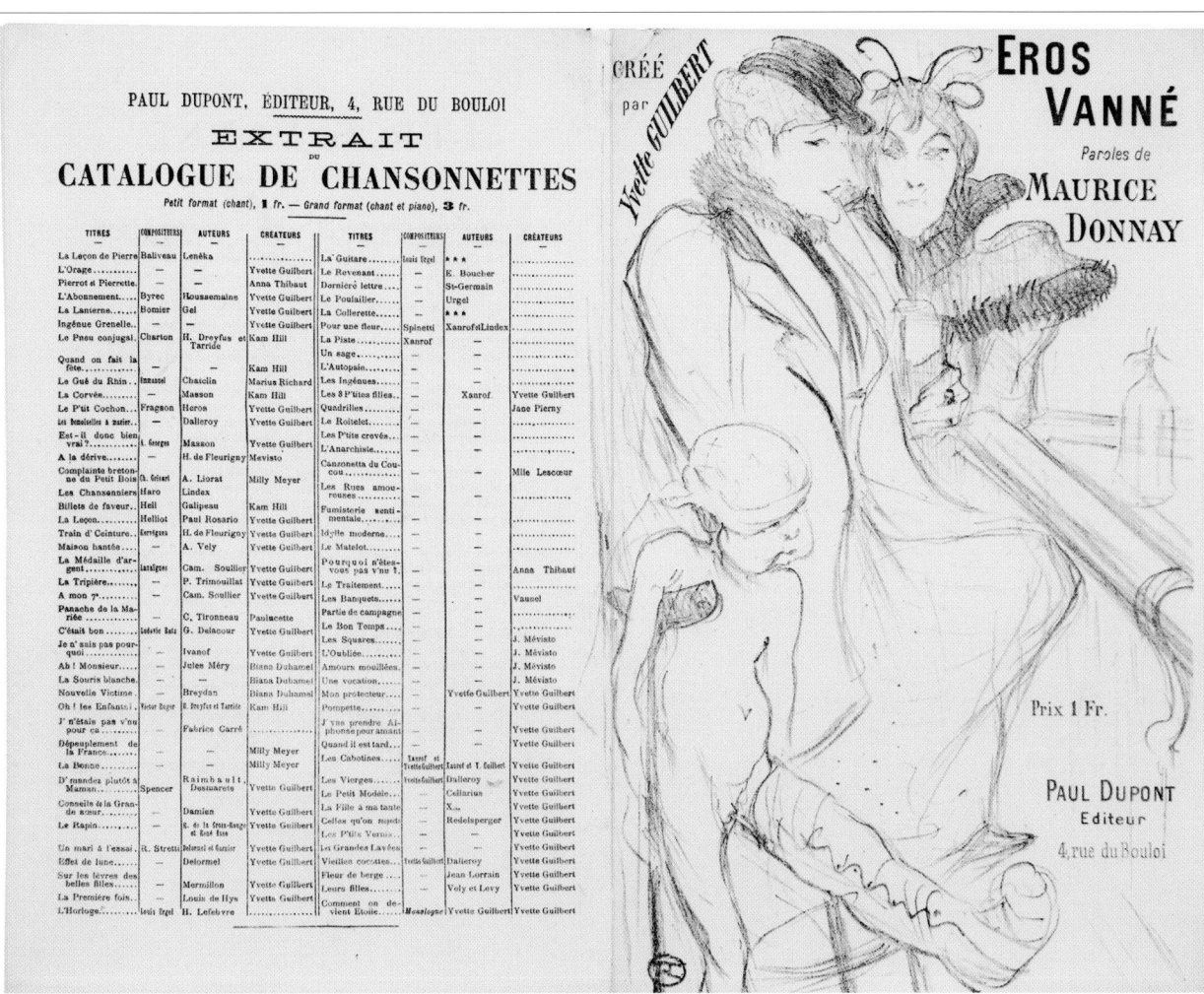

CAT. 115 Henri de Toulouse-Lautrec (French, 1864-1901)

Sheet music for *Eros Vanné*, 1894

Lithograph, 10¾ x 6¾ in. (27.1 x 34.6 cm)

Jane Voorhees Zimmerli Art Museum; Rutgers, The State University of

New Jersey; Regina Best Heldrich Art Acquisition Fund

Photograph by Jack Abraham; 2001.0230

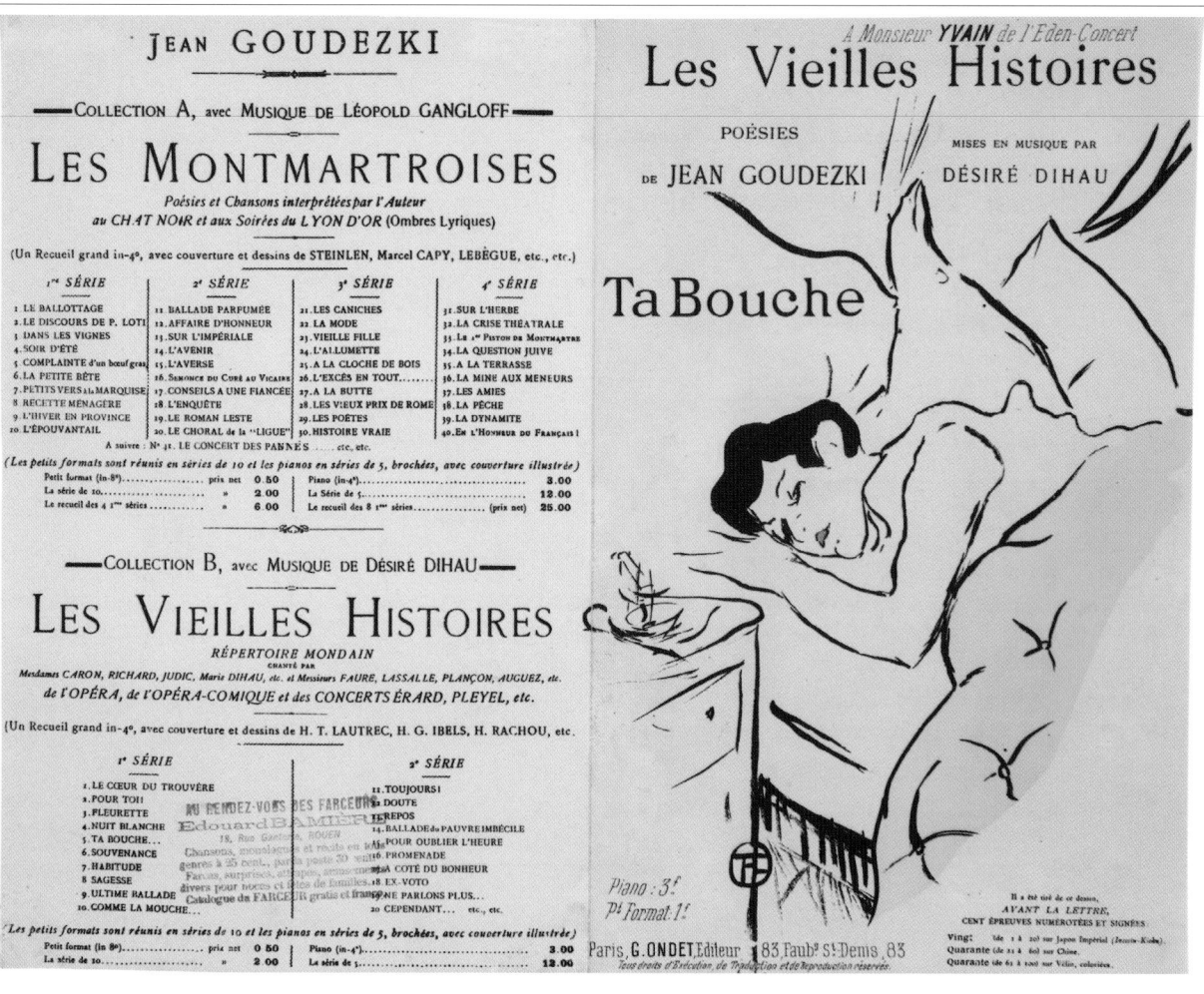

CAT. 114 Henri de Toulouse-Lautrec (French, 1864-1901)

Sheet music for *Ta bouche*, 1893

Lithograph with color applied with stencils; 10⅝ x 13⁹⁄₁₆ in. (27 x 34.4 cm)

Jane Voorhees Zimmerli Art Museum; Rutgers, The State University of

New Jersey; Regina Best Heldrich Art Acquisition Fund

Photograph by Jack Abraham; 2001.0236

Paris 1900
Bibliography

Abbot Suger on the Abbey Church of St. Denis and its Art Treasures. Edited, translated, and annotated by Erwin Panofsky. Princeton, NJ: Princeton University Press, 1979.

Adhémar, Jean. *Toulouse-Lautrec: His Complete Lithographs and Drypoints*. New York: Harry N. Abrams, 1965.

Adriani, Gotz. *Toulouse-Lautrec, The Complete Graphic Works: The Gerstenberg Collection: A Catalogue Raisonné*. London: Thames and Hudson, 1988.

d'Albis, Jean. *Ernest Chaplet: 1835-1909*. Paris: Presses de la connaissance, 1976.

Alexandre, Arsène. *Le Figaro* (28 December 1895): 1.

Allen, Ann Taylor. *Satire and Society in Wilhelmine Germany: Kladderadatsch & Simplicissimus, 1891-1914*. Lexington, KY: University Press of Kentucky, 1984.

Anquetin dessins, peintures (exhibition catalogue). Bordeaux: Centre régional de documentation pédagogique, 1965.

Anquetin, Louis. *De l'art [par] Anquetin*. Edited and annotated by Camille Versini. Paris : Nouvelles Éditions Latines, 1970.

L'Architecture & la sculpture à l'Exposition de 1900, 5 vols. Paris: A. Guerinet, 1904.

d'Argencourt, Louise and Douglas Druick, (eds.). *The Other Nineteenth Century: Paintings and Sculpture in the Collection of Mr. and Mrs. Joseph M. Tanenbaum*. Ottawa: National Gallery of Canada, 1978.

Arwas, Victor. *Alphonse Mucha, Master of Art Nouveau*. London: Academy Editions; New York: St. Martin's Press, 1985.

——. *Alphonse Mucha, The Spirit of Art Nouveau*. Victor Arwas, Jana Brabcova-Orlikova, Anna Dvorak, with an introduction by Ronald F. Lipp and Suzanne Jackson and essays by Quentin Bajac, et al. (exhibition catalogue). Alexandria, VA: Art Services International; New Haven: Yale University Press, 1998.

——. *Art Nouveau: The French Aesthetic*, pts.1-2. London: Andreas Papadakis, 2002.

——. *Belle Epoque: Posters & Graphics*. New York: Rizzoli, 1978.

—— and Veronique Arwas. *Louis Legrand : Catalogue Raisonné*. London: Papadakis, 2006.

Baldick, Robert. *The Life of J.K. Huysmans*. Oxford: Clarendon Press, 1955.

Bantens, Robert James. *Eugène Carrière, His Work and His Influence*. Ann Arbor, MI: UMI Research Press, 1983.

Barazzetti-Demoulin, Suzanne. *Maurice Denis, 25 novembre 1870, 13 novembre 1943* (exhibition catalogue). Paris: B.Grasset, 1945.

Baumgart, E. "La Maufacture Nationale de Sèvres en 1900: Les Biscuits. " *Art et Décoration*, no. 7 (January-June 1900): 139-47.

Bénédite, Léonce. *Exposition universelle de 1900: les beaux-arts et les arts décoratifs, par L. Bénédite, J. Cornély, Clément-Janin, Gustave Geffroy, J.J. Guiffrey, Eugène Guillaume, G. Lafenestre, Lucien Magne, P. Frantz Marcou, Camille Mauclair, Roger Marx, André Michel, Auguste Molinier, Émile Molinier, Salomon Reinach*. Paris: Gazette des Beaux-Arts, 1900.

Benjamin, Walter. *The Arcades Project*. Cambridge, MA: Belknap Press, 1999.

——, Hannah Arendt, (ed.), and Harry Zohn. *Illuminations*. London: Fontana/Collins, 1973.

The Berne Convention for the Protection of Literary and Artistic Works, from 1886 to 1986. Geneva: International Bureau of Intellectual Property, 1986.

Blanche, Jacques-Émile. *Correspondance Jacques-Émile Blanche- Maurice Denis (1901-1939)*. Edited edition, presented and annotated by Georges-Paul Collet. Geneva: Droz, 1989.

Bodelsen, Merete. *Toulouse-Lautrec's Posters*. Copenhagen: The Museum of Decorative Arts, 1964.

"Bodenhausen to Lichtwark" (correspondence: 16 July 1895). Kunsthalle, Lichtwark-Archive, Hamburg.

Bouillon, Jean-Paul. *Maurice Denis*. Geneva: A. Skira, 1993.

Bourget, Paul. *Essais de psychologie contemporaine*, vol. 1-2. Paris: Plon-Nourrit et cie, 1924.

Bridges, Ann, (ed.). *Alphonse Mucha, The Complete Graphic Works*. New York: Harmony Books, 1980.

Brown-Séquard, Charles-Édouard. *Archives de physiologie normale et pathologique*. Paris: V. Masson, 1868-1898.

Brunhammer, Yvonne, et. al. *Art Nouveau, Belgium, France* (exhibition catalogue). Organized by the Institute for the Arts, Rice University, and the Art Institute of Chicago. Rice Museum, Houston (26 March 1976 – 27 June 1976); Art Institute of Chicago (28 August 1976-31 October 1976). Houston, TX: Institute for the Arts, Rice University, 1976.

Buffet-Challié, Laurence. *The Art Nouveau Style*. Translated from the French by Geoffrey Williams. New York: Rizzoli, 1982.

Cailler, Pierre. *Catalogue raisonné de l'œuvre gravé et lithographié de Maurice Denis*. Geneva: Cailler, 1968.

Caillet, H. "Monsieur F. Khnopff's Villa." *The Studio*, vol. 57 (1912): 201-7.

Carabin, François Rupert. *L'Oeuvre de Rupert Carabin: 1862-1932*. Galerie du Luxembourg, (20 May-October 1974). Introduction by Yvonne Brunhammer; text by Colette Merklen-Carabin. Paris: Galerie du Luxembourg, 1974.

Carluccio, Luigi. *The Sacred and Profane in Symbolist Art* (exhibition catalogue). Toronto: Art Gallery of Ontario, 1969.

Carrière, Jean-René. *De la Vie d'Eugène Carrière, souvenirs, lettres, pensées, documents*. Toulouse: E. Privat, 1966.

Cass, Claire and Jason Jacques. *Masterpieces of French Art Pottery, 1885-1910*. New York: Jason Jacques Inc., 2005.

Catalogue du Salon de la Rose + Croix (10 March - 10 April). Paris : Galerie Durand-Ruel, 1892: 7-11.

Catalogue Illustré de l'exposition des Arts Incohérents. Paris: E. Bernard et cie, 1884: 29.

Cate, Phillip Dennis and Sinclair Hamilton Hitchings. *The Color Revolution: Color Lithography in France, 1890-1900*. Salt Lake City: Peregrine Smith, Inc., 1978.

—— and Susan Gill. *Steinlen*. Layton, UT: G.M. Smith, 1982.

Charcot, Jean Martin. *Leçons sur les maladies du foie, des voies biliaires et des reins, faites à la Faculté de médecine de Paris*. Paris: Progrès médical, 1877.

——. *Lectures on the Diseases of the Nervous System, Second Series*. Translated and edited by George Sigerson with an introduction by Walter Riese. New York: Hafner Pub. Co., 1962.

Chassé, Charles. *Le Mouvement symboliste dans l'art du XIXe siècle*. Paris: Librairie Floury, 1947.

——. *The Nabis and their Period*. London: Lund Humphries, 1969.

Chéret, Jules. *La Naissance de l'Affiche Moderne, 1866-1886* (exhibition catalogue). Chaumont: La Maison du livre et de l'Affiche, 1994.

"Chronique," *L'Art décoratif* 1 (February 1899): 250.

Clarke, J.A. "Munch, Liebermann, and the question of etched 'reproductions.'" *Visual Resources* 16.1 (2000): 28.

Clement, Russell T. *Four French Symbolists: A sourcebook on Pierre Puvis de Chavannes, Gustave Moreau, Odilon Redon, and Maurice Denis*. Westport, CT: Greenwood Press, 1996.

Le Courrier français, 15.11 (13 March 1898): 9.

Crauzat, Ernest de. *L'Oeuvre gravé et lithographié de Steinlen: catalogue descriptif et analytique suivi d'un essai de bibliographie et d'iconographie de son œuvre illustré*. Paris: Société de propagation des livres d'art, 1913.

Delevoy, Robert L. *Fernand Khnopff*. Brussels: Éditions Lebeer-Hossmann, 1979.

——. *Symbolists and symbolism*. New York: Skira, 1978.

Delteil, Loys. *Le peintre-graveur illustré (XIX et XX siècles)*. Paris: Chez Lauteur, 1906.

Denis, Maurice. *Journal*, vols. 1-2. Paris: La Colombe, 1957. *Maurice Denis: Earthly Paradise (1870-1943)*. Paris: Éditions de la Réunion des Musées Nationaux, 2006.

——. *Du symbolisme au classicisme; théories. Textes réunis et présentés par Olivier Revault d'Allonnes*. Paris: Hermann, 1964.

"Der Bing'sche Pavillon l'Art Nouveau auf der Weltausstellung," *Dekorative Kunst 3* (1900): 490-92.

Dessins de Steinlen, 1859-1923. XLᵉ exposition du Cabinet des dessins, Paris, 1968. Catalogue edited by Françoise Viatte. Preface by Maurice Sérullaz. Paris: Réunion des musées nationaux, 1968.

Dorra, Henri, (ed.). *Symbolist Art Theories: A Critical Anthology*. Berkeley: University of California Press, 1994.

Dortu, M.G. *Toulouse-Lautrec et son œuvre*, vols.1-6. New York: Collectors Editions, 1971.

Dumont-Wilden, Louis. *Fernand Khnopff*. Brussels: G. van Oest & cie, 1907.

Duncan, Alastair. *Art Nouveau Furniture*. New York: C.N. Potter: Distributed by Crown, 1982.

——. *Louis Majorelle: Master of Art Nouveau Design*. New York: Harry N. Abrams, 1991.

Eemans, Nestor. *Fernand Khnopff*. Anvers: Edited by De Sikkel for the Ministère de l'instruction publique, 1950.

Elderfield, John, (ed.). *Modern Painting and Sculpture: 1880 to the Present at the Museum of Modern Art*. New York: The Museum of Modern Art, 2004.

Fahr-Becker, Gabriele. *Art Nouveau, An Art of Transition: From Individualism to Mass Society*. Translated by Frederick G. Peters and Diana S. Peters. Woodbury, NY: Barron's Educational Series, 1982.

Fanica, Pierre-Olivier. *Charles Jacque, 1813-1894: École de Barbizon: graveur original et peintre animalier*. Montigny-sur-Loing: Art Bizon, 1995.

Fermigier, André. *Toulouse-Lautrec*. New York: Frederick A. Praeger, 1969.

Fernand Khnopff, 1858-1921. Brussels: Royal Museums of Fine Art Belgium, 2004.

Fernand Khnopff and the Belgian avant-garde (exhibition catalogue). Introduction by Barry Friedman. David and Alfred Smart Gallery, Chicago (5 January – 26 February 1984); Barry Friedman Ltd., New York (12 March – 28 June 1984); Delaware Art Museum, Wilmington (12 July –26 August 1984). New York, NY: B. Friedman Ltd., 1983.

Fields, Armond. *Henri Rivière*. Salt Lake City: G.M. Smith/Peregrine Smith Books, 1983.

Finger, Stanley. *Minds Behind the Brain: A History of the Pioneers and Their Discoveries*. Oxford; New York: Oxford University Press, 2000.

Foucault, Michel. "What is an Author?" *Screen*, vol. 20.1 (Spring 1979): 13-29.

Fusco, Peter. *The Romantics to Rodin: French Nineteenth-century Sculpture from North American Collections* (exhibition catalogue). Edited by Peter Fusco and H.W. Janson. Los Angeles: Los Angeles County Museum of Art; New York: G. Braziller, 1980.

Gage, John. *Color and Meaning: Art, Science, and Symbolism*. Berkeley; Los Angeles: University of California Press, 1999.

Gide, André. *Correspondance: 1892-1945*. Edition edited, annotated, and published by Pierre Masson and Carina Schäfer; in collaboration with Claire Denis. Paris: Gallimard, 2006.

Goddard, Linda. "Symbolism (exhibition review)." *Burlington Magazine*, vol. 169, no. 1253 (August 2007): 581-2.

Goldsmidt, Lucian and Herbert Schimmel. *Unpublished Correspondence of Henri de Toulouse-Lautrec, 1864-1901*, 2 vols. Paris: Floury, 1926-1927.

Goldstein, Robert Justin. *Censorship of Political Caricature in Nineteenth-Century France*. Kent: Kent State University Press, 1989.

Goldwater, Robert John. *Symbolism*. London: Allen Lane, 1979.

Goncourt, Edmond de. *La maison d'un artiste*, vols. 1-2. Paris: G. Charpentier, 1881.

The Goncourt Journals, 1851-1870. Edited and translated from the Journal of Edmond and Jules de Goncourt, with an introduction, notes, and a biographical repertory by Lewis Galantiere. Garden City, NY: Doubleday, Doran, & Company, Inc., 1937.

Gounot, Roger. *Charles Maurin, 1856-1914: essai sur le peintre et catalogue de l'exposition de 1978*. Le Puy: Musée Crozatier du Puy, 1978.

Greenhalgh, Paul, (ed.). *Art Nouveau, 1890-1914* (exhibition catalogue). London: Victoria & Albert Museum; Washington, D.C.: National Gallery of Art, 2000.

——. *Essential Art Nouveau*. London: Victoria & Albert Museum, 2000.

Guide to the Berne Convention for the Protection of Literary and Artistic Words (Paris Act, 1971). Geneva: World Intellectual Property Organization, 1978.

Guiffrey, Jules. *L'œuvre de Ch. Jacque, catalogue de ses eaux-fortes et pointes sèches*. Paris: Mlle Lemaire, 1866.

Heller, S. "Late, Great *Simplicissimus*," *Print* 33 (September 1979): 36.

Henri de Toulouse-Lautrec: Images of the 1890s (exhibition catalogue). New York: The Museum of Modern Art: Distributed by New York Graphic Society Books, 1985.

Hoentschel, A.M. Georges. "Notes sur Carriès, " *Art et Décoration*, no. 7 (January-June 1900): 64-73.

Howe, Jeffery W. *The Symbolist Art of Fernand Khnopff*. Ann Arbor, MI: UMI Research Press, 1982.

Huysmans, Joris Karl. *L'Art moderne*. Paris, 1883.

——. *Au rebours* and *Le drageoir à épices*. Preface by Hubert Juin. Paris: Union Générale d'Éditions, 1975.

——. *Certains*. Paris, 1889.

—— and Robert Baldick, (trans.). *À rebours* [Against the Grain]. Harmondsworth, Middlesex, England: Penguin Books Ltd., 1968

J. "Art industriel," *L'Art Décoratif* 1 (March 1899): 250.

Jacob, Mira. *Charles Filiger : 1863-1928*. Strasbourg: Musées de la Ville de Strasbourg, 1990.

Jean Béraud: 1849-1935: un témoin de la Belle Époque: collections du Musée Carnavalet. Musée Carnavalet (5 June-29 July 1979); Mairie-annexe du Ve Arrondissement (28 September-26 October 1979). Paris: Le Musée, 1979.

Jeanne, Paul. *Les théâtres d'ombres à Montmartre de 1887 à 1923*. Paris: Les Éditions des presses modernes au Palais-royal, 1937.

Jensen, Robert. *Marketing Modernism in Fin-de-Siècle Europe*. Princeton: Princeton University Press, 1994.

Joyant, Maurice. *Henri de Toulouse-Lautrec, 1864-1901*, 2 vols. Paris: Floury, 1926-1927.

Jullian, Philippe. *Dreamers of Decadence: Symbolist Painters of the 1890s*. New York: Praeger, 1971.

Jumeau-Lafond, Jean-David, Arcadi Calzada i Salavedra, Pablo Jiménez Burillo and Guillermo Solana. *Un País Ideal El Paisatge simbolista a França* (exhibition). Fundació Caixa de Girona, 2006.

——. *Les Peintres de l'âme: le Symbolisme idéaliste en France* (exhibition catalogue). Uitgeverij Snoeck-Ducaju & Zoon/Gent: Sabam Belgium, 1999.

Juniper, Andrew. *Wabi sabi: The Japanese Art of Impermanence*. Boston: Tuttle Pub., 2003. Krahmer, Catherine. *Pan* 1.2 (June 1895): 99-100.

——. "Pan and Toulouse-Lautrec." *Print Quarterly* 10.4 (December 1993): 392-7.

"Korrespondenzen: Paris," *Dekorative Kunst* 2 (1899): 215.

Lacambre, Genevieve. *French Symbolist Painters* (exhibition catalogue). London-Liverpool: Hayward Gallery, 1972.

Laclotte, Michel and Jean Pierre Cuzin. *Petit Larousse de la peinture*. Paris: Larousse, 1979.

Lacquemant, Karine. "The Bing Art Nouveau Pavilion at the World's Fair of 1900: New Art from Old," in: *The Origins of L'Art Nouveau: The Bing Empire*, Gabriel P. Weisberg, Edwin Becker, and Évelyne Possémé (eds.). Amsterdam: Van Gogh Museum; Paris: Musée des arts décoratifs; Antwerp: Mercatorfonds, 2004: 191.

Lambourne, Lionel. *Japonisme: Cultural Crossings between Japan and the West*. London: Phaidon, 2005.

Laran, Jean. *Inventaire du Fonds Français après 1800*. Paris: Bibliothèque Nationale 4; M. Le Garrec, 1930.

Leen, Frederik, (catalogue compilation). *Fernand Khnopff, 1858-1921* (exhibition catalogue). Brussels: Royal Museums of Fine Art of Belgium, 2004.

Legrand, Francine-Claire and Alistair Kennedy (trans.). *Symbolism in Belgium*. Brussels: Laconti, 1972.

Leipnik, F.L. *A History of French Etching from the Sixteenth Century to the Present Day*. London: John Lane, the Bodley Head, 1924.

Loïe Fuller, Danseuse de l'Art Nouveau. Exhibition organized by the Musée de l'école de Nancy, Musée des beaux-arts (17 May – 19 August 2002. Paris: Réunion des musées nationaux, 2002.

Lost Paradise: Symbolist Europe (exhibition catalogue). Jean Clair and Pierre Théberge. Montreal: Montreal Museum of Fine Arts, 1995.

Lövgren, Sven. *The Genesis of Modernism: Seurat, Gauguin, Van Gogh, & French Symbolism in the 1880's*. Bloomington: Indiana University Press, 1971.

Lucie-Smith, Edward. *Symbolist Art*. New York: Thames and Hudson, 1985.

Mabille, Xavier. *La Belgique depuis la Seconde guerre mondiale*. Brussels: Centre de recherche et d'information socio-politiques, 2003.

Mack, Gerstle. *Toulouse-Lautrec*. New York: A.A. Knopf, 1938.

Madsen, S. Tschudi. *Sources of Art Nouveau*. Translated by Ragnar Christophersen. New York: G. Wittenborn, 1956.

"The Man in the Street," *New York Times* (2 June 1901): SM1.

Marx, Roger. "Lautrec et Maurin." *Le Voltaire* (February 1893).

Mauceley, Baude de. "L'Evénment." (30 October 1895).

Mauclair, Camille. *Jules Chéret*. Paris : M. Le Garrec, 1930.

——. *Louis Legrand: peintre et graveur*. Paris: H. Floury; G. Pellet, 1910.

Maurice Denis. Orangerie des Tuileries (3 June – 31 August 1970). Exhibition catalogue, notes edited by Anne Dayez. Paris: Ministère d'État, Affaires culturelles, 1970.

Maurice Denis. Gemälde, Handzeichnungen, Druckgraphik. Meisterwerke des Nachimpressionismus aus der Sammlung Maurice Denis. (Ausstellung) Kunsthaus Zürich, 29. Jan-12. März 1972 (exhibition catalogue). Zurich, 1972.

Maurice Denis et la Bretagne. Musée de Morlaix (3 July-29 September 1985); Maurice Denis à Perros-Guirec: Maison des Traouïeros, Perros-Guirec (13 July-20 August 1985). Morlaix: Le Musée; Perros-Guirec: La Maison, 1985.

Maurice Denis, 1870-1943. Paris, Musée d'Orsay (31 October 2006 -21 January 2007); Montreal, Musée des beaux-arts de Montréal, Pavillon Michal et Renata Hornstein (22 February – 20 May 2007); Rovereto, Museo di arte moderna e contemporanea di Trento e Rovereto (23 June – 23 September 2007. Paris: Réunion des musées nationaux; Montréal: Musée des beaux-arts de Montréal, 2006.

Meier-Graefe, Julius. "Floral-Linear." *Dekorative Kunst 4* (1899): 169, in: Kathryn Bloom Hiesinger, (ed.), *Art Nouveau in Munich: Masters of Jugendstil from the Stadtmuseum, Munich, and other Public and Private Collections*. Philadelphia: Philadelphia Museum of Art and Prestel Verlag, 1988: 19.

——. *Modern Art: Being a Contribution to a New System of Aesthetics*. London: W. Heinemann; New York: G.P. Putnam's Sons, 1908.

——. "Some Recent Continental Bookbindings." *Studio* 9 (October 1896): 38.

Menon, Elizabeth. "Decadent Addictions: Tobacco, Alcohol, Popular Culture and Café Society," in: Laurinda Dixon, (ed.), *In Sickness and in Health, Disease as Metaphor in Art and Popular Wisdom*. Newark: University of Delaware Press, 2004.

——. "Les Fleurs du mal," in: *Evil by Design: The Making and Marketing of the Femme Fatale*. Champaign-Urbana: University of Illinois Press, 2006.

Millman, Ian. *Georges de Feure: Maître du Symbolisme et de L'Art Nouveau*. Courbevoie, Paris: ACR, 1992.

Milner, John. *Symbolists and Decadents*. London: Studio Vista, 1971.

Moffett, Kenworth. *Meier-Graefe as Art Critic*. Munich: Prestel-Verlag, 1973.

Morris, William. *Art and its Producers, and The Arts and Crafts of Today: Two Addresses Delivered Before the National Association for the Advancement of Art*. London: Longmans & Co., 1901.

——. *News from Nowhere, or, An Epoch of Rest: Being Some Chapters from a Utopian Romance*. Edited with an introduction and notes by David Leopold. Oxford; New York: Oxford University Press, 2003.

Mucha, 1860-1839: peintures, illustrations, affiches, arts décoratifs (exhibition catalogue).Essays by Jiri Kotalik, Michel Laclotte, Marc Bascou, Jana Brabcova and Geneviève Lacambre. Paris, Grand Palais (5 February – 28 April 1980), organized by the National Gallery of Prague and the Réunion des musées nationaux. Paris: Éditions de la Réunion des musées nationaux, 1980.

Mucha, Jiri, Marina Henderson and Aaron Scharf. *Alphonse Mucha*. New York: St. Martin's Press, 1974.

Mucha, Sarah. *Alphonse Mucha*. London: Frances Lincoln, 2005.

Natanson, Thadée. "Œuvres de H. de Toulouse-Lautrec." *La Revue Blanche* (February 1893): 146.

Ockman, Carol and Kenneth E. Silver. *Sarah Bernhardt: The Art of High Drama*. New York: Jewish Museum, under the auspices of the Jewish Theological Seminary of America; New Haven: Yale University Press, 2005.

Péladan, Joséphin. *L'Art idealistique et mystique*. Paris: E. Sansot, 1909.

——. *Introduction à l'esthétique*. Paris: E. Sansot, 1907.

Pianzola, Maurice. *Théophile-Alexandre Steinlen*. Lausanne: Éditions Rencontre, 1971.

Pincus-Witten, Robert. *Occult Symbolism in France: Joséphin Péladan and the Salons de la Rose-Croix*. New York: Garland Pub., 1976.

Post-Impressionist Graphics: Original Prints by French Artists, 1880-1903 (exhibition catalogue, Mary Anne Stevens). London: Arts Council, 1980.

"A Poster Artist: Maurice Biais at the New Gallery of Williams," *New York Times* (19 October 1901): 9.

Proust, Marcel. *A la recherche du temps perdu*. Paris: Gallimard, 1954.

——. *Remembrance of Things Past*, "Swann's Way," "Swann in Love," vol. 1. Translated by C. K. Scott Moncrieff and Terence Kilmartin. New York: Vintage Books, A Division of Random House, 1982.

Ramiro, Erastène. *Louis Legrand, peintre-graveur; catalogue de son œuvre gravé et lithographié*. Paris: H. Floury, 1896.

Reade, Brian. *Art Nouveau and Alphonse Mucha*. London: H.M.S.O., 1967.

Rennert, Jack and Alain Weill. *Alphonse Mucha: The Complete Posters and Panels*. Boston, MA: G.K. Hall, 1984.

Rewald, John. *The History of Impressionism*. New York: The Museum of Modern Art, 1973.

Rodenbach, Georges. *Bruges-la-morte*. Paris: E. Flammarion, n.d.

Roger Marx, un critique aux côtés de Gallé, Monet, Rodin, Gauguin: Nancy, musée des beaux-arts: musée de l'école de Nancy, 6 mai-28 août 2006. Ville de Nancy: Artlys, 2006.

Roy, Alain and Paula Goldenberg. *Les peintures italiennes du Musée des beaux-arts: XVIe, XVIIe & XVIIIe siècles*. Strasbourg: Musées de la ville de Strasbourg, Musée des beaux-arts, 1996.

Salmon, Eric, (ed.). *Bernhardt and the Theatre of Her Time*. Westport, CT: Greenwood Press, 1984.

Sandier, Alexandre. "La Céramique à l'Exposition." *Art et Décoration*, no. 9 (January-June 1901): 62.

Schafter, Debra. *The Order of Ornament, the Structure of Style: Theoretical Foundations of Modern Art and Architecture*. New York: Cambridge University Press, 2003.

Schardt, Hermann, (ed.). *Paris 1900: Masterworks of French Poster Art*. New York: Putnam, 1970.

Schimmel, Herbert D., (ed.). *The Letters of Henri de Toulouse-Lautrec*. Oxford; New York: Oxford University Press, 1991.

Schurr, Gérald. *1820-1920, les petits maîtres de la peinture; valeur de demain*. Paris: Les Éditions de l'Amateur, 1975.

Silverman, Debora L. *Art Nouveau in Fin-de-Siècle France: Politics, Psychology, and Style*. Berkeley: University of California Press, 1989.

Simpson, Juliet. *Aurier, symbolism and the visual arts*. Bern: Peter Lang, 1999. *Le Sourire*, 4.43 (24 May 1902).

[Steinlen Designs]. *Steinlen Cats: Drawings*. New York: Dover Publications, 1980.

——. *Théophile-Alexandre Steinlen, 1859-1926* (exhibition catalogue). Paris: Bibliothèque Nationale, 1953.

——. *Théophile-Alexandre Steinlen. Staatliche Kunsthalle Berlin vom 15. Januar bis 15 Februar 1978*. Edited by Dieter Ruckhaberle; scholarly contributions by Margit Rahl, Klaus Schrenk, and Waldemar Thomas. Berlin: Staatl. Kunsthalle, 1978.

Sterner, Gabriele. *Art Nouveau, An Art of Transition: from Individualism to Mass Society*. Woodbury, NY: Barron's Educational Series, 1982.

Stuckey, Charles F. *Toulouse-Lautrec: Paintings*. Chicago: The Art Institute of Chicago, 1979.

Le Symbolisme en Europe (exhibition). Rotterdam: Musée Boymans-van Beuningen, 1975.

Symbolistes et nabis, Maurice Denis et son Temps (exhibition catalogue). Saint-Germain-en-Laye, Yvelines : Musée départemental du Prieuré, 1981.

Thomson, Richard, Phillip Dennis Cate and Mary Weaver Chapin. *Toulouse-Lautrec and Montmartre*. Washington, D.C.: National Gallery of Art; Princeton, NJ: Princeton University Press, 2005.

Toudouze, Georges Gustave. *Henri Rivière, Peintre et Imagier*. Paris: H. Flaury, 1907.

Trench, Lucy. *Materials and Techniques in the Decorative Arts: An Illustrated Dictionary*. Chicago: University of Chicago Press, 2000.

Troy, Nancy. *Modernism and the Decorative Arts in France: Art Nouveau to Le Corbusier*. New Haven: Yale University Press, 1991.

Varille, Mathieu. *Hermann-Paul, Peintre-Graveur, 1864-1940*. Lyon: Vaucanson, 1941.

Villechenon, Marie Noëlle Pinot de. *Sèvres: Porcelain From the Sèvres Museum, 1740 to the Present Day*. London: Lund Humphries Pub.; Wappingers Falls, NY, 1997.

Viollet-Le-Duc, Eugène-Emmanuel. *The Architectural Theory of Viollet-Le-Duc: Readings and Commentary*. Edited by M.F. Hearn. Cambridge, MA: MIT Press, 1990.

——. *Dessins inédits de Viollet-le-Duc*. Paris: A. Guérinet, (?-1902).

——. *Discourses on Architecture*, vols. 1-2. Translated from the French by Benjamin Bucknall. New York: Grove Press, 1959.

——. *Eugène Emmanuel Viollet-Le-Duc, 1814-1879*. London: Academy Editions; New York: Rizzoli, 1980.

——. *The Foundations of Architecture: Selections from the Dictionnaire raisonné*. Introduction by Barry Bergdoll; translations by Kenneth D. Whitehead. New York: G. Braziller, 1990.

Waller, Bret. *Artists of La Revue Blanche: Bonnard, Toulouse-Lautrec, Vallotton, Vuillard*, Memorial Art Gallery of the University of Rochester (22 January – 15 April 1984). Rochester, NY: The Gallery, 1984.

Weber, Eugen. *France, fin de siècle*. Cambridge, MA: Belknap Press, 1986.

"We Get German Brains for Free," *New York Times* (16 March 1905): 2.

Weisberg, Gabriel P. and Elizabeth Kolbinger Menon. *Art Nouveau: A Research Guide for Design Reform in France, Belgium, England, and the United States*. New York: Garland Publishings, 1998.

Weisberg, Gabriel P. *Japonisme: Japanese Influence on French Art, 1854-1910* (exhibition catalogue). Cleveland: Cleveland Museum of Art, 1975.

——. "Louis Legrand's Battle over Prostitution: The Uneasy Censoring of *Le Courrier Français*." *Art Journal*, 51 (Spring 1992): 45-50.

——. *Manuel Robbe: From Impressionism to Symbolism*. Beverly Hills, CA: Galerie Michael, 1987.

——, (ed.). *Montmartre and the Making of Mass Culture*. New Brunswick: Rutgers University Press, 2001.

——. Review of "Roger Marx un critique aux côtés de Gallé, Monet, Rodin, Gauguin…," Nancy, Musée des beaux-arts: Musée de l'école de Nancy (6 May – 28 August 2006), in: *Nineteenth Century Art Worldwide 6, issue 1* (Spring 2007).

——, Edwin Becker and Évelyne Possémé, (eds.). *The Origins of l'Art Nouveau: The Bing Empire* (exhibition catalogue). Amsterdam: Van Gogh Museum; Paris: Musée des arts décoratifs; Antwerp: Mercatorfonds, 2004.

——. *The Realist Tradition: French Painting and Drawing, 1830-1900* (exhibition catalogue. Cleveland: Cleveland Museum of Art, 1980.

——. "The Urban Mirror: Contrasts in the Vision of Existence in the Modern City," in: *Paris and the Countryside: Modern Life in Late 19th Century France* (exhibition catalogue). Portland: Portland Museum of Art, 2006: 1-61.

Design Notes

This publication was designed using Adobe InDesign CS3; v. 5.0.1. It was printed in an edition of 1500 using 100 pound Gusto gloss as the text paper and 120 pound Centura (with a gloss laminate) for the cover stock.

The text of this publication was set in Fournier regular, italic, and small caps at 11/15. Fournier was cut by French typographer and punch cutter Pierre Simon Fournier (Fournier le Jeune) circa 1742 and called "St Augustin Ordinaire" in Fournier's "Manuel Typographique."